Pavlov

A BIOGRAPHY

B. P. BABKIN

THE UNIVERSITY OF CHICAGO PRESS
Chicago and London

The University of Chicago Press, Chicago 60637
The University of Chicago Press, Ltd., London

Copyright 1949 by The University of Chicago
All rights reserved. Published 1949. New Impression 1960. Third Impression 1971
Printed in the United States of America

No illustration or any part of the text may be
reproduced without permission of The University of Chicago Press

International Standard Book Number: 0-226-03372-4
Library of Congress Catalog Card Number: 49-11887

Твоей памяти, моя Родина, и вамъ

великія Тѣни ея Строителей.

Б. Бабкинъ.

*To Thy Memory, My Country, and the Shades of Thy
Great Builders.*

B. P. Babkin

Foreword

THE following pages, which contain an account of the life and scientific achievements of the great Russian physiologist, Ivan Petrovich Pavlov, must be considered only as material for a future, more comprehensive biography. The interval since Pavlov's death has not been sufficiently long for the collection of all the necessary data on his life and work, even by biographers living in Russia. For me, a resident of Canada, it has been much more difficult to obtain the information I desired. Then, inevitably, the biographer is handicapped by a certain lack of perspective in writing of a great man recently departed. He is, as it were, still among us. We see and hear him as he was at our last meeting; we regard him from a personal angle, which makes it difficult to maintain strict objectivity in the description of his character and work. Nevertheless, I decided to write a biography of Pavlov for the following reasons.

I am Pavlov's senior surviving pupil. I knew him well for thirty-five years—from 1901 to the time of his death in 1936. I served for ten years as his assistant in the Department of Physiology at the Institute of Experimental Medicine in St. Petersburg. Our association in the laboratory developed into a lasting friendship. These circumstances entitle me to speak of Pavlov as a contemporary who was familiar with his scientific activity throughout the greater part of his life. Since the year 1949 is the centenary of I. P. Pavlov's birth, I felt that for me it was a duty as well as a privilege to communicate to those interested in his life and work all that I know about him.

There was another consideration which influenced me in my decision to write this biography. It seemed to me that an account of Pavlov's life by one of his contemporaries who was closely associated with him might be of some value to future students of the cultural development of Russia.

Pavlov belonged to the younger generation of those remarkable men who made possible the astounding cultural development of nineteenth-century Russia. Less than one generation separated Pavlov from such men as Pirogov (anatomist and surgeon), Mendeleev and Butlerov (chemists), Sechenov (physiologist), Botkin (physician), Soloviev (historian), Chicherin (political economist), Turgenev, Tolstoy, and Dostoevski (novelists), Tchaikovsky, Mussorgsky, and Rimski-Korsakov (composers), and many others. Pavlov and his contemporaries continued this brilliant tradition.

The mental development of Pavlov and his attitude toward life in general were formed during the sixties and seventies of the past century. Profound political and social changes were taking place in Russia during the reign of Alexander II (1855–81). The youth of the period was full of idealism and of a sincere desire to serve its country and humanity. Pavlov retained these high ideals all through his life, steadfastly believing in truth, justice, and liberalism and the all-important role of science. In 1917 this astounding cultural development of Russia was suddenly disrupted, and new political and social ideas were forcibly imposed on the country.

This book consists of four parts. Part I comprises the biography proper and my reminiscences of Pavlov. Parts II, III, and IV deal with his scientific achievements in the physiology of the cardiovascular, digestive, and central nervous systems. As far as possible, the scientific material has been presented in a form comprehensible to any intelligent lay reader. I hope, however, that specialists in these fields will also find there certain things which may interest them. I have been sparing in the use of quotations from the scientific literature, referring the reader whenever possible to monographs rather than to individual articles.

In the preparation of the manuscript I have had the help of a number of persons, to whom I should like here to express my sincere thanks. In Part I, I had the assistance of Mrs. Irena Kirkpatrick, Miss Janet F. Oswald, and Miss Helene Kernan. In Parts II, III, and IV, I was assisted by Professor K. A. Griffin of Dalhousie University, Halifax, Nova Scotia; Dr. Louis Notkin; Dr. Simon Dworkin of McGill University, Montreal; and Miss Dorothy Karp, M.Sc. Professor Wilder Penfield kindly read chapters 29 and 32 of Part IV, Professor H. E. Hoff, chapters 19 and 20 of Part II; Professor J. E. Thomas read Part III and Dr. W. C. Alvarez, the whole manuscript. My special thanks are due to an old friend of Pavlov, Dr. A. J. Carlson, emeritus professor of physiology of the University of Chicago, who kindly read the whole biography in manuscript and recommended it to the University of Chicago Press for publication.

The first draft of this biography, which was completed in 1946, was too long, and it was necessary to shorten it for publication.[1] Three of my young friends and former students, Drs. M. H. F. Friedman, S. A. Komarov, and M. J. Schiffrin, assisted me in editing the manuscript. Mrs. A. Gilbert kindly retyped the whole typescript. I greatly appreciate their generous help.

The first chapters of this book were read by me to my daughter, Mrs. Xenia Kernan, during her fatal illness in the summer of 1944. The interest which she showed in the work encouraged and stimulated me to complete it.

B. P. BABKIN

MONTREAL, CANADA
January 26, 1949

Contents

PART I. BIOGRAPHY

INTRODUCTION 3

1. EARLY YEARS. Parentage. Pavlov's Father. Pavlov's Godfather. Life in Ryazan. The Ecclesiastical Seminary. The University. Professor I. Cyon. I. R. Tarkhanov. Assistantship in the Veterinary Institute 5

2. MEDICO-CHIRURGICAL ACADEMY AND BOTKIN'S LABORATORY. The Institute of Postgraduate Study. Botkin's Laboratory. An Account of Pavlov by N. J. Chistovich. Pavlov's Thesis. Formation of Pavlov's Character 18

3. SERAPHIMA VASILIEVNA. Seraphima's Memoirs: Arrival in St. Petersburg. Pavlov Falls in Love with Sara. Ivan Petrovich Proposes to Sara. The Wedding 27

4. MARRIED LIFE. First Troubles. Death of the First Child and Illness. Visit to Professor S. P. Botkin. The Place of Sara Vasilievna in Pavlov's Life. Jealousy. Pavlov as a Traveler. Intimate Life 40

5. PROFESSORSHIP IN THE MILITARY-MEDICAL ACADEMY. The Chair of Pharmacology. The Chair of Physiology. Pavlov, the Teacher. Conflict with the Principal of the Academy . . 55

6. THE INSTITUTE OF EXPERIMENTAL MEDICINE. The Physiological Laboratory of the Institute. Graduate Students . . . 67

7. I ENTER PAVLOV'S LABORATORY. Bechterev's Laboratory. The History of Medicine. How Pavlov Greeted Me. Research Work in Pavlov's Laboratory 74

8. PAVLOV, THE SCIENTIST. Pavlov's Belief in Science. Pavlov's Devotion to Science. Bechterev's "Reflexology." Pavlov's Controversy with Bechterev 84

9. PAVLOV'S INTEGRITY. Pavlov's Sense of Duty. "The Reflex of Purpose." Pavlov's Ability To Concentrate 95

10. PAVLOV'S SENSE OF REALITY AND CREATIVE IMAGINATION. Pavlov and the Americans. Pavlov's Creative Imagination. Pavlov's Legacy to Students 103

CONTENTS

11. THE SCHOOL OF EXPERIMENTAL PHYSIOLOGY. Pavlov's Moral Influence. Pavlov's Temperament 115

12. PAVLOV'S ATTITUDE TOWARD HIS CO-WORKERS. A Laboratory Tragedy. Assisting Pavlov at Operations 123

13. PAVLOV'S DAY—THE NOBEL PRIZE 130

14. PAVLOV, THE WRITER 139

15. CLASSICISTS AND ROMANTICISTS IN SCIENCE. Osler's Theory of the "Fixed Period" 144

16. PAVLOV'S POLITICAL VIEWS 152

17. PAVLOV AND THE BOLSHEVIKS 161

18. PAVLOV'S ILLNESSES AND DEATH. Gallstones. Severe Grippe. The Physiological Congress. Pavlov's Death. Conclusion . . 173

PART II. EARLY PHYSIOLOGICAL WORK
OF PALOV

19. REGULATION OF THE BLOOD CIRCULATION. Centrifugal Nerves of the Heart. Trophic Innervation 187

20. CENTRIFUGAL NERVES OF THE HEART (Concluded). Heart-Lung Preparation. Innervation of the Pancreatic Gland. The Effect of Vagotomy 198

PART III. THE WORK OF THE
DIGESTIVE GLANDS

INTRODUCTION 211

21. PHYSIOLOGICAL SURGERY. The Theoretical Basis of Physiological Surgery. Physiological Surgery of the Digestive Tract . 217

22. NERVOUS REGULATION OF THE SECRETORY ACTIVITY OF THE DIGESTIVE GLANDS. Gastric Glands. The Pancreatic Gland. A New Field of Investigation. The Mammary Glands . . 224

23. SPECIFIC EXCITABILITY OF THE ENDINGS OF THE AFFERENT NERVES IN THE GASTROINTESTINAL TRACT. Evidence in Favor of the Theory of Specific Excitability. Origin of the Theory of Specific Excitability. Beaumont's Influence. The Modern Conception of the Specific Excitability of the Digestive Glands 233

24. SECRETORY AND TROPHIC GLANDULAR NERVES. Adaptation of Pancreatic Enzymes. Katabolic and Anabolic Nerves . . 239

25. SECRETORY INHIBITORY NERVES. Purposiveness of the Physiological Functions. Blondlot's Influence on Pavlov . . 248

[xii]

CONTENTS

26. PAVLOV'S CONTRIBUTION TO THE PHYSIOLOGY AND PATHOLOGY OF THE GASTROINTESTINAL TRACT. Salivary Glands. Gastric Glands. Pancreatic Gland. Discharge of Bile into the Duodenum. Intestinal Juice. Motility of the Gastrointestinal Tract. Experimental Pathology and Experimental Therapeutics . . 261

PART IV. CONDITIONED REFLEXES

INTRODUCTION 273

27. ORIGIN OF THE CONDITIONED REFLEXES. The Evolution of Psychology. The Evolution of the Physiology of the Central Nervous System. Orientation Reflexes. Cerebral Cortex . . 275

28. I. M. SECHENOV 285

29. J. HUGHLINGS JACKSON. The Three Levels of Evolution. The Reflex Mechanism of the Centers. Nervous State and Mental State 293

30. FROM SECHENOV AND JACKSON TO PAVLOV. Conditioned Reflexes 301

31. CONDITIONED REFLEXES AS A PHYSIOLOGICAL DISCIPLINE. Mechanism of the Formation of a Conditioned Reflex. Theoretical Conceptions of Pavlov. Three Systems in the Brain. Conditioned Reflexes and Psychology. Conditioned Reflexes from a Psychological Point of View. Professor Lashley's Point of View 311

32. CONCLUSION. Localization of "Consciousness" in the Brain. Conditioned Reflexes and Consciousness. Conditioned Reflexes and Psychic Phenomena in Man. Voluntary Movements 323

NOTES

NOTES 337

REFERENCES

REFERENCES 347

INDEX

INDEX 357

[xiii]

PART I

Biography

Introduction

THE name of the famous Russian physiologist, Ivan Petrovich
Pavlov, is familiar today to every educated person. However,
few know what Pavlov accomplished in the scientific domain in
which he worked for almost sixty years, how he achieved the results which gave him his world-wide reputation, and what kind of
man he was. It seemed to me that my long association with Pavlov
imposed on me the obligation to share with others what I know of
this famous scientist. It has seemed to me the more necessary to
do so since recently there have appeared several so-called "artistic"
biographies of great men in which the author paints a portrait of
his hero as he sees him and tries to create a precise image.

The addition of artistic details to the facts of a great person's
life-history carries with it the danger of creating a legend, and in
this belief I consider that my recollections of Pavlov might materi-
ally benefit future students of his life. As a contemporary of Pavlov
I shall only impart, without embellishments or panegyrics, what I
have known of him and how he appeared to me during our thirty-
five years' acquaintance. Since it is inevitable that events will be
included in which the biographer himself took part, such an approach will necessarily be subjective at times. However, all that I
may have understood incorrectly or reported inaccurately will be
clarified in accounts of Pavlov's life by others and from other
points of view, with the result that the spiritual likeness of Pavlov
and his work will one day stand in its true perspective.

Owing to my separation from Russia during recent years, the
biographical material concerning Pavlov at my disposal has necessarily been scant. The greater part of the biographical information
about Pavlov, in particular about the early years of his life, was
collected by another of his pupils, my friend, the late Professor
V. V. Savich. An article on Pavlov by Savich, composed with deep
affection and respect, was published in Russia in 1924. This contribution was used to a certain extent by Dr. W. H. Gantt for his

[3]

biographical sketch of Pavlov in his American edition of the lectures and articles of I. P. Pavlov (1928) on *Conditioned Reflexes*. Back in 1925 Professor Savich asked me to arrange for the publication of his article in some American scientific journal. In spite of my desire to help my friend, I was unable to do so since Pavlov was dissatisfied with this biography. He considered that it touched on some intimate details in his life which were not for publication. I think, moreover, that the psychological analysis to which Savich had subjected him in the biography was not entirely agreeable to Pavlov. The analysis was based to a certain extent on factual material, but of course each of us knows much more about himself than any biographer and therefore in many details the analysis might have appeared to Pavlov to be one-sided; also, it could hardly afford pleasure to anyone to be subjected to psychological analysis, or at least to have the results of such an analysis made public, during his own lifetime. Since Pavlov's death, there has been, of course, no reason for withholding the biographical material collected by Savich. Many of the particulars which I have included in my recollections were told to me by Pavlov himself. He freely shared his reminiscences of the past with us who worked with him in his laboratory. In addition, we learned much about Pavlov from our older colleagues who had been his companions.

Two recent biographies of Pavlov, in Russian, which were available to me, one by Professor C. S. Koshtoyanz (1937), the other by Alexis Yougov (1942), unfortunately display a definite political bias and contain many inaccuracies. Moreover, as Professor Koshtoyanz frankly admits, some episodes which never took place were included in his book "to enliven the skeleton of historic events."

When this biography was almost finished, there appeared in the Russian Soviet journal *Novi Mir* (*New World*) for 1946, the "Reminiscences" of Pavlov's widow. Mrs. Pavlov's very valuable memoirs are of a personal character and present little material for judging Pavlov as a scientist. They are primarily concerned with Pavlov as a husband and father and display a true and vivid picture of his intimate life. In the present biography I have included whatever data were possible from Mrs. Pavlov's "Reminiscences."

[4]

CHAPTER ONE

Early Years

PARENTAGE

IVAN PETROVICH PAVLOV was born on September 14(27), 1849,[1] in the town of Ryazan, where his father was priest in the poor parish of Nikola Dolgoteli. In order to understand the traits of Pavlov's character to which he in large measure owed his scientific successes, one must take into consideration Pavlov's clerical origin and the circumstances in which he grew up.

Pavlov was of pure Russian extraction. This was due to a peculiar condition existing among the Russian clergy: from time immemorial the clergy constituted a separate class, whose members intermarried almost exclusively within the limits of their class. Particular attention must also be given to Pavlov's ecclesiastical background. A hundred years ago Russia was almost exclusively an agricultural country. The life of the village clergy differed very little from that of the peasants. The village priest sowed, reaped, and worked his land on the church property as did his peasant parishioners on theirs. Because of the large size of his family his poverty was always great. This condition remained unchanged until the beginning of the twentieth century, at least in many of the northwestern provinces, such as Tver, where I used to go every summer.

Professor Savich has truly remarked that this indefatigable agricultural labor, along with a certain intellectual development of the village clergy, created a mentally strong and physically sound stock. Their characters were formed not in the artificial and humiliating atmosphere of old-type chancelleries or in urban affairs but in a constant and real struggle with nature. True, the diocesan bishop was "Lord Bishop" indeed, but it was not often that he got in touch with the village father. Drought or flood, rain or frost, an insufficiency of grain, a fallen horse or cow, sick children—these are what continually occupied the thoughts of the Russian village

[5]

priest. The more energetic of them struggled out of these onerous conditions and obtained a better position.

PAVLOV'S FATHER

The grandfather of Ivan Petrovich Pavlov was a village sexton. His father, Peter Dmitrievich Pavlov, had already completed a seminary course when he began his service as priest in one of the poor churches of Ryazan. Toward the end of his life he received the distinguished Order of Vladimir, fourth class, and was a much-respected dean and preacher in one of the best parishes in Ryazan.

Peter Dmitrievich Pavlov was undoubtedly a person who stood out from his surroundings. He possessed a strong will and was exacting toward others but also severe with himself. Throughout his life he preserved intellectual interests and a love of learning. Sometimes he even bought books, which in view of his poverty was often not easy. Pavlov frequently recalled the solemn injunction of his father to ready every worth-while book twice in order to understand it better. On the other hand, from his farmer ancestors Pavlov's father inherited a love of the land and of physical toil. In Ryazan he had a vegetable garden and an orchard, in which he loved to work.

Pavlov inherited many of his father's characteristics, although I cannot say that, as I knew him, he had an indomitable will in all matters. He was not a man to bend or break to his will everything standing in his way. Not infrequently, especially in matters of secondary importance, Pavlov agreed to a compromise. But, once convinced of the rightness of his purpose, nothing could change his resolution or weaken his perseverance in the pursuit of any goal he set for himself.

The love of learning was similarly inherited or acquired by Pavlov from his father. Pavlov was not one of those bookish men who read indiscriminately and know a little about everything. In his own specialty, physiology, he read chiefly what had relation to his own work. He read continually, sometimes in the laboratory but usually at home when he had had his after-dinner rest. He read slowly, often rereading whole passages and pages. He derived great pleasure from reading, being interested in literature as well as in scientific writing. On his vacations he always set himself the task of reading or rereading some author. At one time it was Shakespeare, at another Pushkin, and after the Revolution and the appearance of separatist tendencies in the Ukraine, it was Kostomarov.

However, for the laboratory research worker—both for himself and for his students—Pavlov considered experimental work most important. When I wrote my first monograph on the digestive glands, I dedicated it to Pavlov. In his letter of thanks (autumn, 1913), which to my regret I do not now have in my possession, he warned me not to be drawn away by the reading of scientific literature or the writing of scientific books. He wrote that only a very few research workers were able to preserve a balance between experimental and literary work; the majority of those who entered on a scientific literary career ceased to be interested in the laboratory.

Although Pavlov derived great pleasure from reading, a book to him was not only a means of diversion; it satisfied to a certain extent his yearning to know and understand something new. This he himself subsequently called the "instinct for research," and in his student days it undoubtedly directed him into the path of scientific research.

Another characteristic trait which Pavlov inherited from his father was a love of physical toil and especially of toil with the earth. While still a boy at Ryazan he alone of all the family willingly helped his father in the garden and the orchard, and he grew very fond of this work. His life in St. Petersburg, which occupied the period between Pavlov's entrance into the University of St. Petersburg until his death—a period of sixty-seven years—did not, of course, afford him much opportunity for working in either garden or orchard. However, during the famine in St. Petersburg, in the years of revolution, 1918–20, Pavlov with enthusiasm and persistence cultivated a vegetable garden on his part of the allotment set aside for the staff of the Institute of Experimental Medicine on Apothecary's Island (*Aptekarski Ostrov*).

In ordinary times, Pavlov satisfied his passion for work on the land in another fashion. In the city he planted flowers in boxes in the early spring. As I recall, he was particularly fond of stock. Then in the second half of May he made several expeditions to his summer cottage (or *dacha*) in Sillomiagy in Estonia. Here he prepared the flower beds and transplanted his flowers. Pavlov would throw himself into his favorite pastime with great zest, and often he was so exhausted physically that he could not sleep at night. Nonetheless, on his return to St. Petersburg and the laboratory, when he told us of his horticultural exploits and we asked him how he felt after such physical exertion, he always replied: "Splendid! From this kind of work I get 'muscular joy,' which gives me greater satisfaction than 'intellectual joy.' " And if any of the laboratory workers expressed surprise, Pavlov added: "Yes, that is so. I am by nature more of a peasant than a professor!"

This love of physical toil Pavlov preserved to an advanced age (Pavlov, 1940). In a letter to the Youth Organization of the Donetz Valley Conference of Coal Miners, written on January 7, 1936, that is, less than two months before his death (February 27, 1936), Pavlov wrote:

HONORED MINERS:

All my life I have loved intellectual and physical work, and indeed the second even more than the first. But I have felt particularly satisfied when I have introduced into the latter some successful improvization, that is, have united the head with the hands. You have entered on the same path. From my heart I wish you success in advancing farther along this unifying way, which assures mankind of happiness.

With sincere greetings,

I. PAVLOV
Academician

KOLTUSHI
January 7, 1936

PAVLOV'S GODFATHER

Neither Pavlov himself, in his short autobiographical sketches, nor any one of his biographers has mentioned the very great influence which Pavlov's godfather, the Abbot of St. Trinity's Monastery near Ryazan, had on him. We find an account of the boy Pavlov's life with his godfather in the "Reminiscences" of Mrs. Pavlov.

On one occasion the old monk visited the Pavlovs in Ryazan and saw his godson in a pitiful condition. Young Ivan was much the worse for a bad fall. The good abbot took Ivan with him to the monastery and there attended the boy and helped him to recover by seeing that he had a great deal of nourishing food, fresh air, and exercise. Little Ivan, in his turn, helped in the garden and tried to do his tasks around the monastery as accurately and thoroughly as his godfather had taught him.

The old man also had a great spiritual influence over the boy which was, perhaps, even more important. Ivan was greatly impressed by the fact that his godfather worked all the time. If ever the boy woke up in the middle of the night, he saw the old abbot seated at his desk. For a long time afterward Ivan assured his parents that the abbot never slept! This constant labor gave Pavlov an example which he followed all his life.

The life of the abbot was extremely simple and even Spartan. He subsisted chiefly on bread and water, and only when he was ill did he permit himself the luxury of tea with honey. Following this example, Pavlov remained modest in his material requirements all his life.

By reading and storytelling to the boy the well-educated abbot awoke a keen interest for mental work. As his first gift young Ivan received a copy of the *Fables of Krylov*. (Krylov occupies in Russian literature approximately the same position as La Fontaine does in French literature.) Ivan, who possessed a vivid imagination, loved this book, learned almost all of it by heart, and kept it on his desk until he died. When Ivan began to read, he annoyed everyone by endlessly recounting all that he had read. His godfather then gave him a copy-book and told him: "Tell everything you read to this copy-book, and tomorrow I will read what you have written." In this way was Pavlov's ability to express his thoughts in writing developed.

Through the influence of his godfather, Pavlov's character was formed. The thoughtfulness and training of the old monk had almost a greater influence on Pavlov than that of his own father.

LIFE IN RYAZAN

Pavlov's father had a large family. The children were divided into two groups. The older group consisted of Ivan, Dmitri, and Peter, born in succession a year apart and all of sound health. The second group consisted of the youngest children in the family, Sergei and Lydia. An intervening group of six children all died of infectious diseases at an early age. The almost continuous child-bearing, nursing, and supervision of many children reduced Pavlov's mother, Varvara Ivanovna (herself the daughter of a priest), from a strong woman to an invalid. Perhaps in consequence of this the two youngest children did not possess the health or the abounding energy with which the three eldest were endowed. Ivan, Dmitri, and Peter, after finishing their studies at the Ecclesiastical Seminary in Ryazan, entered the University of St. Petersburg. Pavlov, on completing his university course, continued his education in the Medico-Chirurgical (later renamed the Military-Medical) Academy and remained there with a view to attaining a professorship. Dmitri chose chemistry as his specialty and after graduating from the university received the post of assistant in the same institution. Subsequently he was professor of chemistry in the Novo Alexandria Institute of Agriculture (near Warsaw). Of Peter I have no information. Apparently he died young. The youngest brother, Sergei, on finishing his courses at the Ecclesiastical Seminary, did not proceed to a university but became a priest. In his biography of Pavlov, Professor Savich states that Sergei passed his whole life in Ryazan and died there of typhus during the Revolution.

Professor Savich relates several incidents in the early life of Pavlov. He was already eleven years old when he entered the second class in the Ryazan Ecclesiastical High School. This rather late entry is explained by the fact that at the age of nine the boy fell off a fence onto a brick floor, seriously injuring himself, and was long ailing. This was the accident referred to above. At one time it was believed that his lungs had been affected. As a matter of fact, although Pavlov's lungs remained his weak spot throughout his life, he enjoyed, in general, excellent health and was brought low by serious illness on only a few occasions.

The Ecclesiastical Seminary

On leaving the Ecclesiastical High School, Pavlov and his brothers entered the Ryazan Ecclesiastical Seminary. Pavlov remembered the seminary with great affection and often told us in the laboratory of the peculiarities of the instruction there. Strange as it seems, the fact remains that in the sixties of the nineteenth century the clerical seminaries were leading institutions with respect to some methods of instruction. They were free from that pedantry with which instruction was permeated in the classical schools even in my time, that is, in the nineties of the past century. The seminary was interested not in the average pupil who was obliged to succeed in all subjects but in the individual capacities and inclinations of each boy. If a boy distinguished himself by knowledge of or devotion to some one subject, they overlooked his shortcomings in other subjects. Many of the teachers at the seminary were very young people, who experienced the uplift of the sixties. It was a period of transition from the strict autocratic regime of Nicholas I to the more liberal regime of his son, Alexander II. The seminary pupils of the senior classes read *Contemporary (Sovremennik)*, the *Russian Word (Ruskoye Slovo)*, and other liberal periodicals. A very great influence on the youth of that period was exerted by a popular writer and critic named Pisarev. In fact, it was the inspiration of Pisarev that moved Pavlov to select natural science as his subject of study at the university. Impressions received in youth are unusually strong and leave indelible traces in afterlife. So, for example, to the end of his days Pavlov preserved an almost ecstatic attitude toward the teaching and personality of Charles Darwin. And there is no doubt that it was from an article of Pisarev's that Pavlov first became acquainted with the Darwinian theory of natural selection.

All the novelty that, after the repressive regime of the epoch of Nicholas I, was suddenly precipitated on unprepared Russian society naturally aroused endless arguments. Professor Savich graphically describes how groups of seminary students, walking along the streets of sleepy Ryazan, passionately discussed these contemporary questions. One can easily imagine all the noise, laughter, and swearing. Even when paying a visit, the young people did not for a moment cease arguing. Their hosts would join in the discussion, and time would pass unnoticed in some controversy that led to nothing and convinced nobody. I. M. Sechenov in his famous book, *Reflexes of the Brain*, written at the beginning of the sixties, compared such arguments to crackling fireworks, on the conclusion of which the spectator retains only a confused recollection of something noisy and bright but exceedingly indefinite.

Pavlov distinguished himself among the disputants by his earnestness and the sharpness of his remarks, but he himself was the object of frequent merciless attacks. Even in his ripe years he retained his love of argument and often would say that in order to argue successfully one should not give his opponent a chance to collect himself but should "hit him on the head," continuously overcoming him by sheer talk. This, it must be said, is a purely Russian tactic, whereby the opponent cannot open his mouth, or, if he does, nobody listens to him, and everyone shouts at the top of his voice. Constantly in ordinary conversation Pavlov would interrupt his interlocutor with, "No, listen, listen," and would then develop his own line of thought. In spite of such vehemence in dispute, Pavlov was completely at a loss when he had to meet an impudent person. He did not know how to give an impertinent individual the proper rebuff, could not find an answer for him, and was silent or would mutter something meaningless. However, next day in the laboratory Pavlov would pour out all his anger and indignation when telling us of the encounter. Such a retreat before rudeness is explained by Pavlov's unusual bashfulness. Even in the presence of new acquaintances he was somewhat lost.

The University

At the time of Pavlov's attendance at the Ecclesiastical Seminary the seminary students were given the right of admission to the university before completion of the seminary course. This was fortunate for Russian science and was due to reorganization of the seminary curriculum. Many of the pupils availed themselves of this privilege and one of them was Pavlov. Together with two comrades, Bystrov (later professor of pediatrics in the Military-Medical Academy) and Cheltsov (who became a physician in one of the St. Petersburg hospitals), Pavlov traveled to St. Petersburg in 1870 and enrolled in the Faculty of Natural Science in the University of St. Petersburg. Within a year they were joined by Pavlov's second brother, Dmitri. The Ryazan boys stuck together and lived cheaply. They ate in humble restaurants, paying 15 or 20 kopeks for a two-course meal with an unlimited amount of bread.

The Pavlov brothers went home to their father in Ryazan for the summer. Hunting, which was the joy of his brothers, did not appeal to Pavlov, but he was passionately devoted to the game of *gorodki* (a game played by throwing sticks at small wooden blocks). He retained his passion for this game all his life. Years later, at his summer home in Estonia, *gorodki* was one of his chief diversions. When Pavlov's children grew older, they and their friends constituted a group of "sons," who frequently gained the victory over a group of "fathers," which included Pavlov. Dr. W. H. Gantt, who worked in Pavlov's laboratory from 1923 to 1929, writes in his biographical sketch of Pavlov that he was a witness of the zeal and youthful enthusiasm with which seventy-seven-year-old Pavlov played *gorodki* in 1926 (see Pavlov, 1928). His endurance and muscular skill were extraordinary. He not only beat players half his age but when, after three days of play at the rate of eight hours a day, the tournament came to an end, only Pavlov had enough energy left to propose its resumption on the fourth day.

PROFESSOR I. CYON

At the university the man who exerted the greatest influence on Pavlov was the professor of physiology, Ilya Cyon. Cyon was a fine scientist, with a European reputation, and was also a brilliant lecturer. As a physiologist he was the complete master of an exceptional experimental technique; the sureness of his eye and the skill of his hands were extraordinary. Among other things, Cyon (1876) wrote and published the first textbook on experimental physiological technique that was of first-rate quality. Even today it is occasionally necessary to turn to Cyon for accurate instructions on how to carry out this or that experiment.

Cyon so interested the young man in his subject that in his third year of university study Pavlov had already decided to become a physiologist. In a short autobiographical sketch, which Pavlov wrote for a volume in commemoration of the Twenty-fifth Graduation Anniversary (1879–1904) from the Medico-Chirurgical (later renamed Military-Medical) Academy in St. Petersburg, he emphasized what a great impression Professor Cyon had produced on all his students by his masterly lecturing and his really artistic performance of experiments. "Never can such a teacher be forgotten," concluded Pavlov (quoted from Mrs. Pavlov's "Reminiscences"). Like Cyon, Pavlov was an exceptionally skilful operator. An observer was always amazed at the accuracy of Pavlov's surgical methods, his speed, the absence of unnecessary motions in his manipulations, and his delicate treatment of tissues. Professor Robert Tigerstedt (1904) of the University of Helsingfors wrote in the *Jubilee Volume* in honor of Pavlov's twenty-fifth year of scientific activity that Pavlov performed any simple operation so quickly that he was finishing it when the spectator thought that he was just beginning.

On the suggestion of Cyon, Pavlov, while still a student at the University of St. Petersburg, carried out in collaboration with M. I. Afanassiew his first experimental work, on the nerves of the pancreatic gland. This work was rewarded by a gold medal, but the time taken from his curriculum set Pavlov back a year in the completion of his university course. He received his diploma in 1875. Although the subject of the investigation had been suggested by Cyon, he was unable to direct its completion, for he had in the meantime been appointed professor of physiology of the Medico-Chirurgical Academy and had transferred to that institution.[2]

In 1875, when Pavlov graduated from the University of St. Petersburg, Cyon had offered him the post of assistant in his laboratory at the Medico-Chirurgical Academy. Pavlov decided to accept this offer and, while holding the assistantship, to take a course in medicine, for which purpose he entered the third year at the Academy. However, this plan was only partially realized. Pavlov entered the Academy as a student but he did not become Cyon's assistant, owing to the latter's retirement.

I. R. TARKHANOV

After Cyon's dismissal, the Conference of the Medico-Chirurgical Academy appointed in his place Ivan Romanovich Tarkhanov (if I am not mistaken, Prince Tarkhan-Mouravov), who was a former pupil of Sechenov. He was a clever and exceedingly well-bred individual, always elegantly dressed, a good but somewhat affected lecturer, who unfortunately left almost no impression on science.

Tarkhanov offered Pavlov the post of assistant, but Pavlov refused this offer, although at that time he was in extremely difficult circumstances. Professor Savich in his article on Pavlov writes that "Pavlov resolutely refused only because Tarkhanov, not long before, had to the detriment of the truth covered up by his authority the blunders of a person of some importance, occupying a high position."

I do not know what Professor Savich had in mind when he wrote this, but Pavlov related to me the following incident in connection with Tarkhanov which occurred at one of the scientific sessions in the University of St. Petersburg. Professor Ovsyannikov and his assistant Chiriev (later professor of physiology at the University of St. Vladimir, Kiev) were demonstrating on an anesthetized dog an experiment which was designed to show the effect of muscular work on certain functions of the body. The experiment consisted in binding the hind legs of the supine animal to a wheel. When the wheel was turned, the dog's legs bent and unbent at the joints. Pavlov, then still a student, stood up and said that in this (truly foolish!) experiment the muscles performed no work at all, since the movements of the animal's legs were passive, being caused by an external force, and that the muscles themselves were in a relaxed condition due to the anesthetic. Thus the findings of the investigators could not relate to genuinely contracting muscle.

According to Pavlov's account, Ovsyannikov was extremely put out by these comments of a mere student but could find no reply. Thereupon Tarkhanov came to his rescue and in an effort that was hardly convincing endeavored to prove that the muscles in this experiment were, in spite of everything, contracting slightly. Whether or not this incident was the reason for Pavlov's refusal to accept the post as Tarkhanov's assistant, I do not know, but one thing is certain—that Tarkhanov's hypocrisy and truckling to an individual who was then almost a member of the Academy of Sciences produced a repellent impression on such a passionate and incorruptible searcher for scientific truth as Pavlov. Subsequently the relations between Pavlov and Tarkhanov were quite correct and even friendly. To the best of my knowledge, Tarkhanov treated Pavlov, as a scientist, with great respect. He frequently made use of the services of Pavlov's laboratory and borrowed from the Institute of Experimental Medicine, for demonstration purposes in public lectures, dogs with chronic fistulas of the digestive tract. For his part, Pavlov always spoke well of Tarkhanov, which, however, did not prevent him from laughing at Tarkhanov's scientific methods and some of his investigations. For instance, much to

Pavlov's amusement, Tarkhanov called one of the proteins which he discovered "Tata-protein," after his little daughter. In particular Pavlov criticized Tarkhanov's habit of intrusting to others the task of carrying out an experiment, without himself going into all the details of the investigation. As an extreme example of such a system, which makes the research worker dependent upon the vagaries of an inexperienced and irresponsible assistant and naturally may lead to absurd conclusions, Pavlov told the following story.

Tarkhanov became interested in the influence of one of the then fashionable substances (I believe it was lecithin) on the growth and development of young animals. The experiments were intrusted to one Morozov, an attendant in the Physiological Laboratory of the Military-Medical Academy. The puppies in one litter were divided into two groups: the experimental and the control. The puppies for experiment were to be given definite and adequate food rations along with lecithin, while the control puppies *were supposed* to receive the same amount of food but no lecithin. Thanks to the efforts of Morozov, the great benefit of lecithin was clearly proved. The results were amazing. The puppies experimented upon were plump and lively, with shiny coats. To everybody's surprise, the ribs of the control puppies stuck out, their fur was matted, and they could hardly stand on their legs. Morozov evidently was a great experimentalist!

ASSISTANTSHIP IN THE VETERINARY INSTITUTE

While taking his course at the Academy, Pavlov secured a position as an assistant in the Physiological Laboratory of Professor Ustimovich. This was not in the Medical Faculty but in the Veterinary Institute. In the seventies of the last century the Medico-Chirurigal Academy still had a veterinary division, which was later abolished. Pavlov was an assistant in Ustimovich's laboratory from 1876 to 1878. During that time he began several independent investigations, some dealing with the physiology of blood circulation, some with the physiology of digestion. (Incidentally, it was here that he developed a new operative procedure for making a permanent pancreatic fistula, an account of which he published only in 1879.)

The work which Pavlov performed at that time on the circulation of the blood will be examined in detail in Part II of this book. It must be noted here that this work was important not only in its scientific aspect but also in a practical way for Pavlov himself. His investigation of the circulation of the blood had already attracted attention, and his familiarity with experimentation on the cardiovascular system led Dr. J. J. Stolnikov (who was connected with the Academic Medical Clinic of the famous clinician, S. P. Botkin) to recommend his friend Pavlov for the position of director of the Physiological Laboratory in Botkin's clinic.

During the tenure of his assistantship in the Veterinary Institute, Pavlov in spite of his modest means was able to go abroad. He spent the summer of 1877 in the Physiological Laboratory of Professor R. Heidenhain at Breslau. Heidenhain was interested in the subject of digestion, and Pavlov there studied the effects of ligation of the pancreatic ducts in rabbits. This was Pavlov's first published work (Pavlov, 1878).

CHAPTER TWO

Medico-Chirurgical Academy
and Botkin's Laboratory

THE INSTITUTE OF POSTGRADUATE STUDY

PAVLOV graduated from the Medico-Chirurgical Academy on December 19, 1879, being awarded a gold medal. As the result of a competitive examination (known as the "concourse"), he obtained a scholarship for postgraduate study and research at the Academy (1880–84) and was then sent abroad for two years' further study (1885–86).

The "Institute" of Postgraduate Studies for the young graduates of the Medico-Chirurgical (later renamed Military-Medical) Academy existed in conjunction with this medical school. Ten postgraduates, selected each year for a term of three years, were usually called "Institute physicians." At the end of their term, three of the ten candidates were elected by the Academy to be sent abroad for further study for two years.

BOTKIN'S LABORATORY

During his stay at the Academy as a postgraduate, Pavlov's resolution to become a physiologist continued unchanged. However, owing to his previous refusal to take the post of assistant in Tarkhanov's laboratory, his attachment to Professor Tarkhanov's Department of Physiology in the capacity of an Institute physician was precluded.

A fortunate combination of circumstances enabled Pavlov to find conditions of work in which his talents as an experimental investigator could develop fully. Thanks to the recommendations of his friend, Dr. J. J. Stolnikov, Pavlov was invited by Professor S. P. Botkin in 1878 to take charge of the newly opened experimental laboratory connected with the medical clinic of the Academy.

I have very little information about Stolnikov. At one time he and Pavlov worked together, as is evident from work which they published jointly. Professor Tigerstedt (1904) stated in his article in the *Pavlov Jubilee Volume* that he met Stolnikov in 1883 in Ludwig's laboratory in Leipzig, where he and Stolnikov were both working. At that time Stolnikov said to Tigerstedt: "In Russia we have an outstanding physiologist, gifted to the highest degree, who will do something very significant one day. His name is Pavlov." It seems that Stolnikov was himself a very brilliant man and was appreciated highly by Pavlov. Pavlov once told us jestingly that he and Stolnikov were a laughingstock and that people said to them: "The cuckoo praises the rooster for praising the cuckoo." But Stolnikov was right—the rooster grew into a mighty eagle. Stolnikov died at rather an early age.

S. P. Botkin conducted the medical clinic in the Military-Medical Academy. He was the most outstanding Russian clinician of his time and was a representative of the so-called school of "scientific medicine," which strove to replace empiricism in medicine by accurate knowledge of the physiological and pathological relations in the organism. He tried to regulate clinical experience by the experimental working-out of medical problems. His especial interest in physiology never flagged, and he maintained active relations with I. M. Sechenov and with Professor Carl Ludwig. Counterbalancing this trend, the famous school of Professor Zakharin in the University of Moscow had a predominantly clinical outlook.

In view of the special character of the problems which Botkin set himself, he of course needed a laboratory where experiments could be made on animals. He also required a director who would supervise the investigations of his numerous students. In connection with his clinic Botkin organized a laboratory, if such a name can be given to the small wooden building in the garden of the clinic, which was little adapted to the carrying-out of scientific investigations and was very poorly equipped.

The direction of this laboratory was intrusted altogether to Pavlov, since Botkin himself was overloaded with other responsibilities. This is in truth an amazing fact—that a recently graduated science student, who had not yet finished his medical course and who himself should have been studying under another, became the director of scientific investigations (*chef des travaux*) in the most famous clinic of internal diseases in Russia.

During this period Botkin was interested primarily in the action of various substances which could be used in treating the heart and the vascular system. Many of these substances were extracted from plants, such as *Adonis vernalis* (pheasant's-eye), *Convallaria majalis* (lily of the valley), and *Hellebori viridis* (green hellebore); other substances were also investigated, for example, antipirin, cesium, rubidium, and so on. Thus the character of these investigations was primarily, though not exclusively, pharmacological. Botkin merely outlined the problem to his house doctor, but the planning and performance of the actual experiment fell entirely to Pavlov. Sometimes Botkin suggested problems that were quite impossible to work out experimentally, for example, one was to determine the reason for the coating of the tongue during certain illnesses. Even today we do not know for certain why the tongue becomes coated, but sixty years ago this question was quite unapproachable experimentally. Pavlov has told how he tried by various methods to find an experimental solution to this problem, but nothing came of it and the problem had to be abandoned.

Pavlov considered the time spent in Botkin's laboratory very useful for his scientific development. He was quite independent in his work and could devote all his time to research. "I worked there," wrote Pavlov in his short autobiography, "without considering whether I was working for myself or helping others. For months and years all my laboratory activity consisted in participating in the research work of others" (quoted from Mrs. Pavlov's "Reminiscences"). He advised Dr. Savich and me, when we were his assistants, not to worry much about time lost for our own work when helping others. This would broaden our own experience, he said, and give us extremely valuable practice in directing physiological research.

Association with such an outstanding man as Botkin could not fail to leave its impress on Pavlov's scientific views. Botkin ascribed especial importance to the nervous system in the development of pathological phenomena and the role of abnormal reflex influences in the appearance of pathological processes. For instance, he always tried to find the internal cause of some skin affection, presuming that the abnormal condition of the skin might in some cases be the result of pathological processes in some internal organ and not merely a local process. This is only one example of that "nervism" with which Botkin's scientific conceptions were permeated. (The theory of "nervism" postulated that most of the bodily functions are regulated by the nervous system.) The same is true of Pavlov— a tendency toward "nervism" runs through all his scientific works. At the end of his M.D. thesis Pavlov mentioned that it was Botkin who directed his scientific activities toward "nervism."

The influence of Botkin and his clinic on Pavlov was manifested in still another way. Throughout the whole course of his life Pavlov never tired of emphasizing the necessity for co-operation between laboratory and clinic. He often said that he considered it of the utmost importance for a physiologist to go through a medical school. His thoughts might be formulated as follows: "Our experimental imagination and our necessarily rough handling of living tissue can in no measure be compared to the variety and fineness of those injuries which can be produced in an organism by pathological processes. The clinic teaches us how to approach an experimental solution of physiological problems." Pavlov, of course, did not give preference to clinical over laboratory and experimental investigation but, when already in his declining years, showed rather by his own example how important it is for a physiologist to be in contact with a clinic. When he was over seventy-five years of age, he began to study psychiatry as practiced in a hospital, since he found this necessary for a better understanding of his researches in experimental neuroses in dogs.

Life repaid Pavlov in full for his disinterested devotion to his work. Many years later, in 1890, when being considered for the chair of pharmacology in the Military-Medical Academy, one of the circumstances which assisted his appointment to this position was his former direction of Botkin's laboratory. At the Conference meeting, during the discussion of the qualifications of the various candidates, Professor Manassein said:

It is definitely known that Pavlov himself actually directed all the pharmacological and physiological work for the M.D. theses presented from Botkin's clinic. The Conference is, of course, aware of the fact that the esteemed teacher, S. P. Botkin, being a great clinician, did not in later years occupy himself with physiological investigation.[1]

But there is no doubt that, in assisting Botkin's pupils, Pavlov thought least of all of any material gain which might accrue to himself at some future date from this type of work.

An Account of Pavlov by N. J. Chistovich

Professor N. J. Chistovich testifies to the extremely important role played by young Pavlov as director of Botkin's experimental laboratory. Chistovich became an Institute physician in Botkin's laboratory in 1885 and was assigned to study the action of the root *Hellebori viridis* on the heart and circulation. When in 1885 Pavlov left the laboratory and went abroad for two years, Chistovich found himself without laboratory guidance. The only assistance available was from the senior students in the laboratory who were working on analogous problems. The methods in experimental physiology are difficult in themselves, and, moreover, they need to be adapted to each particular problem. Consequently Chistovich's senior friends, being young medical men themselves and not physiologists, were of little assistance to him. Chistovich learned what he could from Cyon's *Physiological Methods*, but this was not enough and he pinned his hopes on Pavlov's return. "My friends consoled me by reminding me that in two years Pavlov would return and then everything would be organized." And so it happened: "At last, the passionately awaited Pavlov returned, and at once our poor, pathetic laboratory came to life."

The experiments which Pavlov and Chistovich carried out were extremely difficult and demanded an exceptional experimental technique, which only Pavlov possessed. To perform these experiments even now, sixty years later, would not be a simple matter. The problem consisted in investigating the action of the extract of the root *Hellebori viridis* on the heart *in situ* but with the systemic and pulmonary circulations cut off. The contraction of the heart and the flow of blood through it had to be maintained without interruption. More will be said about these experiments in Part II.

Pavlov's Thesis

Before going abroad Pavlov completed his own extremely important experiments on the augmentor nerves of the heart. He presented this work as his thesis for the degree of Doctor of Medicine, which he received on May 23, 1883.

This investigation, of which more will be written later, established an entirely new fact, namely, that the various branches of the nerves of the heart, during stimulation by an induction current, are capable not only of retarding or accelerating the heartbeats—which was already known—but also of augmenting or diminishing their force. Thus for the first time in a warm-blooded animal (the dog) it was determined that the nerves of the heart exert a dynamic as well as a rhythmic effect. Contemporaneously and independently of Pavlov, the same conclusions were reached by the famous English physiologist, W. H. Gaskell, in experiments on frogs' and turtles' hearts. These were discoveries of first-rate importance. The present conceptions regarding the action of the nerves on the heart differ somewhat from those held by Pavlov, but the facts established by him remain undisputed.

The experimental technique for demonstrating the various actions of the nerves of the heart in an anesthetized dog is extremely difficult, but Pavlov achieved his aim by the skill and delicacy of his manipulation and by working with great speed.

Pavlov was made a lecturer (*Privatdocent*) in physiology at the Military-Medical Academy on April 24, 1884, and it was about eight months later that he left for two years' study abroad.

FORMATION OF PAVLOV'S CHARACTER

At the time when he was in charge of Botkin's laboratory there were already clear indications of those traits of the inspired and incorruptible scientific investigator which he preserved for the rest of his long life. I have mentioned above how Pavlov looked on his participation in the work of those whose experiments he directed. His chief interest was always exclusively how to solve a particular scientific problem. It was for this reason that no irrelevant considerations, and especially those of a worldly nature, were of any interest to him. This does not mean that he lacked a practical knowledge of life; he knew very well how to deal with difficult matters and situations. But if any conflict arose between the practical demands of life and of science, Pavlov without hesitation took his stand on the side of science.

I shall give a few instances illustrating Pavlov's attitude to his scientific work. One of these episodes was in connection with his Doctor's thesis and was related by Pavlov himself. All those graduating from the Military-Medical Academy received the rank of "Titular Councilor," equivalent to a minor government clerk. The degree of Doctor of Medicine automatically promoted the holder of this title to the rank of a staff officer and carried with it an increase in salary and an appointment as a "College Assessor." Pavlov married in 1881, that is, during his second year as director of Botkin's laboratory. The salary of an Institute physician was about 50 rubles ($25.00) a month, which was a good deal less than modest even for those days. One can therefore easily imagine how difficult it was for Pavlov to live, with his wife and the child (his eldest son Vladimir) who soon made his appearance. Pavlov used to tell how his wife would often beg him with tears in her eyes to hasten to attain the degree of Doctor of Medicine, saying that he was helping so many other aspirants to the degree but was doing nothing to help himself. But Pavlov remained adamant. He wanted to do good work for his thesis and above all to be certain of his results. All this took time, and it was not until 1883, when he made his important discovery of the dynamic nerves of the heart and was completely sure of his facts, that he submitted his thesis for the degree of Doctor of Medicine.

Another incident of which Pavlov told was the following. He had been carrying out an investigation with one of his co-workers (a candidate for the M.D. degree); and, though the results were excellent, it was necessary to perform a control experiment which would confirm or refute the basic facts. The M.D. candidate was nervous, realizing that the fruits of his labor and the very doctorate degree with all its advantages might vanish as the result of this crucial control experiment. He begged Pavlov not to do this experiment. One had to know Pavlov in order to understand with what undisguised scorn and indignation he rejected such a proposition and with what vehemence he conducted the experiment on the following morning. Fortunately for the candidate, the control experiment confirmed the results and the thesis was saved.

Professor N. J. Chistovich, in describing his work with Pavlov in Botkin's laboratory, writes the following:

When recalling those days, I think that each one of us feels deeply grateful to our teacher, not only for his talented direction, but, above all, for the exceptional example which we saw in his person, the example of an individual entirely devoted to science and living only for science in spite of the most difficult financial circumstances, almost poverty, which he had to endure with his heroic "better half," Seraphima Vasilievna, who knew how to uphold him and comfort him in the hardest hours of his life. I hope Pavlov will forgive me if I recount some episodes of those days long past.

At one time, Pavlov was quite penniless. He was obliged to separate from his family and go to live with his friend, Dr. N. P. Simanovski. We, Pavlov's pupils, knowing of his financial straits, thought of a way to help him. We invited him to deliver to us a course of lectures on the innervation of the heart, and, clubbing together to raise some money, we handed it over to him, pretending that this was to defray the expenses of the course. But we did not gain our end. He used the entire sum to buy animals for these lectures and nothing was left for himself....

Another time, after Pavlov returned from studying abroad, he had a grant for one additional year's work at the Academy. The year passed, but Pavlov had not succeeded in finding himself a position at the Academy. There was no vacancy in Botkin's department, but there was one under Professor V. A. Manassein, and it was necessary to go to Manassein to ask for the post. In friendly fashion we urged Pavlov to take this step, but he stubbornly refused, considering it an unsuitable thing for him to do. At last we prevailed upon him and he set out, but instead of going to Manassein's office he returned home. Then we took more energetic measures and persuaded him again to go, and this time we sent the laboratory attendant, Timofei, to see that he did not go home again.

A little later, toward the end of the eighties, Pavlov was a candidate for the chair of physiology in the University of St. Petersburg. But N. E. Vedenski was elected. This misfortune affected Pavlov little, since, as he said, he was at that time completely absorbed in observations on the transformation of a chrysalis into a butterfly. A day or so after his rejection at the university, Pavlov noted to his consternation that the slight sounds issuing from the cocoons, where the insects had been stirring, had ceased. He raised the cocoons to his ear, listened attentively, but could not hear any movement. Evidently the insects were dead. And so it proved. The air in the apartment in which the Pavlovs were living was very dry, and the lack of moisture had killed the butterflies.

It happened that at the moment of this tragic discovery Sera-phima Vasilievna, Pavlov's wife, came into the room and began lamenting his failure to obtain the chair at the University of St. Petersburg. There had been the hope that for Pavlov a wide field of scientific activity would open up if he were elected a professor there and that his family would escape from the unbearable financial straits in which they had existed for so long. And now this hope had vanished. Who does not sympathize with a wife and mother who has suffered poverty, and who could blame her for complaining, good wife and mother though she were! But Pavlov replied (and I quote from memory his actual words), "Oh, leave me alone, please. A real misfortune has occurred. All my butterflies have died, and you are worrying over some silly trifle." This, of course, was not a pose but the veritable anguish of a true scientific investigator.

CHAPTER THREE

Seraphima Vasilievna

ON MAY 1, 1881, about a year after graduating from the Military-Medical Academy, Pavlov married Seraphima Vasilievna Karchevskaya, whose family lived in Rostov-on-the-Don. Seraphima Vasilievna was born in 1855. She came to St. Petersburg to study at the Pedagogical Institute and met Pavlov in 1878 or 1879. At this time Pavlov was living in a small apartment with his brother Dmitri, who had obtained the post of assistant in the Department of Chemistry at the University of St. Petersburg.

In her later years Seraphima Vasilievna suffered from ill health and began to sicken in 1932. The death of her son Vsevolod in 1935 was a severe blow to her. The condition of her heart, which had probably been bad for a long time, made it necessary for her to stay in bed frequently. In a letter dated June 2, 1937, she wrote that Pavlov had always said to her, "Your heart is good for nothing." Her health became worse after Pavlov's death, and, in addition, she developed an eye ailment, glaucoma. Her last letters to us before the war were dictated and merely signed by her. She died in 1947.

I consider Seraphima Vasilievna Pavlov to have been an exceptional woman. She was a true friend and companion to Pavlov and understood and appreciated him. Pavlov, being so little aware of everyday problems, in many respects depended on her completely. She was the mother of four children and loved her family. Her whole life was illumined by sincere religious feelings, and it would seem that, all in all, it was a happy one though often difficult. The first nine years of her marriage were made miserable by financial cares. It was not until Pavlov received the chair of pharmacology in the Military-Medical Academy in 1890 and in the following year the directorship of the Department of Physiology in the Institute of Experimental Medicine that life became easier for them.

From the very beginning of their marriage (according to Pro-

fessor Savich) Pavlov was without means, and Seraphima Vasilievna's sister, E. V. Sikorskaya, helped the young couple. It was
necessary for them to share the small apartment of Pavlov's brother
Dmitri, which must have been very uncomfortable and embarrass-
ing for the young bride. Finally Pavlov and his wife experienced
a period of real want and were forced to live apart with friends or
relatives, wherever they could find hospitality. There is no doubt
that the niggardly salary of an Institute doctor was inadequate for
a married man, and the continual lack of money reduced Seraphima Vasilievna to utter despair. However, spiritual well-being
was of primary importance to them, and their material welfare was
a secondary consideration. The ideal and the spirit of self-sacrifice
which animated Seraphima Vasilievna were strong contributing
reasons why their marriage did not fail.

Religion played an extremely important part in Seraphima Vasilievna's life, and this must be taken into consideration in order to
understand her character. Very few of her letters to us (my wife
and myself) in Canada did not mention God. Her religious faith
was true and deep. Thus, on May 22, 1936, soon after Pavlov's
death, she wrote:

> Do you know why I am especially sad? I say to myself, "You did not
> save him." I devoted my life and all my abilities to him to whom I
> promised before God's altar to be a loyal and faithful wife, and, sud-
> denly, I didn't save him. This is terrible—it is unforgivable. I live be-
> cause I must live for Verochka [her daughter] and for my husband's
> memory....
> Only my faith supports me. It is not for nothing that Ivan Petrovich
> used to say: "I envy no one else, but I envy you your religious faith."
> I used to reply to him: "There is a place prepared for you in God's
> Kingdom since God judges people not by their words but by their
> deeds. You live according to Christ's commandments better than any
> servant of God." His soul was pure and his aspirations were pure also.

In the autumn of 1935 the Pavlovs' youngest son Vsevolod died
of cancer of the pancreas. He was then about forty years of age.
His death was a grievous and unexpected blow to the Pavlov
family, since it was not determined until he was operated upon
that Vsevolod had an unremovable malignant tumor of the pancreas. In her Christmas letter, dated December 23, 1935, Seraphima
Vasilievna wrote us:

[28]

SERAPHIMA VASILIEVNA

Yes, we have suddenly been struck by a bolt from the blue. It has long been time for me to die but Vsevolod was taken instead. I believe, profoundly believe, that God does everything for the best, that we with our puny brain cannot understand His designs and for this reason I pray to Her who Herself experienced human sorrow, and I say, "Help me, for I am suffering." I am somehow quite suddenly old, and I must remain strong and cannot even cry, for the sake of Ivan Petrovich, who is bearing this blow badly, for the sake of Vera [her daughter], who is seriously ill, and finally for the sake of Vsevolod's widow, who is living with us. The poor woman has buried her soul—they were so happy together.

Seraphima Vasilievna was outstanding not only because of her deep religious feeling; she undoubtedly also possessed a great love of literature and a talent for writing. While Pavlov was still alive, she began writing her memoirs of him, saying that they were intended for her grandchildren. She also wished to record her talks with Dostoevski on religious topics. "It would be well for the present generation," she wrote on May 13, 1935, "to think by what faith Christians lived and are living. . . . I do not know if I shall have time to finish. But this is necessary. Nowadays all that is most sacred and pure is considered trivial."

Her recollections of a holiday during the time that she was a student at the Pedagogical Institute in St. Petersburg show her appreciation of Russian literature. Apparently the period described was in the seventies, before she was married to Pavlov. Her impressions of this holiday were written at that time.

It is holiday time. A literary soiree. What an evening! All the great talent is there—writers, singers, musicians. Believe me, it is such joy, enough to drive a young girl crazy, especially one who has spent her time studying books and listening to serious conversation!

I put on my black dress; my friend pins her white lace fichu on me and sets the white monitor's ribbon on my shoulder. I enter the hall and in my excitement do not recognize my friends, who stretch out their hands to greet me. I quickly run to the other entrance, where all the invited guests are arriving.

In the middle of a small room on a long table covered with a snow-white tablecloth, tea is being served, with sandwiches, cold hors d'œuvres, expensive *petits fours*, fruit, candy, and various wines. I am a great lover of sweets, but it does not enter my head to pay attention to the food when in the same room with me are Dostoevski, Turgenev, Plescheev [a poet], Melnikov [a writer], Bichurina [a famous actress of that day], and others. Dostoevski silently walks up and down the room, drinking strong tea with lemon. Turgenev tries to be calm but somehow misses the mark in his jokes with the pretty girl-deputies surrounding him. Melnikov is heartily eating hors d'œuvres, and Bichurina, moving a little carafe of brandy closer, drinks glass after glass. Then Melnikov gets up, comes over to her, pats her on the shoulder, and says, "Stop it, Annushka. Remember you are at a children's party." "Well, it's just to get warm," she replies, rises from the table, and goes into the hall to look at these children. It is simply a magic dream!

The first to read is Turgenev. A distinguished-looking man comes out, with an imposing carriage and a mane of gray hair above a clever and expressive face. We hear a resonant voice. Turgenev reads artistically in different tones of voice and is able to bring each character to life by his intonation. *The Singers* stand before us as in real life. When he has finished, thunderous applause and joyful shouts greet him. When all is quiet again, a little man, pale and sickly, with dull eyes, appears on the platform and begins to speak in a weak, barely audible voice. "Poor Dostoevski—he is finished," I think. But instead, what happens? I suddenly hear a deep, loud voice, and glancing at the stage see the "prophet." His face is completely transformed, lightning seems to flash from his eyes, burning the hearts of his listeners, and his face shines with inspiration. At the end of his reading, a real uproar takes place. The audience shouts, breaks chairs, and calls wildly, "Dostoevski, Dostoevski!"

I do not remember who gave me my coat, under cover of which I cried from deep emotion—I do not know how I reached home or who took me home. All the music, all the singing, were but a prelude to this prophetic speech. All the time I kept saying to myself, "Yes, he has kindled the hearts of people and inspired them to serve truth." Ivan Petrovich [Pavlov] repeated the same thing to me, which brought us closer together. Then and there I decided to go to Dostoevski for advice about my faith, which I later did. I must confess that I never again experienced a similar enchantment, a similar uplift of the spirit.

Unfortunately Seraphima Vasilievna does not tell us what Dostoevski said to her.

Seraphima Vasilievna knew and loved Russian literature. In the last years before her husband's death she was often ill and confined to bed. Though past seventy-five, she still kept alive her interest in literature. Much of the period of her illness she spent in rereading Tolstoy, Dostoevski, Kluchevski, and Turgenev and writing her appraisal of them. In their works she found great comfort. After her husband's death she worked on his biography. "I am trying," she wrote us in an undated letter in 1936, "to write Ivan Petrovich's

biography but doubt my own strength to finish it. . . . There is much to write about, after a life of fifty-six years together, and this was no ordinary man but a great man who has become almost a legend."

SERAPHIMA'S MEMOIRS: ARRIVAL IN ST. PETERSBURG

The "Reminiscences" of Seraphima Vasilievna Pavlov appeared in the spring of 1946 in the Soviet Russian journal *Novi Mir* (*New World*). After reading these memoirs, I was convinced that I had understood this remarkable woman correctly and had properly evaluated the very important place she occupied in the life of her husband. The remainder of this chapter is based largely on these memoirs since I can think of no better source for material about the early days of Ivan and Seraphima Pavlov than what one of them wrote after a life-partnership. Incidentally, in her memoirs Seraphima Vasilievna restricted herself only to details of their intimate life and their relations with each other and wrote very little about the scientific activity and laboratory life of Pavlov.

Seraphima Vasilievna Karchevskaya was the daughter of a navy doctor in the Black Sea Fleet. After the death of Dr. Karchevsky, Seraphima Vasilievna and her mother lived in one of the provincial towns of South Russia. The widow's small pension was inadequate to permit a higher education for the daughter. However, the latter had decided to go to St. Petersburg to attend the Pedagogical Institute even though she knew that she would have to depend on what she could earn as a tutor. Not without difficulty she obtained one pupil, whose home was very distant from the place where she was living. She had to tutor her pupil daily and was paid 15 rubles per month. This was Sara's entire income. Even seventy years ago in Russia, 15 rubles (equivalent to $7.50) per month was a very modest income. In order to pay her tuition fees, Sara was forced to pawn her winter coat and wore an autumn jacket throughout an extremely cold winter. She sold her high-school prize books to get enough money to buy theater tickets. Sara was a girl with high ideals and a strong character and refused help from others.

In St. Petersburg there lived at that time her godfather, Admiral P. P. Semenuta, a friend of the late Dr. Karchevsky. Sara found the admiral to be an exceptionally good and clever man who was

exceedingly kind and wanted very much to help her. However, she never accepted any financial help from him, for this would have been a limitation of her independence!

Sara lived in a room which she rented jointly with her dearest friend, Eudoxie Prokopovich. The girls were often visited by a group of ten or twelve students. Among them were two brothers, Ivan and Dmitri Pavlov; Yegor (George) Wagner, later professor of chemistry in Warsaw University; a medical student, Stolnikov, who was a very talented man and a great friend of Ivan Pavlov; and several others. These boys followed the two girls everywhere —to concerts, theaters, dances, and so on.

Each of these young men had his peculiarities. Wagner had a very determined character and easily settled in a few words the most complicated problems of life. Dmitri Pavlov was the wittiest and gayest member of the group. One Cheltzov spoke beautifully on Plato's philosophy, and so on. Ivan Pavlov liked to discuss more general theories. His beloved author was Herbert Spencer. It always seemed to Sara that Ivan's orations were clever and beautifully constructed and his opinions just and noble.

It was Shakespeare who was responsible for the beginning of an intimate friendship between Sara and Ivan. A famous tragedian, Rossi, came with his troupe to St. Petersburg. It happened that Mrs. Semenuta was suddenly called out of town to her sick mother, but the admiral had already bought two theater tickets for a series of the Shakespearean plays. He proposed that Sara accompany him to the theater instead of his wife. He stipulated, however, that on the evening of each performance Sara was to come to her godfather and have dinner with him and explain to him the contents of each play. Rossi's company was an Italian one, and the admiral did not understand Italian.

"There was no limit to my delight," wrote Mrs. Pavlov. "I saw the Shakespearean heroes, whom I have known since my childhood, portrayed most artistically." She added very modestly: "Perhaps my enthusiastic talk about Shakespeare attracted the attention of Ivan Petrovich. He himself was a great admirer of Shakespeare and remained so to his last day."

At this time they frequently discussed the different problems in which the young people of that age were very much interested.

Some of the subjects undoubtedly were of a revolutionary character, and even then Pavlov was inclined to stick to more moderate political opinions. At the beginning, his conservative judgments on current events somewhat surprised Sara, who probably had more radical political views than he, but gradually she became more and more interested in what he was saying.

Certainly it was not Shakespeare and political discussions only which made Sara so dear to the heart of Ivan Petrovich. She was a very pretty, vivacious, and clever girl. Here is a typical scene which shows clearly the character of Sara at this period.

One Christmas Day the lady in whose apartment Sara and Eudoxie rented a room (she was the sister of the famous anarchist Bakunin) invited them to dinner. The girls were stunned by the magnificence of the feast, probably because their own meals were more than modest. Soup was served with a *pirog;* roast goose stuffed with apples and buckwheat gruel followed, and then, oh! delight! Spanish cream in abundance. After dinner there arrived a nephew of the hostess who was a student at Moscow University. He was probably a philosopher, and for this or other reasons was very gloomy and continually spoke of the "Absolute." Another peculiarity was that he wore what are now called "boots" (in Russian, *botiki*) but which were not boots in the ordinary sense of the word. Real Russian boots reach up to the knee, whereas *botiki* cover only the ankles. For some reason, probably adhering to the fashion of the moment, the Moscow students were wearing such *botiki*, whereas the St. Petersburg students were satified with the ordinary high boots. (Of course, the high boots were worn under the trousers, which covered them completely.) The witty Sara gave George, the Moscow student, whom everybody called Yousha, the nickname of *botiki-absolutiki* ("boots-absolutes"!).

Yousha's aunt asked him: "How do you like my young company?"

"Lina is a real beauty," answered Yousha; "Eudoxie is also beautiful; Katia is pretty . . ." and then stopped.

Katia tapped him on the shoulder and said: "Why didn't you say anything about Sara Vasilievna?"

Yousha answered gloomily: "Sara Vasilievna is better than any beauty!"

"*Botiki-absolutiki!*" exclaimed Sara. "Write this down and give me a beauty certificate!"

"Ah, it's *you* who gave me the name *botiki-absolutiki*. I will not write anything for you!" answered Yousha.

Yousha then got up and gloomily asked to be excused because he had to leave in order to finish a philosophical discussion with somebody. However, he did not go very far. At the door he was met by Pavlov's friends, who brought him back, and the whole evening he and his "Absolute" were a target for the jokes of the young people.

PAVLOV FALLS IN LOVE WITH SARA

From the "Reminiscences" of Mrs. Pavlov it is evident that love touched Ivan Petrovich's heart first. It was much later, about two and a half years after their first meeting, that Sara Vasilievna became seriously interested in him.

Pavlov began to show his affection for Sara but, being extremely shy, never did this in a direct way.

On one occasion the young people danced a square dance (quadrille) in the apartment where Sara and Eudoxie lived. Ivan Petrovich had no partner for the dance. He was sitting on a window sill behind a curtain in deep melancholy. Many years later he told Sara Vasilievna what he was thinking about that evening: "What a man this Yegor [Wagner] is! He has known her for only two months and already he has told her how fond he is of her. And I don't dare tell her what she means to me. If she were not here, I would never come!"

However, someone soon pulled Pavlov out from behind the curtain and made him take part in the square dance too.

Among the guests that evening there was a young medical student who had a beautiful baritone voice. He was madly in love with Eudoxie and gazed at her continuously. Suddenly he got up, approached Sara, and told her that he had been asked to sing to her Gremin's aria from Tchaikovsky's opera *Eugene Onegin:*

> "Onegin, I cannot hide from you
> That I love with all my heart Tatiana."

He sang this aria and during the singing he looked sadly at Eudoxie instead of at Sara. When he finished, Sara asked him who had requested him to sing the song to her. He answered that he was not permitted to reveal this secret, but Dmitri Pavlov, who knew the truth, pointed to his brother Ivan, who was again sitting on the window sill behind the curtain!

About three years after their first meeting, Sara really began to notice Ivan Petrovich. She saw now that he was tall, slim, and very agile; that he had curly fair hair and a long beard—in the fashion of that period—and blue eyes and a sincere smile which showed sparkling white teeth. She became aware also that his conversations were always interesting and stimulating and that one felt he possessed a hidden spiritual force. To put it simply, Sara fell in love with Ivan Petrovich.

IVAN PETROVICH PROPOSES TO SARA

Sara was in her last year at the Pedagogical Institute when this new interest in Ivan Petrovich was aroused. At that time she was reading August Comte, and Pavlov gave her a great deal of useful advice. He always added, however: "It would be better if you could begin with my favorite author Spencer."

That winter the brothers Pavlov lived with their mother, who was anxious to have them marry rich girls. She made her wishes known very clearly; and when Sara and her girl friend came to see the two boys, Mrs. Pavlov opened the door herself and angrily said: "They are not at home."

A few minutes after the disappointed girls had left, they heard quick steps behind them and the excited voices of the two brothers: "Stop! Come back!" Of course, the girls refused to return and, instead, invited the boys to come to their apartment, and their invitation was accepted very willingly.

The academic year 1879–80 was drawing to a close. Sara was graduating from the Pedagogical Institute that spring and planned to leave St. Petersburg for good. Pavlov still did not propose to her! At last, on June 13, 1880, he did summon up his courage enough to ask her to marry him.

That evening Sara had spent with the two Pavlov brothers. At eleven o'clock Ivan Petrovich took her home, and on the way he asked her to become his wife. They walked the streets until four o'clock in the morning. (In June, there are practically no nights in

St. Petersburg.) Sara did not go to bed at all but sat just as she was in her overcoat and hat at the window, thinking about the great change which was to take place in her life. Her godfather, Admiral Semenuta, found her still there in the morning.

"Where are you going so early?" he asked.

Seraphima Vasilievna writes that she was delighted to answer: "Congratulate me; I am going to be married!"

"Well, it is too early yet to congratulate you. Have dinner with us at our *dacha* [country house] and bring your fiancé! Then I shall see whether you deserve congratulations or not," replied her godfather.

When Pavlov learned that he was to go with Sara to her godfather's, at first he refused to do so. After a long exhortation by Wagner and Dmitri, he at last gave in and accompanied her. After dinner, the admiral took Pavlov for a walk in the garden and by every means tried to show him how worthless Sara was. He expressed great astonishment that Pavlov had decided to marry such a good-for-nothing girl.

"She is penniless," said the old man. "She is lazy and fond of luxury. She is not pretty at all and will be a hopeless housewife!"

"Don't try to scare me any more," exclaimed Pavlov. "I have known her almost three years. Not only her life but all her thoughts have passed before my eyes. I know that we suit each other!"

The old man embraced Pavlov and said: "I see that you have made a decisive choice!"

When they returned to the house and joined Mrs. Semenuta and the other guests, the admiral did not say a word. Suddenly champagne was served. The admiral kissed Sara tenderly and said:

"Now I may congratulate you and wish you a happy life. I approve of your choice."

The young people decided to postpone the wedding for one year. Sara wanted to "serve the people" in the capacity of a teacher in a primary village school. The idea to help the common people actively in any possible way was dominant among the youth of this age. Ivan Petrovich was studying that year for his M.D. examinations. So they parted. It seems that Pavlov did not study too much, though he passed his examinations successfully. Most of his time, according to the testimony of his brother Dmitri, was spent in writing letters to Sara or reading hers.

At Christmas, Sara came to St. Petersburg for two weeks to visit her fiancé. She stayed with the Pavlov brothers. They still were living with their mother, who had been so unfriendly toward Sara. The Rev. Mr. Pavlov and Mrs. Pavlov were very much against their son's marriage to Sara, but in spite of this disapproval Ivan Petrovich and Sara had a lovely time together. Knowing that she was inclined to spend money too freely, Sara gave the hundred rubles that she had brought with her to Ivan Petrovich. The young people went to the theater and to concerts, and Pavlov presented Sara with candies, pastry, and other delicacies. The only thing which Sara bought for herself was a pair of shoes. Later, she very much regretted that she had trusted Pavlov with her money, for when the time came for Sara to leave St. Petersburg, he declared that he had spent all her money as well as his own and proposed that he might borrow from his mother. Sara was decidedly against this and asked her friend Eudoxie to lend her money for the return trip. Eudoxie herself was short of money and could give Sara only a very little. During the railway trip back to the south, the train was held up by a snowstorm. Half-starving, Sara at last reached her destination. When she opened her trunk to look for her new shoes, to her surprise she found only one shoe. She wrote to Pavlov at once and soon received this answer from him: "Don't look for your shoe. I took it as a remembrance of you and have put it on my desk."

Sara was touched by this expression of affection on the part of her fiancé, but Dmitri continually teased his brother by advising him to drink tea from Sara's shoe!

THE WEDDING

The next summer, Pavlov went to Rostov-on-the-Don, where Sara was living with her married sister. The weather was beautiful, the moon was shining on the river, which flowed like a glittering ribbon, and the flowering acacias filled the air with the aroma of their blossoms. Everything seemed shrouded in mystery, but better than anything were the words of Ivan Petrovich. He declared that Sara and he would strive to achieve the highest aims of the human spirit and that they would serve not only their own Russian people but all humanity.

"I had an unlimited belief in the intellectual strength of Ivan Petrovich," wrote Sara Vasilievna fifty to fifty-five years after her wedding. "I felt that his strong hand was helping me to enter a fairy kingdom. Even now the memory of these conversations inspires me." She remained true to her love and to her belief in her husband all her life.

Were Ivan Petrovich and Sara Vasilievna only dreamers? Were the words which Pavlov spoke only the beautiful but empty words which every young man in love utters so easily? I do not think so. Pavlov to the end of his life kept his idealism, his belief in truth, in liberalism, and in science which, according to his conviction, was to bring happiness to suffering humanity. Like her husband, Sara Vasilievna never gave up her high ideals, her deep religious faith, her devotion to her husband and to her family. And all this in spite of the fact that the first ten years of the Pavlovs' married life were darkened by real and humiliating poverty. No doubt the clash between high ideals and the crude realities of everyday life made Ivan Petrovich and Sara Vasilievna wiser. They learned how difficult it is to achieve high aims as most young people do learn (if they have such aims!). Nevertheless, until the end of their lives they remained idealists.

At last came the day of the wedding. Sara's wedding attire did not cost her a penny. The dress was given by one sister, the shoes by another, and the veil and flowers by a third.

"For what are you praying?" asked Ivan Petrovich during the wedding ceremony in the church.

"For your happiness," said Sara.

"I am doing the same," answered Pavlov.

Sara was true to her vow all her life. She sacrificed all her personal interests and ambitions and created, as far as it was in her power, a happy life for her husband. Not only was she a devoted wife and model mother, but she became the true life-companion of Ivan Petrovich. There is not the slightest doubt that in no small part Pavlov owed his great scientific success to his wife, who organized their home life in such a way that he was never bothered with everyday domestic worries and was able to devote all his time to his work.

Long before her marriage, Sara had had this desire to serve a great cause. The following episode, when she met the great novelist Turgenev, shows this clearly.

A year or two before Sara was engaged to Ivan Petrovich, she occasionally met Turgenev at the home of Mrs. Mordvinov, one of the lady-patronesses of the pedagogical courses.

Turgenev asked Sara one day: "Have you read any of my writings?"

Sara was somewhat offended by this question and answered that as a student in her last year of high school she and her class were asked to write an essay on "A Submissive and an Indocile Woman according to Turgenev."

"Unquestionably, you had a good teacher!" said Turgenev. "Whom did you choose from my heroines?"

"I took Liza from the *Nobleman's Nest* and Marianna from *Virgin Soil*."

Then Turgenev asked: "Who is dearer to your heart?"

"Certainly Liza," answered Sara without any hesitation.

Turgenev was extremely pleased with such an answer. He remarked that only a Russian woman knows what to do with her education, as she will be true to her ideals and will carry them throughout her life.

Mrs. Mordvinov and another lady-patroness (Mrs. N. V. Stasov) were rather doubtful about this point and said that the opinion expressed by Sara was heard very rarely.

"Since my childhood, my beloved heroine has been Tatiana" (from Pushkin's *Eugene Onegin*), declared Sara.

Turgenev smiled and asked, "Is it because of her words:

> 'But I became another's wife:
> I shall be true to him through life'?"

"Yes!" answered Sara. "These words show that Tatiana did not forget her vows and devoted her life to the care and happiness of the one to whom she was married."

Sara, too, was true to her vow all her life.

[39]

CHAPTER FOUR

Married Life

SARA VASILIEVNA begins the chapter on her family life with a quotation from the poet Tiutchev: "Your destiny was hard, but joyous." The Pavlovs' difficulties began immediately after the wedding: Ivan Petrovich had no money either for the wedding or for the return trip to St. Petersburg. Sara Vasilievna's explanation that this was due to his contempt for financial matters was the explanation of a loving heart!

Professor Savich, in his biography of Pavlov, wrote that Sara Vasilievna's sister Mrs. Sikorsky provided the young couple with money, but Sara Vasilievna gave another account of this unpleasant situation. Not wishing her relatives to consider Ivan Petrovich an irresponsible person, she did not expose his carelessness and used her own modest savings for the return railway trip and for their life together during the month of August at a *dacha* (summer home) near St. Petersburg.

When the summer was over, the Pavlovs returned to St. Petersburg absolutely penniless. Fortunately, Pavlov's brother Dmitri, as one of Mendeleev's assistants, had a tiny apartment in the Chemical Institute of the University of St. Petersburg. Later the Pavlovs took a small apartment which they shared with Eudoxie, Sara Vasilievna's student brother, and his friend. They had an old Finnish servant, Gustava, who was a very careful manager. No matter what Sara Vasilievna asked her to prepare for dinner, she would answer: "We will not have this. It is too expensive for us." She fed them chiefly on liver, which was very cheap.

Pavlov's entire income was only 50 rubles per month, earned by lecturing to the male nurses in St. George's Red Cross Hospital. This hardly covered current expenses, let alone the cost of some furniture and other household effects. Sara Vasilievna suggested that she could find a job and thus help them to balance their budget, but Pavlov was decidedly against this plan. He wanted Sara, who had worked since childhood, to remain at home so that they could enjoy the family life about which he had always dreamed. He obtained a few pieces of furniture which belonged to him from his brother's apartment, borrowed 200 rubles from friends, and somehow the Pavlovs managed to furnish their room and to clothe themselves.

In spite of a chronic lack of money, the young Pavlovs and their companions lived very happily. According to all testimonies, Pavlov in his early years was an extremely pleasant and gay companion. At times, however, their financial difficulties, which were close to real poverty, were unbearable. Pavlov, who was accustomed to a Spartan life, probably suffered less than Sara Vasilievna. His complete inability to manage his financial affairs forced Sara Vasilievna to shoulder all such problems. The last drop in the bucket —a rather substantial one—was the following incident.

When Pavlov became the head of the Department of Physiology in the Institute of Experimental Medicine in 1891, he was, for some reason, immediately given 720 rubles, which at that time was considered a very large sum of money. He declared to Sara Vasilievna that he could not trust her with such a large amount of money and that he would take care of it himself. The result was that the Pavlovs lost this money forever. An unscrupulous couple, acquaintances of Ivan Petrovich from Ryazan, learned somehow that the Pavlovs had received this money. The wife asked Sara Vasilievna to lend them the money, but Sara Vasilievna refused. The husband was more successful. The next day he went to see Pavlov in his laboratory and borrowed 700 rubles from him. When in the evening Sara Vasilievna brought her husband a list of things which were needed urgently for the children, for the house, and for themselves, he could give her only 20 rubles. He was very much upset and said: "Well, from now on you had better manage our money affairs yourself." And this she did for the remainder of their lives together.

First Troubles

Sara Vasilievna sacrificed all her personal interests for the interests of her husband and children. Pavlov was not an easy man to live with. Being always concerned with his own thoughts and his work, he paid little attention to the interests of those around him. His nature was passionate, he always wanted to have complete possession of anything that he was interested in at the moment, be it a scientific problem, his own wife, a game of *gorodki* or cards, or a collection of butterflies or stamps. The following shows how little he thought about other people.

Sara Vasilievna was expecting her first baby. Ivan Petrovich liked to take long walks with his wife. He walked extremely fast, so fast, indeed, that he could outdo the horse-drawn carriages. To keep pace with her husband, Sara Vasilievna was forced to run after him. The result of this extreme exertion was that Sara had a miscarriage. Both Pavlov and Sara Vasilievna were very much grieved by this misfortune. When, sometime afterward, Sara Vasilievna was again expecting a child, Pavlov showed the greatest care and attention toward her. He did not permit her even to climb the stairs but carried her in his arms to their fourth-floor apartment.

DEATH OF THE FIRST CHILD AND ILLNESS

The misfortunes of Sara Vasilievna did not end with her miscarriage. The second baby arrived safely—a lovely boy whom the Pavlovs called Mirchik and whom his mother adored.

However, their poverty continued. Presumably there was no money to arrange for Sara Vasilievna and Mirchik, whom she nursed herself, to stay in the country somewhere near St. Petersburg. It was decided that Sara Vasilievna and Mirchik would go to the south to visit her sister. The brothers Ivan and Dmitri scraped up as much money as they could. Unfortunately, it was only enough to purchase a third-class ticket to Ryazan where the Rev. Mr. Pavlov and his wife lived. Sara Vasilievna had to visit the old Pavlovs since the priest had been asked in advance by his son to supply her with money for the remainder of the journey. Unpleasant as it was, Sara Vasilievna had to agree to meet these two who continued to dislike her and who still believed that their son should not have married her. The stingy and harsh old man carefully estimated the cost of a third-class ticket to Rostov-on-the-Don and gave her the money for it, but he did not add anything for food or for other traveling expenses. Those who have never traveled in Russia by third class can hardly imagine what a horror it was. Poor Sara Vasilievna arrived at her destination half-alive. However, in the country, living with her sister's family, she quickly recovered and Mirchik flourished. But alas! Very soon after and very suddenly he died, probably from some children's summer disease.

There was no limit to the despair of Sara Vasilievna after the death of Mirchik, her first child. She had no more desire to live, and it was with difficulty that her brother-in-law was able to persuade her to return to St. Petersburg.

Visit to Professor S. P. Botkin

In spite of the wish of Sara Vasilievna to be useful to her husband, she became a great worry to everyone who was fond of her. She was in such a terrible state of mental depression, being unable either to eat or to sleep, that Mrs. E. P. Shumov-Simanovsky, the wife of Professor Simanovsky and Pavlov's co-worker, forced her to go to the famous clinician Sergei Petrovich Botkin.

It is interesting to see how a medical man without benefit of vitamins, hormones, or pills could restore the shattered health of his physically run-down and mentally depressed patient.

This conversation took place between Professor Botkin and Sara Vasilievna.

"Do you like milk?"

"No, I don't like it and never drink it."

"However, we shall drink it." [The plural "we" was the manner of expression used by the old doctors.] "You are from the south and probably you are accustomed to having a glass [of wine] during your meal?"

"Never a single drop! I detest alcohol."

"However, we shall drink. Do you play cards?"

"What are you talking about, Sergei Petrovich! Never in my life!"

"Well, we shall play cards. Have you read any of Dumas's stories or such wonderful books as *Rocambole?*"

"But what do you think of me, Sergei Petrovich? I recently graduated from the Pedagogical Institute, and we were never interested in such trash."

"Splendid! Therefore you will drink milk daily, starting with half a glass, increasing the amount of milk gradually until you will drink eight glasses per day. Then you will gradually diminish your milk ration and return to the initial half-glass. To each full glass of milk you will add a teaspoonful of brandy."

"But it is disgusting!"

"Is it more disgusting than taking medicine? After your dinner you will lie quietly for one to one hour and a half. You will play daily two to three rubbers of *wint* [the Russian modification of whist], and you will read Dumas's stories. You will walk daily, in any weather, not less than an hour, and every night before going to bed you will sponge yourself with water of room temperature, and you will rub your body with a rough peasant sheet. It is a shame that a man with medical training has forced his wife, in the first period of her married life, to run with him through the woods like a hunter with his hound and has permitted such a tremendous loss of the vital forces to occur that it has resulted in complete exhaustion!"

Sara Vasilievna began to cry and asked Botkin:

"How do you know this?"

"I was told about everything by Mrs. Shumov-Simanovsky. Don't cry, I did not say anything insulting about Ivan Petrovich. He is a physiologist and not a practitioner, and I know that he took great care of you when you were expecting your second baby. A loving husband must treasure his wife. Goodbye. I am sure that you will be quite well again."

Following Professor Botkin's prescriptions exactly, Sara Vasilievna regained her health in three months.

There is a postscript to this story. When Dmitri Pavlov saw that Sara Vasilievna was reading Ponson du Terrail's novel *Rocambole*, he asked her to lend it to him. He took it to the chemical laboratory at the university. Passing through the laboratory, Mendeleev saw the book and borrowed it from Dmitri Pavlov. This happened at two or three o'clock in the afternoon. He appeared next day at the laboratory very late, about four o'clock in the afternoon. He threw *Rocambole* on the bench and said: "It is nonsense, incredible nonsense! But when I began to read it, I could not stop until I had finished." Then, turning to his assistants, he added: "You have all probably read it already?"

Dmitri Pavlov explained to Mendeleev that it was Botkin who had prescribed this book for his seriously ill sister-in-law to read.

"Yes, one can see how clever Botkin was to do so," concluded Mendeleev.

THE PLACE OF SARA VASILIEVNA IN PAVLOV'S LIFE

In writing of the illness which was brought on by Mirchik's death, Sara Vasilievna described herself as melting away like a burning wax candle. It was during this time that Ivan Petrovich often said to her:

"Believe me, if you die, I shall leave forever the science that I love so much. I shall bury myself in the most obscure provincial town and will become a country doctor."

Sara Vasilievna always replied with conviction:

"The will of a dying person is sacred and must be fulfilled absolutely. My last wish is that you will continue to serve science and humanity."

It is very improbable that Pavlov himself started this kind of conversation. Probably Sara Vasilievna spoke about death and received the above reply from Pavlov. But this strong belief in her husband's great scientific future is typical of her, and it was a belief in which she was not mistaken.

When in 1904 Pavlov received a letter from Professor Tigerstedt, notifying him that the Nobel Committee had awarded him the prize, he was exceedingly surprised by this distinctive honor. Sara Vasilievna, on the other hand, found it perfectly natural that at last there had come proper appreciation of her husband's great work. Pavlov was very much displeased with this idea of Sara Vasilievna's and told her that she had forgotten the commandment: "Thou shalt not make unto thee any graven image or any likeness of anything. Thou shalt not bow down to them nor serve them." Yet she did both!

"There is nothing exceptional in my work," added Pavlov; "it is all based on facts from which logical conclusions were drawn. That's all."

To understand the character of Sara Vasilievna, it is important to note that very soon after the wedding she organized their family life so that Pavlov could devote all his time to scientific work. She reminded him that in his letters to her before their marriage he himself had complained about the lack of strong rules and of order in his life. She asked him to promise her three things: first, never to take alcohol in any form; second, never to play cards; and, last, to receive friends on Saturday only and to go to the theater and to concerts only on Sundays. (In Russia, even in my time, anyone, at any time, could visit his friends, which very often was extremely inconvenient and even annoying.) Pavlov gladly promised Sara

Vasilievna to do as she asked him and kept his promise to the end of his days. (However, all his life, for relaxation he liked to play a children's card game called "Fools." There were several of his friends who played with him, and especially strict rules for the game were worked out. They were sometimes called "Fools' Constitution"!)

The devotion of Sara Vasilievna to her husband and her unshakable belief in him were repaid by Pavlov's great love for her and his true friendship.

Here is an example of Pavlov's attitude toward his wife. It happened after Sara Vasilievna's second child was born, that is, several years after their marriage.

Long ago I wanted to talk to you [Ivan Petrovich said once to Sara Vasilievna] about our relationship. You probably remember that for a long time I dreamed of your participation in my scientific work. Many times I told you how highly I valued your capacity for observation and your ability to adjust yourself under any circumstances. Your illness and the difficulty of our life interfered with this plan. Now I see how seriously you have fulfilled the duties of a wife and mother. I have always found in you an interesting and congenial companion as well as a friend who took care of me and freed me of everyday worries. Nothing could be more pleasant and useful to me than the atmosphere that I breathe at home, which you have made a place where I can rest from my scientific thoughts. It would be pretty hard to breathe the same physiological air in the laboratory and at home!

Such conversations occurred often, especially when some experimental work was nearing completion and doubts of its validity and correctness tortured Pavlov.

Here is an example. In 1894, when his work on the digestive system showed some new and important results and at the same time created doubt in Pavlov's mind, he once came home completely upset and could not sleep. Sara Vasilievna knew these paroxysms of doubt in her husband and tried to comfort him by expressing a firm conviction in the correctness and strength of his logic. He answered in this particular case thus:

How wrong I was when I insisted on your participation in my experimental work! You would be only my co-worker and undoubtedly you would share all my opinions. Now you are speaking to me quite independently and therefore convincingly. You have freed me from the eternal physiological atmosphere of the laboratory and created in me a great interest in my own family which refreshes me and gives me a rest from the laboratory tension. Today you have also calmed me. Put your hand on my head and sit near me until I fall asleep.

"This was the happiest period of our life," writes Sara Vasilievna.

JEALOUSY

There is no doubt that Pavlov had an extraordinary wife! One may say with justice, however, that it was not easy for a vivacious, gay, and clever girl, such as Sara Vasilievna had been before her marriage, to be transformed into a stolid matron who sacrificed all her interests for the happiness of her husband and children. I remember Sara Vasilievna (or at that period Seraphima Vasilievna) only as a very quiet and composed woman. She gives the evidence herself in several pages of her "Reminiscences" of how this transformation occurred.

The Pavlovs already had two children (Vladimir and Vera), and Sara Vasilievna devoted all her time to her husband, her children, and her home. She attended parties seldom, since Pavlov was always displeased when she was present at social gatherings. On such occasions, Sara Vasilievna was forced to listen to very unpleasant reproaches from her husband, who was jealous of the time she spent with other people. The following incident will illustrate my point. It was a day when the children had behaved well, Ivan Petrovich was in a good mood, and the couturier had brought Sara Vasilievna a simple but very becoming dress. That evening the Pavlovs were invited to Professor and Mrs. Simanovsky's. Pavlov asked Sara Vasilievna to go there by herself with the understanding that he would join her at the party after the meeting of the Society of Russian Physicians was over.

There were many old friends at the Simanovskys'. Sara Vasilievna was in excellent spirits, very witty, animated, and talkative. At last, when Ivan Petrovich arrived, Professor Simanovsky reproached him for hiding his wife from them all, who was so gay and gave so much pleasure to everybody. Pavlov frowned, said that he was very tired, had a headache, and declared that he was going home at once. He proposed that Sara Vasilievna stay and enjoy herself, but of course she joined her husband and left with him.

Knowing that Ivan Petrovich would spend a sleepless night, Sara Vasilievna at once told him the contents of the conversations at the Simanovskys' and promised him never to go anywhere again without him. In spite of this Pavlov was in a bad mood for two days.

"This was so painful to me," writes Sara Vasilievna, "that I told myself that I would not take so much interest in dresses and that I would make a vow of silence. This attitude on my part brought extremely good results. Ivan Petrovich was spared sleepless nights and saved from unpleasant and painful thoughts. Nevertheless we lived in a friendly atmosphere and very happily."

PAVLOV AS A TRAVELER

Besides such presumably numerous cases of unjustifiable jealousy which reveal Pavlov's difficult temperament, there were other occasions when Pavlov's behavior was far from perfect. Here is a picture of him as a traveling companion.

After the International Congress of Medicine in Paris in 1900, the Pavlovs made a tour of Switzerland, Italy, and Austria. Nothing pleased Pavlov. He was indifferent to the beauty of Paris, and in the midst of Switzerland's magnificent scenery he stubbornly insisted that Sillomiagy (his summer home in Estonia) was much more beautiful.

"With this refrain sounding in my ears, we traveled all over Switzerland," writes Mrs. Pavlov. In Italy he found the food too terrible to eat. He used to say that he always felt that someone had washed their hands in his soup! He found Venice dirty and smelly. In Vienna the Pavlovs stayed only two days because Ivan Petrovich decided that he was tired of looking at foreign wonders and wanted to return home as soon as possible. At the Russian border station Pavlov bowed low to his country and exclaimed:

"At last I will be able to have a plate of *shti!*" (Russian cabbage soup).

In 1903 before leaving for the International Physiological Congress in Madrid, Pavlov proudly showed Sara Vasilievna the two round-trip tickets to Madrid, Granada, Seville, Cadiz, then by sea to Venice, Bologna, Rome, and back to Russia. The tickets were very expensive, but Pavlov presented them to his wife as compensation for her life of continued seclusion at home. When young,

Sara Vasilievna had always dreamed about traveling, and especially she wanted to see Italy and Rome.

Pavlov's behavior during this trip was as bad as his behavior during the first one. He was constantly irritable, as he detested the life of a traveler and thought only about returning home as quickly as possible. In Bologna, where the Pavlovs stayed at a poor hotel, Pavlov was so upset by the conditions that he rushed out into the street, shouting at the top of his voice that it was not a hotel but a den! It can be seen that his wife derived very little pleasure from the trip that was meant to reward her for her dull existence at home. Only the angelic disposition of Sara Vasilievna could withstand her husband's outbursts of moodiness.

After the Revolution of 1917 Pavlov traveled abroad a great deal. He even visited America twice. It seems that he enjoyed meeting foreign scientists and visiting laboratories and institutions. However, it would be better to ask his son Vladimir, with whom Pavlov traveled during that period, how his father enjoyed traveling. The difference between these trips and his early journeys was that they were scientific visits and not pleasure trips.

INTIMATE LIFE

I know very little of the intimate side of the Pavlov's family life, but the stories of friends and my own personal observations have led me to think that, generally speaking, Pavlov and his wife's life together was happy and that they were imbued with mutual respect. Pavlov, when speaking to others, would jokingly refer to his wife as "my dearest half" or in more intimate talks as "Sara" (an abbreviated form of her name which she disliked).

Pavlov depended very much on his wife's care, since all the family problems fell on her shoulders. Seraphima Vasilievna even bought his clothes for him. He never carried money with him. All that he ever had in his pocket was 15 or 20 kopeks for the horse trams and later for the electrically driven streetcars when they appeared in St. Petersburg. In all probability this money was given him by Seraphima Vasilievna every morning along with his lunch, wrapped in a clean little napkin, and I think that she must have accompanied him to the hall door every morning, for once she said that it was her "privilege" to help her husband on with his coat.

Money had little interest for Pavlov, but he hated to spend it, not from avarice but because he had passed through the grim school of poverty and valued the labor which earned it. Sometimes in the laboratory he would complain that Seraphima Vasilievna spent too much money—only yesterday he had given her his salary from the Academy and today she was demanding his pay from the Institute of Experimental Medicine! He grumbled mainly because, in order to get this money, he had to put on his coat and rubbers and go to the treasurer's office in another building, thus losing five or ten minutes of the laboratory's time. (Nevertheless he always fulfilled her requests.)

Although she took care of all other family matters, one thing she could not do was to buy the winter's wood supply for their apartment, which was leased to them "without wood." This duty fell on Pavlov. He discharged it without enthusiasm but with the thoroughness with which he did everything. Usually on a September morning he went down to the Neva or the Fontanka River, where the "wood" barges were tied up, or to the storehouses near there and bought his supply for the winter. The wood vendors were not distinguished by polite manners, refined speech, or honesty, and had to be carefully watched or else they would cheat and try to pass off inferior wood and in smaller quantities than had been agreed upon.

The following story, which Pavlov told me in Montreal in 1929, shows how indispensable Seraphima Vasilievna was to his well-being. He was telling us that St. Petersburg at night had become a desolate, lonely city, poorly illuminated, and dangerous for pedestrians. If someone was assaulted, no help or defense could be expected. He was especially worried when his daughter Vera had to cross the Nikolaevski Bridge over the Neva River on returning home in the evening, even if it was still early. "There is no one on the bridge, and it is dark," he said. "It would be easy to rob her, take off her coat, and then throw her over the parapet into the Neva—she is so little. I worry; I can do nothing," he continued, "and my only comfort is my wife. I look at her, and, if she is calm, then little by little my cares go from me."

I would not be telling the truth if I were to say that Seraphima Vasilievna's life was a continual idyll. The chief hardship of her married life, so far as I can gather, arose from the fact that Pavlov was an extraordinary man. Every great man finds himself in the grip of some dominating idea; everything else is relatively unimportant. This makes living, and even casual relations, with such a person very difficult. Pavlov, moreover, was easily irritated and quickly aroused. Because of his passionate nature, his emotional outbursts were often out of proportion to the provocation. Though in general he was extraordinarily reserved and firm, little things easily annoyed him. In such cases, silence was the best defense since argument only poured oil on the fire. But when the last traces of smoke from such an explosion had cleared and all his wrath was spent, it was easy to explain one's point of view and to insist on one's opinion. Pavlov was a fair man; he always admitted when he was at fault and never insisted on his opinions in order to "save face." He was never malicious, but there was little softness in him, although essentially he was a kind and responsive person. For those who did not know him, however, his kindness was masked by his irritability and a sort of tenseness in everything he did.

Here is an incident told me by Pavlov's son Vladimir in a private conversation but in the presence of his father and mother and testifying to the fact that Pavlov's irritation with something outside his home was often turned against his family—a kind of "irradiation of excitation."

Once, when Vladimir was a little boy, his father grumbled at Seraphima Vasilievna and his son all through dinner, complaining about a certain Dr. Mett, who was working at that time in his laboratory (1889). Dr. Mett had in some way disgraced himself that day and had done something wrong during an experiment. The little boy turned to his father and said: "Papa, how are mother and I at fault because Dr. Mett's experiment was not successful?" Of course, this rebuke from a child immediately stopped Pavlov's scolding.

It was interesting to watch Pavlov's face while his son told this story. He looked at Vladimir with an expression either of reproach or of apprehension, as though thinking, "What next will he be saying about me?"

I was a witness and to some extent a victim of a similar "irradiation of excitation" when Pavlov and his son Vladimir were in

London in 1923. They were preparing to return to Leningrad and for some reason had chosen the route through Finland. The Finnish consul in London, however, refused to give them a transit visa. At that time everyone feared bolshevism, the Finns especially, and Pavlov's name meant nothing to the Finnish diplomat. I arrived at the house where the Pavlovs were staying, that of our mutual friend, the late Miss Rose M. Paul, just as they returned from the Finnish consulate. Pavlov's face was dark and grim, and Vladimir was trying to appear cheerful. Finally Pavlov could restrain himself no longer and poured out his anger to me. "Did you ever see a son like this," he said, "who would abandon his old father, unfamiliar with the language, in the middle of a strange city?" It appeared that Pavlov was so cross at having been refused a visa that on the street going home he began to complain about the consul and then to scold Vladimir for not having arranged things better. Pavlov expressed his anger in thunderous sentences and, as was his custom even in ordinary conversation, by waving his hands about so much that the English passers-by, unused to such methods of discourse, turned to look at them or even stopped to watch. Seeing this, Vladimir threatened to leave his father and go home by himself if he did not stop shouting at once. Pavlov kept quiet then and said not another word during the whole trip home, but when he saw me he could contain himself no longer and told me of his son's "heartlessness." Probably owing to the fact that he did not find me very sympathetic, he suddenly descended on me. The subject was not in the least relevant to the problem of a transit visa. Why had I "introduced" to the study and technique of conditioned reflexes one of my colleagues in the University of Odessa who now, it seemed, was only creating confusion in this field? I replied that any person has the right to work on any problem that he chooses and that, since I could not stop this man from working on conditioned reflexes, it was much better that I should watch over his experiments. My reply, of course, did not satisfy him. Indeed, no reply would have pacified him at that moment. He muttered something, and our conversation soon turned into a more peacful channel.

With what yardstick can one measure Pavlov as a man? If he had been an ordinary man, he would be considered an egotist, for whom personal interests were of such paramount importance that everyone and everything had to serve them. However, such a yardstick cannot be applied to a man of genius. Pavlov served an ideal of the highest and noblest character. He firmly believed, until the end of his life, that only through science can humanity be made happy. He did not require much for himself; the simplest life, a plate of cabbage soup (*shti*), a game of *gorodki*—things which his humblest countryman was able to have—satisfied him completely. All those who lived and worked with him, including his wife, had to sacrifice their own interests for his, if they wanted to remain with him, for his own interests were not his personal interests in the strict sense of the word but lay outside him, so to speak.

Another example of a man with an incomparably greater egotism than Pavlov, and without his crystal honesty, who subdued everything and everyone for the achievement of his high ideal, was Richard Wagner. He actually sacrificed his health and life for the creation of a new era of musical drama. Neither Pavlov in his belief that science alone will bring happiness to humanity nor Wagner in his belief that the true form of art is a combination of drama and music was correct. (Newman[1] [2:193, 1937] defined Wagner's ideal as "music, poetry and visible action all cooperating to one end in the theatre.") Nevertheless they both achieved great things, one in science, the other in art. (This does not mean that all men of genius are of the Pavlov-Wagner type and are difficult to deal with. There were other men of genius, no less great than these two, who possessed a most kind and friendly character. Thus, for instance, W. Ostwald in his book *Grösse Männer* [1909] spoke of Faraday as a man exceptionally gentle and full of sympathy toward other people.)

When King Ludwig of Bavaria (the so-called "mad king," but whose madness actually was never proved) learned about the death of Wagner (1883), whose work he had supported, he exclaimed: "It was I who was the first to understand this artist, the death of whom the whole world now mourns: it was I who rescued him for the benefit of the world."

Newman, Wagner's biographer, comments as follows on the above: "This is no more than the simple truth; it was to him and after him to Cosima, that the world was indebted for the preservation of Wagner and the completion of his life's work. These two never doubted his mission, suffered with him and for him, never forsook him, never shrank from any sacrifice for him."

One has to regard such women as Sara Vasilievna Pavlov and Cosima Wagner with the greatest respect and admiration. They gave up their own lives to serve their husbands or, more exactly, the high ideals toward which their husbands were striving. Both these women were intelligent, even talented (Cosima was an accomplished musician), but both of them saw their destiny in the support of those whom Fate gave them as life-companions.

CHAPTER FIVE

Professorship in the Military-Medical Academy

THE year 1890 marked the beginning of a new period for Pavlov, a period when he could devote himself wholly to scientific work and when he entered on the path which was to lead to world fame.

The first institution to acknowledge Pavlov as an outstanding and promising scientist was the University of Tomsk in Siberia. Dean Florinski offered him the chair of physiology, but the minister of education, Delianov, appointed another candidate, a certain Dr. Veliki, who was recommended by some influential person. Florinski then offered, and Pavlov accepted, the chair of pharmacology. However, on April 24, 1890, the very next day after his official appointment, Pavlov was also elected by the Conference of the Military-Medical Academy to the vacant chair of pharmacology in the Academy. Here he assumed his duties on June 15, 1890. The conditions for work were certainly more favorable at the Academy than in the recently opened University of Tomsk. Less than a year later (June 13, 1891) Pavlov, at the invitation of Prince Alexander Petrovich Oldenburg, became director of the Physiological Department of the Institute of Experimental Medicine, which opened in 1890. At the Institute, Pavlov found exceptional opportunities for developing his scientific activities, and here he carried out his scientific work on the digestive glands and on conditioned reflexes.

The Chair of Pharmacology

From the very first year of his professorship at the Academy, Pavlov made radical changes in the teaching of pharmacology there. In his lectures he emphasized the main action of medicinal substances and avoided petty details, and he introduced demonstrations during lectures. All this was necessary because in the eighties and nineties of the last century pharmacology was one of the most backward of the medical sciences. It was made up of countless unrelated and unsystematized facts, some important but mostly unimportant and burdensome to the memory of the student.

Dr. Kamenski (1904), former assistant of Pavlov in the Department of Pharmacology, informs us that Pavlov eliminated all unessential details from his course and, being a physiologist, classified all the most important drugs according to their basic physiological action. Thus he grouped together drugs which stimulate the central nervous system and drugs which paralyze it, substances which stimulate the muscles and those which paralyze them, and so on. Unquestionably this method of teaching introduced some order and clarity into the heterogeneous material of pharmacology, so that Pavlov's presentation was more akin to the present-day methods of teaching. Moreover, Pavlov did not strive to inform his students about all the latest drugs but considered it more important to examine in detail the mechanism of the action of drugs already known. He taught his students to consider the action of drugs from the physiological viewpoint and not the purely empirical knowledge concerning their effects on the organism. In order to evaluate correctly the method of teaching which Pavlov introduced into pharmacology, we must not forget that this happened more than fifty years ago. Since then physiology and experimental pathology have made tremendous advances and opened up new avenues of approach to the study and understanding of the action of drugs.

Pavlov (1894) expressed his views on the problems of pharmacology in a paper in memory of N. I. Pirogov on "The Defects of Contemporary Physiological Analysis of the Action of Drugs," read at the Fifth Convention of Physicians. In this report Pavlov described pharmacology as a branch of science bordering on physiology, on the one side, and clinical therapy, on the other. A conflict often arises between pharmacology and the clinic when the pharmacologist is unable to confirm in experiments on animals the therapeutic effect claimed for some drug while the clinician often finds that the results of some laboratory research is not applicable to the cure of a sick person. Pavlov considered that the greater fault lies with the pharmacologist who investigates the action of drugs only on the functions of the organism known to contemporary physiology. He believed it desirable to widen pharmacological experimentation and to open new fields of pharmacological investigations. He stressed, for example, the importance of studying the action of various substances on the peripheral endings of different nerves, the specific character of which he emphasized. This problem interested him in connection with his work on the physiology of the digestive glands. Pavlov also recommended strongly the study of the effect of drugs on the central nervous system and on the processes of restoration of tissues after their activity.

In the five years during which Pavlov was head of the Department of Pharmacology twelve M.D. theses and several papers on pharmacological problems were issued from his laboratory. A short review of these may be found in an article by Dr. Kamenski published in 1904.

THE CHAIR OF PHYSIOLOGY

Pavlov was in charge of the Department of Pharmacology actually for a little less than five years, since he was appointed on May 29, 1895, to the chair of physiology vacated by Professor I. R. Tarkhanov, who was dismissed.

Tarkhanov's dismissal and Pavlov's transfer was the work of V. V. Pashoutin, principal of the Military-Medical Academy at that time. This was attributable to Pashoutin's unfair and personal motives. He had a tendency to patronize his own former students and to help them by all possible means to obtain chairs at the Academy without regard to their scholastic merits. Thus, P. M. Albitsky was appointed professor of general and experimental pathology (a chair occupied by Pashoutin himself before he was made principal of the Academy), and a chair of encyclopedia and history of medicine was created for Skorichenko. Another former student of Pashoutin's, Kosturin, was professor of pharmacology in the University of Kharkov.

Pavlov suspected nothing of these maneuvers behind the scenes. He was far removed from intrigue, and Pashoutin's offer to transfer him to the chair of physiology came as a complete surprise to him. He told us that after his talk with Pashoutin he thought: "Even though Pashoutin is a scoundrel, he evidently respects science and appreciates me as a physiologist." Pashoutin himself had been a promising scientist but ruined his career by becoming an administrator and yielding to that passion for power which creates so much evil in the world. Disappointment in Pashoutin's "respect for science" came very soon, for immediately after Pavlov's transfer to the chair of physiology Kosturin was appointed to the chair of pharmacology. Kosturin died not long afterward, in the spring of 1899, and N. P. Kravkov was elected to the chair of pharmacology.

Upon becoming professor of physiology, Pavlov immediately reorganized the method of teaching this subject at the Academy. He placed the main emphasis on demonstrations during lectures. Each lecture was intended as an explanation of the experiment which the students were watching. Later, some of the students wrote up, and Pavlov edited, the experiments and published them under the title of *Physiology in Experiments*.

Almost every lecture that Pavlov gave to the students was accompanied by one or two experiments. Everything possible to demonstrate in a classroom was shown. Many of the experiments were extremely difficult; and, in order to prepare for them, it was necessary for some of the staff to come to the laboratory at six or seven in the morning, since the lectures began at nine. There were five lectures in physiology each week, one on Thursday, two on Friday, and two on Saturday. These were for students in the second year. During his first year as professor of physiology Pavlov himself came early in the morning and took part in the preparation of the experiments. Later this was the responsibility of Vartan Ivanovich Vartanov, the prosector (an assistant of higher rank) in the Department of Physiology.

Cyon had introduced into the physiology course lecture demonstrations on laboratory animals. Sechenov, it seems, did not like to make experiments on warm-blooded animals. But it was Pavlov who made lecture experiments the basis of the teaching of physiology.

This method of teaching had great advantages and also some disadvantages. There is no doubt that knowledge strengthened by facts actually witnessed made an indelible impression on the student. But, unfortunately, only the students in the front rows could see all that was going on in an experiment. The majority of the students in the auditorium had to rely on the lecturer's words. Pavlov usually called on one of the students to come to the table on which the animal lay. The student had to testify that a truthful representation of what was going on in the experiment was being passed on to the audience. In jest Pavlov called this student his "honorable witness." The latter, either from embarrassment or because the complicated experiment was so difficult to follow, usually stood by either dumb or nodding his head, not always at the right time. But the chief shortcoming of this method of teaching physiology in the Military-Medical Academy was the absence of practical work.

The main reason why no practical classes were held in the Department of Physiology (at least up to the end of the War of 1914) was the absence of the requisite space and facilities, an inadequate number of assistants, and the pathetically small laboratory budget (300 or 400 rubles, or $200 per annum). Pavlov considered that his course of "Physiology in Experiments" to a certain extent took the place of practical work—an opinion with which it is difficult to agree.

The physiological laboratory was transferred in 1905 to a fine new building on Lomanski Street, but, if I am not mistaken, practical classes in physiology were not introduced by Pavlov at the Academy until 1920.

During the time when I was a student at the Academy (1898–1901), there were, in addition to the general course in physiology for the students in the second year, special optional courses of lectures open to all students, given in alternate years by Pavlov and the professor of physiological chemistry, A. J. Danilevski. Thus, for example, in 1898 or 1899 Pavlov, during the course of his lectures, explained and demonstrated in classroom experiments all that was then known about the functions of the vagus nerve. The lectures were especially interesting since Pavlov had contributed so much to the elucidation of the role of the vagus nerves in the body.

PAVLOV, THE TEACHER

Pavlov's method of lecturing was unique for his day. He expounded his subject very simply and clearly, achieving this mainly by emphasizing the most essential points and omitting details. He was never theatrical or pretentious, but his lectures reflected a deep and sincere interest in his subject, which often warmed to real enthusiasm. His classes were always full of students, who soon became infected with his sincere interest in physiology. Pavlov's language was exact and picturesque. He often used descriptive phrases. He would say, "acid forces out the pancreatic juice," instead of "acid stimulates the secretion of pancreatic juice," or "bile knocks out pepsin," instead of "bile arrests the action of pepsin," and so on. He did not use notes when lecturing or when he read his papers in Russian at different meetings, since his memory was extraordinarily good. However, he was no orator, and he said that he passed on to his listeners only what he had thought over earlier.

He permitted students to interrupt him during his lectures and gladly answered their questions. Sometimes he asked questions himself, to make sure that the students were following him and to find out whether they were thinking or merely listening passively. Dr. S. A. Komarov told me that once, when Pavlov was speaking of how difficult it was to collect pure gastric juice, he asked the students how they would set about obtaining it. One student volunteered an answer and gave a correct account of a very difficult operation which can be performed on a dog in order to isolate part of the stomach to form a "stomach pouch." Although the pouch described was one which Pavlov himself had devised, Pavlov was not at all pleased with this answer and said: "You have not thought that out for yourself but have merely read about it."

He delivered his lectures seated in a chair before a table, not standing, as most lecturers did in my time. This was no doubt the survival of the "chair," on which professors always sat in former days.

When the lecture was accompanied by an experiment, Pavlov became extremely animated and, if all went well, was genuinely pleased. It made no difference whether he had seen the same experiment performed a thousand times; he was invariably delighted to see it again. Often he would take the electrode or test tubes out of his assistant's hand and start to stimulate a nerve or collect the flowing juice, and sometimes his interference upset the progress of the experiment. Then he would become greatly irritated—with the assistant of course. If an experiment was for some reason unsuccessful, Pavlov without hesitation would begin blaming the assistant then and there, to the great delight of the students, who loved such a "circus." This scolding would go on after the lecture, behind the scenes, and the worst reproach that Pavlov could level against the guilty assistant was to say that he was "not a physiologist."

At that time it was still the custom at the Academy, for all the assistants, some of the *Privatdocenten*, and many of the research workers to be present at lectures even when no demonstration was being given. Since the same lectures were repeated year after year, it was somewhat tedious at times to have to sit through them. Very amusing incidents often occurred when Pavlov in the middle of a lecture suddenly asked an assistant something and the assistant was unable to reply, his thoughts having roamed far from physiology.

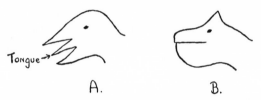

Fig. 1.—*A*, Head of a dog drawn on the blackboard by Pavlov. *B*, Head of a dog drawn on the blackboard by me.

One such incident happened to me. Pavlov was giving a lecture on the salivary glands (he always began the course with the subject of digestion) and was speaking of the most elementary things. I do not know where my thoughts had wandered, but, though present in body at the lecture, I was absent in spirit. All of a sudden Pavlov turned to our group of assistants and asked if someone could draw a dog's head on the blackboard. Pavlov never used any charts or slides but drew what he needed on the board during the lecture. He was a very bad draftsman and his drawings were a source of great amusement to the students. This time he had drawn the head of a dog with outstretched tongue. He had to show the tongue, since he was speaking of reflexes from the mouth cavity to the salivary glands. The drawing was something like that shown in Figure 1, *A*.

Apparently this time the students' laughter at such an extraordinary dog hurt Pavlov's feelings, and he turned to us with the request that one of us would draw a dog's head for him. Nothing of what had been going on had penetrated my brain. But, as often happens when one returns suddenly to reality, I thought wrongly that the question had been addressed to me and, not being anything of an artist myself, I drew the accompanying monster with a huge jaw (Fig. 1, B). The students' delight was unbounded. "Hey," shouted Pavlov, "why did you offer to draw when you draw worse than I do? And where is this dog's tongue?"

Pavlov loved to have an audience and to lecture. In a letter dated January 29, 1928, he wrote me as follows: "And now concerning worldly matters. I will tell you of my taste. I used to like lecturing very much and I gave this up with reluctance owing to the 'purge.' When you are trying to pass something on to someone else, you enlighten yourself because it is impossible to teach others that in which you yourself are not well versed. And furthermore the excitement of a lecture often puts new ideas into one's head."

The reference to "purge" in his letter concerns Pavlov's voluntary resignation from his professorship at the Military-Medical Academy in 1924. At that time the Bolshevist authorities did not permit the children of the clergy to have a higher education. Pavlov explained his resignation by saying that he was himself the son of a clergyman and considered it a great injustice to deprive these young people of the right to a higher education.

Pavlov always wore civilian dress, even though the professors at the Academy usually wore military uniform. For his lectures he would put on over his civilian waistcoat and trousers a military frock with epaulettes but never bothered to button it. He kept his uniform hanging in his laboratory, and I think that during his thirty-four years of service at the Academy he owned only two military frocks. He would have managed with only one, had not the laboratory attendant Morozov gambled away his first, for which misdemeanor Pavlov dismissed him.

Once, when it was announced that the minister of war, General Kuropatkin, would in all probability attend the lecture on physiology that day, Pavlov decided, after much swearing, that for this occasion he would have to put on not only the military frock but the trousers as well. He arrived in the auditorium in complete military dress, with his coat buttoned. The students greeted him with laughter. The reason for this hilarity was that there was still attached to the trousers, which Pavlov had never worn before, one of those slips of paper on which Russian tailors put the measurements of their clients. "What are they laughing at?" Pavlov asked crossly. When it was explained what was the matter, he tore the paper off angrily and said: "The devil only knows all the foolish things one has to do!" by which he expressed his disgust at having to put on the uniform. Incidentally, General Kuropatkin did not appear at the lecture.

CONFLICT WITH THE PRINCIPAL OF THE ACADEMY

Pavlov was not only an honest and independent person but a fighter by nature. At no time was this streak in his character more clearly apparent than in his official dealings with the principal of the Academy, V. V. Pashoutin.

During the time when his predecessor (Bvkov, I think) was in office, Pashoutin was the honorary secretary of the Academy; he was very popular with the professors and was considered an outstanding scientist, an excellent secretary, and a good colleague. He was elected principal of the Academy by the Conference (council or senate) of the Academy. His appointment as principal was hailed with satisfaction by the professors. However, their joy soon turned to dismay. The passion for power, hidden deep in Pashoutin's nature, came to light in a series of infringements on the regulations of the Academy and in many unjustifiable actions.

The chair of general and experimental pathology became vacant when Pashoutin was appointed principal of the Academy, and his method of filling it showed at once his dictatorial tendencies. He wanted this chair to go to either Albitsky or Kosturin, both former students of his. Since both these men were extremely weak candidates and there was a possibility that neither would be elected by the Conference of the Academy, Pashoutin invented the following extraordinary method of balloting. Only one ballot box was provided. On one side of the box appeared Albitsky's name, and on the other Kosturin's. Since the professors were given only one ballot ball, no matter where the vote was cast, one or the other candidate was sure to be elected.

This ruse, which violated all the voting rights of the professoriate, made Pavlov so indignant that he lodged a personal protest and demanded that his views be included in the official records. As a result he was reprimanded by the minister of war, Vannovsky. Pavlov made the following statement: "I consider the method of balloting on professors Albitsky and Kosturin at any rate incorrect; for instance I wanted to put a white ball in the ballot box for each of them, but I could not do this as I had received only one ball. Thus I undeservingly offended Doctor Kosturin."

The resolution of Minister Vannovsky in reply to Pavlov's statement ran as follows: "I consider the statement made by Professor Pavlov at any rate incorrect, since professor Pashoutin had the right to replace the chair, which he occupied with such glory, by one of his pupils and thus to preserve his own line of scientific research."

P. M. Albitsky was elected to the chair of general and experimental pathology and the department was buried in deep sleep for at least twenty years.

The reprimand which Pavlov received from the minister of war in no way chastened or deterred him, and he continued to wage war against the ever increasing ambitions of Pashoutin. To be on the side of the law, Pavlov learned the Academy regulations by heart and carried the book of regulations in his pocket so that he would always be prepared to raise objections to Pashoutin's illegal actions at the Academy Conference meetings.

Many of the Conference members sympathized with Pavlov's stand but lacked courage to support him openly. He struggled alone and in vain against Pashoutin and the group of professors who formed the principal's party. Every conceivable difficulty was put in his way. Thus, it was not until 1897—seven years after he had accepted the chair at the Academy—that Pavlov was given the rank of "Ordinary Professor," together with an increase in salary. What disappointed Pavlov more than the delay in his promotion was the fact that none of the Institute doctors attached to his department was ever elected for study abroad.

Notwithstanding all that has been said to the contrary, Imperial

Russia, so often called a "police state," was slowly and with many delays reaching toward democratic development. It is not fair to blame only the government for political backwardness. Those who had privileges did not value them or defend them. Here is an example taken from the affairs of the Military-Medical Academy.

When four outstanding professors were retired by Pashoutin from the Academy, Pavlov organized a dinner by subscription for them.[1] Out of thirty-five professors twenty-five gave their signatures. Pashoutin expressed his displeasure apropos of this dinner, and most of the professors refused to attend it. There was no limit to Pavlov's indignation. Among other things he said: "If from the very beginning we had defended our rights and our dignity, Pashoutin would have been forced to give up. But now the situation is such that the one holding the stick is master, and the stronger this stick is, the lower everyone has to bow his head. Here is no moral dignity, only the servility of slaves!"

After each Conference meeting Pavlov came home completely broken. Two of Pavlov's friends (Professors Simanovsky and Sirotinin) once reproached Mrs. Pavlov for not restraining her husband in his quarrel with Pashoutin. "But I admired the courageous behavior of Ivan Petrovich, who fought for truth," wrote Mrs. Pavlov in her "Reminiscences."

Pavlov's fearless attitude to Pashoutin was therefore all the more extraordinary when compared with the servility of the rest of the Academy professors. He rated independence higher than any other human attribute. I think that I may be permitted to quote here a letter which Pavlov wrote me after I had been appointed to the chair of physiology at Dalhousie University, Halifax, Nova Scotia, in 1924.[2]

VASILIEVSKI OSTROV, 7TH LINE
October 23, 1924

DEAR BORIS PETROVICH:

I thank you with all my soul for your sincere greetings. I feel indeed that your letter comes straight from your heart. I repeat, I am happy that you have at last found a position. And not only because you have the chance to work independently, are provided for, and so on. This is obvious. But also because this has come to a person who has kept his personal integrity intact, for, having received an insult, you kept sternly

[65]

remembering it and refused to return to Russia in spite of all offers, at a time when your position was very hard abroad.

I am amazed at the absence of this feeling of integrity in those around me. A person is thrown once, twice, three times into jail, chained like a dog, but he soon forgets this and seems to be unaware that he has been insulted.

I was happy to read in your letter about the flame of research.

Write to me in your next letter, as promised, details of all the facts of your life.

Yours,
I. Pavlov

Pashoutin suddenly collapsed and died at one of the meetings of the Academy Conference in 1900. He was succeeded as principal by the professor of anatomy, A. I. Tarenetski, and the conduct of affairs at the Academy changed for the better. Pavlov now stopped carrying the book of Academy regulations in his pocket when he went to the Conference meetings.

CHAPTER SIX

The Institute of Experimental Medicine

PAVLOV used to carry on his research work not at the Military-Medical Academy but in another physiological laboratory, at the Institute of Experimental Medicine. Up to 1905, when a new and spacious physiological laboratory was opened at the Military-Medical Academy, almost all the work which was done under his direction was carried on at the Institute.

The Institute of Experimental Medicine was founded in St. Petersburg by H.R.H. Prince Alexander Petrovich Oldenburg in 1890. The creation of this fine institution was without doubt a repercussion of the brilliant discoveries of Pasteur and the successes of the newly established science of bacteriology. From the very beginning of its existence, one of the departments in the Institute was called "Pasteur's Station" because it was engaged in the production of vaccine against rabies. I do not know who suggested the name of the Institute, but undoubtedly its choice was influenced by the ideas of Magendie and Claude Bernard. For a long time the Institute of Experimental Medicine was the only one of its kind in Europe in addition to the Pasteur Institute in Paris. Subsequently, the Lister Institute was opened in London in 1901 and the Kaiser-Wilhelm-Gesellschaft zur Förderung der Wissenschaften, with its numerous laboratories, in Berlin in 1911.

Up to the time of the Revolution of 1917 there were seven departments in the Institute. The heads of the departments when the Institute was founded were I. P. Pavlov, physiology; M. V. Nencki, biochemistry; O. N. Vinogradski, general bacteriology; P. V. Ouskov, pathology; H. I. Gelman and then A. A. Vladimirov, epizoötiology; E. F. Sperk, syphilidology; V. A. Kraushkin and V. G. Ushakov, Pasteur's Station. The Department of Syphilidology had ceased to exist in my time (1901–12) but had been replaced by the Department of General Pathology, directed first by Lukianov and afterward by Podvisotski. Both these men served in turn as directors of the Institute. In addition to the above-mentioned departments, there was a clinic for the study of skin diseases, which was opened while I was at the Institute.

The Institute of Experimental Medicine was established on a solid basis. It was made a state institute, and the prince persuaded Czar Alexander III to bestow on it the title of "Imperial." This gave prestige to the new center of learning, putting it at once on a level with older educational establishments.

The choice of heads for the Institute departments was extremely successful, since Pavlov, Nencki, and Vinogradski were at that time already considered first-class scientists. I was told that at first the brothers A. J. and V. J. Danilevski were considered as prospective heads of the Departments of Biochemistry and Physiology, respectively, but, fortunately, Pavlov was chosen to be head of the Physiology Department, and he, it seems, recommended Nencki to the prince for the chair of biochemistry.

It is difficult to exaggerate the importance of the Institute of Experimental Medicine, which became a model for similar institutions in pre-revolutionary Russia. After the Revolution the basic plans of its founder were not altered but merely enlarged. The Institute of Experimental Medicine was reorganized as the All-Union Institute of Experimental Medicine located at Moscow. The St. Petersburg Institute became a branch of the All-Union Institute.

THE PHYSIOLOGICAL LABORATORY OF THE INSTITUTE

At the beginning of the twentieth century Pavlov's laboratory in the Institute of Experimental Medicine appeared to many, and especially to visiting foreigners, as small and dirty. Compared with the palatial American laboratories, it was a mere hovel. Nevertheless, in the nineties of the last century, it was unique and far in advance of the times. Here Pavlov's idea of adapting aseptic surgical methods to the study of physiological function in animals and in particular to the study of the functions of the digestive tract was realized for the first time. As an alternative to the old physiological method of "acute experiment," where an experiment is performed on an anesthetized animal which is not allowed to survive but is painlessly destroyed, Pavlov introduced the new method of "physiological surgery." In this method an aseptic operation is per-

INSTITUTE OF EXPERIMENTAL MEDICINE

formed on an animal in accordance with all the rules of surgery. The animal comes out of the anesthetic and is given the utmost care after the operation, and when fully recovered it is used for so-called "chronic experiments." By this term is meant repeated experimentation, sometimes over many years, without the slightest pain to the animal, which is in normal or nearly normal state. Pavlov established a special surgical section in his laboratory for the carrying-out of such operations on animals. The two methods of performing physiological experiments will be explained in greater detail in Part III. I should only mention here that nowadays a physiological or experimental pathological laboratory without a special department for the performance of aseptic operations on animals is rare, but at the end of the nineteenth century this was a great innovation.

Other important factors which aided Pavlov in the full development of his talents were the allocation to his laboratory of an adequate budget and provision for the services of assistants and laboratory attendants. We must not forget that this took place more than fifty years ago, when Russia was a poor country, and that the laboratory arrangements cannot be judged according to present-day American standards. In my time, that is, 1902–12, Pavlov's biochemical assistant was E. A. Hanike, and his physiological assistant was A. P. Sokolov, and later myself.

The annual budget of the laboratory was in the neighborhood of 2,000 or 3,000 rubles ($1,000 or $2,000), which was something unheard of in Russia, since other university laboratories received only a few hundred rubles a year to cover all their expenses. Over and above this grant, Pavlov's laboratory had a special source of income in the sale of gastric juice, which brought in, I believe, another 2,000 rubles. As will be explained later, Pavlov by the method of "sham feeding" was able to obtain from dogs large quantities of pure gastric juice, as clear as water. He recommended its administration in cases of hyposecretion or gastric achylia, where there was an insufficient flow of the patient's own gastric juice.

From time to time the Institute administrators sought to deprive Pavlov of this income from the sale of gastric juice, which they wished to apply to the general needs of the Institute. Their efforts

[69]

always called forth stormy protests from Pavlov, and he invariably defended the right of his laboratory to use funds gained from the sale of a product obtained by his own method. Of course, he himself did not receive a penny from this undertaking, and, as far as I know, he never patented his method of procuring gastric juice. Notwithstanding Pavlov's authority for its use and the truly beneficial effects produced by gastric juice in some gastrointestinal disorders, this remedy was never widely adopted. The main reason why gastric juice did not become popular as a medicine either with patients or with doctors was the inconvenience of its administration. Even though twice diluted with water, it still had an unpleasantly sour taste. The juice had to be taken in large quantities, being sucked through a glass tube so that its acid would not damage the teeth.

GRADUATE STUDENTS

The success of Pavlov's work in the Institute of Experimental Medicine was due in part to the fact that in his laboratory there was always a full complement of medical graduates working for the degree of Doctor of Medicine. Until the War of 1914, at least three M.D. theses were completed every year in the physiological laboratory of the Institute. The Doctor's degree was conferred by the Military-Medical Academy. These M.D. candidates were drawn mainly from two sources, one group consisting of military doctors attached to the Military-Medical Academy, the other comprising civilian physicians from St. Petersburg or the provinces. In addition to these, some of the Institute doctors attached to the Military-Medical Academy and also physiologists from other universities worked in Pavlov's laboratory. Although the physiologists were comparatively few in number, they became, so to speak, members of the school of physiology headed by Pavlov, whereas for many of the graduate students the work they did under Pavlov was a passing, if important, phase in their lives.

The steady influx of young doctors into Pavlov's laboratory up to 1914 may be attributed to several factors. First, Pavlov was widely known in Russia as a scientist from the time of the publication of his *Lectures on the Work of the Principal Digestive Glands* in 1897. Second, it was confidently expected that after one year's work in Pavlov's laboratory the thesis would be written and the degree of Doctor of Medicine would be received. This certainty was based on the unique manner in which experimental work in Pavlov's laboratory was organized. Each doctor, on joining the laboratory, was allotted a subject, which was usually the continuation of a problem worked on by his immediate predecessor. It required very little work on the part of the novice in order to become acquainted with the literature on the subject, since almost all of it had already been written up in Russian in previous theses. The doctor was given one, two, or more dogs, often laboratory veterans, for the care of which an experienced attendant was responsible. The assistant showed the student the techniques of some rather simple experiments, for instance, the hourly collection of some particular type of digestive juice and the determination of the ferments it contained. The assistant also prepared all the solutions of chemicals required for the experiment. Pavlov personally supervised the majority of the experiments. However, he always discussed the results of each experiment with the research student who performed it, so that there was a joint consideration of every problem by Pavlov and the student. Third, research work at the Institute was conducted under exceptionally favorable conditions. The fees payable by research students at the Institute were astonishingly moderate. According to the regulations, the research workers were required to pay the Institute 25 rubles ($12.50) a year for the privilege of using the laboratory, but in practice many were released from this obligation. All physiological difficulties were solved by Pavlov or by his assistant, and all questions pertaining to chemistry were disposed of by the kindly co-operation of E. A. Hanike. The attendants in many cases gave absolutely invaluable assistance. The asepectic operations and the preparation of animals for acute experiments were always done by Pavlov himself or by his assistant. Under such exceptional conditions all that was necessary for a doctor's success was that he should perform his work carefully, bringing to it all his concentration and understanding, as indeed many did.

With the help of these graduate students Pavlov, as it were, multiplied the results that could be produced by his own two hands, since the whole laboratory was occupied with his problems. Only in exceptional cases did Pavlov admit a new worker who wished to carry on independent research on his own problems.

Pavlov's relations with the senior workers in his laboratory were much closer and more intimate than they were with the graduate students. This permitted real and extremely stimulating co-oper-ation between Pavlov and his co-workers—a complete union of thought and experimental inventiveness. Here, too, in most cases Pavlov dominated the scene.

Professor Savich in his article on Pavlov relates the following incident, which happened in 1905 during the Russo-Japanese War, when Savich, in the role of an army doctor, was at the Manchurian front, where he met one of Pavlov's former co-workers.

After the battle of Laoyan, during the disorder which always accom-panies an army's retreat [writes Savich], I met a doctor in Mukden, a typical senior army doctor of former days. This type of man falls far behind in medical progress and becomes narrow and officious. On seeing me, he began to talk joyfully and enthusiastically of Pavlov's laboratory. He remembered his dogs, especially Hector, who always satisfactorily "showed" the experiments conducted on him. Not one word about the war or the Japanese. Such was the impact of Pavlov's enthusiasm in the laboratory that it could arouse an interest in the search for truth even in a man like that!

(I remember that this military doctor, not long before the Russo-Japanese War, had been working in Pavlov's laboratory in the In-stitute of Experimental Medicine toward the M.D. degree. Savich intentionally used the incorrect expression "the dog 'showed' an experiment." This was the particular expression always used by that doctor—as if the experiment were some trick!—and we all made fun of him in the laboratory about it.)

The research carried on in the physiological laboratory of the Institute of Experimental Medicine, from the time it was opened in the nineties of the last century until the beginning of the twen-tieth century, dealt almost exclusively with the physiology of the digestive glands. From 1902, when Pavlov began to work with Dr. I. F. Tolochinov on conditioned reflexes, the laboratory began gradually to adapt itself to this type of research, and about 1910 research on digestion ceased there. But the so-called "gastric-juice factory," involving the collection, filtering, and distribution of canine gastric juice, continued at the Institute. All Pavlov's co-workers at the Institute were now working on the subject of conditioned reflexes. At the same time part of this work was carried on in the new physiological laboratory of the Military-Medical Academy. It was there that the research on digestion was now concentrated. Pavlov had ceased to be interested in the latter, since he was completely absorbed in studying the functions of the central nervous system. The study of digestion was carried on by V. N. Boldyreff, V. V. Savich, N. P. Tichomirov, and myself, and later by G. V. Volborth. After the Revolution of 1917 there were also many of Pavlov's students working on conditioned reflexes in the spacious laboratory of the Academy of Sciences.

In the period from 1910 to 1913 the Institute of Experimental Medicine, with the generous assistance of the Society for Furthering the Progress of the Experimental Sciences and Their Practical Application, sponsored by X. S. Ledentzov of Moscow, enabled Pavlov to realize his dream of building a special laboratory with soundproof rooms for the study of conditioned reflexes in dogs.

It is not surprising then that the physiological laboratory at the Institute of Experimental Medicine was Pavlov's favorite place of work, since it was veritably his offspring.

CHAPTER SEVEN

I Enter Pavlov's Laboratory

IN THE following pages I shall attempt to describe Pavlov as I knew him. I must apologize to my readers for beginning my story with a reference to certain events concerning myself. This is necessary as it will insure a better understanding of Pavlov's attitude toward his pupils and toward the work on which he lavished all his energy.

After the competitive examinations in November, 1901, I remained at the Military-Medical Academy to take a postgraduate course in medicine. The department in which I elected to work was that of the History of Medicine, the head of which was Professor Skorichenko. My choice, which came as a surprise to many of my friends, was motivated not by an interest in Skorichenko's personality or lectures but by entirely different considerations. It was determined by two factors: my early interest in history (in the high school) and lack of interest in clinical medicine.

When I began my clinical studies at the Academy—walking the hospital wards, examining patients, day and night duty, and so on —I realized that the career of a practicing doctor was not to my liking, although the medical studies interested me. Even now, I consider that a medical education, on account of its breadth and scope, gives the student a better understanding of life and people than does any other science. By a happy chance, when I was in the third year, I saw in the Academy vestibule an announcement of a competition in which a gold medal was to be awarded for the best essay. It was held every year at the Academy, entrants being given the choice of three subjects. The work had to be completed in one year. The Academy Conference judged the work, and the successful competitor was awarded a gold or silver medal according to its merit. The experimental problem appealed to me more than the other two, which were clinical. It was "The Influence of Artificial Sutures of the Skull on Its Growth and Development in Young

Animals." The object of the study was to determine whether the capacity of the skull in growing animals is increased if a narrow lóngitudinal (sagittal) or frontal slit is made in the calvarium. This is called an "artificial suture." The problem was inspired by an operation suggested not long before by the French surgeon Lanne-long for the cure of microcephalics. Lannelong, in accordance with the scientific opinions of his day, considered that the small skull and state of idiocy in the microcephalic are the result of premature ossification of the natural sutures of the skull. To allow the compressed brain freedom to develop, Lannelong suggested the making of artificial sutures of the cranium.

BECHTEREV'S LABORATORY

I betook myself to Bechterev's laboratory. Those who once saw Bechterev never forgot him. He was a thick-set man of medium height with a typically Russian cast of features and a large bushy beard. In 1898 he still wore his straight black hair parted Russian fashion in the middle and let it fall on either side of his face. He looked more like a coachman than a professor of nervous and mental diseases. Later, as more liberal ideas spread, Bechterev wore his hair shorter and with a side parting which greatly detracted from the purely Russian style of his appearance.

Bechterev was an outstanding figure in the scientific world, at least in Russia. He had tremendous energy, and his activities were many and varied. At the time of my studies in his laboratory, he had published about half a thousand papers and a two-volume work on the conductive tracts in the spinal cord and brain. Subsequently, many more articles and books were added to his long list of contributions. He combined his intensive scientific productivity with lecturing, direction of psychiatric and neurological clinics, editing of a scientific journal, private practice, the organization of the Psychoneurological Institute in St. Petersburg, and after 1905 with political activities as well.

I do not know how clinical work was conducted by Bechterev, but he supervised the experimental investigations of his students very little, if at all, although he set the problems. Bechterev usually dropped in at the laboratory for half an hour once or sometimes twice a week, but he was always in a hurry to go off somewhere—

to see a patient or to attend a meeting. The research workers would surround him, each trying to tell him about his experiments or microscopic research. These fleeting discussions were of little help. It was especially hard for me, a student, when all the rest of the workers were doctors. I had therefore to decide for myself all questions which arose during the course of my work and to suffer my doubts in silence. In addition, Bechterev was strangely absent-minded. When he listened or spoke, it was evident that his mind was on something entirely different.

I suffered the same fate as everyone else in Bechterev's laboratory; I was left entirely to my own resources. When I arrived at the appointed time for my first interview with Bechterev, with my chosen subject for the gold medal competition, he accepted me at once as a worker in his laboratory. On my expressing the fear that such work might be beyond my powers, he replied with the cynical phrase: "It is not the gods who fire the pots." After this he said that the attendant Peter would help me. Thus Peter became the director of my first research work. Nobody else in the laboratory was interested in me or my work, though in fairness to Bechterev I must say that he was always very nice to me, or perhaps merely indifferent, and he listened patiently to my occasional reports on the progress of my work. He never advised me on any essential points, however.

Although Peter knew as much about laboratory technique as any intelligent and experienced attendant, his help to me consisted chiefly in cheating and robbing me. When I needed puppies for my work, he would charge me the unheard-of sum of 5 rubles ($2.50) for a pregnant dog, although the price of an ordinary dog was usually 30 to 50 kopecks (15 to 25 cents). It was useless to argue with him; for, when I protested about the high price of the dogs, he threatened to stop working for me, and I did not want to complain to Bechterev. The kennels at Bechterev's clinic were in a most unsanitary condition; after the operation on their skulls many of my puppies died prematurely of distemper. More and more 5-ruble pieces were required for dogs, and it was not easy for me to ask my father for this money every time.

However, there were advantages to be gained from this independent work. I had to search and puzzle over the literature by myself, since Bechterev had mentioned to me only two or three articles to which I might refer. Experiments had to be planned and conclusions drawn from them without help or advice from anyone. I thereby tasted all the joys and most of the sorrows of experimental research. But my work was finished on time, written up, and presented to Bechterev for approval. He returned it without a single mark, which I interpreted as a sign that he had never read it. I then presented it for the gold medal award. The judge who had to give a verdict on my work was the professor of anatomy, A. I. Tarenetski. I received the medal, or rather a diploma stating that I had been awarded the gold medal, and my work (again uncorrected by Bechterev) was published in Russian in the *Kazan Neurological Journal* (*Nevrologicheski Vestnik*) in 1901.

This, my first scientific investigation, disturbed my peace of mind for many years to follow. I was only twenty-one years old when I did this work quite independently, and the more experience I acquired in experimental physiology, the more anxious I was to verify my results of long ago. But this remained impossible for many years because of the pressure of other work. It was not until forty-five years later, in 1943–44, that I was at last able to repeat this work, with the help of two of my co-workers in the physiological laboratory at McGill University, Professor Norris Giblin and Miss Armine Alley. I suggested that they investigate the effect of artificial sutures of the skull in puppies, and to my great satisfaction they confirmed all the main results of my youthful study.

Although my experimental work in Bechterev's laboratory interested me, I was deeply disappointed, as only a young enthusiast can be, in the atmosphere of the laboratory and in Bechterev himself as a director of scientific research. I remained in his laboratory for about six months longer. He gave me another problem to investigate—the physiological function of the flocculus of the cerebellum. Again Peter had to direct my work, but, since I had little interest in it, I made no progress, and soon I left Bechterev's laboratory for good.

THE HISTORY OF MEDICINE

Possibly it was because I needed to be enthusiastic about something that I returned to my old love, history. Disappointed with the conditions of work in Bechterev's laboratory, though not with experimental research, which gave me great satisfaction, I decided to make a compromise. I would become a medical historian but would learn medicine in a more vital way and not merely from books. When I shyly mentioned to Professor Volkov my tentative desire to devote myself to the study of medical history (Volkov, whom I knew personally, was professor of medicine in the Women's Medical Institute), he became very enthusiastic. He said that it was an excellent idea and that there should be a chair of medical history in every medical school but that preparation for a career in medical history ought to be organized along special lines, combining the study of history with work in the laboratory and clinic. Since I hoped to remain at the Academy to do postgraduate work, he advised me to enter Pavlov's laboratory in order to familiarize myself with experimental methods, to be an intern in his own clinic so as to learn the fundamentals of medical practice, and in addition to study history and the history of medicine. It was not surprising that a student in his fifth year, as I was, should be carried away by such enthusiasm, envisaging himself already as a professor of medical history!

I remained at the Academy after graduating, and in the autumn of 1901 was at last ready to start postgraduate work. I informed Professor Skorichenko of my desire to specialize in the history of medicine and of my plans for study. He was so surprised that an Institute doctor should wish to be attached to his department that he agreed to all my proposals without demur. Along with my history studies I began working in Professor Volkov's medical clinic. Then, one day, at the beginning of December, I went off to the Institute of Experimental Medicine to talk things over with Pavlov, flattering myself that he, like Volkov, would think me a very serious and original young man and would be struck with admiration at my ambition.

HOW PAVLOV GREETED ME

Pavlov received me in the large main laboratory, where several people were working and into which a number of doors opened.

"What do you want?" he asked me.

I explained to him that I was an Institute doctor, taking a postgraduate course, and began outlining my plan to study the history of medicine. I was unable to finish, for he interrupted me with shouts and gesticulations so that I had to back away from him until finally I was right up against the wall.

"History of medicine!" he shouted. "How absurd! This is utter nonsense—all medical history leads to the same thing. In one century the cure was cold water and in another hot. How could such a crazy idea enter your head? Do you want to be a bookworm? ..." and so on.

Everyone in the room stopped working, and curious heads appeared in the doorways, but Pavlov still continued shouting. Suddenly he stopped.

"Why are you silent?" he cried. "Explain what this history of medicine can teach us."

Completely bewildered by such a reception, I began to make some pointless remarks. After a minute he interrupted me with the words: "Eh, all this is nonsense!" And then more calmly, with some irony and perhaps even sadness, he asked, "And what is it you intend to do in my laboratory? To watch what we are doing and how we work?"

"No," I replied, "I want to work here and do just as your students do."

"Very well then," said he, "come here after the [Christmas] holidays." With that, Pavlov turned and left me. I went into the vestibule, and, as I was putting on my coat, I heard him say to someone, with his voice still raised: "The devil only knows what this is. He wants to become a medical historian!" Later, as he passed me without seeing me, he said aloud (Pavlov often talked to himself audibly), "We'll see what comes of this history of medicine!"

When I left the laboratory, I drew several deep breaths of frosty air in order to regain some of my composure. What was I to do now? I did not want to talk matters over with someone else and perhaps change my plans. Pavlov's words had not offended me; they had only shown that there could be different points of view on the subject. Pavlov's conviction and sincerity, instead of alienating me, served rather to attract me to him. Who was right—the famous scientist or I, a young man recently awarded his Doctor's diploma? I did not want to capitulate and go to some more friendly laboratory to acquaint myself with experimental methods, nor was I prepared to alter my original plan of studying the history of medicine. In talking with Volkov, I touched very lightly on my conversation with Pavlov, and I decided to present myself at the appointed time (namely, on January 2, 1902) at the physiological laboratory of the Institute of Experimental Medicine, secretly hoping to convince Pavlov of the importance of medical history and of the soundness of my decision to study it.

The talk which I had with Pavlov serves to indicate Pavlov's character. Without doubt he needed research workers for his laboratory, especially Institute doctors, from whose ranks real physiologists might be recruited to carry on his work. Nevertheless, he did not dissemble and receive me with open arms into his laboratory, where conceivably he might aim at cooling my enthusiasm for the history of medicine and at making a physiologist out of me. His refusal to compromise and his harshness to me might be taken as an attempt to frighten me away. I understood and appreciated all this much later, when I had at last emerged from my private world of fancy and self-conceit and come face to face with grim reality.

In justification of Pavlov's attitude to the history of medicine, if justification is necessary, I should say that during the whole course of his life he was a tireless seeker after truth, a great observer of the functions of nature. What could the history of medicine add to the knowledge of nature? Nothing! Only now do I realize how bitterly disappointed Pavlov must have been to find a young man who failed to take advantage of an exceptional opportunity for scientific work and decided instead to dedicate himself to work which from Pavlov's point of view was entirely useless!

RESEARCH WORK IN PAVLOV'S LABORATORY

I began work in Pavlov's laboratory in January, 1902. At this period the laboratory occupied itself almost wholly with problems of digestion. The spring term of that year was a very difficult time in my life. I seemed to be in a cul-de-sac from which there was no exit.

I would wake up at six o'clock in the morning and drowsily read history and the history of medicine. Toward nine o'clock I hurried to Volkov's clinic on the Petersburg Side. In 1902 there were still no electric trams in St. Petersburg, and it was necessary to travel by horse-drawn streetcar. I left the clinic about 1:00 P.M., with my work often unfinished, just when tea was served and the professors, assistants, and doctors gathered and usually discussed the more interesting clinical cases. I then hastened to the Institute of Experimental Medicine on Apothecary's Island, only to be confronted with Pavlov's cross face. The nature of the experiment required early attendance at the laboratory, but I began my experiment there three or four hours after the normal time and stayed in the laboratory until late at night, when it was completed. My dog, equipped with a fistula of the pancreatic duct, was of course very hungry. The experiment usually did not run well and had to be repeated interminably.

Pavlov had a special system for training a new research worker. The newcomer was given one or two dogs which had been operated upon previously and on which he repeated the experiments of his predecessor. After about a month, Pavlov gave him a problem to investigate.

There is no doubt that at first Pavlov subjected me to a special disciplinary regime. I was obliged to spend four months alone with my dog, repeating the same old experiments. During all that time Pavlov came only two or three times to see what I was doing. Our personal relations were limited to "How do you do?" and "Goodbye." Pavlov never spoke to me in a friendly manner during this time, and for my part I avoided any general laboratory discussions, thinking that I might be laughed at for my ignorance or rebuked for my interest in the history of medicine. In spite of this, I became more and more interested in physiology and experimental methods. Evidently the independent experimental work I had done in Bechterev's laboratory had made a deep impression on me. But in Pavlov's laboratory I at least saw and understood how research work should be conducted. The laboratory atmosphere created and sustained by Pavlov was very stimulating. Here the strain of scientific thought went hand in hand with simplicity of relationships, absence of dictatorship in the chief, familiarity with the work of other students, and the unified trend of the laboratory research. A further satisfaction to me was the growth of friendships with many young co-workers in the laboratory and of real comradeship with that extraordinarily warmhearted man, Dr. V. V. Savich. This attachment lasted until Savich's death in 1936. On the other hand, the medical clinic and patients began to lose their interest. Volkov was displeased with me because I did not give sufficient time to the clinic. My study of the history of medicine ceased entirely, since, on returning home from Pavlov's laboratory often at 10:00 or 11:00 P.M. after a day of stress, I was incapable of thinking about science, and at 6:00 o'clock in the morning I could not muster enough energy to read medical history as I had done formerly. And so my carefully laid plan for studying the history of medicine collapsed in all directions.

At last in May, 1902, Pavlov gave me a problem—the influence of soaps on the secretion of the pancreatic gland. Pavlov mobilized his whole laboratory that spring in order to present as many papers as possible at the Congress of Northern Naturalists and Physicians in Helsingfors. In 1901 there began to circulate rumors that Pavlov was an outstanding candidate for the Nobel Prize, which had only recently been founded. It seems that Robert Tigerstedt, a distinguished physiologist of the University of Helsingfors, had great influence in the award of the prize for physiology by the Karolinska Institutet. Tigerstedt was Pavlov's friend and a great admirer of his scientific work. In an article dedicated to the memory of Tigerstedt, published in the *Skandinavisches Archiv für Physiologie* in 1925, Pavlov called him his "best friend." My seniors in the laboratory told me that before my arrival a special Nobel Committee, headed by Professor Tigerstedt, had visited St. Petersburg in order to become acquainted with the work being done in Pavlov's laboratory and his experimental methods.

Pavlov naturally wanted to present as many papers as possible from his laboratory at the Helsingfors congress, which would be attended by the Swedish scientists. Besides a contribution by Pavlov in collaboration with S. V. Paraschuk, six other papers from his laboratory were read.[1] However, Pavlov did not receive the Nobel Prize that year. The prize was awarded in 1901 to Emil von Behring, in 1902 to Ronald Ross, in 1903 to Niels R. Finsen, and not until 1904 was it bestowed on Pavlov.

My investigation of the effect of soaps on the secretion of pancreatic juice had proceeded very well, and I was even able to establish some new and important facts. Pavlov was pleased with the results, and I reported them at the congress in fairly good French. This only partly broke the ice in my relations with Pavlov. That my first experimental work in Pavlov's laboratory turned out so successfully was in great measure due to Pavlov's having suggested a problem carefully thought out by himself. It was an important event in my life, for it helped me to find myself. I decided to become a physiologist.

It was not difficult to break off my connection with Volkov, since he understood that to work simultaneously in the clinic and in the laboratory was impossible. In May, 1902, I talked the matter over with him, and we parted on friendly terms. It was hard to renounce a cherished and carefully considered idea, but I took courage and in the autumn of 1902 told Pavlov that I wanted to become a physiologist and remain in his department. "Well, remain then," said he. "There are no physiologists now, and they are needed."[2] And thus our conversation ended.

I knew Pavlov well enough by then not to be offended by his lukewarm manner of accepting me as an Institute doctor. He never allowed sentiment to enter into laboratory relationships. But I still did not know whether he considered me a good-for-nothing or hoped that something could be made of me. However, soon afterward one of the laboratory workers, Dr. Z. I. Ponomarev, reported to me a remark of Pavlov's which encouraged me: "It seems that Babkin is a serious man, since he has decided to leave this nonsense—the history of medicine—and become a physiologist!"

Never again did I talk to Pavlov of my ambition to devote myself to the history of medicine. It was not until 1912, when I was appointed to the chair of animal physiology in the Agricultural Institute of Novo Alexandria, that Pavlov again referred to it, jokingly asking me: "Well, aren't you sorry that you did not become a medical historian?"

CHAPTER EIGHT

Pavlov, the Scientist

PAVLOV'S scientific achievements will be described in detail in Parts II, III, and IV of this book. For the present it will suffice to say that Pavlov's work on the physiology of the cardiovascular system, the digestive tract, and the central nervous system not only made him famous during his life but undoubtedly inscribed his name for all time on the pages of the very history of medicine which he appreciated so little.

Was ambition the motive which impelled Pavlov to work energetically at scientific research? It certainly was not vanity, if by vanity is meant desire for distinction, influence, and position. Pavlov did not possess this trait. He was by nature very modest and detested pose and, above all, was averse to exhibition of his merits. He naturally desired that his achievements in scientific research should be recognized by others, and he valued such recognition and probably was proud of it. In spite of his innate modesty, Pavlov would not permit anyone to underestimate the significance of the work of his laboratory.

Pavlov was absolutely indifferent toward rank and position. He did not take an undue pride in having attained the rank of professor, a fellowship in the Academy of Science, and the status of a privy councilor; in fact, these things mattered as little to him as the color of the suit he wore. This is exemplified by an incident that occurred when Professor R. Tigerstedt was in St. Petersburg and had been invited to dinner at Pavlov's home. Pavlov's two sons, Victor and Vsevolod, then small boys, appeared before the famous guest, one wearing the Stanislav star and the other the Stanislav ribbon. After being awarded the Stanislav decoration of the first class, Pavlov had given it to the children to play with!

His indifference to outward distinction is shown by another incident. Once he was performing an aseptic operation on a dog's brain but was very pressed for time. He was due at a conference of the dignified and highly respected Academy of Science. Not waiting to see whether the brain hemorrhage had completely stopped, he closed half the wound and walked out. I remained to finish the operation, and seeing that the bleeding continued (a brain hemorrhage can be very persistent and insidious at times), I opened the wound and tried to stop the bleeding. With his coat on and ready to leave for the Academy, Pavlov stopped to take a look at the operation. "Are you almost through with the operation?" he asked me. "Not yet," I answered; "the wound had to be reopened on account of hemmorhage." "Well done," he commented and remained standing there, deep in thought. The next minute he began to abuse the Academy of Science, exclaiming bitterly, "I did not ask them to elect me. Attending these conferences only distracts a man from his work. Wait for me." So saying, he disappeared. He quickly returned, wearing an operating gown, and, after washing his hands, he completed the operation. Naturally he was not present that day at the Academy of Science.

How highly the government rated the members of the Academy of Science may be seen from the fact that they were placed in the fourth class of honors (Table of Ranks) of the Russian Empire. On official occasions they wore a gold-braided uniform, white trousers with a gold stripe, and a three-cornered hat. But apparently none of this grandeur appealed to Pavlov, for he never acquired the uniform with the gold braid or the white trousers. Yet, how many scientists in Russia and elsewhere have dreamed of wearing such plumage in some form or other!

Pavlov's Belief in Science

As a true son of the nineteenth century, Pavlov believed in science to the fullest extent. Science, unrestricted in its investigations, should, according to the materialistic philosophy of the latter half of the nineteenth century, be able to answer all questions pertaining to life and to replace religion. Traces of these ideas were discernible in Pavlov. In his speeches and articles Pavlov very often likened the living organism to a machine. At the Thirteenth International Medical Congress in Paris in 1900, where he discussed the methods of keeping dogs alive after double vagotomy (i.e., cutting of both vagus nerves), he stressed particularly the justifiability and correctness of treating the living organism as a machine. "Indeed," he remarked, "in all stages mentioned in our discussion, the living organism showed itself to be merely a machine—a very complicated one, of course, but just as submissive and obedient as any other machine." In an address on "Natural Science and the Brain," given in Moscow in 1909, Pavlov said: "As a part of nature, every animal organism represents a very complicated, closed system, the internal forces of which, at any given moment, as long as it exists as such, are in equilibrium with the external forces of its environment. . . . The time will come, be it ever so distant, when mathematical analysis, based on natural science, will include in majestic formulae all these equilibrations and, finally, itself" (Pavlov, 1928, p. 120).

Nowhere does Pavlov express his belief in science so strongly as in the Preface to his collected papers and reports, *Twenty Years of Objective Study of the Higher Nervous Activity (Behavior) in Animals*, which was translated by W. H. Gantt under the title *Lectures on Conditioned Reflexes* (Pavlov, 1928). This is his profession of faith. Pavlov speaks of doubts which he had concerning the appropriateness of studying the functions of the cerebral cortex by the purely objective physiological method rather than by the psychological.

Gradually, with the progress of our research [he wrote], these doubts appeared more rarely and now I am deeply and irrevocably convinced that along this path [of conditioned reflexes] will be found the final triumph of the human mind over its uttermost and supreme problem— the knowledge of the mechanism and laws of human nature. Only thus may come a full, true, and permanent happiness. Let the mind rise from victory to victory over surrounding nature, let it conquer for human life and activity not only the surface of the earth but all that lies between the depth of the seas and the outer limits of the atmosphere, let it command for its service prodigious energy to flow from one part of the universe to the other, let it annihilate space for the transference of its thoughts—yet the same human creature, led by dark powers to wars and revolutions and their horrors, produces for itself incalculable material losses and inexpressible pain and reverts to bestial conditions. Only science, exact science about human nature itself, and the most sincere approach to it by the aid of the omnipotent scientific method, will deliver man from his present gloom, and will purge him of his contemporary shame in the sphere of interhuman relations [Pavlov, 1928, p. 41].

These lines were writen by Pavlov in 1922. Seventeen years later World War II broke out, and science, instead of tempering human relationships, made them more cruel than ever. This is the fault not of science but of those who used its achievements for the sake of evil. In the same way the very name of Christ at times has been used to cover the most wicked deeds committed on earth. Will science at some future time, no matter how distant, improve human relationships as Pavlov believed? Or are other forces also necessary?

PAVLOV'S DEVOTION TO SCIENCE

Pavlov's belief in science was wholehearted, and he devoted himself entirely to it. He was not the scientist in whose estimation science shared a place with equally important spiritual interests. To him science was the essence of his life; he "served" it. He of course had also other spiritual interests and deep feelings, such as a great love for his native land and a keen interest in art, but in his mind science dominated everything else. A man of strong principles, he was on the whole tolerant and indulgent toward human weaknesses. For instance, he was opposed to capital punishment; he was loath to give students a low mark in examinations; he restrained others from condemning people for their failings. However, he was absolutely implacable, even pitiless, if an offense was committed against his sanctum sanctorum—science. Later on I shall relate how particular Pavlov was that there should be no flaws in his work and what painstaking effort he demanded from himself and his collaborators. Here I shall mention only a few examples of his reaction to the violation of scientific truth or of scientific traditions or merely to a negligent attitude toward duties in the laboratory. The most outstanding example of Pavlov's attitude was his struggle with Bechterev over conditioned reflexes, a struggle which lasted many years.

BECHTEREV'S "REFLEXOLOGY"

When Pavlov's first work on conditioned reflexes appeared in print, Bechterev at once appreciated the importance of the new theory. Bechterev carried over bodily into psychology the conception of the objective method of studying the complex functions of the brain which Pavlov had introduced into physiology. In his book, *Objective Psychology*, Bechterev (1907) wrote: "This science purports to study and explain only the relationship of a living being toward the surrounding conditions affecting it in some way or other and does not pretend to clarify those internal or subjective experiences, known by the name of conscious processes, which are open only to self-observation" (quoted from Ivanov-Smolensky, 1929, p. 103).

In later editions Bechterev renamed *Objective Psychology*, first, *Psycho-reflexology* and, then, simply, *Reflexology*. Bechterev tried to squeeze into the frame of "reflexology" all that was known of human behavior, including subjective psychology and behaviorism. *Objective Psychology* was translated into French and German in 1913. The third Russian edition of *Reflexology* was translated into German and was published in 1926, that is, a year before the publication in English of Pavlov's *Conditioned Reflexes* (1927). Bechterev changed the designation "conditioned reflex" to "associative reflex," while such psychological concepts as "attention," "memory," "will-power" he replaced by the terms "concentration or reflex of concentration," "reproduction," "personal activity," and so on.

Bechterev did not confine himself to theoretical treatment of psychology from the point of view of conditioned reflexes. He and his pupils applied this method, which they called the method of "associative reflexes," to animals and man. Instead of the salivary reflex reaction employed by Pavlov and his associates, they utilized the motor reaction in dogs. For the unconditioned stimulus they used an induction current of moderate strength, which acted upon one of the front paws and produced a quickening of the respiration and flexion of the stimulated extremity; both were registered on the kymograph. The conditioned reflex was formed when an electrical stimulation of the paw was combined with some other stimulus, for instance, a sound. Then the sound alone produced flexion of the paw. Work done by one of Bechterev's collaborators, V. P. Protopopov (1909) on the *Associative Motor Reaction to Acoustic Stimuli* was well conceived and thorough, which should be credited to the serious attention given to the subject by Protopopov himself.

PAVLOV, THE SCIENTIST

PAVLOV'S CONTROVERSY WITH BECHTEREV

We now come to a very unpleasant period in the history of Russian science, when scientific competition, usually so desirable and stimulating, took the form of polemics conducted in an atmosphere of vituperation. Essentially it was a conflict between two diametrically opposite characters. On one side was Pavlov, whose ultimate aim was scientific truth; on the other, Bechterev, to whom scientific data served only as material for a new and interesting theory. Pavlov paid scrupulous attention to the accuracy of the facts upon which he based his conclusions. Becherev was not at all particular in the choice of experimental data from which to derive his conclusions. Bechterev took for granted, without critical examination, all the experimental data obtained by his pupils, the majority of whom were quite inexperienced in physiological research. As a result, any good work produced in Bechterev's laboratory, such as that of Protopopov, was completely lost sight of in the large number of carelessly and hastily conducted investigations. Of course, it was not a question of who made any particular discovery first, though undoubtedly Pavlov would not let anyone deprive him of due credit for his discoveries. As Pavlov repeatedly said, Bechterev was "debasing science," and the opposition which Pavlov led against him was in the name of science. It would have been much worthier and more appropriate on Pavlov's part, in view of his position as a world-renowned scientist, if he had paid no attention to Bechterev's actions.

However, it was not in Pavlov's nature to compromise, and he preferred to fight Bechterev. As often happens, this controversy did not convince anyone but only caused hard feelings, though in due course it eventually became clear who was right. Pavlov attacked Bechterev, and Bechterev defended himself to the best of his ability. The disputants did not confine themselves to pointing out in the scientific literature that this or that claim of the opposing side was incorrect but often carried on their arguments in public at scientific meetings.

It all began when Pavlov tried to discover the nerve paths which transmit conditioned stimulations through the cerebral cortex. As a starting point Pavlov based his own experiments on the results of

Bechterev's investigations. It might be conjectured, for instance, that in the case of a visual conditioned reflex the visual stimulation is transmitted from the visual area situated in the occipital part of the cerebral cortex, via the cortical center for taste, to the salivary cortical center, and thence to subcortical regions and the salivary center in the medulla oblongata. Pavlov naturally was interested in the cortical center for taste and the cortical salivary center. If indeed a nervous process, originated as a result of some conditioned stimulation, passed through them, then the extirpation of one of these centers ought to have destroyed the conditioned reflex in question. The cortical centers of taste were described by one of Bechterev's pupils, Gorshkov (1901). The discovery that the secretion of saliva results from stimulation of certain regions of the cerebral cortex was made by Lepine and Bochefontaine (1875) and was confirmed by Bechterev and Mislavski (1888, 1889) and by several of Bechterev's pupils (see Babkin, 1928). Finally, in 1906, another of Bechterev's pupils, Belitski, claimed that after surgical extirpation of the cerebral cortex in the region of the salivary centers all conditioned reflexes disappeared. The experiments of Belitski were the first experiments of Bechterev's laboratory to be checked in Pavlov's laboratory, the work being done by Dr. Tichomirov (1906). Contrary to Belitski's conclusions, Tichomirov showed in experiments on dogs that, after extirpation of the so-called "cortical salivary center," various natural conditioned reflexes were fully preserved, as well as an artificially formed conditioned reflex to slight irritation of the skin by means of a small brush (called a "scratcher"), the application being combined with the pouring of a solution of hydrochloric acid into the dog's mouth. Tichomirov's results were later confirmed by Dr. Orbeli, another of Pavlov's pupils (Pavlov, 1928, p. 97). Further, Tichomirov (1906) and Pavlov himself (1928) have shown experimentally that conditioned reflexes of the gastric glands are not destroyed through extirpation of the cortical centers of gastric secretion, the existence of which centers Bechterev's pupil, Gerver (1900), considered as proved. This was contrary to Gerver's assertion that such extirpation would abolish the conditioned reflexes in question.

The negative results obtained by Pavlov and his co-workers in attempting to confirm the findings of Bechterev and his pupils made Pavlov very critical of all experimental and physiological work which emanated from Bechterev's laboratory. Disgusted by the inaccuracy of the results reported by Bechterev's pupils, Pavlov decided to submit the dispute between the two laboratories to public judgment. It was at one of the meetings of the Society of Russian Physicians in St. Petersburg that Pavlov reported on "The Cortical Test Center of Dr. Gorshkov" (Pavlov, 1928, p. 99). On the basis of Tichomirov's and his own experiments he absolutely refuted Gorshkov's findings. He considered them a "result of prejudice and inexact observation" and some of them even "altogether fantastic."

In order to make his extremely low opinion of the experimental results of Dr. Gorshkov more apparent, Pavlov compared himself with the latter. He read from I. M. Sechenov's autobiography the passage in which Sechenov says that according to the general opinion the best experimenter in Europe at that time was Pavlov (I quote from memory). "Whom, then, shall we believe," said Pavlov, "myself or Gorshkov?"

This last utterance produced rather an unpleasant impression on me at the meeting. It seemed to me both superfluous and lacking in modesty, since no one doubted Pavlov's authority as a physiologist and experimenter. However, as Gorshkov's thesis had been written in Bechterev's laboratory, Pavlov's words obviously meant, "Whom do you believe, myself or Bechterev?" In justice to Bechterev it should be stated that in public he was always polite toward Pavlov.

The blunt statement on Pavlov's part that the results of Gorshkov's investigations were fantastic forced Bechterev to defend publicly the discoveries made in his laboratory. During the next three meetings of the society, Bechterev and his pupils attended regularly and attacked the results obtained in Pavlov's laboratory (the discussions at those meetings are quoted from the *Collected Works* of I. P. Pavlov, 1940).

At one of these meetings papers were presented by two of Pavlov's co-workers. Eliason (1907–8) spoke on "The Acoustic Functions of the Dog under Normal Conditions and after Partial Bilateral Extirpation of the Auditory Area" and L. A. Orbeli (1908) on "The Localization of Conditioned Reflexes in the Central Nervous

System." Others taking part in the discussion were W. M. Bechterev and his two co-workers, A. P. Ostankov and L. M. Poussep. They attacked mainly Orbeli's statement that, on extirpation of a certain part of the cortex, the corresponding conditioned reflexes disappear.

Ostankov insisted that Orbeli's experiments did not afford sufficient grounds for the conclusion that the coupling of the arc of a conditioned reflex takes place entirely in the cerebral cortex. He suggested that other, as he called them, "coupling apparatuses" for conditioned reflexes might be present in the subcortical centers. This criticism was valid, since several years later it was demonstrated that conditioned reflexes, though very primitive ones indeed, could be found in decorticated dogs (see Part IV).

Bechterev formed his objections on a wider basis. He maintained that the method of conditioned reflexes which had just been introduced into science had been of extremely little help in the study of localization of functions in the cerebral cortex. "So far it has introduced us merely to the *A B C* of this well-established and well-developed branch of science," said Bechterev and added maliciously: "The only new feature is the denial of certain results obtained by other authors." Bechterev's remarks about the results of other authors referred, of course, to the experiments by his own pupils Belitski, Gerver, Gorshkov, and others. He maintained that, besides the method of conditioned reflexes, there were other methods which had already been tried out, such as the method of electrical stimulation of the cerebral cortex or extirpation of its parts with subsequent observation of the reactions and of the behavior of the animals. The negative results obtained by Pavlov's laboratory were attributed by Bechterev to the fact that the time of observation after the extirpation of one center or another in a dog had been too short. According to Bechterev, Pavlov was ignoring the ability of the central nervous system to compensate the lost functions and in his investigations did not take into account the possibility that after extirpation of certain cortical centers some stimuli may act via the subcortical ganglia.

Pavlov's reply to Bechterev was very blunt. He said that he was an experimenter and that he believed in facts only. "One should argue by means of facts, not words," said he and challenged Bechterev to produce experimental evidence in support of his co-workers' results which Pavlov's laboratory had failed to confirm, in particular the existence of the salivary center in the cerebral cortex, as claimed by Belitski. Pavlov did not deny that stimulation of a certain point in the front part of the cerebral cortex by means of an induction current causes the secretion of saliva, but he could not agree that the presence of this portion of the cortex was absolutely necessary for the transmission of the stimulus from the periphery to the salivary glands in a conditioned reflex. Pavlov also pointed out that, though he did not deny the mechanism of compensation in the central nervous system, yet it was necessary to prove first that such a mechanism really exists, for, if in an animal a reaction or a conditioned reflex which had disappeared after a brain operation reappeared, this might be due not to the compensating activity of other parts of the brain but to a gradual elimination of the postoperative inhibition.

During the next two meetings of the Society of Russian Physicians, at which papers from Pavlov's laboratory were read, heated discussions between Pavlov and Bechterev or his pupils continued.

After the third meeting neither Bechterev nor his pupils participated in the discussions when papers from Pavlov's laboratory were read. This caused some disappointment to many members of the Society and the public (meetings of the Society were open to the public). The bulk of the audience understood very little about the proceedings and looked on at such encounters with interest and amusement to see who would get the upper hand. Conditioned reflexes were at that time quite a novelty; their importance was not fully appreciated by the clinicians and general practitioners and even by representatives of other theoretical medical sciences.

However, Bechterev accepted Pavlov's challenge and decided to verify the experiments of Pavlov and Tichomirov involving extirpation of the cortical salivary centers. In two dogs with permanent salivary fistulas the cortical salivary centers were extirpated on both sides by one of Bechterev's pupils, Dr. Spirtov (1909), and it was claimed that these animals had completely lost all conditioned reflexes. The dogs were exhibited during a meeting at Bechterev's clinic, at which Pavlov and all his assistants, including myself, were present.

One could see at once that Bechterev, who did not concern himself very deeply with the matter, or perhaps did not care to do so, relied completely upon the obliging Spirtov. An assistant was slowly rotating a glass jar containing several lumps of sugar in front of the dogs. The jar was sealed with an air-tight stopper. Consequently the sugar in the jar acted on the dogs almost exclusively through their vision, without affecting their sense of smell or hearing. This weak stimulus in fact produced no secretion of saliva. Bechterev triumphed.

Then Pavlov rose from his seat and firmly demanded a weak solution of hydrochloric acid. He had a resolute appearance, with his lips set and his brows knitted. When he was given the acid, he sat down in front of the dogs and, disregarding all protests on the part of Bechterev and Spirtov, he poured acid into the dogs' mouths several times. This produced an abundant salivary secretion. After the secretion had stopped, the mere sight, smell, or splash of the acid in a test tube without fail caused the secretion of saliva, that is, a conditioned salivary reflex to the acid was formed in Spirtov's dogs notwithstanding the absence of the cortical salivary centers. After this, Pavlov did not pay much attention to the proceedings and soon left.

It was indeed an enthralling spectacle! Pavlov was so certain of the correctness of his theory and so convinced that it was necessary to finish once and for all with these false and erroneous statements that he did not consider the possibility of failure, which might conceivably have happened at a crowded meeting under environmental conditions to which the animals were quite unaccustomed. However, the most amazing sequel to this meeting was that Spirtov's paper was published notwithstanding.

CHAPTER NINE

Pavlov's Integrity

PAVLOV'S integrity was beyond dispute. He was honest in his scientific research, in his relationships with people, in his political convictions. Usually he was sharp in censure and did not consider the feelings of his companions; but, when he disagreed with someone whose susceptibilities he did not wish to hurt, he merely kept quiet. He was frank in expressing satisfaction or dissatisfaction. He praised his co-workers but rarely and meagerly, holding to the rule that, if you praise a Russian, he will at once become conceited and "spoiled." But he generously scolded those who made mistakes and did not mince words on such occasions. Strangely enough, in spite of all the commotion which he was capable of raising and which made him such a formidable figure, he was extremely hesitant in coming to a decision when it was necessary to dismiss some really unsuitable assistant or attendant. One consideration which forced Pavlov to tolerate the presence of an undesirable individual was when such a man had a family to support and Pavlov did not wish the family to suffer because of the mistakes or carelessness of the breadwinner. The matter usually ended in Pavlov's shouldering the useless assistant's work until he left the laboratory of his own accord.

The fact that everyone knew what was expected of him and realized that the professor's words never carried any hidden meaning made it easy to work with Pavlov. Of course, unpleasant situations would sometimes arise through Pavlov's vehemence, but these were mere incidents which were quickly smoothed over and in no way disturbed the atmosphere of mutual trust.

Pavlov's attitude toward scientific truth is well illustrated by his reaction toward the discovery of "secretin" by two English physiologists, Bayliss and Starling. This discovery shattered the very foundations of the concept, held in Pavlov's laboratory, that the secretory activity of the pancreatic gland and of the digestive glands in general is regulated exclusively through the nervous system. After being convinced that Bayliss and Starling were right, Pavlov always spoke of secretin as a normal stimulant of the pancreatic gland and acknowledged the possibility that in some cases stimulation might be conveyed from the digestive tract to the digestive glands through the blood (by so-called "humoral transmission"). Of course, he did not discard the theory of the nervous regulation of the digestive glands. This dualistic concept in regard to some of the secretory functions of the digestive tract has been maintained in physiology to this day. But there were many physiologists, such as Popielski and Verigo, who stubbornly refused to recognize the humoral mechanism of pancreatic secretion, although they contributed little or nothing to the physiology of the digestive glands. (The story of secretin will be more fully discussed in Part III.)

Pavlov's Sense of Duty

Pavlov's sense of duty was extremely strong. He always arrived punctually for lectures or meetings. Except on days when he lectured at 9:00 A.M., he would reach the laboratory of the Institute of Experimental Medicine about 9:30 A.M., and he always left at 6:00 P.M. sharp. Over a period of ten years I cannot remember that he was ever late in arriving at the laboratory without good reason. A delay caused by reading his newspaper too long—and we lived in troubled times—or by talking too long to a friend on the street could never have occurred with him. Whether Pavlov had had the same traits in his youth as he had at the time I knew him, I cannot say.

Pavlov never put anything off unless it was absolutely necessary to do so, but his weak point was letter-writing, which he detested. His letters were very brief, and he usually delayed replying until, as he himself said, some slight and harmless but not quite truthful excuses had to be made—a cold, much work, and so on. I think, however, that he always replied to important letters at once.

Since science and laboratory work were for Pavlov not only a source of continuous joy but a means of serving truth, he regarded his work very seriously. His advent always brought a certain amount of strain to the laboratory. Every worker was on the alert when Pavlov approached, since he would not allow any carelessness or inaccuracy in the conduct of experiments, and this put all the workers on their mettle. Although working with Pavlov consequently brought anxious moments, to be associated with him was indeed inspiring, for it drew one closer, if only in a small degree, to this great aim of serving truth.

As an example of Pavlov's conception of duty and his demands on his co-workers in this respect, here is an account of his relations with Dr. V., who was a great friend of the late V. V. Savich and of myself. Dr. V., I am sure, will not object if I recall the past.

Dr. V. was a very talented and cultured pupil of Pavlov's. At the time of my story he was acting as a prosector (senior assistant) in the Department of Physiology in the Military-Medical Academy, and it was his duty to prepare the experiments for the lectures, which began at 9:00 A.M. Being a young man, Dr. V. did not always retire at an early hour, for it is not so easy, when you are very young, to don the gown of a scientific monk and renounce such harmless distractions as the theater, dances, and parties with friends. As a result he was sometimes not ready in time for the lectures, or the demonstrations were not properly prepared. Of course, Pavlov was dissatisfied with Dr. V.'s work. However, there was no limit to his indignation when he learned the cause of V.'s dereliction of duty. V. paid dearly for his love of pleasure, since life in the laboratory became veritable torture to him. Pavlov literally never left him alone, upbraiding him whether he deserved it or not. Outside the laboratory Pavlov was as kind to him as to the rest of us, but as soon as Pavlov crossed the threshold of the laboratory and saw V., he would begin to find fault with him. In this way two years went by. During that time V. changed from a pleasure-seeking young man to an excellent and reliable scientific worker, and he married and became the father of a child. But Pavlov could not forget that V. had once preferred night life to the laboratory. A strong negative reflex had been formed in Pavlov's mind in relation to Dr. V.! The situation had become unbearable and depressed V. extremely, especially since he was much attached to Pavlov. In an altruistic moment V. V. Savich, who was working at that time in the physiological laboratory of the Military-Medical Academy, went to Pavlov and bluntly told him that he was wrong in his attitude toward V. and that it was unfair to treat him as if he were a criminal when he had long ago radically changed his ways and become an exemplary worker. There were three minutes of painful silence. As Savich told me later (I was a professor in Odessa at that time), Pavlov turned his face away, so that Savich could not see what effect his interference was having. At last Pavlov said: "You are right. I am fond of V., but I was continually influenced by his former unruly behavior. It is my mistake." Next day Pavlov apologized to Dr. V., which brought tears to the eyes of the young man, and Pavlov remained his friend both in and outside the laboratory to the end.

"THE REFLEX OF PURPOSE"

One of the characteristics that helped Pavlov to realize his scientific aspirations was his extraordinary persistence. In his oft-quoted article Professor Savich remarks that in his youth Pavlov's stubbornness in working out any problem he had selected was already strongly developed. Pavlov's father installed a little gymnasium in the garden for his children. After the usual period of enthusiasm, Pavlov's brothers quickly cooled toward their new recreation and only Ivan Petrovich continued to practice systematically. He had a good reason for doing so. His constitution was not strong in his early youth, and in the ecclesiastical seminaries of that time there were many fights among the students. Pavlov had to develop his muscles for self-defense against bigger boys who could beat the weaker ones with impunity.

Pavlov remained the same all the rest of his life. In work or play he never deviated from the path which he had set himself, except when he became convinced that the goal was wrong. But in such cases, as I have already mentioned, much proof was needed before he would change his position.

A typical example of Pavlov's tenacity was seen when he devised the operational method of the "Pavlov gastric pouch." The operation consists of the formation of a small pouch or pocket, which is excised from the animal's stomach so that its nerves are preserved. It is provided with an opening leading to the outer surface of the body. The isolation of a gastric pouch by Pavlov's method is a very complicated operation and requires considerable surgical skill. When in 1893 or 1894 Pavlov first conceived the idea of constructing his isolated gastric pouch in dogs, he failed nineteen times, because for different reasons the operation was unsuccessful. It was only at the twentieth attempt that he achieved his aim. The problem of studying gastric secretions in dogs with an isolated pouch had been assigned to Dr. P. P. Khijin, who was working in Pavlov's laboratory. He was quite panic-stricken by these misfortunes and thought that he would never have time to complete his research and write his thesis for the degree of Doctor of Medicine. Pavlov, however, persevered and won. Dr. Khijin shared in his triumph, since the results obtained on the twentieth dog (called "Pal" [*Drujok*] in gratitude for its survival!) not only enabled Dr. Khijin to secure his degree but, what is much more important, led to the establishment of facts concerning the work of the digestive glands which have become classic in physiology.

There are many examples of such perseverance in Pavlov's life. He attributed special importance to the resoluteness which enables a person to attain a desired goal. This quality always impressed him. His views on the ability of people to reach a predetermined objective were formulated in a paper, "The Reflex of Purpose," given at the Third Convention of Experimental Pedagogy in Petrograd, on January 2, 1916 (Pavlov, 1928, p. 275). By the "reflex of purpose," or the instinct for achieving an aim, Pavlov meant the desire of a man or an animal to possess some object which at the moment is of interest to him, or, speaking physiologically, stimulates him. Man's life, as he said, consists in the pursuit of variable aims, important or trivial. We cannot help observing the fact that often there is no commensurate relationship between the importance of the aim and the amount of energy expended on achieving it. A paradoxical situation then arises in which the emphasis is laid on the *pursuit* of the aim and the aim itself is a secondary factor. One of the most outstanding examples of a "reflex of purpose" is the passion for collecting, which certain people possess and which can also be observed in animals.

In analyzing the collecting habit, Pavlov came to the conclusion that it is based on a desire to possess objects that for some reason have a strong attraction for the person concerned. It always has the aim of acquiring or gathering parts of a huge whole which is usually unattainable *in toto*. Collecting is a variation of the "grasp-

[99]

ing" instinct or reflex. It has much in common with the food instinct, one of the most important factors in self-preservation.

" 'The reflex of purpose,' " remarked Pavlov, "is of tremendous significance in life. It is the basic form of life energy in each one of us." Life has meaning only when we have a goal or goals which we continually try to reach. As soon as the objective disappears, life ceases to be of interest. Pavlov compared the Anglo-Saxon, who possessed the reflex of purpose to the highest degree, with the Russian, in whom this reflex was developed poorly, if at all. Whereas an obstacle only serves to increase the determination of the Anglo-Saxon to achieve his aim, to a Russian "circumstances excuse and justify everything."

In conclusion, Pavlov advises us to guard the "reflex of purpose" in ourselves as a precious part of our lives and to develop and strengthen it in our youth.

Pavlov's Ability To Concentrate

Another faculty which aided Pavlov in utilizing and developing his talents was his amazing power of concentration. This ability to focus his attention on a subject was so great that over a period of many years he could remain occupied with the solution of a number of problems in one branch of physiology, and in this way he worked on the physiology of the digestive glands for some fifteen years. The same thing occurred when he dedicated himself and his laboratory to the study of conditioned reflexes, which absorbed his attention and thoughts completely during the last thirty-four years of his life.

It would be incorrect to say that Pavlov neglected other branches of physiology while studying digestion or the physiology of the central nervous system, but his interest in such was necessarily more superficial than in his own current research work. If one of his workers told him of some investigation which had no relation to the work going on in the laboratory, Pavlov would listen inattentively or brusquely interrupt with the statement: "I am not interested in that!" In 1902 and 1903 the younger members of the laboratory, N. V. Strajesko, J. A. Buchstab, V. V. Savich, and myself, were full of the fashionable new side-chain theory of Ehrlich and attempted to explain the activation of inactive digestive ferments by this theory, but it was absolutely impossible to interest Pavlov in these complicated though intriguing questions.

With his inherent modesty, Pavlov often told us that his scientific success was due to constant and unrelaxing meditation. "In this continual thinking lies my main strength," he used to say. Once he remarked: "When I was working on digestion, I pondered on my experiments day and night." Another time he said that it was necessary to "possess the lucky gift of being able to concentrate on a problem, or the knowledge of how to do so," if one was to achieve results in science. Probably this ability to concentrate on one problem instead of jumping from one investigation to another was inborn in Pavlov, but he strengthened and developed it to the utmost degree. Once, when he had attended a performance of *La Bohème*, by Puccini, at the Marinski Theater, I asked the next day whether he had enjoyed the opera. "Yes, I think I did," he replied; "however, I cannot give you a definite answer. It was extremely difficult to concentrate on the stage, since my thoughts kept switching to conditioned reflexes!" This concentration of attention on one single problem was not a narrow-mindedness but a method of scientific work.

Pavlov often reiterated that it was a great mistake to scatter one's interest in various directions in scientific research, as was done and is still done in some laboratories. In view of the growing tendency in physiology toward specialization, there are fewer and fewer "universal laboratories." Up to a point, this guarantees the soundness of the results coming from these laboratories, but we must not forget that extreme specialization and thinking in only one direction narrow the scientific horizon of the research worker.

An outstanding example of how an unbiased conception may suddenly solve a seemingly hopeless enigma in science was the discovery by Bayliss and Starling of pancreatic secretin, of which we have spoken above. Neither before nor after their discovery of secretin did Bayliss and Starling carry out any research on the physiology of the external secretion of the digestive glands.

While Pavlov was obliged to acknowledge that Bayliss and Starling were right as to the method whereby stimulation of pancreatic secretion is effected by hydrochloric acid, nevertheless in his Preface to the second (Russian) edition of his *Lectures on the Work of the Digestive Glands* (1917) he characterized this discovery as the result of a "chance experiment" which led the English physiologists to establish a "completely unique and unexpected mechanism." This judgment can hardly be accepted as fair. The discovery of secretin did not result from a "chance" experiment but was the result of the brilliant conception of creative experimental minds and was a masterpiece of experimental research. The significance of this discovery in the realm of the physiology of the digestive tract and the impetus it gave to all future research in this connection were very great.

Pavlov, of course, recognized this. From their work and from his personal acquaintance with Bayliss and Starling, he knew them to be outstanding physiologists and had the highest regard for them. But the kind of persons he could not tolerate were those he called "riders." This was the name he gave to those energetic young men who, on becoming acquainted with the results of systematic research in some school, begin to work independently on the same lines. After completing one or two, usually quite insignificant, studies in this field, they do not return to the same questions but transfer their attention to the work of another group of investigators in order to learn from them their technique and ideas. Such scientists reminded Pavlov of "circus riders." Around the circus ring runs a horse with a big flat saddle. Suddenly the performer in his spangled trunks runs out from behind the curtain and jumps on the horse. He does tricks to exhibit his obvious art and win applause, then, waving goodbye, he jumps from the horse and runs off, while the horse continues to circle calmly around the ring. The horse is science continuing undisturbed along its appointed path, and the rider is one of those light-minded research workers who cannot contribute anything to change the course of science but merely want to gain applause.

Fear of being troubled by such "riders," who in Pavlov's own words only "cluttered up" science and did not assist its progress, was one of the reasons why few of the early reports of his laboratory on conditioned reflexes were published in foreign languages. The only exceptions were Pavlov's own papers and orations, mostly of a general character, which he read at various international congresses.

CHAPTER TEN

Pavlov's Sense of Reality and Creative Imagination

PAVLOV possessed a unique intellect rarely met with in the Russia of his day. His was a realistic mind. Combined with his faculty of acute observation, this sense of reality with which nature had endowed him, and which he developed to the full, revealed to him much that was hidden from others. Pavlov himself described such a mind as "directed toward reality." He attributed great significance to the power of observation. The words "Observation, Observation, and Observation" were inscribed in large letters on the outside of the main building of the Biological Station at Koltushi, near St. Petersburg, which was constructed according to Pavlov's design during the Soviet regime.

Pavlov incorporated his views on the human mind in a public lecture which he delivered in the spring of 1918 in St. Petersburg. This lecture, on the subject of "The Mind in General and the Russian Mind in Particular," was an outstanding event, since at that time northern Russia was in the power of the Bolsheviks, and Pavlov did not hesitate to criticize their activities publicly.

In his public lecture Pavlov defined the various types of mind that are found in men: realistic or unrealistic, accurate or inaccurate, systematic or unsystematic, and so. One of the important functions of the brain, he said, consists in the establishment of correct relationships between the body and the external world which acts upon it from every side. If the nervous system does not safeguard the interests of the body in an animal or man, then the organism will invariably suffer or even perish. What is true for the individual also holds true for human society in general. "At the present time," said Pavlov, "an experiment is being tried in Russia in which no attempt is being made to establish correct relationships between the different sections of the population and between one man and another. There is very little justification for this experiment, for it does not follow the most elementary rules of experimentation." There was so little to be said in its favor and so much against it, that he, Pavlov, would not have sacrificed even one laboratory frog for it. (Pavlov's words proved to be prophetic. This was a period of militant communism, when attempts were made to abolish family, religion, trade, and money. However, no communism in the true sense of the word was established in Russia. The Bolsheviks, two or three years after coming to power, were obliged to compromise, and introduced the "New Economic Policy," known as NEP, in which actually there was nothing new but which to a certain extent constituted a return to the pre-revolutionary order.)

According to Pavlov, the Russian mind was not given to realism but strove to establish things that were impracticable. As an example of this, he mentioned in his lecture the peace treaty then recently concluded between the Bolsheviks and the Germans at Brest Litovsk. Pavlov concluded the lecture (if I am not mistaken, there were actually two lectures) with a few observations which he called "poetry in prose." He said that conservatism and liberalism are legitimate and necessary forces in human society. It is bad if one is dominant and the other is crushed. He expressed the ardent hope that at some time in the future the extreme conservatism of the former Imperial regime and the excessive radicalism of the present would blend together in a rational progressive movement under which the innate abilities of the Russian people would develop and contribute to their happiness.

Pavlov admired realism in all things. In 1902 and 1903 I was enthralled by Ibsen. His symbolic dramas, such as *When We Dead Awaken, The Woman from the Sea*, and *The Wild Duck*, produced a specially strong impression on me. I was naturally curious to know Pavlov's views on Ibsen and asked him which of Ibsen's dramas appealed to him most. He replied that he was most interested in Ibsen's realistic dramas like *Hedda Gabler* and *A Doll's House* and that he did not care so much for the symbolic plays.

Pavlov's realism was evident in his critical attitude toward new facts or recent events. He took nothing for granted but first of all made sure that the fact reported was true or that the event spoken of really did take place. When he was told of some result obtained in an experiment in the laboratory, he would ask repeatedly, "Is it really so? Are you absolutely sure that you are not mistaken? Do you know that for a fact?" When Pavlov was satisfied that the worker was not mistaken in his observation, he went to see the experiment himself.

PAVLOV AND THE AMERICANS

Pavlov's realism was unquestionably responsible for his special interest in Americans and the respect in which he held them. The United States of America and its people continually intrigued him. In his view, Americans presented a vivid contrast to Russians, and he was amazed at their practical attitude to life, their diligence, and their love of hard work. These qualities were rarely met with among the Russians of Pavlov's time. He was deeply disappointed and indignant at the passivity and indifference of his countrymen and at the fruitless fantasies which represented their approach to the realities of life.

It is true that in the Russian character this was offset by a positive characteristic—idealism. Among educated Russians idealism was not uncommon, but unfortunately in the majority of cases it was of an unpractical turn. Among the minority of the Russian youth, before the Revolution of 1917, idealism was united with revolutionary maximalism and so destroyed itself. Some of these young people became fanatics, who in the name of a high ideal even went the length of assassinating the czar and other members of the government, sacrificing their young lives for this ideal. These political murders, especially that of Alexander II, brought nothing but misery to Russia. Pavlov always remembered with anger and horror the first of March, 1881, the day the emperor was assassinated.

The majority of the idealistically inclined youth compromised and came to terms with their consciences. The university students sang revolutionary songs and organized strikes and demonstrations, but after graduating they soon calmed down and were absorbed into the current of Russian life; numbers of them entered the government service and became obedient and colorless officials. Some of them retained their idealism throughout their lives, but, to Russia's great misfortune, many of these high-minded and honorable people were unrealistic in their attitude to life, for they were dreamers. Among them, however, were men who, like Pavlov, had both the inclination and the knowledge to combine high spiritual aspirations with the stubborn pursuit of a definite goal and a well-balanced attitude toward life. Why conditions in Russia at that period should have produced characters of such different types is a question we cannot go into in these pages, but it was so.

It thus becomes clear why passive and dreamy natures irked Pavlov and led him to protest and why, on the other hand, action in any sphere of life aroused his admiration. In regard to Americans, what especially impressed Pavlov was the contrast between their practical minds, which presumably should have transformed them into a race of callous materialists, and their exalted humanitarian ideals, which were in the last analysis altruistic.

Pavlov had several friends among the American scientists, of whom can be mentioned P. A. Levene of the Rockefeller Institute, Professor W. B. Cannon of Harvard University, and Professor A. J. Carlson of the University of Chicago. Pavlov greatly appreciated their scientific work and enjoyed their friendship. On their part they paid him a high tribute as world dean of physiology and as a tireless, scientific explorer (see Fig. 2).

I remember, for instance, that at one of the meetings of the International Physiological Congress (in Edinburgh in 1923), when Pavlov appeared at the chair to deliver his communication, Professor Carlson got up, waved his hand, and the whole audience arose as one man and greeted Pavlov with long applause.

Notwithstanding Pavlov's enthusiasm for Americans and his admiration for their "business-like" methods and "practical approach to life," he and his son Vladimir proved ill adapted to American life. They experienced some very unpleasant moments while sojourning in the United States, although, generally speaking, their two visits gave them much pleasure. Pavlov and his son told me of three adventures which befell them in the United States.

The most unfortunate event was the theft of $800 from Pavlov. In August, 1923, Pavlov and his son Vladimir were in New York, where among other places they visited the Rockefeller Institute for Medical Research. This was of special interest to Pavlov, since the director of the Biochemistry Department at the Institute was

FIG. 2.—A photograph taken at the meeting of the Thirteenth International Physiological Congress in Boston, Mass., in August, 1929. From left to right are Drs. A. C. Ivy, A. J. Carlson, I. P. Pavlov, B. P. Babkin, A. B. Luckhardt, and V. N. Boldyreff. (Courtesy of Dr. A. B. Luckhardt.)

PAVLOV'S SENSE OF REALITY

Dr. P. A. Levene, a former student of his at the Military-Medical Academy. He and his son were setting out for Boston from the Grand Central Station, New York. As they were boarding the train, several men surrounded Pavlov and began jostling him on the platform of the car. "Volia,[1] what are they doing to me?" cried Pavlov to his son. "Never mind, never mind—come inside quickly," Vladimir called back. When at last they recovered from the bustle, the heat, and the crowds, Pavlov put his hand in his inside jacket pocket and found that the $800 was missing.[2] He was unaware at that time of the existence of travelers' checks and always carried paper money with him. Because of New York's usual August heat, Pavlov had worn a light summer suit, through which his pocket-book could be clearly seen, bulging with money. Evidently the American thieves could not resist such an extraordinary sight and realized that this was a wonderful opportunity to demonstrate their "practical approach to life"! The travelers looked foreign, especially Pavlov, with his beard and whiskers, which stuck out like a cat's, and no doubt looked like easy victims. Both father and son were shaken by this calamity, but succor was at hand. When Dr. Levene heard of their misfortune, the Rockefeller Institute at his request replaced the stolen sum and even added to it.

On this same trip the Pavlovs lost a suitcase in New York, while on the way from the dock to the hotel. Anyone who has arrived in New York from Europe knows the docks as a veritable inferno. It was not surprising that the Pavlovs, dazed by the noise and the hustling crowd, lost their suitcase. Unfortunately, all their dress suits were in this suitcase. Later in England they ordered new ones, but these were not completed in time for the Eleventh International Physiological Congress at Edinburgh in August, 1923. Sir Edward Sharpey Schafer, then professor of physiology in the University of Edinburgh, gave a formal dinner to which he invited all the foremost physiologists in the world. Pavlov, who was one of the most distinguished guests, appeared at the dinner in a gray summer suit, while the rest of the guests wore full evening dress.

A little episode with a happier ending involved the disappearance of Pavlov's boots. This happened in 1929 during a second trip which he made to America with his son Vladimir. (Vladimir acted as his father's interpreter.) They were staying at a hotel in New

York and at night on retiring left their boots in the corridor outside their room to be cleaned, according to the European custom. Pavlov woke first in the morning, and, remembering the "business-like" methods of the railway thieves, he looked outside the door for his boots and Vladimir's shoes, only to find to his horror that they were gone. This seemed a real tragedy, for Pavlov, since breaking his hip in 1916, had had to wear high orthopedic boots, and this was his only pair. Fortunately Vladimir had two pairs of shoes with him. Dressing quickly, Pavlov's son hurried to the hotel desk to inquire about the missing footgear and was told that these had been put safely away by the chambermaid on their floor. They were requested not to leave their boots in the corridor again. In America this was never done, for there were special shoeshine parlors in the hotels!

Pavlov's Creative Imagination

It is customary to think that only artists, in the broad sense of the term, use their creative imagination to attain the results they achieve, while scientists merely observe facts and analyze them, relying almost exclusively on the inductive method. This is not so. Of course, a scientist must have an analytical mind, but he must also possess a creative imagination; otherwise there could be no forward movement in science. Pavlov was endowed with an exceptionally keen scientific imagination. When a new fact was observed, he incorporated it into the scheme of facts already established. If the new fact stubbornly refused to enter into the already existing framework, the latter was discarded and a new one substituted, incorporating all the facts. Pavlov constructed hypotheses freely and easily when an intractable new fact had to be dealt with. But he did not stop there. More and more facts were demanded to strengthen the new scheme. It was gradually overlaid with facts and transformed from a hypothesis into a theory based on all the facts now available. Finally, Pavlov subjected his new conception to merciless theoretical and experimental analysis.

It may be recalled that Pavlov entertained grave doubts when he began to study the functions of the cerebral hemispheres by the method of conditioned reflexes. He spoke of this in the Preface to his *Lectures on Conditioned Reflexes* (1928, p. 41). In current work he was equally critical of results achieved in the laboratory and of theories that might be put forward regarding them. He often told us that a theory is good only if it can connect facts for a period of six months at least. If the facts do not fit the theory, then that theory must be replaced by another.

He publicly expressed his views on the importance of theory in experimental work when he spoke of his research on the structure and functions of the brain:

> It is too early yet to speak of any definite plan of a functional type of brain. Consequently one should now limit oneself to the collection of facts. However, at any given time one must have a general conception of a subject, in order to have a framework on which to hang the facts, to have something on which one may build, and in order to have a hypothesis for future investigations. In scientific work, such conceptions and hypotheses are indispensable [Pavlov, 1928, p. 115].

At the same time, Pavlov was not a slave to facts. He was always able to evolve a sound structure out of them. It is true that his theories were often criticized, but his facts remained undisputed. It must be admitted that some of Pavlov's theories eventually proved to be completely or partially incorrect, but his mistakes are to be attributed more to the influence of the epoch in which he worked than to any inexact or hurried mental conclusions made by him. However, theoretical conjectures of Pavlov's in their day gave inspiration to countless workers in the tireless search for new facts. For this reason Pavlov's theories, despite their shortcomings, may be regarded as generally sound, since they produced such a harvest of facts. After all, it was not by secrecy that Pavlov made his multitudinous discoveries!

Pavlov could never understand how it was possible to conduct research in physiology without making use of an appropriate theoretical conception, even though only a temporary one. To him every new fact that was revealed in the laboratory was like a link in a chain that was being pulled out of a dark hold. One link was connected with another and inevitably led to the appearance of the next. Research must follow some guiding idea and not be a blind investigation of different possibilities.

Such were Pavlov's methods of research. Others may employ

different methods, but Pavlov is one of those of whom it is singularly appropriate to say: "By their fruits ye shall know them."[3]

PAVLOV'S LEGACY TO STUDENTS

Pavlov expressed his views on scientific work and the relationship between the factual and theoretical sides of research perhaps more clearly than anyone else has done. At the beginning of his last illness, when he was still carrying on his work, an organization of Russian youth (the Komsomol) asked Pavlov to write an article for their journal. He acceded to this request, submitting a short contribution, which may now be considered in the light of a legacy to students—not to Russian students only but to students of all lands. Here is what he wrote:

This is the message I would like to give to the youth of my country. First of all, be systematic. I repeat—be systematic. Train yourself to be strictly systematic in the acquisition of knowledge. First study the rudiments of science before attempting to reach its heights. Never pass on to the next stage until you have thoroughly mastered the one on hand. Never try to conceal the defects in your knowledge even by the most daring conjectures and hypotheses. Practice self-restraint and patience. Learn to do the drudgery of scientific work. Although a bird's wing is perfect, the bird could never soar if it did not lean upon the air. Facts are the air on which the scientist leans. Without them you will never fly upward. Without them your theories will be mere empty efforts. However, when studying, experimenting, or observing, try not to remain on the surface of things. Do not become a mere collector of facts but try to penetrate into the mystery of their origin. Search persistently for the laws which govern them.

The second important requisite is modesty. Never at any time imagine that you know everything. No matter how highly you are appreciated by others, have the courage to say to yourself, "I am ignorant." Do not let pride possess you.

The third thing that is necessary is passion. Remember that science demands of a man his whole life. And even if you could have two lives, they would not be sufficient. Science calls for tremendous effort and great passion. Be passionate in your work and in your search for truth.

All his life Pavlov remained faithful to the branch of science that he had chosen in his youth, namely, experimental physiology. Pavlov said of himself: "I am an experimenter from head to foot. My whole life has been given to experiment" (see chap. 17). He dreamed of living to a ripe old age in order to finish his experimental work on conditioned reflexes—as far as it is possible to finish anything in science—and then to begin writing. He often repeated this in talk with us. It has been noted likewise by Frolov (1938, p. 11) and Gantt (Pavlov, 1941, p. 11).

Pavlov always remained devoted to experimental research and did not, like many retired professors, yield to the temptation to philosophize and write philosophical treatises, which true philosophers for reasons best known to themselves usually do not consider seriously. His experimental work was brought to a conclusion by his last illness. This fidelity to the subject that he had embraced in his youth illustrates the vigor and tenacity of Pavlov's mind and its extraordinary freshness.

Such was Pavlov. With the exception of those moments which he gave to his family, Pavlov's whole life was dedicated to the laboratory. This was not a life rich in events that would make his biography vivid and picturesque. Of course, many things happened during his life, bringing him joy or sorrow. But not for one day did any of these things make Pavlov forget the problems to which he had dedicated his life.

In a letter which I received from Pavlov's wife in 1936, soon after his death, she wrote: "This was no ordinary man but a colossus, an almost legendary figure." Indeed, he was a colossus in both a spiritual and a scientific sense. Relations with him were not always easy, but they were inspiring and pointed the way to upright living, hard work, and civic duties, which is the path that everyone should travel through life.

Pavlov's method of directing scientific work was different from that usually employed by laboratory chiefs. As a rule, when a graduate student arrives in a laboratory, it is not long before he is given a problem to work on. The professor himself or his assistant helps him to perform his first few experiments, and then he is left to carry on by himself. From time to time, but not very frequently, the student comes to the professor to report on the results he has achieved and to discuss further plans. This system, if it is not abused, as it was in Bechterev's laboratory, is a reasonable one and has certain advantages, the chief of these being that the beginner learns to surmount the difficulties of scientific investigation and gradually develops in himself the requisite qualities of a scientist and an experimenter.

As it was mentioned above (chap. 6), a different system of training of the new workers existed in Pavlov's laboratory. After a few days of watching other investigators, the newcomer received dogs with one or another type of salivary or gastrointestinal fistula on which he repeated the experiments of his immediate predecessor. This was a double check—on the results of the previous worker and on the ability of the new collaborator to master the experimental technique. Only after a few weeks of this preliminary training, which some of the new workers considered a mere waste of time, would Pavlov give to the student his problem. Such a long initial period of training was partly due to the fact that Pavlov gave most careful thought to each question that he was planning to investigate with a new collaborator, and this required time. From the moment that a problem was allotted to a worker, Pavlov took a most active interest in it and inquired about its progress almost daily. Often he would sit for an hour or more in the worker's room observing an experiment. He would examine the protocols and often remembered the figures previously obtained better than did the worker himself. Finally, if he was especially interested in the work, he would participate in the experiments himself.

Here is an example of Pavlov's interest in the case of my own research work. When I was investigating the inactive lipolytic enzymes of the pancreatic juice, it was necessary to observe continuously the process of the splitting of fat (monobutyrin) by the pancreatic juice and not to allow the water incubator to remain unattended for one minute. When the time came for lunch, I naturally wanted to leave my experiment and go to the Institute dining-room. This was in 1902, when I had a healthy appetite. So I would go to Pavlov's study and ask him to look after my test tubes. He would never consider such a request strange and would break into his own short recess to come and replace me. I can see him yet, with his tall figure and the pince-nez on the tip of his nose, conscientiously observing the test tubes in the water incubator.

I am sure that many of those who worked in Pavlov's laboratory could remember such incidents. I am also sure that there was not another chief or *Geheimrath* in the world who made so little distinction between the interests of the worker and those of the laboratory.

When Pavlov was present at an experiment being performed by one of his collaborators who was working on a dog with a chronic fistula, he usually talked to the worker about his problem. During such discussions it was as if Pavlov were thinking aloud. Sometimes he would suddenly ask a question concerning the validity of some view which was entirely opposed to his own ideas, in order to receive a negative answer and be reassured once again that he was right in his original assumption. On other occasions Pavlov would enthusiastically talk over details of experiments or future research with some newcomer to the laboratory and would try, usually without success, to draw the other into discussion. Once I asked Pavlov whether it was worth losing time to talk with a man who seemed unable to follow the drift of the discussion. "Of course it is," replied Pavlov. "The beginner's brain is not cluttered up as ours is with all sorts of theories; his hands and feet are not shackled by his scientific past, as our are. He can look at a subject from the outside and express some original thought." I am afraid that Pavlov rarely encountered any original thoughts among the beginners in the course of his long career. However, these seemingly useless talks were just another way in which Pavlov could confirm his own ideas. While describing new phases of laboratory work in language as simple and clear as possible, he again thought over all aspects of the results which had already been obtained.

When the facilities of Pavlov's laboratories were greatly extended by the opening of the Physiological Laboratory at the Military-Medical Academy about 1905 and by the removal of the laboratory of the Academy of Science to a new and larger building after the Revolution of 1917, there were about forty people working with Pavlov on conditioned reflexes. In a letter to me dated December 22, 1923, he wrote: "My work progresses on a large scale. A great many workers have gathered, and I cannot accept all those who want to come." Pavlov had therefore to use other methods in directing his numerous co-workers. As Professor Savich has aptly expressed it, Pavlov now resembled a chess player, playing on several boards at once. The data obtained by one worker could be confirmed and carried a step further by the research of another worker. I am not familiar with this period of Pavlov's work, since I left Petrograd for good in the summer of 1918.

CHAPTER ELEVEN

The School of Experimental Physiology

FROM the foregoing it might be concluded correctly that Pavlov initiated the research work of his students and constantly supervised them. The students for the most part followed plans previously drawn up by Pavlov. (Such continual control presumably might deaden scientific initiative, but this was far from the case in Pavlov's laboratory.) The young research aspirants who entered the laboratory usually had had no experience in experimental research. There they were initiated into the techniques and methods and learned to be accurate in the details of their research. They considered it a privilege to acquire operational technique from a master such as Pavlov. Under the influence of the exceptionally original creative mind of Pavlov they underwent an excellent training in experimental thought, which set an indelible stamp on all their future independent scientific activity. If we also take into account the enthusiasm with which Pavlov infected most of them and the mental satisfaction which they received from thinking in conjunction with him about their work, then it is not surprising that, far from resenting his interference, the workers were deeply disappointed when for some reason or other he ceased for a time to show interest in their experiments.

Pavlov himself considered his method of work the only correct one. It was not dictatorship on the part of a laboratory "chief" to compel his co-workers to do what he wanted—to work, in fact, for him—since Pavlov was, after all, the teacher and the young research workers were his pupils. Notwithstanding Pavlov's active participation in the work of his students, the scientific co-operation between teacher and pupils was in many cases interesting and stimulating, since Pavlov, when reviewing and analyzing experiments with his workers, tried to make them think independently and to draw them into discussing the facts they had arrived at. Pavlov not only allowed himself to be contradicted but was anxious to be contradicted, and to bring this about he argued vehemently with his students, trying to find out during these disputes the real nature of the observed phenomenon. He was always delighted if a pupil added something of his own to the solution of an experimental problem. Any attempt to alter this organization of his laboratory would have been considered by Pavlov as a violation of his scientific freedom. Such an attempt was indeed once made. After the Revolution of 1917 one of Pavlov's assistants suggested organizing a laboratory council, made up of laboratory assistants with the director of the laboratory as chairman. This council was to have selected problems for new co-workers and to have directed their work. Pavlov was so indignant at this plan that he emphatically condemned it not only in the laboratory but also in public in the lecture which he gave at the Tenishevski Technical School on "The Mind in General and the Russian Mind in Particular" (chap. 10).

When a young scientist had matured and was able to formulate his own ideas and plans for research, work with Pavlov became difficult. Subjects which had no direct relation to the work of the laboratory did not interest him, and often he would even refuse to discuss them. If the scientific interests of the young co-worker coincided with those of Pavlov, every new idea of the former was incorporated into the general fund of laboratory knowledge and was lost sight of among the ideas of other workers and especially those of Pavlov. Of course, the name of the originator of the idea appeared in the published work, but little remained of the original idea after the refining process which it underwent in Pavlov's mind.

In the Introduction to his *Lectures on the Work of the Principal Digestive Glands* Pavlov (1897) expressed his position very clearly. He stated there that in discussing some fact he used the expression "we," as if speaking for the whole laboratory—that is, he did not distinguish between his co-workers and himself.

While constantly mentioning the author of a special experiment when discussing its object, its significance, and its place among other experiments, I speak collectively, mentioning no authors, when I discuss ideas and opinions. . . . This basic viewpoint is the final viewpoint of the laboratory; it embraces all the facts constantly experienced, minutely examined, and thus the most correct. Such an opinion is, of course, also that of my co-workers, but it is a joint work and the result of the general laboratory atmosphere, to which each one gives something and which is imbibed by all.

Pavlov was not greatly interested in the general education in physiology even of his most earnest pupils. Once, at the very beginning of my work in his laboratory, I asked his advice on how best to learn physiology. He quickly replied: "Read the *Ergebnisse* [*der Physiologie*] and so approach the subject gradually" and at once turned the conversation to laboratory matters. It is quite probable that, being himself self-taught in physiology, he considered that others should do likewise.

In summing up the influence exerted by Pavlov, a man of strong and original character, on his co-workers, we might say that his influence was both mental and moral. The extent of his influence was, of course, determined in each case by the strength of character of the co-worker. Even those who were not easily swayed adopted to some extent his method of thinking. Others even went so far as to copy his manner of speech and his gestures. Pavlov's technical style naturally was imitated also, but during my time in his laboratory nobody could compare with him in operational technique.

The most powerful influence exerted by Pavlov was a mental one, which was felt especially by his co-workers of many years' standing. Observing day by day how Pavlov followed the progress of experiments, listening to his discussion and the conclusions that he drew from them, perceiving how he formulated new problems on the basis of the results obtained and at once determined the proper experimental approach, we, unnoticed to ourselves, assimilated our teacher's method of thought. This was truly a school of scientific thought, and we, his pupils, should be grateful to Pavlov for this above all else.

Pavlov's method of reasoning could be described as experimental. When he thought about a subject, he imagined its future development in the form of an experiment. Every supposition or theory at once took shape in his mind as an experiment which had to affirm or disprove a new conjecture. The desired solution was not always attained, but his thoughts were thereupon at once directed to a new experimental plan. I do not mean to imply that this kind of "experimental thinking" was the sole method used by Pavlov, but it did play a considerable part in his mental processes and was the basis of his realism. When he observed some experiment that deviated from the normal course, he was not usually satisfied in obtaining only a theoretical explanation of this deviation but planned a new experimental attack.

"As you know," he said, "I am an experimenter from head to toe. My whole life has consisted of experiments" (from his address at the government reception of delegates to the Fifteenth International Congress of Physiology, in Moscow, August 17, 1935). An experiment was the only thing which could convince Pavlov that some supposition or theory was correct. Theories he regarded as the framework needed to construct a building, but the actual edifice was erected with facts obtained through experimentation. What Pavlov built was a structure inspired by some great idea and not a mere storehouse for building materials.

Work in the laboratory was to Pavlov unquestionably a labor of love. He greeted the discovery of a new fact with jubilation, and failure only made him more determined in his pursuit of any problem. The final goal he continually strove to reach was the establishment of scientific truth and ultimately the good of all mankind. The immediate motive that prompted Pavlov to make experiments and thereby attain an understanding of the physiological processes of the organism was the pleasure he derived from the work. He once spoke to me of this when visiting us in Montreal in 1929. "Of course, we strive to reach the highest goal in science," he said, "but do you not agree that what so strongly impels us to work in the laboratory is the satisfaction that we get from our work?" I agreed wholeheartedly, since I have always experienced this feeling in the laboratory. The life of an experimenter is interesting and full because he is always confronted with the unknown, which he has to investigate and understand. Thus he satisfies that spirit of adventure which most of us possess.

PAVLOV'S MORAL INFLUENCE

It was not only in sphere of scientific research that Pavlov's influence was felt by his co-workers. A man of prodigious intellect, Pavlov was bound to affect spiritually anyone who worked with him for a considerable length of time. His manner of judging different matters, his reaction to events great or small, his firmness in adhering to his principles of moral behavior, were all involuntarily absorbed in various degrees by his associates in the laboratory, especially by the younger ones.

Imperceptibly, without pretending to educate anyone, Pavlov taught us by his example, at a time when there was much that was abnormal in Russian life. It was the end of the nineteenth century, a time of transition, when many Chekhov characters still existed. Some of these characters were honorable but were dreamers and lacking in will-power; others were coarse and ruthless predatory types. There were a few people with strong and noble convictions and the will to realize their aims. Pavlov was one of these. He grew up in an entirely different atmosphere from that in which the youth of the intelligentsia were educated. He had passed through a stern school of experience, and he early acquired a realistic outlook on life and disapproved of everything that was not realistic. There was no weakness nor indecision in him, and he hated to find these qualities in others.

When someone in the laboratory remarked that one of the distinctive traits of the Russian character was softness, Pavlov indignantly denied this. He asserted that what might be taken for softness in many Russians was merely weakness of character, which caused them to close their eyes to wrong and to remain indifferent to every event, wishing merely to be left in peace.

Pavlov did not go to extremes in his admiration of the West like those who considered anything Western better than its Russian counterpart; neither was he a Slavophile who believed in the special virtues of the Russian soul and longed to proselytize the West. Pavlov was a Russian patriot in the best sense of the word, that is, he believed that Russia, like many other nations, had contributed much to the world and that she would again contribute something of her own, something original and precious, to the general sum of the world's culture.

Pavlov's Temperament

Earlier I mentioned that Pavlov was a man of uneven temperament and not always easy to get along with. One of the traits which sometimes made it difficult to work with him was his irritability, expressed in outbursts of uncontrollable anger. These flare-ups were accompanied by loud shouting and, in earlier days, before I joined the laboratory, also by strong language. But Pavlov's anger was short-lived, and he soon regained his composure.

Pavlov's behavior was not exceptional in the Russia of his day. For some reason all Russian officials, with the possible exception of the more polished St. Petersburg officials, considered it necessary to instil fear into their subordinates by raising their voices. In other countries, too, officials considered it necessary to shout in order to assert authority, and the Germans were worse in this respect. It was only when one arrived in England that one was amazed to find that much better results were achieved without raising the voice at all.

PROFESSOR CHISTOVICH'S STORY

Professor N. J. Chistovich in his article on Pavlov in the *Pavlov Jubilee Volume* (1925) relates the following incident, which occurred in the eighties.

In his personal contact with his workers, Pavlov succeeded in combining strict authority with quite simple, friendly relations. I will tell of a little incident which took place between us. When he had successfully carried out the experiment of isolating the heart in a dog, Pavlov wanted to demonstrate it to S. P. Botkin and so invited him to the laboratory. Everything was prepared beforehand. The dog had been operated upon, and only the last steps of the operation remained to be performed in Botkin's presence: the ligature had to be tied around the inferior vena cava and the arch of the aorta, and the forceps had to be removed from the jugular vein to release the blood from the reservoir. Pavlov asked me whether everything was ready and, on my replying in the affirmative, he quickly tied the ligatures. But the flow of blood from the subclavian artery suddenly ceased—I had forgotten to remove the forceps from the jugular vein! Seeing what was the matter, Pavlov grasped the forceps and hastily removed them in such a way that the vein was severed and the blood gushed out, and the experiment failed. Anyone acquainted with Pavlov can imagine how he turned on me: I was guilty of every misdemeanor known to man, because I had forgotten to remove the forceps! I replied that he was guilty too, since he should have been more careful in removing the forceps and should not have pulled them off the way he did. By degrees our quarrel reached such proportions that we acknowledged the impossibility of working together in the future and parted, disillusioned and upset. In the evening I received a note from Pavlov, which read: "Invective is not an obstacle to work. Come tomorrow to do the experiment."

There is no need to add that all of us whom Pavlov railed at with the choicest expressions were deeply attached to him and were not at all put out by his weakness in blaming us for every misfortune, knowing his sincerity and his scrupulously honorable soul.

SWEARING

Pavlov at one time had the habit of swearing. This he probably acquired in seminary, where in the sixties morals were of the order of those described by Pomialovski in his *Ecclesiastical Seminary* (*Bursa*), that is to say, they were crude or even worse.

In my time Pavlov never swore. It is true that he often mentioned the devil in his conversation, but this was a habit many of us had in Russia. I must add that the Russian devil is not as awesome, merciless, and evil a creature as the foreign varieties like Beelzebub, Lucifer, and Mephistopheles, the very mention of whose names is offensive and even insulting. Of course, the Russian devil tries to make trouble for everyone, but he is not very clever and is easily outwitted, since in Russian fairy tales the peasant always wins a victory over him. Often, when something turned out well, Pavlov would gleefully say: "All the devils must be sick at this!" meaning that, no matter how hard the devils had tried to spoil his work, they had not succeeded and therefore were now sick with disappointment.

I believe that it was Professor N. Riazantsev of Kharkov Veterinary Institute who cured Pavlov of his swearing habits. Once, while assisting Pavlov in an operation, Riazantsev, who at the time was working in the physiological laboratory of the Institute of Experimental Medicine, was unable to stand Pavlov's talk any longer. He began to answer Pavlov with the familiar "thou" and in the same coarse language. Pavlov fell silent, but after the operation he remarked to Riazantsev that there must be an end to swearing because it was a very objectionable habit.

"WHITEY"

Here is another illustration of Pavlov's character. The incident took place during the first or second year after I joined Pavlov's laboratory, when I was still a young Institute doctor. It was a Sunday, but like most of the research workers I came to the laboratory on Sundays, since Pavlov himself never missed a day's work between September 1 and May 31. On this particular Sunday, however, for some reason there were few people in the laboratory and everything was quiet. I was in my room collecting pancreatic juice from a dog which stood harnessed to its special stand on the table. (Dogs thus equipped with a fistula of the pancreatic duct may live for years.) Pavlov sat alone in the large laboratory at his favorite place by the window, where I could see him through the open door of my room. "Whitey," as the dog was called, whined continuously. I was used to this, since I had been working with "Whitey" for several months, but this whining evidently prevented Pavlov from thinking. All at once he jumped up from his chair, rushed into my room, seized a towel that was hanging over my shoulder and struck the dog with it. He then went back to his place by the window. Hardly five minutes had passed before he returned to my room and, shaking his finger at me, said in a very cross voice, "Boris Petrovich, never, never, beat a dog." I replied that I never had beaten one. "I know, I know, but this should never be done," he replied in quite a different, more gentle tone of voice. After that, "Whitey" could whine to his heart's content without punishment.

Notwithstanding his fiery temperament, those who were most closely associated with Pavlov and worked with him did not fear him. It was disagreeable when he was angry with one of us, but this was usually due to some mistake that had been made in the work. His irritated tone of voice was regarded as a passionate expression of displeasure rather than as active anger. At all events, neither I nor any of my friends in the laboratory were afraid of Pavlov. Perhaps the attendants feared him at first, but even they got used to his ways in time and learned that the loud expression of his annoyance carried with it no unpleasant consequences. No one in the laboratory "trembled" when Pavlov was angry, contrary to the assertion of Yougov (1942). This writer, who is very little concerned with the truth, gives a fantastic picture of the reaction of the laboratory workers to Pavlov's anger: "The faces of the oldest and most trusted of his workers turn pale ... the veins freeze when Pavlov's face changes and becomes gloomy and terrifying."

attitude

CHAPTER TWELVE

⌐s Attitude toward His Co-workers

PAVLOV'S research could not have been carried out on so large a scale without the assistance of many co-workers. When, in the twenties, the Medical Research Council in London offered Pavlov a grant for the rest of his life if he would continue his work in England, he refused, preferring to remain in Soviet Russia; and I am inclined to think that one of the reasons for his refusal was the impossibility of having a sufficient number of co-workers in England. There were, of course, other factors to be considered if he migrated to England, such as love for his country, the necessity of leaving some of his family in Russia, and his inability to speak English. (Pavlov read English with ease but pronounced the words just as they were written.) If his work had been handicapped by a lack of co-workers, Pavlov would have been utterly unhappy. This must have played an important part in his decision to remain in Russia.

As I have already stated, the atmosphere of Pavlov's laboratory was friendly. It was created by Pavlov himself, who kept on simple and amicable terms with his students and co-workers without losing his dignity or lessening his authority. Since the majority of the research workers in his laboratory were postgraduate students who remained only for a year or at most for a year and a half, these friendly relations were naturally for the most part of a superficial kind, and it was only in his associations with his permanent co-workers that real friendship sometimes developed. Such ties, originating in the laboratory, were valued highly by Pavlov. This is evident from the following letter, which he wrote me on January 29, 1928, on the publication of the second edition of my book, *Die äussere Sekretion der Verdauungsdrüsen*. In the first edition of 1914, the book, which was published both in Russian and in German, had been dedicated to Pavlov as my "teacher," but now I had asked his permission to call him also my "friend." He replied: "I am very pleased by your addition of 'friend.' I always very much wanted laboratory relationships and encounters to develop into friendship but unfortunately this seems to happen rarely in Russia." So my dedication of the second edition was as follows: "Meinem hochverehrten Lehrer und Freund, Herr Professor Dr. I. P. Pavlov, gewidmet."

Pavlov was friendly with all his laboratory staff, and it was difficult to determine who were his favorites. Everyone knew which workers Pavlov considered good, which moderately good, and which poor. Pavlov never favored "yes men" or flatterers. Those he regarded most were the men whose work was progressing well and whose experiments promised to furnish new and interesting results. Since there was good progress only when the work was conducted by talented and thinking men, Pavlov naturally was interested in them to a certain extent, but the work was the main thing.

I remember two cases illustrating Pavlov's interest in the work and the worker which occurred while I was his assistant in the Institute of Experimental Medicine. One of these was the problem of "disinhibition" of the conditioned reflexes, which Pavlov worked out with Dr. I. V. Zavadsky; another, the elaboration of the conception of irradiation and concentration of the conditioned inhibition on the basis of Dr. N. I. Krasnogorsky's experiments (see Part IV). He sat through Zavadsky's and later through Krasnogorsky's experiments by the hour and thought and spoke exclusively of them. It was extraordinary to see such youthful enthusiasm in a man of sixty-two over the success of a scientific investigation. He looked like a happy lover, for whom nothing existed but the object of his love and to whom all else was of secondary consideration. Pavlov was a true scientist, a scientist by God's grace!

When Pavlov's interest in a man's research work was transferred to the man himself, this interest was only temporary. As soon as a new and important fact had been established and it was no longer necessary to expend all his intellectual energy and all the subtlety of his experimental technique on its analysis, Pavlov abandoned his "temporary favorite" without compunction and began to show interest in the work of another co-worker. Often these young men were under the impression that Pavlov had a special interest in them rather than in their work. Although Pavlov maintained lasting friendships with some of his co-workers, such as V. V. Savich, N. I. Krasnogorsky, and others, he never allowed personal relationships to interfere with scientific work.

Among the workers in the laboratory there were many different types, and some of them tried to attract Pavlov's attention and to produce a specially good impression on him. I remember a certain doctor, probably one of the temporary scientific "favorites," who attempted rather crudely to flatter Pavlov. He had already received his M.D. degree and now rarely came to the laboratory. He had worked with Pavlov during the period when the latter was enthusiastic about the idea of purposiveness in the functions of the alimentary canal. By the time that I joined the laboratory Pavlov had cooled considerably toward the idea of purposiveness, the significance of which he had before stressed with great persistence. However, this doctor was still thinking in terms of former days. Pavlov would speak of some experiments, and the doctor from habit would murmur, "How purposive!" We younger workers used to wait with interest for this "How purposive!"—but Pavlov would only frown.

There was one graduate student who displayed greater finesse in his campaign to win Pavlov's attention. His work progressed exceptionally well, and Pavlov would sit in his room for hours observing the experiments and, as usual, speaking and thinking aloud. The next day the young man would come to the laboratory and announce that he had slept badly, since all night long he had thought of nothing but his experiments. With some variations, he would then repeat to Pavlov what Pavlov himself had said to him the previous day. Perhaps from naïveté or because he did not at once see through this little artifice, Pavlov believed everything the young man said. He would remark to us in the laboratory: "How strange it is—N. N. and I think exactly alike in regard to his experimental work!" Generally, however, Pavlov understood people very well, and it was difficult to deceive him for long.

Pavlov did not seek to create any intimacy between his co-workers and himself. Once or twice a year the Pavlovs gave a big dinner, to which only the assistants and the senior co-workers were invited. Unfortunately, even these more intimate meetings with Pavlov and his family usually coincided with the arrival of some foreign scientific visitor at the laboratory. We used to call such visitors "distinguished foreigners," although many of them were not at all outstanding in science.

At the New Year and at Easter, according to the Russian custom, many of us would pay a call on Pavlov's wife and remain for ten or fifteen minutes. Pavlov himself would not be at home, since he never missed a day at the laboratory during the scholastic year.

It may be seen that Pavlov drew a sharp dividing line between his laboratory relationships and his personal ones when I say that Pavlov met my wife for the first time twenty-two years after I had first entered his laboratory, although I was then already a married man. The meeting took place in 1923 in London, where we were living as refugees. Pavlov and his son Vladimir had come to England for the Eleventh International Physiological Congress, which was held that year at Edinburgh. As for Pavlov's wife, she never met my wife, since we were never invited to their home together; and on those very rare occasions, of which I have spoken above, when the Pavlovs entertained the senior members of the laboratory staff, I was invited alone. The same applied to my married colleagues. Many years later, after we had come to Canada, Pavlov's wife, Seraphima Vasilievna, corresponded with us both and also separately with my wife. She wrote very warm letters, telling us that we were among her family's best friends. It is impossible to imagine such formal relations existing in university life in England, Canada, or America. It probably never occurred to Pavlov that it might be derogatory to a young wife not to be invited along with her husband to the home of his chief.

A Laboratory Tragedy

An unwelcome period of readjustment began for Pavlov when a graduate student completed the experimental part of his work. Usually the student, who had known very little physiology when he entered the laboratory, had by doing his work well during a whole year become a quite useful research worker. Then suddenly, often at the most interesting stage of his research, he had to cease work, since the period of his postgraduate study was coming to an end. He had to spend the remaining time in writing his thesis, having it printed, and preparing the material for its public defense.

Usually Pavlov bore this misfortune in silence and began to train some newly arrived student to carry on the work, reconciling himself to the unavoidable delay in the progress of his investigations. But if any student who had finished his work tried to hurry Pavlov into reading his handwritten thesis or the material for its defense, Pavlov would lose his temper and would begin shouting uncomplimentary remarks at the student making the request. It must be said that there were some graduate students who came to Pavlov's laboratory for the sole purpose of obtaining their M.D. degree in the short space of one year. Such students would listen to the bitter reproaches of Pavlov, probably thinking: "Let the old man rave. I'll get my own way in the end"—which, indeed, they did.

The reading of the handwritten thesis was a very dull occupation for Pavlov. He consented to it only because he naturally wanted the results obtained in the laboratory, and the experiments on which they were based, to be reported correctly in the printed work. The author of the thesis read it aloud to Pavlov while he sat in his study in an armchair with his head thrown back, probably listening with no great attention, even though sometimes interrupting the reading with a correction.

Pavlov must have found this task very irksome. I remember that I was once conducting an experiment in which he was interested. He told me to call him when a certain point was reached, and he himself went to his study on the second floor of the laboratory to hear someone read a thesis. When the appointed moment arrived, I ran up to Pavlov's room, but the door was half open and I could hear the monotonous voice of the student reading. I was still a newcomer at that time and did not dare to disturb him. In a little while Pavlov himself came running down and reproved me for not having called him. I excused myself by saying that I had come to his study at the appointed time but that he was busy listening to the reading of the thesis and I did not wish to interrupt. "What nonsense you are talking!" he exclaimed. "Do you think I was busy—listening to that twaddle?" The poor student, who was standing there, could only blink!

There was one little tragicomedy which was enacted in the laboratory when a certain graduate student, now long dead, had to stop his experimental work. This incident provided much amusement for all except Pavlov and the student himself. The latter was a very pleasant provincial Jew, full of good humor, somewhat naïve, and probably not very clever. Our hero was very talkative and liked to boast. When Pavlov sat with him during his experiments, he amused the chief with stories of his romantic escapades with the wife of some provincial magistrate in a far-off province, where he had served as a doctor. How much truth there was in his stories it is hard to say, but evidently Pavlov, who rarely went to the theater and seldom read any literature during the winter, found these stories entertaining and readily listened to the doctor. All this ended very sadly. The doctor one day informed Pavlov that he would have to stop his research work, because he had spent almost all the money that he had saved for his graduate study, only a small sum now remaining for the printing of his thesis. Pavlov was very angry. He walked up and down the laboratory, muttering indignantly: "The devil knows what this is! He spent all his money on the magistrate's wife and now he can't continue his work!" This attitude was rather unfair, since Pavlov was making the romance the public property of the whole laboratory, and previously he himself had listened with interest to the doctor's stories without rebuking him for his wastefulness. As for ourselves, and especially V. V. Savich, we teased the poor doctor about the magistrate's wife for a long time, but he took our jokes in good part.

Assisting Pavlov at Operations

As I have mentioned before, Pavlov was an exceptionally skilful surgeon. He performed operations very quickly; all his movements were exact and his eye was extraordinarily true. For example, he never made two rows of stitches in a cut in the abdominal organs but was satisfied with one. He would adjust the edges of a wound so closely that the tissues grew together perfectly. He did this even in an organ such as the intestine, where the slightest inaccuracy in bringing the edges of a cut together might form a tiny crack, from which the intestinal contents could drip into the abdominal cavity, resulting in peritonitis and the death of the animal.

It was not easy to assist Pavlov when he was operating. He did not like to call out the name of the instrument he wanted at a given moment or to say what he would do next, and at the same time he was extremely impatient. The instruments were handed to him by the very able young laboratory attendant, Vania Shuvalov, who knew the procedure of the operations perfectly and gave Pavlov the required instrument at the right moment. But the assistants, especially the newcomers, often failed to give Pavlov the help he wanted or gave it at the wrong time. Then he would push the assistant's hand away and say: "I speak with my hands—you must get used to that," or he would begin to mutter irritably: "Well, hold this, hold this!" or some such words. He had no patience with new assistants, which was quite understandable, and they would feel altogether at a loss during an operation and would give him even less help than they were capable of. In a little while, however, the operator and the assistant would get used to each other and the work would begin to run smoothly.

Although Pavlov performed many operations on animals, he always became extremely nervous at the sight of blood. He acknowledged this fact himself, and for this reason he always insisted that the wound be kept dry and free from bleeding.

In the summer of 1902, Dr. W. H. Thompson, who was professor of physiology in (if I am not mistaken) the University of Dublin and who was then making an English translation of Pavlov's book, *Lectures on the Work of the Digestive Glands*, arrived in St. Petersburg. Pavlov wanted to demonstrate to him the operations of isolating a stomach pouch (Pavlov pouch) and making a fistula in the main stomach of a dog. Unfortunately, the permanent laboratory assistant, A. P. Sokolov, was not in the city at the time and Pavlov had to operate with the assistance of us newcomers. Despite this, the operation was carried out successfully. The isolation of the stomach pouch in one dog was completed in one hour and twenty minutes, a record at that time even for Pavlov. Pavlov then moved to another operating table on which lay an anesthetized dog and made a fistula in its stomach in fifteen to twenty minutes. Naturally Pavlov wanted to display his skill to the foreign visitor.

After Professor Thompson left the laboratory, Pavlov, pleased with his success, to our great delight remarked with all seriousness: "Well, well, everything went satisfactorily, even though I did have to operate with the help of a lot of riffraff!" We accepted this strange expression of thanks without any rancor whatsoever.

CHAPTER THIRTEEN

Pavlov's Day—the Nobel Prize

DURING the years 1901–12, when I was a member of Pavlov's laboratory, Pavlov, if he did not have to lecture in the morning at the Military-Medical Academy, used to arrive at his laboratory in the Institute of Experimental Medicine between 9:30 and 10:00 A.M. To the left of the entrance was a vestibule with a coat rack running along the wall on one side. Each member of the laboratory had formed the habit of hanging his coat on the same peg every day, and Pavlov would glance around the vestibule in the morning to see who had not yet arrived. He never missed a day at the laboratory and did not like anybody to be absent or late.

On the twentieth of each month the Russian officials received their salaries. Pavlov was displeased when those members of his laboratory who were attached to the Clinical Military Hospital of the Military-Medical Academy first went to collect their salaries and thus did not reach the laboratory until about 11:00 or 11:30 A.M. on that day. I do not know how these matters are arranged in Soviet Russia today, but in my time salaries were paid in cash. The treasurer of the Clinical Military Hospital set off on the morning of the twentieth by coach, accompanied by a soldier from the hospital guard with a rusty revolver, which he probably did not know how to use. They went to the State Treasury, or perhaps to the Treasury of the War Ministry, and there collected gold, silver, and paper money, to be brought back in suitcases. Since the treasurers of all the St. Petersburg garrisons visited the Treasury on that particular day, it is easy to understand why we did not receive our salaries until quite late in the morning. In the meantime Pavlov prowled about the noticeably empty laboratory and ironically called this "St. Civil Servant's Day." He himself received his salary at the Administration Office of the Military-Medical Academy after his lecture, which was always on a Thursday or Friday. If the twentieth fell on a Saturday, then the professors, being privileged persons, received their salaries from the treasurer of the Academy before or during the Conference, held on Saturdays from three to six o'clock. Pavlov also received a salary from the Institute of Experimental Medicine. He hated to waste time on these matters, and I have no doubt that his wife had to remind him when the twentieth came around that, after all, one could not live without money!

The archaic method of paying salaries in cash rather than by check was retained in Russia during the Imperial regime because the petty government officials were always very poor and, if they saved any money, they usually deposited it in special savings banks. In Soviet Russia everybody avoided going near a regular bank. To keep money in a bank was equivalent to being a "capitalist" and "counterrevolutionary" and carried with it all the disagreeable consequences which this entailed. There were no private banks in Soviet Russia; all the banks were government institutions.

On a day when gastric juice was to be collected from the dogs, Pavlov first went to the section of the laboratory (called the "gastric-juice factory") where this was done. The gastric juice was collected from six or eight dogs which had undergone esophagotomy (a special operation on the gullet) and were equipped with a gastric fistula. The dogs were fed raw minced meat, which, because of the esophagotomy, fell out of the upper end of the gullet into a dish. The animal bent its head, took the same meat in its mouth and swallowed, and again the meat fell into the dish. The dog could never know the reason why it might continue eating indefinitely and yet become more and more hungry. By this method of "sham feeding" a large quantity of gastric juice can be collected from an empty stomach, and the juice so obtained is uncontaminated with saliva or food. This secretion of gastric juice is due to a reflex from the mouth cavity on the gastric glands. Large, hungry dogs could produce up to 1,000 cc. of gastric juice at one session. Gastric juice was collected from an animal every other day so as to allow the animal's organism time to replenish the water, salts, and proteins lost with the secretion.

After spending some time in the "gastric-juice factory," Pavlov would go and watch some experiment being performed by one of his co-workers. When one o'clock approached, he withdrew to his study, where he lunched on a sandwich brought from home and tea without milk. It is uncertain how many mugs of tea he drank, since after lunch he was in the habit of walking through the laboratory, carrying his mug, which he would replenish several times. He drank his tea while biting on a lump of sugar which he took from his pocket. Pavlov used to say that the reason why he drank so much tea was in order to cleanse his system of all unnecessary or harmful products of metabolism, but the real reason was that, like all Russians, he was very fond of tea.

Pavlov ate little. His one substantial meal was dinner at 6:30 in the evening. He liked soup very much and used to say, "Yes, it's a weakness of mine! I love soup." In his youth he trained himself to eat sparingly for fear of becoming stout, since there was a tendency to corpulence in his family.

After lunch Pavlov, mug in hand, came down to the large room on the ground floor of the laboratory and, seating himself in his favorite place by the window, began to talk with the research workers. Sometimes the conversation was general; sometimes topics of the day were discussed; but most often current problems concerning the laboratory research were debated.

In the afternoon, if Pavlov remained in the laboratory, he might again observe some experiment that was being carried out or perform an operation or read for some time in his study, then go home about 6:00 P.M.

After the new physiological laboratory at the Military-Medical Academy was opened in 1905 and the number of research workers studying conditioned reflexes increased, Pavlov usually went there at about three in the afternoon. On Saturdays he again went to the Military-Medical Academy at three o'clock—not to the laboratory but to attend the meetings of the Conference, which he never missed.

At home in the evening after dinner Pavlov took a nap. He woke about 8:30 and proceeded to the dining-room, where the samovar was already hissing. Always served in the evening in Russia was tea with lemon and biscuits or with jam which the housewife had prepared at her *dacha* during the summer. Pavlov was not satisfied with tea just once in the evening, and at 10:00 P.M. a second samovar was brought in. I do not know whether any of his family shared his great addiction to tea-drinking. When the rest of his family retired, Pavlov read or, on finishing his tea, went to his study to write. He retired to bed late, at about 1:00 A.M. Breaking up the day into two parts with a short nap, as Pavlov did, is a useful habit. It seems to make two days, though of unequal length, out of one.

In his later years Pavlov organized his life in much the same way as during the time when I was a member of his laboratory. The writer Logansky (quoted from Frolov, 1938) describes how Pavlov spent his day.

Pavlov woke at 7:30 in the morning. At 8:00 he was having his morning tea with bread and butter. He sat in his armchair until 8:30, quietly admiring his pictures, for during his lifetime he collected about a hundred paintings by Russian artists. He then retreated to his study, where he worked until 9:30 or 9:50 A.M. Pavlov considered these morning hours the most productive for mental work. On Tuesdays and Saturdays he went to the Institute of Experimental Medicine and on Fridays to the Biological Station at Koltushi, outside St. Petersburg, where he remained until 5:30 P.M.; or he might go to the laboratory of the Academy of Sciences or to the Neurological and Psychiatric Clinic at the Institute of Experimental Medicine. If Pavlov was spending the forenoon at the laboratory of the Academy of Sciences, he would walk home for lunch at about 12:30. After lunch he rested for at least an hour, again looking at his pictures or listening to the gramophone. From 2:00 to 6:00 P.M. Pavlov was again to be found at one of his laboratories. After dinner he rested until 9:00, when he arose and drank his evening tea; then from 10:00 P.M. until about 1:30 A.M. he worked in his study. One of his pastimes was solitaire, which he would play after lunch or dinner. This regular alternation of work and rest was repeated without variation day after day. Doubtless the octogenarian Pavlov rigidly maintained this routine in order to save his strength as much as possible and to preserve himself for a long period of productive scientific work. After the Revolution and the Civil War the number of Pavlov's co-workers increased so considerably that it became physically impossible for him to observe and discuss each worker's progress individually. Consequently, in 1924 Pavlov inaugurated a special kind of colloquium, known as the "Wednesdays." Every Wednesday morning all the workers met together and joined with him in discussion of some phase of the work being carried on in the laboratories.

Another place besides the laboratory where in my time Pavlov's colleagues and students could meet him—this time on an equal footing—was the Physicians' Athletic Society in St. Petersburg. Pavlov was a member and one of the chief supporters of this organization. Every Monday evening the members of the society met in one of the gymnasiums in St. Petersburg and exercised on the various kinds of gymnastic apparatus. This society had very few members and Pavlov tried to persuade the doctors working in his laboratory to join it. The attendance was poor mainly because transportation was unreliable in St. Petersburg at the beginning of the twentieth century. The horse-drawn trams moved at a maddeningly slow rate, and the price of a private cab was prohibitive to a young student. In order to arouse a competitive spirit and induce the members to attend more regularly, Pavlov bestowed various titles on them. Those who never missed a meeting were called "pillars" of the society; those whose attendances were irregular but fairly frequent were called "supports"; and those, like myself, who came once and then failed to put in an appearance for half a year were called simply "riffraff"!

There were also other forms of exercise from which Pavlov derived pleasure, but they were possible only in the summer. (As was mentioned in chap. 1, Pavlov loved to work in his garden in the summer, to play the game of *gorodki* strenuously with his friends, and to organize excursions.)

The Nobel Prize

Pavlov was awarded the Nobel Prize for physiology in December, 1904. He journeyed to Stockholm to receive the award, presented to him by the king of Sweden. Up until the time the award was announced, hardly anyone knew that Pavlov had been selected as a laureate of the Nobel Committee on Physiology and Medicine in 1904. Pavlov, of course, was informed of the matter in advance but with the stipulation that the committee's decision be kept secret until a certain date.

I have very little firsthand knowledge of the kind of reception that was accorded Pavlov in Sweden or of the impression the land

and its people produced on him, since I left St. Petersburg for a two-year period of study abroad very soon after Pavlov's return from Stockholm. However, in her "Reminiscences" Mrs. Pavlov speaks at some length about the awarding of the Nobel Prize to her husband.

When Professor Tigerstedt of the University of Helsingfors communicated with Pavlov from Stockholm, informing him that the Nobel Committee had awarded him the prize for his work on the physiology of the digestive glands, he was positively stunned, as Mrs. Pavlov writes. He had no thought that his work would receive such exceptional recognition, especially since his book on the *Work of the Digestive Glands* had not met with great success. The demand for it greatly increased after Pavlov received the Nobel Prize.[1]

"We ordered for Ivan Petrovich," states Mrs. Pavlov, "a suit of full evening dress and for myself two dresses and a very good winter coat." Tigerstedt, who was one of Pavlov's best friends, both personal and professional, invited the Pavlovs to spend a week in Helsingfors to celebrate Pavlov's success before going to Stockholm.

The whole week in Helsingfors was spent in festivities. The Pavlovs were entertained in a most lavish and friendly fashion by many people. "I may say," adds Mrs. Pavlov, "that there was such wholehearted participation in our rejoicing as we would have expected only from our nearest relatives. Ivan Petrovich cherished the memory of this reception to his last day."

In Stockholm the Pavlovs were met by Professor (Count) Mörner and Emmanuel Nobel. The latter played a very important role in the establishment of the Nobel Prize. When his uncle, Alfred Nobel, bequeathed huge sums of money for the establishment of prizes for the most outstanding work in medicine and physiology, physics, chemistry, and so on, his family, the whole of Stockholm society, and even the king himself disapproved. They considered that it was not wise to drain the country's finances by giving away such large sums of money in prizes every year. It was Emmanuel Nobel who insisted on executing the will of his late uncle.

Many parties were given in Stockholm in honor of the Pavlovs, but the main event was the presentation of a diploma and gold medal to each laureate by the king himself. Each candidate was welcomed in his own language. Professor Mörner took some lessons in Russian in order to make the official address to Pavlov. When Pavlov was presented to the king, the latter also spoke to him in Russian, with the words, "Kak vashe zdorovie [how is your health], kak vi pojivaete [how are you], Ivan Petrovich?" Pavlov, who certainly did not expect to be greeted in Russian, was so astounded that for a moment he could think of nothing to say. Afterward he learned that the king had spent a long time studying the correct pronunciation of these words. Later the king remarked to Emmanuel Nobel, "I am afraid of your Pavlov. He does not wear any orders. Surely he is a socialist."

After their return home a practical-minded friend advised the Pavlovs to increase their capital by buying some stocks. Pavlov was indignant at the idea. "This money," he said, "I earned by incessant scientific work. Science never had and never will have anything in common with the stock exchange."

In 1904 the Nobel Prize consisted of about 73,000 gold rubles, or about 36,000 gold dollars, a very considerable sum in those days. Pavlov deposited the money with the St. Petersburg branch of Nobel's Russian firm. During the Revolution of 1917 he lost all this money, since the Bolsheviks liquidated all stocks and bonds of value. Pavlov applied to the head office of the Nobel firm in Russia for a refund of the 73,000 rubles which he had deposited. He was informed that the firm itself had lost everything, including his money, and that to their great regret they could not return any of it to him.

In connection with Pavlov's visit to Stockholm, it is noteworthy that in the address which he gave as a recipient of a Nobel Prize he did not attempt to enlarge upon his achievements in the field of gastroenterology or to describe in general and picturesque terms the investigations for which he was receiving the prize. On the contrary, he spoke about conditioned reflexes, which had only just been discovered and the conception of which was based on a few facts in Pavlov's possession. He bravely discussed this new method of studying the most complicated functions of the cerebral cortex, speaking with as much confidence in the validity of his new theory as does an explorer who is setting out to discover strange new lands and fearlessly asserts that success will crown his undertaking. Pavlov entitled his address: "The First Sure Steps along the Path of a New Investigation."

On the surface, Pavlov remained quite unchanged after receiving the Nobel Prize. His attitude toward his friends, his colleagues, and his students was absolutely the same as before. No superiority or conceit was apparent in his behavior. He was still the same Ivan Petrovich, always completely engrossed in some scientific idea and giving little thought to the outward conditions of life. Being the first physiologist to receive the Nobel Prize, an award which acknowledged him as the foremost physiologist of the day, undoubtedly gave Pavlov great satisfaction and increased confidence in his ability to blaze new paths in science. This encouragement was especially necessary to him then and came at an opportune time, when he had just embarked upon the difficult and controversial research on the functions of the cerebral cortex by the method of conditioned reflexes.

Although the winning of the Nobel Prize did not change Pavlov, it changed the attitude of some of his colleagues toward him. Most of them truly respected and appreciated Pavlov, but there were some who, while they expressed their admiration openly, envied him in their hearts. Since Pavlov's studies of digestion had been considered worthy of the highest scientific award, they began to be talked of as really important scientific achievements. At the same time nobody hesitated to criticize and even joke about the study of conditioned reflexes. The reading of reports on conditioned reflexes by Pavlov and his colleagues at the meetings of the Society of Russian Physicians was regarded by most of the members as an unwelcome necessity. Their attitude was that it was their duty out of respect for Pavlov to listen to these quasi-scientific papers, which were basically of little worth.

Since I left St. Petersburg on my appointment as a professor in the Novo Alexandria Agricultural Institute in the autumn of 1912, I do not know all the details of subsequent events, but Professor Savich's article provides us with some facts. An event which caused Pavlov much unpleasantness occurred in 1913. A thesis presented by one of the graduate students in Pavlov's laboratory, although accepted for defense, was declared by the Conference of the Military-Medical Academy to be so poorly written that the candidate was required to rewrite it and have it printed over again in its corrected form.

"Of course," writes Savich, "he [Pavlov] understood perfectly that all this was done with the intention of hurting him. About the same time one of his students returning from abroad was rejected when he sought to obtain the rank of *Privatdocent*. A very exceptional occurrence, indeed!" Moreover, owing to some intrigues, Pavlov was forced to resign from the presidency of the Society of Russian Physicians.

CHAPTER FOURTEEN

Pavlov, the Writer

TWO books by Pavlov, *Lectures on the Work of the Principal Digestive Glands* (1897) and *Lectures on Conditioned Reflexes* (1926), are written in entirely different styles. The pictorial language of the first book and the overflowing enthusiasm which is evident in every line were replaced after twenty-nine years by more restrained but less brilliant writing in the second book. Nevertheless, the author displayed the same enthusiasm for his subject, the same deep conviction that he was on the right path, as in the earlier work.

The years 1890–99 were probably the happiest time of Pavlov's life. In 1890 he received the chair of pharmacology at the Military-Medical Academy, and in 1891 he was appointed director of the Physiology Department of the Institute of Experimental Medicine. Both these institutions were in St. Petersburg, where Pavlov had now been living for twenty years and where both his scientific and his personal connections were strongest. These would have had to be broken if Pavlov had been obliged to take an appointment at some provincial university. Finally, after a humiliating period of extreme poverty, the livelihood of Pavlov and his family was at last made secure and, most important of all, the opportunity had now arrived for him to realize his most cherished scientific plans. In the same period his family was increased by the birth of three more children, a daughter, Vera, and two sons, Victor and Vsevolod, which gave Pavlov and his wife great happiness.

The acknowledgment of Pavlov as a scientist worthy to occupy two such important positions, the resultant financial security which freed him from the necessity of worrying about where their next meal was coming from, and family happiness gave Pavlov the opportunity of devoting himself wholly to scientific work, which he did with extraordinary enthusiasm. Now he could study the subjects in which he was interested, instead of working on the problems of others, as in Botkin's laboratory, where he had to teach experimental technique and probably often solve the problems of the young, inexperienced clinicians who had been working under his direction. From 1891 onward, graduate students who wished to complete their studies for the degree of Doctor of Medicine and true students of physiology, such as Walther, Lobasov, and Popielski, came to join Pavlov's laboratory either at the Military-Medical Academy or at the Institute of Experimental Medicine.

Pavlov himself described the time between 1890 and 1899 as a period of exceptionally earnest and, I would even say, inspiring experimental work in his laboratory, when discoveries of cardinal physiological facts followed one another in quick succession. In the Introduction to the second Russian edition of *Lectures on the Work of the Principal Digestive Glands* in 1917, Pavlov stated that the book was published in the form in which it had first appeared in 1897 for the following reasons:

The *Lectures* were written at a time when there was great excitement in the laboratory regarding their subject matter, and this has set its stamp on the book and given it a special warmth and freshness. I have long since departed from that subject and my keen interest is devoted to an entirely different physiological field. Now I could not write about the old theme in the same manner. For this reason, if I wanted to correct and add to the new edition in accordance with what has happened during these past twenty years, the book would appear "patched up." I did not wish to spoil its first enthusiastic tone.

Unfortunately, I did not witness this happy and productive period of Pavlov's laboratory work. I entered his laboratory in 1902, and at that time Pavlov's scientific interests were divided. The laboratory continued to work on problems connected with the secretion of the digestive glands, and co-workers now came from all over Russia and from abroad to study these problems. However, during the winter of 1901–2 the psychiatrist I. F. Tolochinov came to the laboratory once or twice a week from the Emperor Alexander III Hospital (in Oudelnaïa, a suburb of St. Petersburg), where he worked. He collaborated with Pavlov in the first experiments on the effect of different substances "acting from a distance" on salivary secretion in dogs (conditioned reflexes).

Pavlov's final decision to study the functions of the brain by the method of conditioned reflexes was probably reached in the beginning of 1903. In April of that year he gave an address at the general meeting of the International Medical Congress in Madrid entitled: "Experimental Psychology and Psychopathology in Animals" (Pavlov, 1928, p. 47). In writing this address he made use of the small store of experimental material which he had collected with the assistance of Dr. Tolochinov. In it Pavlov was already expressing his firm conviction that the manifestation of psychic activity in animals should be studied by physiologists and, even more important, should be studied by means of objective physiological methods.[1]

The *Lectures on Conditioned Reflexes* is written in quite a different style from the *Lectures on the Work of the Principal Digestive Glands*. The former has none of the brilliance and youthful enthusiasm which Pavlov had at forty-eight years of age, when he was writing his first book. However, the clarity with which the complex question of cerebral function is presented is just as impressive as was his treatment of the functions of the digestive glands. Moreover, the author's firm conviction of the correctness of the approach made to the study of the nervous activity in the use of the method of conditioned reflexes is apparent on every page of the book. At the same time, Pavlov is very careful in the deductions that he makes.

Although I had worked on conditioned reflexes myself for several years and knew what was going on even when I was abroad, Pavlov's book, which I read in Russian, produced a great impression on me. I wrote Pavlov a letter in which I expressed my admiration of his work. On August 28, 1927, in reply to this letter he wrote: "You praise my latest work too highly. This is understandable between friends of long and intimate relations. But how will outsiders react? The book, as you probably know, came out in English in June."

Unfortunately, not very many "outsiders" valued the great labor of Pavlov. Probably the work was too much of an innovation and too radical for the majority of psychologists, psychiatrists, and even physiologists.

Pavlov's third book (1923), entitled *Twenty Years of Objective Study of the Higher Nervous Activity (Behavior) in Animals*, ran into five editions in Russia up to 1932. This book is a collection of the addresses, articles, lectures, and reports which Pavlov made on conditioned reflexes from 1903 on. It was translated into English by Dr. W. Horsley Gantt under the title of *Lectures on Conditioned Reflexes* (Pavlov, 1928) and is furnished with a short biographical sketch of Pavlov by the translator, along with many notes which help the reader who is little acquainted with conditioned reflexes to understand the meaning of separate, sometimes isolated, articles written by Pavlov. This book had two English editions.

In a literary sense this anthology seems ill assorted. Along with excellently written orations such as that on "Natural Science and the Brain," the Madrid address of 1903; the Groningen address of 1913, "The Reflex of Purpose"; and others, there appear notes on verbal reports, which are sometimes not given verbatim but apparently were hastily made by the secretary of the society at which they were presented. Some of them are not sufficiently explicit, and some are too repetitious. The articles which had obviously been dictated by Pavlov are the best. He liked to dictate, and once or twice I had to take down what he dictated, although I have now forgotten what it was.

As a whole, however, this collection is valuable as an aid to understanding the development of Pavlov's creative thought. The collection was made at the insistence of Pavlov's friends and closest co-workers, especially V. V. Savich. The desire to have all Pavlov's articles and addresses assembled under one cover was engendered by the fact that Pavlov year after year postponed writing a systematic presentation of the principles of conditioned reflexes in book form. He started this work at the beginning of 1917, but his book on conditioned reflexes (first Russian edition) was not given to the world until 1926.

As if apologizing for the appearance of this anthology, Pavlov says in his Introduction that it would be difficult for those who wished to become acquainted with the study of conditioned reflexes to do so through the numerous individual theses and articles of his co-workers. A collection of his own articles would to some extent replace a systematic report which he intended to write.

His hesitation in presenting this new field of science in a systematized form and his extreme deliberation in writing the book is to be ascribed not to Pavlov's age—he was then seventy-five—but to his great sense of scientific responsibility.

Pavlov's fourth book, *Conditioned Reflexes and Psychiatry*, is the continuation of the *Twenty Years of Objective Study, etc.* (in Russian) or of the *Lectures on Conditioned Reflexes* (the same in English). In this book Dr. Gantt collected all the last articles of Pavlov.

CHAPTER FIFTEEN

Classicists and Romanticists in Science

AT THE beginning of the twentieth century the Leipzig chemist, Wilhelm Ostwald, one of the founders of physical chemistry, wrote a book called *Great Men*. This book was soon translated into Russian and enjoyed great popularity. In Pavlov's laboratory everybody including Pavlov had read it, and it was hotly discussed. In his book Ostwald sought to define scientifically what constitutes genius in a scientist. He based his conclusions as much as possible on an unprejudiced and impartial analysis of the lives and activities of six great scientists: H. Davy, J. R. Mayer, M. Faraday, J. Liebig, C. Gerhardt, and H. von Helmholtz. His research led him to the conclusion that there are two types of scientific research workers and that these may be classified as classicists or romanticists.

The chief difference between the classical and romantic types of scientists lies in the speed of their mental processes. As a rule, the mental development of a classicist is slower than that of a romanticist: he is a slow thinker. The classicist usually works alone; he has very few students or none at all. He is unsuccessful as an instructor or as a director of research, since it is difficult for him to stoop to the level of a student's knowledge. The classicist usually concentrates on one problem, working at it until he has developed it to such an extent that neither he himself nor anyone else can add anything to it for a considerable time. For this reason the work of the classicist endures for a long time and, strange as it may seem, impedes the progress of knowledge in the sphere of science in which it belongs, since it is so fundamental, so carefully reasoned, and so exhaustive. Ostwald cited Newton as an example. For a century and a half after the publication of his works nothing substantial was done in the realm of his investigations. The works of a classicist continue to be indissolubly bound to his name for a long time and do not acquire an identity of their own in the common storehouse of science. The classicist works more for himself than for others. He will not publish his work unless he is entirely satisfied with it. *Pauca sed matura,* said the "classicist," the great mathematician Gauss. The classicist does not seek popularity but regards his work as his own personal possession. For this reason, questions of priority of achievement and of disagreement with other research workers have great significance for a classical scientist. As a result of these characteristic traits, the genius of a classicist often remains unacknowledged for a long time.

The romanticist in science has entirely different characteristics. The quick tempo of his mental processes insures his early development. He is interested in many different subjects and at an early age feels the urge to create. The romanticist, working more quickly and productively, achieves a greater output than the classicist, but his works lack the depth of the latter's. His mental activity bubbles over, and for this reason he requires the assistance of co-workers in order to develop the theories which he is ceaselessly formulating in his mind. Since the romanticist is abounding in true inspiration and fervor, he spontaneously transmits his enthusiasm to others and infects all who come into contact with him. The romanticists in consequence often found "schools," something which classicists are entirely incapable of doing. The student becomes imbued with his teacher's enthusiasm and, although the subject of his research is allotted to him and the investigation is conducted under his teacher's immediate guidance, he becomes so engrossed in his work that he considers it his own. Ostwald notes that the romanticist is not interested in teaching beginners; he leaves that to others. This is understandable, since the romanticist has need of co-workers, not beginners, in order to accomplish his scientific aims during the short span of his life. Although romanticists are usually good lecturers on account of their enthusiasm, which engages the attention of their listeners, they are basically not pedagogues. Their true sphere of activity is the laboratory. Here they teach their students, guiding their research and working with them, and help to solve the theoretical and technical difficulties of their co-workers. Classicists act quite differently. That great man of genius, Helmholtz, was extremely poor at supervising his students' work. He rarely answered a co-worker's question at once but would provide the solution a week later, and the answer was often so complex and so abstractly formulated that it seldom helped the student out of his difficulties!

A superabundance of new ideas, plans, and possibilities forces the romanticist to hasten the completion of one problem in order to start the next. Often before he has completed one problem the romanticist undertakes another because it so intrigues his mind that it gives him no rest. This switching from one subject to another is what the classicist endeavors at all costs to avoid. For this reason, questions of priority, which are so important to the classicist, are of little interest to the romanticist. The general advancement of science is more important to him than personal motives. If he indulges in controversy, it is in order to remove obstacles from the path of science.

The romanticists are scientists who through their labors and personal actions exert a great influence on the scientific thought of their age. They, as it were, revolutionize science. As for the classicists, their scientific activity usually produces no such direct effect. But, on the other hand, their works in time may completely change the scientific conceptions of their epoch.

The fire and brilliance of the romanticist's mind, his talent as a lecturer, the crowd of students and followers he attracts, all contribute to bring about the recognition of his genius early in his career. However, scientists of the romantic type pay dearly for their success: the constant mental and physical strain to which they are subjected burns out the energy of many of them and causes a break in their work. The classicists, who are of more even temperament and work systematically, do not so commonly show the effects of strain.

We can, of course, disagree with Ostwald's classification and consider that his division of outstanding scientists into classicists and romanticists is artificial and that, if it is applicable at all, then it applies only to some scientists, such as those whom he has selected to prove his theory. Again, it can be argued that the terms "classicist" and "romanticist" belong in the realm of art and are not applicable to scientific workers. Romanticism in art to a certain extent arose as a reaction to classicism, and in particular to the false French classicism with its lifeless formalism. Romanticism laid stress on deep feeling, passion bordering on pathos, and the originality and adventure of an interesting story.

All these objections to the classification of scientists are legitimate, but we must not forget that Ostwald himself did not present his suggestions as the only possible ones. Furthermore, Ostwald's characterization of the group of scientists whose biographies he analyzed is a real masterpiece and entirely convincing.

To which group did Pavlov belong, according to Ostwald's classification—the classical or the romantic?

Professor Savich, in the days of our eager arguments over Ostwald's book and many years later, in 1924, when he wrote his biographical article on Pavlov, classed him as a romanticist. I was never in agreement with this view, and in this I was supported indirectly by Pavlov's own disagreement with Ostwald's classification. It is possible that Pavlov examined Ostwald's definition in relation not only to other scientists but also to himself and found that Procrustes' bed did not fit him!

Pavlov's scientific enthusiasm, which infected others, his sociability, his habit of collaborating with his co-workers, his passionate attention to the subject in which he was currently interested, and his complete coolness toward it a little later may coincide with the characteristics of the romantic scientist. However, there was much in Pavlov, the scientist, which corresponded to the typical characteristics of the classicist.

Pavlov enjoyed teaching and was a good but not a brilliant lecturer or one who attracted great numbers of students by his eloquence. We have seen who composed the ranks of his many co-workers before the Revolution of 1917. Few of his students had dedicated themselves wholly to the study of physiology. With the advent of the Soviet regime there came a change. Instead of ten or twelve co-workers, he now had up to forty, many of whom probably aimed at becoming professional physiologists. It must be remembered, however, that the conditions governing scientific work in Soviet Russia were fundamentally different from those existing before the Revolution. In Soviet Russia every worker is an employee of the state, and the government pays him a salary. Owing to the great demand for teachers and scientific research workers to staff the many new universities and other institutions, it is not surprising that Pavlov's laboratories were filled to overflowing. One must also consider the psychological effect produced by Pavlov's growing fame in Russia and throughout Europe, which naturally attracted to his laboratory many young people who wanted to become "students of Pavlov."

Moreover, Pavlov did not possess the creative fire which the romanticist was supposed to possess. The working of his mind was more akin to the persistent and searching mental processes of the classicist than to the unpredictable flights of scientific fantasy which make the romanticist. Although Pavlov was endowed with a fertile scientific imagination, he never allowed himself to be satisfied with the superficial verification of a hypothesis. He subjected it systematically and relentlessly to experimental analysis. Furthermore, facts which seemed to be solidly established were verified over and over again.

Finally, the fact that he concentrated all his scientific efforts on a single subject at one time refutes any suggestion of "romanticism" in Pavlov. If we exclude the initial period of his scientific activity, when he worked on various subjects under the direction of others (Cyon, Heidenhain, Ludwig), we find that during all the rest of his life, that is, a period of more than fifty years, he studied only three questions: circulation, digestion, and the functions of the central nervous system. In other words, he did not jump from subject to subject but changed over only after studying one theme for years. Helmholtz, that classicist of classicists, worked in the same manner, studying one subject exhaustively before embarking on another: first, muscle and nerve physiology and, then, the physiology of the eye and ear and, finally, abandoning physiology and devoting himself wholly to the study of physics.

There was another characteristic possessed by Pavlov which indicates that he cannot be placed arbitrarily in one of these special categories, namely, his undiminished energy and continual scientific creativeness, which he retained even in his old age. When he was about eighty years old, Pavlov began to study psychiatry, both theoretically and in hospital patients, and through his experimental work on neuroses exploded the conception of the purely psychological basis of certain mental diseases.

Ostwald asserted that a scientist of the "romantic school" through overtaxing his mental capacities and ceaselessly expending his energy soon exhausts his strength. A break occurs in his work, or he even stops work altogether during what are relatively the best years of his life, when he is between forty and fifty years of age. Pavlov's mental energies were subjected to great strain during the many years of his life, but in spite of this he did not lose a single day's work except on account of sickness. Thus Pavlov was a special blend of the classical and the romantic. It seems impossible to put ready-made clothes on every genius.

Osler's Theory of the "Fixed Period"

Pavlov's indefatigable scientific work during a period of more than sixty years likewise disproves the theory of the famous clinician Osler, who believed in "the comparative uselessness of men above forty years of age." Osler pointed out of what "incalculable benefit it would be in commercial, political, and professional life if, as a matter of course, men stopped work at sixty years of age" (Cushing, 1926, p. 667). Osler formulated this belief in his famous farewell address, entitled "The Fixed Period," which he gave on leaving Johns Hopkins University for Oxford University, and based his remarks on the fact that most great masterpieces had been created by young people under forty and that, if everything in the world was discarded which had been done by men over forty, the world would be left with almost all the spiritual wealth it has today. There is much truth in this belief, with which Ostwald concurs, but it is not the whole truth. In earlier centuries men often died from disease before reaching the age of forty, and it is open to conjecture what would have been created in later life by Raphael (who died at thirty-seven), Mozart (at thirty-five), Pushkin (at thirty-eight), Bicha (at thirty-one), and many others. On the other hand, entirely new vistas in science of great benefit to mankind have been opened up by men well over forty. For example, if Pasteur had died at forty years of age, his work on spontaneous generation would not exist; the method of pasteurization would be unknown; his work on the diseases of the silkworm would have remained undone; the bacteriological nature of chicken cholera and anthrax would not have been determined; and antirabies inoculation would not now be in use. Pasteur's great discoveries in bacteriology, for which mankind is indebted to him, were begun only in 1876, when he was fifty-four years of age.

In art, too, the best creative work is not always done before the age of forty. The last novels of Dostoevski do not fall below his earlier works in literary worth or in profundity of thought. In music it is almost always the rule that the later compositions of a great composer are better than those written before he is forty, for example, Beethoven's *Ninth Symphony* and Tchaikovsky's *Sixth*. In politics we have the example of sixty-three-year-old Franklin D. Roosevelt and seventy-year-old Winston Churchill, who between the ages of thirty and forty undoubtedly could not have accomplished the great work that they did during World War II.

Pavlov himself is a contradiction of the Osler-Ostwald theory. Although one part of his great lifework, the investigation of the functions of the digestive glands (the innervation of the pancreatic gland, 1888) was begun when he was thirty-eight or thirty-nine years old, nevertheless, all the most important work of his laboratory was done after he had reached his fortieth year (the innervation of the gastric glands, 1889; the psychic secretion of gastric juice, 1892; the Pavlov pouch, 1894; secretions of the salivary gland, 1895; the survival of dogs after vagotomy, 1895; the secretion of pancreatic juice, 1896; enterokinase, 1899; and so on). Pavlov was born in 1849. His famous *Lectures on the Work of the Principal Digestive Glands* was published in 1897, when he was forty-eight years old. Admittedly this was the most brilliant period of Pavlov's experimental creativeness, but his scientific activity did not stop there; as we know, it continued with extraordinary intensity for thirty-nine years longer, until his death in 1936. About 1901 or 1902 Pavlov, when already fifty-two or fifty-three years of age, began to study the functions of the central nervous system by the method of conditioned reflexes, which has had and will continue to have a great influence on physiology, psychology, psychiatry, and pedagogy. It is true that Pavlov's interest in the study of conditioned reflexes was inspired by I. M. Sechenov's book, *The Reflexes of the Brain*, which he had read in his youth, but the difference between an impression received and active scientific work is as great as the difference between dreams and their realization.

Osler, an outstanding clinician of the end of the nineteenth and the beginning of the twentieth century, was an exceptional man. If we apply Ostwald's classification to him, he appears to be a typical romanticist. His interests were many and varied. He was not only a first-rate clinician, who taught students and doctors at the bedside of the sick, but was at the same time an outstanding medical writer, historian of medicine, bibliophile, and lover of literature. As a typical romanticist, Osler influenced all those around him and founded a large school of followers. All these diverse activities required boundless energy. True to type, Osler quickly burned up his energy and toward his fiftieth year felt very tired, almost a finished man. When he was invited to become regius professor of medicine at Oxford University, where the work would be much less strenuous than at John Hopkins Medical School in Baltimore, one of the chief reasons for his acceptance was his great fatigue. In his letter of June 21, 1904, to Professor Burdon-Sanderson, he wrote: "In many ways I should like to be considered a candidate [for the chair at Oxford]. While very happy here and with splendid facilities, probably unequalled in English-speaking countries, I am over-worked and find it increasingly hard to serve the public and carry on my teaching. I have been in harness actively for thirty years and have been looking forward to the time when I could ease myself of some of the burdens I carry at present" (Cushing, 1926, p. 644).

Perhaps this extreme fatigue of Osler's, resulting from his ceaseless activity during thirty years, partly accounts for his theory that a man over forty is almost useless and at sixty should stop working entirely. Even during his Oxford period, when Osler was over fifty, he did far from little work.[1]

The conclusion that might be drawn from Ostwald's theory, based on the study of the lives of six great men of science, is that the nature of the brain and its peculiarities in men of genius are much more complex than would at first appear. Those classical and romantic traits which Ostwald so subtly noted can occur in various combinations in men of great talent. Pavlov was without doubt a combination of the classicist and the romanticist, but he was not an intermediate type, which is usually colorless. His nature was vividly individualistic and original by virtue of its spiritual and mental makeup.

CHAPTER SIXTEEN

Pavlov's Political Views

IN HIS political views Pavlov, throughout his long life, was a moderate liberal. There often arose in his laboratory, through which passed many people with the most diverse political opinions, discussions about the political evils of the time. The most heated discussions before 1914 concerned particularly the events of the Russo-Japanese War and the first Revolution of 1904–5. Frequently Pavlov took part, but he always expressed moderate liberal views. He was opposed equally to the courses of the extreme right and the extreme left. As an example of this we may notice his attitude to one of the most influential Russian newspapers, the *New Times* (*Novoe Vremia*).

The publisher of the *New Times* was a very intelligent and talented journalist, A. S. Suvorin. Suvorin was not a man of rigid principles, and there was even a touch of cynicism about him. He was no devotee of the Imperial regime and did not respect the government. In his paper he supported now this cause and now that, flattered first one individual and then another, yet always carefully displayed his own patriotism. Furthermore, the *New Times* had a distinctly anti-Semitic tone. Nevertheless, the paper had a large circulation because it possessed an exceptionally good news service and had several interesting contributors on its editorial staff.

Between 1902, when I entered his laboratory, and 1905 Pavlov did not read the *New Times*. Moreover, even when the reading room of the Institute of Experimental Medicine conducted its annual referendum among the workers at the Institute about subscriptions to newspapers, Pavlov used to dissuade his colleagues from voting for the *New Times*. However, after the Revolution of 1905, Pavlov took to reading the *New Times*. He sometimes found fault with it, but he still continued to read it, since the moderate trend of Suvorin, who had now become a constitutional-

ist and had greatly moderated his anti-Semitism, was more acceptable to him than the radical opinions of the leftist newspapers.

When the decree establishing the Consultative (so-called Bulyginsky) Imperial Duma was promulgated in August, 1905, Pavlov said that such a parliament was sufficient for Russia in the first
instance.

During the troubled autumn days of 1905 political conferences
were held in various circles in St. Petersburg. One group met at
the home of Professor Bauman. Pavlov was invited to take part in
these conferences, but he soon ceased to attend, although in all
probability no one more leftist than the members of the Consti-
tutional Democratic party, called the Cadets, was present. In conversation with me (I had come to St. Petersburg for Christmas
during my tenure of a foreign scholarship) he said that he considered his participation in these conferences pointless since those
attending were all "dreamers," as he termed them.

Pavlov found the Russo-Japanese War of 1904–5 very hard to
endure. Professor L. A. Orbeli (1940) in the Introduction to the
Collected Works of I. P. Pavlov writes that, in referring to the
catastrophic disasters of this unhappy war, Pavlov said: "No, only
a revolution can save Russia. The government which has brought
the country into such disgrace deserves to be overthrown." When
at last, in October, 1905, the resistance of reactionary circles was
broken and Russia received the Duma (parliament), Pavlov accepted this as an undoubted step forward in Russia's political
development. However, even after October 17, 1905, he remained
critical of the efforts of the "dreamers," who wished to leap at once
from an unlimited autocracy, to which he was no less opposed than
they, to a responsible ministry or even a republic. He did not join
any of the political parties, but his political opinions in general
outline were the moderate views of the best representatives of the
Octobrist party.

I do not think that Pavlov could have welcomed with much joy
the February Revolution of 1917. Yet as a true patriot and a free-
dom-loving individual he could not but have grieved at the dis-
organization, or rather collapse, of the government during the war
and been aroused by its illegal activities. The following episode is
evidence of this.

During the whole winter of 1916–17 the Imperial government kept putting all kinds of obstacles in the way of calling the first All-Russian Congress of Physiologists, which was to meet in St. Petersburg. The Ministry of Internal Affairs, at the head of which was Protopopov, feared all manner of demonstrations and even that the Congress of Physiologists might turn into a political meeting. From this fear came completely foolish restrictions applied to the purely scientific sphere and activity of the congress, for example, that the city governor (*Gradonachalnik*) was assigned the role of censor of the physiological reports. At last at Easter, 1917, the congress was permitted. However, Pavlov could not take part in it as he was confined to bed with a fractured hip. (On the previous December 27, 1916, while going along Lopukhinskaia Street—now Academician Pavlov Street—toward the Institute of Experimental Medicine, he slipped and fell, as a result of which he sustained a fracture of the hip. Subsequently Pavlov always limped.) In view of his inability to open the congress personally, Pavlov sent the following message of welcome.

We have just passed through a gloomy, harassing time. It suffices to state that this congress was not permitted before Christmas and was allowed at Easter only on the written undertaking of the members of the organizing committee that there would be no political resolutions at the congress. Not only that. Two or three days before our revolution the final permission came through with the stipulation that abstracts of the scientific papers should be presented on the day before to the city governor. Thanks be to God that this is all past, we hope never to return.

The period preceding the February Revolution was indeed "gloomy" and "harassing." It was felt that the life of the country, already complicated by the war, had been tied in a knot, the untying of which could not be accomplished by a city governor. Only a completely radical alteration of government policy would have been able to ward off revolution, on the condition that social groups and political parties came to a reasonable compromise. Neither the former nor the latter was done. A mighty empire crashed and buried under its debris not only that which had hindered its development but also that which had made it great.

The last sentence in Pavlov's communication is significant, "Thanks be to God that this is all past, we hope never to return."

Did Pavlov fear that reactionary forces would again take the upper hand? Or was he convinced that Russia after the February Revolution had come out on the highway of free democratic development? If he was convinced, then there was no need to hope that gloomy and harassing times would not return. I have good grounds for believing that Pavlov experienced torturing anxiety for the fate of his fatherland. Here are a few facts that bear this out.

On one occasion long before the Revolution of 1917 (probably about 1910) Professor S. S. Salazkin for some reason or other dropped in at the laboratory at the Institute of Experimental Medicine. He began to assert that life under the Stolypinski regime was impossible and that a second revolution was needed in order to put an end to the Imperial regime forever. An argument arose in which V. V. Savich and I became heatedly involved. We both, although we were convinced constitutionalists, stood a little to the right of the Cadet party, to which Salazkin belonged. We asserted that for Russia the one revolution of 1905 was enough and that with such a Duma as then existed one could but wish that Russia would last twenty-five years, and then it would be possible to think of a responsible ministry and other changes. Pavlov listened to us approvingly, and it was clear that he did not agree with Salazkin. In conclusion, Pavlov remarked that, if Russia had a second revolution, then Russia would perish.

My second anecdote is of a later date. In his public lecture on "The Mind in General and the Russian Mind in Particular," of which mention was made before and which Pavlov gave after the Bolshevik coup d'état, he deliberately stressed the importance of a balance between conservatism, as represented in Russian life by the Imperial regime, and the new liberal and even radical tendencies, which gained the upper hand after the February Revolution and more particularly after the October Revolution of 1917. At that time Pavlov displayed no sympathy whatever with the acts of the Bolshevik authorities, and he spoke his mind so boldly and openly that many of us were alarmed for his personal safety.

The following are a few episodes which depict Pavlov's attitude toward the Bolsheviks and their deeds.

The world-famous Russian chemist, V. N. Ipatieff (1945), at present residing in Chicago, tells in his autobiography (*Life of One*

Chemist) how the Bolsheviks in 1929 reorganized the old and re-
nowned Russian Academy of Science, which had existed for more
than two hundred years. In that year the Academy underwent
a radical change. Not only was the number of academicians increased up to one hundred (I think at the present time the number
is even greater), but the principal task of the Academy was completely modified.[1] The chief duty of the academicians now was
not science and the development of scientific knowledge in general
but participation in the building of the socialistic state. Therefore
the work of the members of the Academy had to be in close relation with industry. Many of the old academicians looked on this
reform as a disaster but probably were not strong enough to oppose
it without the support of society, which was absolutely deprived of
the right to express its opinion under the Bolshevist regime. The
reform was put into effect, and new members were appointed. The
scientific achievements of many of these newcomers were rather
meager, but they were forced into the Academy by the Bolshevik
authorities owing to their political pro-Soviet tendencies (Ipatieff,
1945, 2:525 ff.). One such case was the election of a bacteriology
professor, Zabolotny, which was strongly opposed by Pavlov. The
scientific achievements of Zabolotny were not great, but he was
known chiefly on account of his participation in the liquidation of
different epidemics and especially of one epidemic of plague in
the southern provinces of Russia before the War of 1914. At the
meeting of the Physical and Mathematical Section of the Academy,
when Zabolotny's candidature was discussed, Pavlov strongly criticized Zabolotny's scientific papers, in which he could find nothing
scientific whatever. "If we admit such scientists to our Academy,"
he said, "it will not be a scientific institution but God knows what
it will be. The Academy has been reorganized by people who do
not understand anything about science and do not realize what
the Academy should stand for. Just recently some Georgian from
Moscow came to see me—I cannot remember his name, I only know
that he was red-haired, and also that he tried to show that he was
very much interested in the Academy" (Ipatieff, 1945, 2:529).
This red-haired man, Ipatieff adds, was none other than Enukidze,
secretary of the Central Executive Committee (ZIK), who was
one of the highest officials in the U.S.S.R. and was second only to

Kalinin, the president of the ZIK. Pavlov was very little concerned about this and about the possibility that his words would come to the knowledge of the Bolshevik authorities.

In spite of Pavlov's protest, Zabolotny was elected to the Academy. At one time, about 1920–21, Zabolotny held the chair of bacteriology in the University of Odessa and I, being then a professor in the same university, had an opportunity to observe his attitude toward the Bolsheviks. He showed himself to be more than loyal, and this was probably the reason why the Bolshevik authorities wanted to have such a man among the members of the Academy of Science.

Ipatieff (1945, **2**:530) quoted another instance where Pavlov showed independence and a complete lack of fear of the Bolsheviks. He was not afraid to express his critical attitude toward the Bolshevist regime at students' lectures. In one of his lectures, after he returned from America, Pavlov told the students of the Military-Medical Academy that he had crossed Europe, visited America, spoken to many people, but had never heard anything about the world revolution. "Nowhere are people living under such poor conditions as in the U.S.S.R., and in no country is freedom of thought so restricted as in Russia." Some agents of the GPU (secret police) were present at this lecture, and soon Pavlov was summoned to the office of the GPU. He was interrogated by an official about his lecture; and, when his answers, criticizing the Soviet regime, were all put down on the questionnaire, he was asked to sign it. There were two lines in the questionnaire on which a signature could be put: one for the accused person, another for a witness. Pavlov asked where he must sign. The official replied, "Sign as a witness."

Undoubtedly the scientific prestige of Pavlov at home and abroad stood so high that he enjoyed complete immunity from prosecution by the Bolsheviks. This to a certain degree prevented him from evaluating properly the Bolsheviks' attitude toward the scientific workers of the old regime who remained in Russia after the Revolution of October, 1917. Their policy may be expressed in one sentence: it was to use these scientists until a new generation of "Soviet" scientists had grown up and then to destroy them.

This example of the Bolsheviks' attitude toward non-Communist scientists and intellectuals in general is enlightening. Comrade Kopilov, a president of the Sovkhos (agricultural unit) of the district of Kaluga, said at a meeting: "We need the bourgeois specialists, but only for a certain length of time. As soon as the members of our party have learned all that they can from these specialists, we shall liquidate them. At the present time we are treating them like cows destined for the slaughter: we take care of them and feed them better than other people; but, when the time comes, we shall finish them off as we did the other bourgeois." Of course, Comrade Kopilov was not an important Bolshevik, but, lacking finesse, he blurted out what the Kremlin was silently contemplating and systematically carrying out. The so-called "Lysenko's controversy" of 1948 (see chap. 17, Postscript) showed that Comrade Kopilov's prediction was quite correct.

I am afraid that Pavlov stood somewhat apart from real life and happenings in Soviet Russia and did not realize that the Bolsheviks were using him partly as window dressing to impress the Western world.

Toward representatives of the Imperial authorities, on the other hand, Pavlov cherished no enmity or ill-will, beyond a passing irritation aroused by such of their acts as did not correspond with his political views. And we have all known occasions when Russians, who were liberally inclined but not even socialists, have been literally infuriated by a single reminder of the reigning house. When speaking of the reaction which had crept into the reign of Alexander III, Pavlov often repeated, "We ourselves created it. We, the youth of the seventies and eighties, yes, and not only the youth, literally hounded Alexander II to death. There was no other name for him but 'frightened crow' [in connection with the numerous attempts on his life] until this folly led to the first of March" (the date of the assassination of Alexander II).

But even at that early date Pavlov clearly displayed moderation. In discussion of the acts of Alexander II he said that he could not follow some extremely leftist friends of Seraphima Vasilievna, whom he was then courting.

Pavlov was twelve years old at the time of the liberation of the serfs, in 1861. In his student years and later, such an intelligent individual as he could not but see how much Alexander II did for his people, beyond any doubt more than any other Russian sovereign. True, he did not surrender his autocracy; nevertheless, partly under the pressure of circumstances and public opinion but also in no small measure voluntarily, he, single-handed, directed Russia onto the path of democratic development. At least eight attempts were made on the life of Alexander II, beginning with the attack of Karakozov in 1866. Shots were fired at him, bombs were thrown, and attempts were made to blow up the train in which he was traveling and also his palace. Several conspiracies against his life were forestalled. Alexander II was in no instance a "frightened crow," as was shown by his intrepidity in all the assaults on him. He perished on March 1, 1881, only because he did not heed the advice of his attendants to drive as quickly as possible from the scene of the first bomb thrown at him. When he descended from his carriage and approached the wounded Cossacks of his escort, a bomb thrown by a second revolutionary wounded him fatally.

During Pavlov's stay in Montreal in 1929 I asked him on one occasion whether it was true that the memorial statue to Alexander III, the work of Troubetzkoy, on Znamenski Square in St. Petersburg, had not been destroyed by the Bolsheviks but that on its pedestal, as I had been told, there had been cut a disgusting inscription, "Here stands a chest of drawers, on the chest a hippopotamus, and on the hippopotamus sits an idiot." Pavlov replied, "I do not know," and after a little reflection added, "That would be extremely unjust." Pavlov could not help approving of Alexander III to some extent. In spite of his reactionary policy, this sovereign was the first of the rulers of Russia to understand that the Germans were not the friends but the enemies of Russia. More than any of his predecessors, Alexander III sped the emancipation of Russian life from German influence and encouraged Russian national culture. In consideration of his patriotism Pavlov forgave Alexander III much, since he too loved and believed in Russia.

Even the unfortunate and colorless Nicholas II awakened in Pavlov a feeling of sympathy. Pavlov himself told me that at one time, when the Soviet authorities were showing him special attentions, they sent him a carriage harnessed with horses from the former Imperial stables. He was taken daily from the door of his apartment at Seventh Line, Vasilievski Ostrov (Island), to the Institute of Experimental Medicine, situated on Aptekarski Island. The same coachman always came, and during the long drive friendly conversations took place between him and Pavlov. The coachman lamented that times had changed and that people had now become rough and cruel. Indeed, he said, the late sovereign always had a kind word or a smile even for such a humble individual as a coachman. Pavlov finished his story with the comment: "Evidently the sovereign was really a kind man."

Pavlov said that he completely failed to understand how many of his acquaintances in St. Petersburg could jest, enjoy themselves, and seek distractions while all around in Russia such violence and injustice were being done.

Moderate liberalism was Pavlov's political credo during his whole life. He went firmly along a definite middle road, making thrusts, when necessary, to right or left, fighting for legality, freedom of thought and word, and human dignity. But for three or four years before his death, that is, from about 1932 or 1933, he apparently betrayed the convictions of his whole life and approved that against which he had so resolutely rebelled previously.

What was the reason?

CHAPTER SEVENTEEN

Pavlov and the Bolsheviks

PAVLOV believed the Bolshevist Revolution to have been the greatest misfortune sustained by Russia. He did not refrain from saying so either in private conversations or in public utterances. At one of the inaugural lectures in the physiology course delivered to the students of the Military-Medical Academy he said, and afterward repeated at a public lecture he gave in the Tenishevski School: "If that which the Bolsheviks are doing with Russia is an experiment, for such an experiment I should regret giving even a frog."

The last time that I saw Pavlov in Russia was in the summer of 1918 (we met abroad in 1923 and 1929). Therefore I am not able fully to set forth and prove with actual details the relationship of Pavlov to the Bolshevist regime during the eighteen years which he lived after this date. But it is undoubted that his attitude toward it underwent an evolution, since toward the close of his life Pavlov was much more tolerantly disposed to the Soviet authorities than at the beginning of their regime.

The first, unfavorable period in Pavlov's relationship with the Bolsheviks, embracing approximately sixteen years (from 1917 to 1933), will probably not find a recorder for a long time and possibly never. People who lived in Soviet Russia contemporaneously with Pavlov, and who are still living there, will not be able for various reasons to write of Pavlov's reactions to the deeds of the Bolsheviks. The second short period, representing Pavlov's more favorable relations with the Soviet authorities (from about 1933 until his death in 1936) has already been very much overstressed by writers and even by scholars living in Soviet Russia (for example, Professor L. A. Orbeli).

The chief documentary evidence of his changed attitude to the Soviet socialistic experiment, for which he earlier was not willing to sacrifice even a frog, is Pavlov's address delivered at the reception held by the Soviet government for the delegates attending the Fifteenth International Congress of Physiologists on August 17, 1935, in the large Kremlin Palace in Moscow. Pavlov said:

You have heard and seen what an exceptionally favorable position science has in my fatherland. The relations that have been established between the government authorities and science I wish to illustrate simply by an example. We, the directors of scientific institutions, are really uneasy and alarmed when we ask ourselves whether we shall be in a position to justify all the resources which the government places at our disposal. As you know, I am an experimenter from head to foot. My whole life has been given to experiment. Our government is also an experimenter, only in an incomparably higher category. I passionately desire to live, in order to see the completion of this historic social experiment. [Amid stormy applause from those present Pavlov proposed a toast to "the great social experimenters."]

How is one to explain such a radical change in Pavlov's attitude to the Soviet regime? Let us try to consider this complicated question with the greatest objectivity possible.

Does this speech of Pavlov's give evidence of a real change in all those convictions in which he had lived for eighty-two years? Were there not some additional motives which forced Pavlov at such an advanced age to look approvingly on the endeavors of the Bolsheviks radically to alter by means of revolution the social structure of Russia, endeavors against which he had openly fought up to this time?

It is rather improbable that Pavlov changed his unfavorable views on revolutions in general. In the Foreword to the *Lectures on Conditioned Reflexes* (see Pavlov, 1928) he wrote that wars and revolutions "bring a reversion to bestial conditions." Even the taking of an animal's life in the laboratory with a purely scientific aim, that is, for the benefit of humanity, aroused strong repulsion in Pavlov and was accepted by him as a grievous but unavoidable necessity. He wrote on the subject of vivisection in 1904, "When I dissect and destroy a living animal, I hear within myself a bitter reproach that with rough and blundering hand I am crushing an incomparable artistic mechanism. But I endure this in the interest of truth, for the benefit of humanity" (quoted by A. Yougov, 1942). By extension, is it permissible, in the interest of a truth which is still to be established, to make a sacrifice not of dogs or rabbits but of thousands and thousands of people?

On September 28, 1929 (i.e., four years before he changed his attitude to the Bolsheviks and six years before the address that he delivered at the congress), Pavlov had written to me, "This autumn we are going to celebrate worthily the centenary of the birth of Ivan Michailovich Sechenov. These landowners, these priests, these merchants, now so defamed and deprived of rights in general and of the right of entry into universities in particular, were, nevertheless, the creators of Russian culture." (Sechenov, an outstanding scientist, the father of Russian physiology, was the son of a landowner; Pavlov himself was the son of a priest; and the noted clinician S. P. Botkin came from the merchant class.)

It is difficult to understand how a person of such exceptional intellect and so unusual a sense of honor as Pavlov could in the short space of four or five years completely renounce that which he had believed during his whole long life and which he had held to be the truth. However, this fact confronts us: the eighty-five-year-old Pavlov passionately desired to live in order to see the completion of the historic social experiment of the Bolsheviks! One need not suggest that there was any weakening of Pavlov's intellectual powers in his final years. On the evidence of the most impartial observers, Pavlov preserved unusual intellectual freshness up to his last moment. Also it is absolutely out of the question that Pavlov had any motives for flattering the Bolsheviks and currying favor with them.

Some Soviet writers and one of Pavlov's pupils endeavor to represent the change in his views about the Soviet regime as a later but genuine recognition of the services of the Bolsheviks to Russia. So, for instance, Pavlov's talented pupil, Professor L. A. Orbeli, in the Introduction to the *Collected Works of I. P. Pavlov*, published in 1940 by the Academy of Science of the U.S.S.R., explains thus the unfavorable attitude of his teacher to the Bolshevist "experiment." This experiment (with all its ghastly excesses, I add) aroused in Pavlov "repeated fits of alarm for the fate of his country, apprehension for the fading role, as it were, of the Russian people, dread of cultural and political degeneracy, and so on." At last, at the end of his life, Pavlov understood and appreciated the truth of communistic ideas. Now he no longer expressed on the subject of the Bolsheviks' acts "random and ill-considered thoughts and imaginings," which were snatched up and greatly exaggerated by elements hostile to the new order.

Pavlov's psychology was probably considerably more complicated than Soviet writers depict it. The Soviet authorities had actually done much for the development of scientific research in Russia. Many new universities had been opened and new research institutes organized or extended. An enormous number of people had been attracted to scientific work, and the resources expended on it were great. Pavlov could not have failed to appreciate this. He was a true son of an age when science acquired almost religious significance. Pavlov firmly believed that only through science would the reconciliation of nations and the true brotherhood of peoples be achieved. True, science in Soviet Russia was not free; in accordance with Marxist theory it must serve the government; "science for the sake of science" must not exist as such; Soviet scientists must reason in accordance with the rules of dialectical materialism; Mendelism, for instance, was considered an injurious heresy, and so on. However, Pavlov probably believed these to be temporary restrictions. The course of Soviet policy was continually changing, and no doubt the time would come when no dam would be able to hold back the stream of free scientific creativeness. Pavlov could not but be pleased that interest in scientific research in Soviet Russia was extraordinarily intensified. So, for example, his collected speeches and papers, entitled *Lectures on Conditioned Reflexes* (see Pavlov, 1928), had five editions in Russia within ten years (from 1922 to 1932), and 21,200 copies were distributed, perhaps most of them free to various institutions.

Pavlov knew from personal experience how benevolently the Soviet authorities could be disposed toward science and scientists. Very soon after the accession of the Bolsheviks to power Pavlov's teachings on conditioned reflexes were recognized by them as affirming that the intellectual life of people can be radically reconstructed and that the world-wide proletarian revolution would create a new human society. Even in 1921, when life in Russia was in a state of complete chaos, the Soviet of People's Commissars extended to Pavlov very exceptional advantages for his scientific work and also personal privileges, as set forth in the following document.

DECREE OF THE SOVIET OF
PEOPLE'S COMMISSARS

Taking into consideration the very exceptional scientific services of Academician I. P. Pavlov, which have enormous significance for the workers of the whole world, the Soviet of People's Commissars has decided:

1. To form on the basis of representations of the Petrosoviet [that is, the Soviet of the city of Petrograd] a special committee with broad powers, having the following personnel, Comrade M. Gorky, Comrade Kristi, director of higher educational institutions, and Comrade Kaplun, member of the Board of Direction of the Petrosoviet, and to direct this committee to create as soon as possible the most favorable conditions for safeguarding the scientific work of Academician Pavlov and his collaborators.

2. To direct the Government Publishing House to print in the best printing office of the Republic an *édition de luxe* of the scientific work produced by Academician Pavlov, also to vest in I. P. Pavlov the right of property in these publications both in Russia and abroad.

3. To direct the Committee of Provisions for Workers to supply to Academician Pavlov and his wife special rations equal in caloric content to two academic rations.

4. To direct the Petrosoviet to assure to Professor Pavlov and his wife the perpetual use of the apartment occupied by them and to furnish it and Pavlov's laboratory with the maximum conveniences.

> V. ULIANOV [LENIN]
>   *Chairman of the Soviet of People's Commissars*
> N. GORBUNOV
>   *Director of Affairs of the Soviet of People's Commissars*
> M. GLIASSER
>   *Pro Secretary*

MOSCOW, THE KREMLIN, January 24, 1921

Later, in the thirties, a special laboratory for research in experimental genetics of higher nervous activity was built for Pavlov in the village of Koltushi, near Leningrad, and also a country house for himself and his family. In 1936 the Soviet government expended 1,000,000 rubles on this laboratory and, in 1937, after Pavlov's death, 1,500,000 rubles and again in 1938, 2,400,000 rubles (I quote from an article by I. Andronov in the newspaper *Izvestia* [1938]). I do not know the purchasing power of the Soviet ruble in the years 1936–38, but, at all events, the sums expended on the laboratory at Koltushi were very considerable.

In honor of the eighty-fifth anniversary of Pavlov's birth (September 27, 1934) the Soviet of People's Commissars of the U.S.S.R. decided "to found an annual government prize of 20,000 rubles in the field of physiology, to be called after Academician I. P. Pavlov, and to found five scholarships, each of 500 rubles a month, also to be called after him, with the object of raising the scientific qualifications of young scholars in the field of physiology. In addition to this the *Sovnarkom* decided to publish a collection of the works of the biological station at Koltushi" (*Evening Red Newspaper*, September 27, 1934).

The Presidium of the Leningrad Soviet decided on the same occasion "to found in the Leningrad Institutions of Higher Learning five scholarships, to be called after Academician Pavlov, for the most advanced students, and to rename Lopukhinskaia Street [on which the Institute of Experimental Medicine is situated] 'Academician Pavlov Street' " (*Evening Red Newspaper*, September 27, 1934).

Pavlov did not refuse all these exceptional privileges but accepted them as expressions of the Soviet authorities' support of the scientific research which he was conducting and which was so dear to him. This is clear from the fact that the Bolsheviks were showering their favors on him at the very time when he was continuing to react very unfavorably to their activity. I do not doubt that Pavlov accepted with a heavy heart this special benevolence shown by the Bolsheviks to him and his work. He could not but recognize that there were in Russia other scientists and other fields of knowledge which deserved the support of the government. Probably only in the very last years of his life, when he was mistakenly convinced that the Soviet authorities were genuinely anxious to support science in general and all scientific institutions in Russia, did he deem it possible to come to terms with them. However, I have every reason to think that as late as 1932 the Pavlovs, both husband and wife, recognized the abnormal conditions still prevailing in Russian life at the time and the special difficulties of their own personal situation.

Pavlov's definitely unfavorable attitude to the Bolsheviks con-

tinued until approximately 1933. What happened then? In that
year Hitler came to power in Germany, and Pavlov, according to
my deep conviction, was one of the first to understand the terrible
danger that threatened Russia, as openly expressed in *Mein Kampf*.

Pavlov's love of his native land was genuine and deep. He took
pride in Russia's great past, rejoiced at her successes, and was
grieved at her failures or at the injustices done by her. He would
never have renounced the past history of his country, whatever it
was, and he believed in her great future. Thus, when, just before
the War of 1914, the minister of education, Kasso, completely and
perhaps even ostentatiously ignored Russian scientists and organized courses to be held at different foreign universities (particularly in Germany) in various sciences, with the object of preparing
young Russians for scientific activity, Pavlov's indignation knew
no bounds. There is no question that his very unfavorable attitude
to Kasso's provocative scheme lent force to the declaration of the
Academy of Science that the proposed measure of the Ministry of
Education was an insult to Russian science and Russian scientists.
(I quote from memory.)

After World War I a decided change had come about in Pavlov's
attitude to the Germans, among whom until then he had had many
scientific friends. So, for example, he did not hesitate to refuse the
proposal of the Soviet government to call in the best German surgeon for a gall bladder operation which he had to undergo at that
time (see chap. 18).

The following is another clear example of Pavlov's patriotism.
One of my Russian co-workers in the physiological laboratory at
McGill University traveled to Europe in the summer of 1936 to
visit his relatives. On his passage through Berlin he called at the
Institute of Professor X,[1] who is very well known. I had met Pro-
fessor X before World War I in the home of the Pavlovs in St.
Petersburg, and I can bear witness that the relations between Pro-
fessor X and the Pavlovs were then of the friendliest.

Professor X was so kind as to invite my colleague to his home for
lunch. There were also among the guests several of his assistants and
fellow-workers who were employed in the Institute, among them
two Nazis. Professor X was definitely opposed to naziism. He said
that he was not in agreement with the policy of the German gov-

ernment and that he was negotiating for leave to emigrate, as he could not work under the conditions in which Hitler's government had placed him. He also said that many of his best assistants had been Jews and that in general, with the exclusion of the Jews from science, technology, and applied chemistry, the Germans "had reduced the weight of their brains" by 40 per cent. Without these valuable specialists German technique could not compete with the technique of other countries, and there was no use even talking of the rapid progress of science in Germany. The two Nazis looked extremely uncomfortable, and the other guests, obviously from caution, kept silent.

When the conversation veered to the subject of Pavlov, Professor X said that Pavlov had been his friend but that to his great grief the friendship had been broken off after the war (that is, World War I). Professor X related how he had met Pavlov at one of the international scientific conferences, which had taken place not long before, and that he had gone up to him with outstretched hand, wishing to renew the friendly relations that had been interrupted by the war. Pavlov had refused to take his proffered hand and had said with irritation that the Germans were traditional enemies of Russia and that this would not permit him to re-establish his former relations with his German colleagues. The sorrow and misfortune which the Germans had brought to Russia were so great, he said, that this had killed all friendly feelings in him.

What Pavlov must have felt and how he must have feared for the fate of Russia when there came to power in Germany such an open and merciless foe as Hitler! Pavlov did not just repeat what he had read in his morning newspaper. He saw more and further than many others. In 1918, in days especially gloomy for Russia, when her whole southern half had been occupied by the Germans and Austrians, Pavlov had already said, with a face that was literally distorted, that in the long run her neighbors would dismember Russia. At that time this had not occurred, since the Central Powers fell; but who would prevent Hitler from doing this?

I have preserved several letters from V. V. Savich, which he wrote me when Pavlov was seriously ill in the spring of 1935. In his letter of June 13 Savich wrote of having seen Pavlov, who was recovering from his illness but was still very weak. Nonetheless, Pavlov had spoken with enormous interest "about the political situation on a world-wide scale" and had pinned his hopes on the "ability of the Britishers to settle matters." Only two years after Hitler's accession to power Pavlov was already alarmed for the fate of Europe and the world. He told Savich that we were living at an exceptionally interesting time and that he would like to see how all this turned out. (Savich was also pessimistically inclined. In a letter dated April 6, 1935, he wrote, "Ahead I see wars and wars. Hitler cannot do without a war, and this portends early or late, and more likely early, a series of wars. An excellent army is in itself a cause of war. Not for nothing has England begun to be uneasy.")

Pavlov, of course, understood that the thread of the democratic development of Russia had been broken in 1917. What moved Pavlov later to change his attitude toward the Soviet authorities?

Had not Pavlov the right to calculate that the Bolshevist regime, to which he was unfavorably disposed, was also transitory, like every other regime in Russia? How many of them had succeeded one another! In spite of this Russia had survived as a state for more than a thousand years, and her people had not fallen apart but had remained the same Russian people as they had been during the whole course of her long history.

Therefore Pavlov could be thankful to the Bolsheviks not for communism with its experiments but because they had united the Russian people and had pulled together a disintegrating Russia. It would be an entirely different thing if the Germans should seize the south of Russia, the Ukraine, the Crimea, the Caucasus, as Hitler planned, and should turn it into *Lebensraum* for themselves. This would be the final and irretrievable ruin of the struggles of a thousand years and the labors of countless generations of Russian folk.

For Pavlov, as for every Russian who dearly loved his native land, there was no choice: everything had to be done to aid Russia and to avoid introducing dissension in the hour of her mortal peril. When he had welcomed the delegates, at the opening of the Fifteenth International Physiological Congress in Leningrad on August 9, 1935, Pavlov made an appeal for the comity of nations and stressed the Soviet government's love of peace as though sensing the approaching catastrophe. Among other things he said:

I can understand the greatness of a war of liberation. However, one cannot at the same time deny that war in essence is a bestial method of deciding our vital differences, a method unworthy of human intelligence with its immeasurable resources. At present there is in evidence almost a world-wide desire and effort to avoid wars, and, truly, through more reliable means than has been the case up until now. I am happy that the government of my mighty country in fighting for peace has announced for the first time in history, "Not an inch of foreign soil." We, of course, must especially sympathize and co-operate with this. As seekers after truth we must add that in international relationships it is essential strictly to observe justice. But this is the chief and real difficulty [*Izvestia*, August 10, 1935].

On the one hand, Pavlov was reconciled to the Bolsheviks by their support of science, which, according to his deep conviction, was due in the long run to resolve all world conflicts. On the other hand, Pavlov was rendered more tolerant of the Bolsheviks by his alarm for the fate of his country, which stood under the shadow of Germany's iron fist. However, there are not sufficient data to assert that Pavlov recognized the Bolsheviks as the best Russian national authority. Pavlov's democratic convictions remained. To him, no kind of organization of society could be acceptable in which there was not personal freedom and in which a small group of people had power over all the rest.

Pavlov's change of attitude to the Bolsheviks can best be compared to the change of attitude of the Russian *émigrés* abroad to the Soviet authorities after Russia was drawn into the War in 1941. With rare exceptions, the great majority of *émigrés* put aside their hostility to the Bolsheviks to assist the Russian people in every way possible to them.

POSTSCRIPT

How mistaken was Pavlov when he believed that the Bolsheviks honestly supported science in Russia is shown by the almost incredible events which took place in August, 1948, in the Soviet Union.

No less a body than the Central Committee of the Bolshevik party (ZK) declared that the teaching of Weismann, Morgan, and Mendel on heredity is a heresy and that the only correct genetical teaching is that of a certain Mitchurin, according to whom there is an unlimited possibility of creating new kinds of plants and new species of animals, which implies that the acquired characteristics can be inherited. The chief exponent of this theory is a Soviet plant physiologist, Lysenko, whom Professor H. J. Muller of Indiana University (1948), a geneticist and an outstanding scientist (Nobel Laureate), in his letter of resignation (September 24, 1948) from an honorary membership in the Soviet Academy of Science, called a charlatan.[2]

Lysenko did not find sympathy for his view among the great majority of Russian scientists. But he declared that the "bourgeois" science to which many Soviet scientists adhere is inimical to the real Soviet science and is against the expansion of the idea of "unlimited planning" in biology. The Academies have forgotten, he said, the first principle of each science—its link with the policy of the party (communistic); they have become objective and apolitical. "The Academy of Science in the U.S.S.R. first of all must support clearly and systematically Lenin-Stalin's idea that each science must follow the [Bolshevik] party line" (Shwartz, 1948).

This point of view attracted the attention of ZK (Central Committee of the Bolshevik party) and suited very well the Bolsheviks' dream of the creation of a new, certainly communistic human society. With the blessing of the ZK and Stalin himself there was permitted and duly organized a real debacle of the Academy of Science, of the Agricultural Academy, and of all other scientific institutions of Soviet Russia. Many members of the Academy of Science were dismissed from their posts, some laboratories were closed, the projects of experimental research had to be revised in the spirit of Mitchurin's teaching, and so on. The ultimate fate of the disgraced scientists, of course, cannot be predicted. It is quite probable that some of them will finish their lives in one of the concentration camps as did the outstanding plant physiologist N. I. Vavilov.

Nobody dares in Soviet Russia to oppose or even to criticize the decision of the ZK. So the scientists who were against Lysenko's teaching quickly retreated. One of the typical examples of that sort is Professor Zhebrak's confession. Zhebrak is a member of the Communist party and before the "purification" of the biological sciences was a staunch supporter of the Mendel-Morgan theory of heredity. He wrote a letter which was published in the party newspaper *Pravda* (August 15, 1948) in which among other things he said, "When it became clear to me that the fundamental principles of Mitchurin's Soviet genetics were approved by ZK, I, as a member of the party, did not find it possible to adhere to my previous views, which were found faulty by the Central Committee of our party."

Another scientist who felt the results of "purification" was Pavlov's pupil Orbeli. He was accused of patronizing the Weismann-Morganists, of filling, like other anti-Mitchurinists, his laboratory with them, and of helping with the publication of their papers. He was dismissed from his post as secretary of the Academy of Science and was forced to apologize for his faulty attitude before the plenary meeting of the Academy of Science (*Izvestia*, August 27, 1948). This happened in spite of the attempts of Orbeli to please the Bolshevik authorities. In the above-quoted Introduction to the *Collected Works of Pavlov* (1940) he wrote among other things that at last Pavlov was able to "enter into the common structure of life created by the Great Proletarian Socialistic Revolution under the wise leadership of the party of Lenin and Stalin" (pp. 20–21).

Recently Julian Huxley reviewed in Nature (Vol. 163, June 18 and 25, 1949) the whole Lysenko controversy. He rightly considered that the major issue of this event was that "a great scientific nation has repudiated certain basic elements of scientific method, and in so doing has repudiated the universal and supranational character of science."

The attack of the Bolsheviks on the biological sciences was the last link in the subjugation of free thought to the "general line of Stalinism" because philosophy, history, literature, and even music (Denike, 1948) had already been cleansed from "heresies." Russia indeed returned to the darkest period of the Middle Ages, when the scientists were burned alive as heretics for their scientific discoveries and thoughts.

CHAPTER EIGHTEEN

Pavlov's Illnesses and Death

PAVLOV was seriously ill in 1927, 1935, and 1936. His last illness ended with his death on February 27, 1936. I have kept the letters which I received from Pavlov, his wife, his daughter, and V. V. Savich concerning these periods. From these and other sources the salient features of his illnesses and their effects on Pavlov's physical and mental well-being can thus to a certain extent be re-created from firsthand knowledge.

GALLSTONES

In 1927 Pavlov suffered from stones in the gall bladder. This was not determined immediately; at first it was thought that he was suffering from malaria, and later cancer of the liver was feared. The following is an excerpt from a letter from his wife, dated February 7, 1927, in which she speaks sadly of the illness of her family and especially that of her husband:

Our chief worry is Ivan Petrovich's health. He has lost a great deal of weight and is weaker, but he goes to the laboratory and works as usual. I do not remember whether I wrote you before about his illness. Last July he began to suffer from attacks of the following type. Severe chills came on, usually after dinner, and were accompanied by pains in the stomach; we relieved him with a hot-water bottle but the chills continued for an hour or an hour and a half. He then felt better, though his temperature was 39°0 or 39°6 C. While in the fever he fell asleep, and the next day he went back to the laboratory. He had two attacks of this nature during the summer. From September onward things went from bad to worse. He was examined and x-rayed, and five or six times his urine was analyzed. His blood pressure was checked, his blood was tested during these attacks and also when he was well, and it was decided that he had malaria. When I said: "Could it be liver?" Ivan Petrovich got angry and asked me to keep my medical ignorance to myself! On January 16, after an attack, he turned yellow (up to that time only the whites of his eyes had turned slightly yellow), and then everything became clear: Liver–gallstones. These are the kind of diagnosticians

[173]

there are nowadays! Any fool would have known it was liver after he turned yellow, but, previously, when I told them that after the attacks the urine was brown, they said it was due to the fever. From the middle of January the attacks occurred every two weeks and. . . .

(Here the letter breaks off.)

I am continuing my letter of the 8th, which was interrupted because Ivan Petrovich returned from the Institute (where he worked from nine in the morning until six at night) thoroughly ill. He had had another attack, this time after nine days instead of two weeks. The trouble is that he will listen to no one, and there are no doctors with authority here. I think that we shall have to go to Karlsbad. You can understand what anxiety we are living in. The trouble is that Ivan Petrovich refuses to work less; he spends the day in the laboratory and the evening at his desk, as he used to do formerly. Do you know, I have noticed in him, as never before, an access of spiritual strength. One is amazed at the beauty and clarity with which he expresses his thoughts. It is a long time since I have heard him give such poetic explanations of his work. He is continually excited, and this excitement prevents him from feeling his illness except during these attacks. He expends his strength as if he still had much left to expend.

Apart from the exact description of the symptoms of Pavlov's illness, her letter is valuable as witness of Pavlov's spiritual strength. Pavlov was angry when his wife suggested that he might have a liver ailment, probably because he feared the possibility of cancer and did not want to give up the idea that he had malaria, a disease much less dangerous to life.

I am inclined to think that the confused diagnosis made by the Leningrad doctors was not so much the result of ignorance as evidence of their lack of progress, resulting from the artificial isolation of Soviet Russia from the rest of the world. Van den Bergh's test for the presence of bile pigments in the blood was known in 1924, while Graham's test for the detection of gallstones in the bile ducts or gall bladder by means of tetraiodophenolphthalein was in use by clinicians in 1925 (see Babkin, 1928; and Graham, 1933–34). A correct diagnosis of jaundice with gallstones in the bile duct could have been made by 1927 without difficulty. It was not the fault of the Russian physicians that they were ignorant of these methods. The wall dividing Soviet Russia from the rest of the world was too thick and too firmly established. With the exclusion of Western ideas, which in the opinion of the Communists are so harmful to Soviet citizens, beneficial scientific advances likewise were prevented from entering Russia.

In a letter dated April 10, 1927, written during Holy Week, Seraphima Vasilievna wrote:

Our life is still unsettled. Ivan Petrovich is ill; he is getting weaker and thinner but is still cheerful. He was alarmed at his loss of weight and has stopped weighing himself, so we cannot say how matters stand in that respect: he appears to be getting thinner. The strange thing is that before and after an attack he loses his voice. Yesterday during dinner he felt well, was gay, and ate his modest meal with appetite, but we were all expecting an attack because he had lost his voice. Today, since morning, his temperature has been 37.3 C. (usually it is 36.3 or 36.2 C.), he has felt poorly, lost his voice and his appetite, and hasn't eaten. He was lying down with a hot-water bottle, and toward six o'clock (temperature 36.6 C.) he again had a desire to eat and, generally speaking, felt better. That is how we live—first well, then sick—and only my faith supports me.... We plan to be in Karlsbad toward the first of July. What will the Karlsbad doctors find?

Up to April, 1927, Pavlov's illness had not been correctly diagnosed, and both husband and wife feared the worst: cancer of the liver. This fear was probably the reason why Pavlov stopped weighing himself. The Pavlovs did go to Karlsbad but not until after Pavlov had been operated on by Professor Martinov in Leningrad. In her "Reminiscences" Mrs. Pavlov gives the following account of her husband's operation: Early in 1927 a Congress of Russian Surgeons was held in Leningrad, and some of the most outstanding Russian surgeons, such as Grekov, Fedorov, Napalkov, Martinov, and Rosanov, came to visit Pavlov. It was decided that he must be operated on, and Mrs. Pavlov was told that the best thing to do was to invite a German surgeon from Berlin to perform the operation. But Seraphima Vasilievna was sure that her husband would refuse to accept the services of a foreign doctor; and, indeed, when Pavlov heard the proposal of the consultants, he said: "I don't consider the German surgeons any better than ours and would never permit a German to operate on me when we have the very best surgeons here. I understand how difficult it is for a friend to operate on a friend," he added. Then he looked at the doctors around him and pointed to a doctor he saw for the first time, a Professor Martinov from Moscow, and asked him to be his surgeon.

Pavlov was placed in Obukhov's Hospital, and Seraphima Vasilievna was also given a room there. She spent all her time at the bedside of her husband. Besides Dr. Martinov, who performed the operation, there were also present Dr. Grekov, Dr. Fedorov, and several other surgeons.

After the operation Dr. Grekov entered Mrs. Pavlov's room, holding in his hand a gallstone which had just been removed from her husband's common bile duct, and said cheerfully, "Everything is fine. The only thing we removed was this gallstone. All of us looked and could not find a trace of cancer. There is only one thing left now and that is for Ivan Petrovich to recover!"

Pavlov, notwithstanding his seventy-eight years of age, came through the ordeal well, but the postoperative period was complicated by pneumonia. When this soon disappeared, Pavlov commenced a gradual course of recovery.

In July, Pavlov and his wife went to Karlsbad. Seraphima Vasilievna wrote from there on July 27, 1927: "Ivan Petrovich has begun to get better; not so much, I think, from the treatments as from the good forest air and the complete rest. After dinner he rests for an hour or an hour and a half, and I write or read."

I received a letter (dated August 28, 1927) from Pavlov from Berlin, when he and his wife were returning to Russia. In it he wrote: "The operation has freed me in a marvelous way from all symptoms of illness: two weeks after it I was completely well. This astonishing fact is one more proof of the law that the organism should be treated like a machine. Exactly like a speck of dust in a watch!—the stone was removed and the machine resumed its normal functions! My doctor friends needlessly shipped me off to Karlsbad: there was little more to do."

Pavlov wrote further that they would await their son Vsevolod in Berlin until September 5 "and then hasten to St. Petersburg, to the laboratory. With the return of strength, enthusiasm for work has also returned. Thank God, it seems to me that despite my almost eighty years, if my head is still clear (of this it is hard for me to judge—my memory has suffered), at least my interest in my work is in no way lessened."

Pavlov was never again troubled with gallstones.

PAVLOV'S ILLNESSES AND DEATH

Severe Grippe

In the spring of 1935 Pavlov again fell seriously ill. This time a very severe attack of grippe, which developed into pneumonia, laid him low. The letters that we received from Seraphima Vasilievna and Vera Ivanovna gave a full description of Pavlov's illness. Seraphima Vasilievna wrote on May 13, 1935:

On March 28 Ivan Petrovich became ill. At first nothing serious was suspected, but as time went on the grippe became worse—the lungs, kidneys, digestive organs, and bladder were affected, and then both his ears. The situation was so grave that the doctors despaired of his life. Since May 1 the danger to his life has passed, but he is still in bed and very weak, with a temperature which often rises to 37°0 or 37°4 C. and a pulse of 76–80. His ears are still full of pus. His humor is either very gay or very depressed. This is the explanation of my silence. During his illness I became convinced that my feeble services were not needed by him, so well was he taken care of by our government. Three doctors came every day, morning and evening; a nurse and doctor were on duty day and night, and on the critical nights one of the professors was on duty too. The only thing left for me to do was to pray and look after trivial matters. The best medical man, Professor Pletnev, came three times from Moscow. Recovery is extremely slow, but all the same I am going about with a senseless smile and beginning to sleep peacefully.

Vera Ivanovna in a letter dated April 26, 1935, gave a more detailed account of her father's illness:

A month ago father fell ill. It turned out to be an extremely virulent form of grippe and infection, which did not leave one part of his organism untouched. The fight against it was terrible. The illness began with bronchitis, then turned into pneumonia and dry pleurisy. The whole respiratory system was affected, which caused choking. Then the digestive tract was affected, and this was accompanied by intestinal spasms. Finally he suffered from purulent otitis in both ears. Only father's iron constitution could sustain all these terrible attacks at the age of eighty-five. At last, when the central nervous symptoms subsided, arrhythmia caused by exhaustion of the heart muscle appeared. Yet throughout the illness his heart was in good condition. This last complication was especially grave since by this time his general weakness was extreme. It was necessary to give him injections of glucose, but since yesterday the crisis has passed and recovery has begun. We have all suffered greatly, but all's well that ends well. The ears are still suppurating, and he can hardly hear; the digestive symptoms remain—

[177]

he has no taste or appetite and forces himself to eat. He says he has to learn how to eat all over again. The personnel of the Obukhov Hospital took charge of his treatment and care, and everything and everybody were wonderful. I am writing you in order to share the happiness of his recovery with you.

V. V. Savich, in five letters which he wrote to me on April 6 and 12, May 7 and 19, and June 13, 1935, sent me detailed reports of this illness of Pavlov's. In his first letters Savich expressed anxiety over Pavlov's growing weakness because of the disturbance of the digestion and the impossibility of feeding the patient by mouth. Feeding per rectum was even considered, but whether this was done or not Savich does not mention in his letter (April 12, 1935). On May 7 Savich reported that the patient's condition was better, since the trouble in the lungs had cleared up and the temperature was normal, but that the otitis still continued and both ears were discharging pus. On May 19 Savich wrote that Pavlov "little by little has come through, so that the immediate danger has passed." On June 6 Savich saw Pavlov for the first time since his illness. Pavlov was in quite good spirits, although his voice was rather weak. Despite this he discussed "the political situation in the world" with great interest (see chap. 17).

Savich correctly estimated the fatal significance of this illness for Pavlov. In every letter he stressed the fact that the illness had so undermined the strength of the eighty-five-year-old man that it might well be considered the beginning of the end. And, indeed, less than a year later, on February 27, 1936, after a slight cold which developed into pneumonia, Pavlov died. Savich was tortured by these gloomy forebodings. In his letter of April 6, 1935, he wrote:

Although Ivan Petrovich is as full of spirit as before his illness, nevertheless his strength has failed perceptibly and, because of the increased requirements of his body since his illness, a deficit may result. And Ivan Petrovich plays such a big role in the lives of all of us! In the most difficult moment of discouragement or disillusionment, the thought of him always sustains one, infuses energy into one, and is a stimulus to work. It is terrible to think that he might go from us. He has such great significance for us all owing to the example he sets us.

THE PHYSIOLOGICAL CONGRESS

The Fifteenth International Physiological Congress was to be held in Leningrad and Moscow in August, 1935. Pavlov was president of the committee in charge of the organization of the congress and also president of the congress itself. In view of his recent serious illness, he was unable to take a large part in the work of organization, and, according to Savich, the burden fell mostly on the shoulders of Professors L. A. Orbeli and K. M. Bykov, two of Pavlov's pupils.

Pavlov spent the summer at Koltushi and recovered his strength to such an extent that just before the congress he journeyed to London to attend the Neurological Congress there. On the eve of the Physiological Congress (held from August 9–16, 1935) he was cheerful and energetic, and it was impossible to imagine that a few months before he had been at death's door.

Dr. L. A. Andreyev, who had worked with me for a time at McGill University, was commissioned by Pavlov to meet Professor W. B. Cannon of Harvard University and his wife in the Ural Mountains. They were coming to the congress via Siberia, and Andreyev was to show them European Russia. They visited the Ural foundries, passed through Ekaterinburg, Kazan, Nizhnii Novgorod, and Moscow and finally reached Leningrad. "We were met at the station," wrote Andreyev to me on August 8, 1935, "by Ivan Petrovich, who had returned only two days before from London, where he attended the Neurological Congress. He was lively and cheerful, the same as he used to be before his illness. There were no visible signs of weariness—he did not look at all as one who was recently so sick."

However, this seeming recovery was deceptive, as future events showed: he died half a year later (February 27, 1936). After Pavlov's death V. V. Savich wrote me: "I did not like his appearance during all this time." In the summer, against his rule, and despite the serious illness Pavlov had gone through in the spring, he took no holidays. Savich thought that Pavlov had some premonition of his approaching death and that this was the reason why he hurried so with his work, fearing that he would not have time to finish it.

PAVLOV'S DEATH

We received the following letter from Seraphima Vasilievna, dated March 22–25, 1936, in which she gave us particulars of Pavlov's last illness and death.

DEAR FRIENDS:

I send you my very deepest thanks for the way you have shared my grief. . . . As you see, I am continuing my letter on the evening of the twenty-fifth, since I am still being plagued by various formalities, for which, I must confess, I am glad—they leave me no time to think, and a friend who is a neurologist keeps telling me: "Your salvation lies in not thinking." Like a wounded animal I want to crawl into my corner, see no one, hear nothing. . . . I will tell you the following facts about Ivan Petrovich's last illness. We were all sick at home with grippe, and the first to catch it was Ivan Petrovich. It was a slight attack, the highest temperature he had was $37^\circ 2$ C. (I had $37^\circ 3$ C.), and we all stayed on our feet. After three days of normal temperature, he went to his laboratory in the Academy of Science and made four trips, since he came home for lunch.

The only thing wrong was that he coughed all the time, although he assured me that it was only something in his throat. This was on February 20. On Friday, February 21, against all our persuasions, he went to Koltushi at nine o'clock in the morning, worked there all day, and did not return home until dinnertime. He was gay, joked, and laughed, and ate pancakes with enjoyment. (He was very fond of pancakes.) After dinner he rested, and the evening passed as usual, except that at eleven o'clock he asked to have his bed made ready as he was tired, and at midnight he lay down never to get up again. . . . The next day, the twenty-second, his temperature was $38^\circ 3$ C., and matters were going from worse to worst. When he breathed, there was a wheezing sound in his chest, and Professor Bock found deep-seated bronchitis to be present. Cups and warm fomentations were applied. Then Professor Pletnev [the most famous physician of the day] arrived from Moscow and confirmed Bock's diagnosis. On the twenty-fourth pneumonia appeared, and his temperature went up to $39^\circ 7$ C. Everybody became greatly alarmed, but the patient felt well and did not think of death. I, however, lost hope. On the twenty-sixth at two o'clock, Ivan Petrovich asked to see his granddaughters, joked with them, and told them to come and see him on Sunday, March 1, to receive a kiss [probably a candy!], but on the first of March we buried him. On the night of the twenty-sixth I was sitting holding his hand and at 2:40 in the morning I asked him to press my hand. He pressed it so hard that it hurt, and at 2:52 everything was over.

It was evidently impossible to save Pavlov this time. His organism was weakened by his previous illness, and his resistance to severe infection was, of course, lowered by his age. In 1936 preparations of sulpha drugs were not yet in use for the treatment of pneumonia. (Sulfapyridine was first used for pneumonia in May, 1938.)

The following account of Pavlov's illness, which I quote from the Soviet newspaper, *Star of the East*, will serve to amplify the description of Pavlov's last days given in Seraphima Vasilievna's letter:

On February 22, during an attack of grippe which had not been long in evidence, Ivan Petrovich's temperature suddenly went up, and at the same time signs of a more serious infection were discovered. On Saturday, February 22, Dr. M. M. Bock found that there was bronchitis of the large and middle bronchial passages, although the patient's general condition was satisfactory and the action of his heart was good. Professor D. D. Pletnev was called from Moscow and later M. V. Tchernoruchkin. Up to the night of February 25–26 his illness ran a normal course, and in some respects there was even progress toward recovery. This night the patient passed restlessly. For the first time during his illness the pulse rate sharply increased, independently of the temperature. On the morning of February 26 the doctors in consultation found that double pneumonia had developed, affecting practically the entire inferior lobes of the right and left lungs. The discomfort of the patient continued to increase. He became semiconscious and suffered from hiccoughs and extra-systoles. His pulse was sometimes as high as 130. M. P. Nikitin, who had been invited to take part in the consultations, did not find any change in the nervous system. Toward the evening of the same day his pulse had become so rapid that it was necessary to administer subcutaneous or intravenous injections of cardiac drugs without delay. At the evening consultation a considerable spreading of the pneumonia was found to have occurred, along with a fall in temperature and a decided weakening of the heart action. At ten o'clock in the evening a serious collapse occurred, the pulse was filiform (150), and there was cold sweat and cyanosis. By a series of energetic measures it was possible to rally the patient temporarily from his state of collapse. At 2:45 in the morning the collapse recurred, and at 2:52 the patient died.

Thus ended the life of a great man. Pavlov died at his post. Only four days before his death he was working all day in the laboratory, and doubtless, if he had lived longer, he would have continued to work and create, since his mind remained clear to the last moments of his life. An autopsy was performed, which revealed that the brain of this man of eighty-six was hardly touched by sclerosis.

Pavlov's death was a great loss to the whole world but especially to Russia. Credit must be given to the Soviet government for doing everything possible to pay due honor to this great Russian at his death and to perpetuate his memory.

Pavlov's memory was preserved by the Soviet government in the following manner (*Star of the East*, February 29, 1936):

PRESERVATION OF THE MEMORY OF ACADEMICIAN IVAN PETROVICH PAVLOV

In acknowledgment of the exceptional service rendered to the workers of the U.S.S.R. by the late Academician I. P. Pavlov, who was a true classical investigator and a world-famous scientist, the Soviet of the People's Commissars of the U.S.S.R., with the object of preserving his memory, decrees:

1. That a monument be erected in Pavlov's memory on one of the central squares in Leningrad, the Leningrad Soviet to fulfil this assignment.
2. That it approves the suggestion of *Narkomzdrav* (R.S.F.S.R.) that the name of the First Leningrad Medical Institute be changed to that of the Pavlov Institute.
3. That the Academy of Science of the Soviet of the U.S.S.R. should publish Pavlov's collected works in four languages—Russian, French, English, and German.
4. That Pavlov's brain be kept in the Brain Institute in Moscow.
5. That the laboratory and study of I. P. Pavlov in the Institute of Experimental Medicine on Pavlov Street in Leningrad be kept as a museum.
6. That Pavlov's widow, Seraphima Vasilievna, be given a personal pension of 1,000 rubles per month.
7. That the government will furnish the expenses connected with Pavlov's funeral and the perpetuation of his memory.

Pavlov's funeral was "grandiose," as V. V. Savich wrote to me.

The coffin, after the church services at home, was taken to the Tavricheski Palace, now Uritski's Palace. It was visited by a great multitude of people who wished to pay their final respects. It is said that up to one hundred thousand came to see it. [Pavlov was lying in state.] On the day of the funeral (March 1) people were allowed to enter by ticket only, and even so there were a great many who attended. The choir sang the Requiem, and then the coffin was taken to Volkov Cemetery and buried beside the graves of Mendeleev and Pavlov's son. There were orations at the grave, and then three salutes were fired. Of course, there were many wreaths. The speeches were strictly limited, which was the correct procedure, for otherwise there would have been enough speakers to go on until the next day. Many articles dedicated to Pavlov's memory are making their appearance in the newspapers [continued Savich]. To tell the truth, they please me very little. They are panegyrics which make a demigod or even a god out of Pavlov, and there is a very unwelcome tendency on the part of writers to attribute to him personal psychology of their own, since Pavlov is no longer here, and there is no one to contradict.

Savich was one of Pavlov's most devoted friends and one of his oldest pupils. It is easy to understand how shocked he was at such unceremonious coloration of the truth. I must add that those few Russian articles on Pavlov which I have read created the same unfavorable impression on me. It will not be easy for a serious biographer of Pavlov in the future to find his way through the mass of undocumented material invented for the moment and even deliberately *ad hoc.*

In the same letter Savich wrote that Seraphima Vasilievna found it hard to bear her loss, especially since she had so recently lost her son (1935). He also mentioned that the Soviet government had shown great concern over Seraphima Vasilievna's future, as at one time it had done in regard to Countess Sofia Andreyevna Tolstoy.

The Academy of Science extended an offer to Seraphima Vasilievna to keep Pavlov's archives after the relatives had gone through his papers and kept what was precious to them, in addition to letters and documents of a personal character. Savich began to help the Pavlovs to go through these archives, but he did not long survive the teacher to whom he was so devoted. On July 5, 1936, he died in his sleep from a cerebral hemorrhage.

Conclusion

The biography of Pavlov may best be concluded with these sentences taken from a short autobiographical sketch which he wrote in 1904 for a volume commemorating the twenty-fifth graduation anniversary from the Medico-Chirurgical Academy.

Truly, I consider that my life has been a happy and successful one. I have received the highest reward which one may ask from life—the complete realization of those ideals with which I started it. I hoped to derive complete satisfaction in intellectual activity and science, which I have already found and continue to do so now. I looked for a suitable life-companion and found her in my wife Sara Vasilievna, born Karchevsky. She patiently withstood all the great difficulties of our life before I received the professorship and always supported me in my scientific aspirations. She devoted her whole life to our family, as I devoted mine to the laboratory. I was able to renounce the practical side of life, with its cunning and not always irreproachable methods. I see no reason to regret my decision, since it has always given me a great deal of happiness. Above all, I thank my father and mother, who taught me to live simply and modestly and who gave me the possibility of obtaining a higher education.

PART II

Early Physiological Work of Pavlov

CHAPTER NINETEEN

Regulation of the Blood Circulation

PAVLOV'S first experimental investigations dealt with the processes of the digestive secretions. However, as a student at the St. Petersburg University, in collaboration with Veliki (1874), he established the existence of the centripetal accelerator fibers in some nerve branches attached to the heart. Later, when a student in Ustimovich's laboratory, he commenced a cycle of experiments on the cardiovascular system which was to occupy his attention for more than ten years. With the exception of a study carried out in Heidenhain's laboratory on the antagonism of the muscles in the sea mussel *Anodonta cygnea* (Pavlov, 1885), the circulatory system was the sole field of his studies.

Pavlov's work on circulation during the period of his assistant-ship to Ustimovich (Pavlov, 1878d; 1879a and b) was based on the theory propounded by Ludwig's school that the blood vessels adapt themselves to different volumes of circulating blood without affecting the blood pressure markedly. This adaptability of the blood vessels was considered by Ludwig to be of a nervous nature.

Pavlov tried to confirm this theory by diminishing or increasing the amount of fluid in the circulatory system. In both sets of experiments he employed an unusual method. He trained his dogs to lie absolutely quiet on a table and connected one of the superficial arteries on the inner side of the knee joint with a manometer. This operation, a superficial, minute cut through the skin, took 2 to 3 minutes and was painless. Measuring the blood pressure at several regular intervals during a month, Pavlov found a remarkable constancy of the blood pressure in each dog. On the average it was equal to 130 mm. Hg and as a rule did not oscillate more than 20 mm. in either direction.

In one set of experiments Pavlov (1879a) gave animals who had been fasted for 24 hours a meal of dry bread or meat. He argued that if there is an adaptation of the blood vessels to the volume of blood, after such a meal there should not be any great change in the blood pressure of the cutaneous artery connected with the manometer. This would happen in spite of the dilatation of the abdominal vessels and the great transfer of fluid from the blood vessels into the cavity of the alimentary canal in the form of digestive juices. As a matter of fact, 20 to 30 minutes after feeding with dry food the blood pressure fell by not more than 10 mm. Hg and stayed at this level for 2½ hours. Pavlov thought that there was a compensatory reflex vasoconstriction in other regions, such as the skin.

A reverse experiment was performed by Pavlov (1879b) when his dogs drank a large amount of fluid (from one-nineteenth to one-eighth of the body weight), in the form of warm meat broth. As a rule, for 10 to 30 minutes after the ingestion of a huge amount of fluid the blood pressure did not change; later it decreased by 10 mm. only and remained at this new level during the whole experiment (up to 4 hours and 30 minutes). Among the principal mechanisms which dealt with this inundation of the body, one of the most essential was the adaptation of the blood vessels to the unusual conditions. Other mechanisms were temporary deposition of the fluid in the tissues and increased activity of the kidneys.

This early work by Pavlov is of interest for two reasons. The first is that Pavlov employed and recommended a new physiological technique by performing his experiments on unanesthetized, normal animals, without inflicting pain which would disturb them. The second is that this work shows that Pavlov foresaw clearly the future development of science. Practically nothing was known about the normal blood pressure in man and its variations under various circumstances, and physicians in no small measure based their judgment of the conditions of the circulatory system upon the investigation of the pulse. Pavlov deplored the lack of knowledge about the variations of the blood pressure during different phases of life. What was only a desideratum in the last quarter of the nineteenth century has now become a standard procedure: the systematic measurement of the blood pressure in health and in disease.

Much later, in the nineties, when Pavlov was absorbed in the studies of the secretory processes in the gastrointestinal tract and was engrossed in the theory of the specific nature of the afferent nerve endings, he made an attempt to apply this theory to the sensory nerves of the blood vessels.

As was mentioned in chapter 5 of Part I, at the Fifth Pirogov's Medical Convention of 1894 he presented an address on the "Inadequacy of the Modern Physiological Analysis of Drugs" (Pavlov, 1940). In this address, among other things, he spoke about the desirability of a pharmacological investigation of the reaction of sensory nerve endings "which are present in all organs and in all tissues of the body." In support of this idea Pavlov's student, Dr. I. L. Dolinski, spoke about the specific excitability of the gastrointestinal mucous membrane, and Dr. V. G. Ushakov presented data on the specific response of the depressor nerve endings to curare.

CENTRIFUGAL NERVES OF THE HEART

The most important work performed during this period is incorporated in Pavlov's M.D. thesis, *The Centrifugal Nerves of the Heart*, which he presented to the Military-Medical Academy in St. Petersburg in 1883. Four years later this was published with some additions in the *Archiv für Physiologie* (1887*b*) under the title "Über die centrifugalen Nerven des Herzens." In the same volume there appeared also another article by Pavlov, "Über den Einfluss des Vagus auf die Arbeit der linken Herzkammer." This latter work was performed in Ludwig's laboratory at Leipzig. After his return from abroad, Pavlov published several papers in Russian on the centrifugal innervation of the heart and especially on the augmentor nerve to the heart (see, e.g., his long Russian article in the *Weekly Clinical Gazette* of 1888).

The main conclusion from these investigations was that the rhythm and the strength of the contractions of the heart are controlled by different fibers of the cardiac nerves. According to Pavlov, the heart is supplied by four kinds of nerves: (1) those which inhibit and (2) those which weaken its contractions, both reaching the heart along with the vagus nerve; (3) those which accelerate; and (4) those which augment them. The latter two nerves are derived from the sympathetic nervous system. The general opinion was, and still is, that there are only two nerves—vagus and sympathetic—which produce all these and other effects on the heart.

The impetus for this work was given by the investigation performed by Pavlov (1882) in which he established that under various conditions, such as dyspnea, apnea, hemorrhage, etc., there is no constant relationship between slowing up the heartbeats and the height of blood pressure. From these experiments he concluded that the vagus nerve does not produce parallel double effects on the rhythm and the strength of cardiac contractions but that these are two separate functions of the nerves, which are conveyed to the heart through different nerve fibers. Pavlov conceived the idea of rhythmic and dynamic nerves of the heart and began to investigate systematically the effect of stimulating different nerve branches going to the heart on the rhythm and strength of the cardiac contractions. A discovery about that time by Gaskell (1882) and Heidenhain (1882) of the augmentation of the heart contractions upon stimulation of the vagosympathetic nerve in the frog supported Pavlov's hypothesis concerning the existence of different heart nerves (see the next chapter).

To separate the different fibers in the cardiac nerves of the dog, Pavlov used two methods—pharmacological and anatomical. The intravenous administration of the tincture of *Convallaria majalis* (lily of the valley) permitted Pavlov to separate the inhibitory fibers from the weakening ones in vagus nerves. After injection of the tincture, stimulation of the vagus lowered the blood pressure but did not affect the rhythm of the heart. Pavlov thought that this could not be due to the diminished excitability of the vagus because only one of its functions was selectively abolished; it seemed to him more logical to suppose the existence in the vagus of two different kinds of nerve fibers.

A more satisfactory procedure was the anatomical one of isolating different branches of the vagal and sympathetic cardiac nerves (Fig. 3) and studying the effects of their faradization. The most striking effect observed by Pavlov was that stimulation of different nerve fibers had different and distinct effects. These effects were rarely that of pure inhibition (or acceleration) and diminution (or augmentation) but were most often mixed. Thus, Pavlov never could find a branch which would produce a pure weakening effect upon stimulation. More consistent results were obtained by stimulating the "strong inner branch," as Pavlov called it (Fig. 3,

3), which he isolated from all other nerve branches. As a result of faradization of this branch, there could be observed a rise of the blood pressure (up to 40 per cent) without much change in the

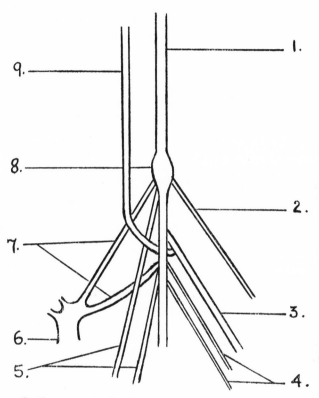

Fig. 3.—Cardiac nerves in the dog. Right side of the chest. *1*, Vagus nerve. *2*, Upper inner branch. *3*, Strong inner branch (augmentor nerve). *4*, Lower internal branches. *5*, Upper and lower external branches. *6*, Stellate ganglion. *7*, Ansa Vieussenii. *8*, Inferior cervical ganglion. *9*, Inferior laryngeal nerve (Pavlov, 1887*b*).

heart rhythm. Upper external (Fig. 3, *5*) and upper internal (Fig. 3, *2*) branches seldom gave this effect. In special experiments Pavlov showed that the rise in arterial blood pressure which resulted from the stimulation of the strong inner branch (*3*) was not due to a dilatation of the pulmonary blood vessel and to a greater transfer of blood from the right to the left heart. To exclude the effect of the vagus, atropine was administered to the animal.

Although in some experiments the stimulation of the "strong inner branch" produced both rise of the blood pressure and acceleration of the heartbeats, Pavlov insisted on the existence of two separate cardiac nerves (an augmentor and an accelerator), since in some dogs he found nerve branches which provoked one or the other of these effects. By dissection of the strong inner branch Pavlov could separate in some dogs the augmentor fibers from the accelerator ones. The accelerator fibers leave the common nerve trunk rather early and pass to the auricles, whereas the augmentor fibers run farther and penetrate into the ventricles. Stimulation of the strong inner branch below the accelerator fibers produces a pure augmentation of the heart contractions. The accelerator and augmentor nerve fibers are derived from the sympathetic nervous system. Stimulation of the vagus nerve never produced an augmentation of the heartbeats.

The accelerator and the augmentor fibers affect the course of the heart contractions differently. Whereas stimulation of a pure accelerator branch forces the heart to beat faster and leads to an almost complete disappearance of the pause between the two contractions, under the influence of an augmentor nerve the systole becomes shorter and the pause longer.

Stimulation of a pure accelerator branch (usually the lower external) (Fig. 3, 5) produced a dissociation between the contractions of the auricles and ventricles. The former contracted twice as fast as the latter, which retained their original rhythm. As a result of this dissociation, the blood pressure fell. Under these circumstances, stimulation of the augmentor nerve (strong inner branch, 3) restored the normal relations between the contractions of the auricles and ventricles and returned the blood pressure to its previous level.

What is the nature of the augmentor nerve? It may be a vascular nerve, or it may be a nerve which has direct relation to the cardiac muscle and is able to raise its excitability and thus to improve the activity of the heart. Pavlov admitted both possibilities. He made a supposition, which many years later was proved to be correct. He presumed that the vagus, stimulation of which usually resulted in a weakening of the heartbeats, supplied the heart with vasoconstrictor fibers, whereas the sympathetic augmentor nerve was a vasodilator. Other facts, however, pointed to a direct action of the augmentor nerves on the cardiac muscle. Thus, e.g., a heart, the contractility of which was paralyzed with *Convallaria majalis,* could be made to contract by stimulation of the augmentor nerve. Again, stimulation of different nerve branches in the excised dog's heart (not perfused!) showed that the external branches evoked contractions only of the auricles, whereas the right and left strong inner branches (Fig. 3, *3*) induced contractions of the ventricle on the corresponding side. As the years passed, Pavlov was more and more inclined to look upon the augmentor nerve as a "trophic" nerve which has a special relation to the metabolism of the heart muscle.

To obtain definite proof that the rise of blood pressure on stimulation of the augmentor branch (Fig. 3, *3*) was due to the changed activity of the heart itself and not to any other cause, Pavlov repeated his experiments with the faradization of the cardiac nerves in Ludwig's laboratory in Leipzig. (This work was performed by Pavlov in 1885–86 during his stay abroad.) For this purpose Pavlov modified and improved Stolnikov's apparatus for measuring the output from the left ventricle (Pavlov, 1887*a*). All other nerves which could have any influence on the work of the heart or on the blood pressure were cut. Stimulation of the strong inner branch (augmentor nerve) increased the volume of the blood ejected from the left ventricle. Pavlov concluded that this augmentation of the discharge of blood could be due only to the increased activity of the ventricle itself. Pavlov made two suppositions concerning the cause of this phenomenon: either greater ventricular relaxation occurred during the diastole and thus the ventricle received more blood, or more blood was ejected from the ventricle during systole as a result of a stronger contraction of the heart muscle. Probably a result of the moderating influence of Ludwig, these conclusions were far more modest as compared to the definite statement concerning the nature of the augmentor nerve which Pavlov made in his M.D. thesis. This supposition seems to be corroborated by the fact that, after his return to Russia, Pavlov spoke again more fully and in greater detail about the augmentor nerve as a trophic nerve of the heart.

At this point mention should be made of an interesting fact observed by Pavlov in Ludwig's laboratory. While using Stolnikov's apparatus, Pavlov dealt almost exclusively with the pulmonary circulation, and he noted that blood lost its capacity to coagulate. This fact was explained much later when Howell in 1918 discovered in the liver a special substance, heparin, which prevents the coagulation of the blood; more recently heparin has been found in even greater amounts in the lungs.

TROPHIC INNERVATION

On his return from abroad in 1886 Pavlov resumed his duties as director of Botkin's laboratory at the Military-Medical Academy. He continued to direct the pharmacological work of Botkin's interns, and he himself continued his studies of the functions of the augmentor nerve. Only at the end of his directorship in Botkin's laboratory did he again become interested in the problems of digestion.

In the papers on the effect of the augmentor nerve on the heart published by Pavlov after his return from abroad, very few new facts were added. Pavlov now emphasized more and more the special trophic function of the augmentor nerve and believed this nerve not only dilated the blood vessels of the heart but also had a relation to the intimate mechanism of the heart muscle. This belief in the trophic nature of the augmentor nerve was based on the fact that under its influence ventricular systole became shorter. Moreover, the tonus of the heart muscle during the stimulation of the augmentor nerve was increased. Thus the augmentor nerve strengthened two vital properties of the heart muscle (Pavlov, 1888).

This work aroused a controversy between Pavlov and Gaskell. Gaskell (see 1900, pp. 203 ff.) considered that the heart, functionally, had only two nerves: an inhibitory one (vagus), which inhibited and weakened the contractions, and an augmentor nerve (sympathetic), which accelerated and strengthened them. He regarded the vagus as a katabolic nerve and the sympathetic as an anabolic nerve, since stimulation of the sympathetic exhausts the heart muscle.

Pavlov disagreed with Gaskell's interpretation (1888). It is true that one could perceive an exhaustion of the heart after stimulation of the nerve branches which contained the accelerator fibers; nevertheless, the augmentor branch always improved the condition of the heart. Pavlov therefore insisted that the sympathetic nerve to the heart contained two distinct types of fibers and that there was a fundamental difference between the accelerator and the augmentor nerves of the heart.

Not being able to deny the vascular nature of the augmentor nerve and at the same time being inclined to regard it as a trophic nerve, Pavlov (1888) proposed a compromise explanation of its effect on the heart. According to him the functional properties of the vasodilator and trophic nerves have very much in common, and there exists an intimate relationship between the vasodilator nerves and the tissue. He based his assertion on the analogy with the so-called "Vulpian-Heidenhain phenomenon." (After section and degeneration of the hypoglossal nerve, stimulation of the chorda tympani, which conveys the vasodilator fibers to the tongue, produces a slow and prolonged contraction of the muscles of the tongue.)

Pavlov's interest in the trophic effect of nerves was dominant, and he was fascinated by this problem all his life. Unfortunately, the conception of the "trophic" innervation of tissues and organs is very vague. In clinical terms the word "trophic" refers to a nutritional state of the tissues, the disturbance of which may lead to pathologic changes, such as formation of ulcers and even gangrene. However, it seems that the causes of such pathological states are multiple. Far more experimental and clinical proofs are necessary to ascribe these pathological changes to the abnormal functioning or lack of function of a special system of "trophic" nerves with their corresponding centers in the central nervous system. However, Pavlov was strongly convinced that trophic nerves did exist. He himself summarized his views on this problem in his article on "Trophic Innervation" written as late as 1922.

Pavlov defined trophic nerves as those efferent nerves which regulate the intensity of vital chemical processes in tissue. The excitatory trophic nerves intensify these processes and thus raise the vitality of a tissue; on the other hand, the inhibitory trophic nerves weaken the vital processes and, in cases of abnormally strong stimulation, they lower the ability of the tissue to resist noxious influences. From time to time Pavlov observed various pathological phenomena in some of his experimental animals with different fistulas of the gastrointestinal tract, such as lesions of the skin or of the mucous membrane of the mouth, tetanus, paresis, and other disturbances. He considered all these diseases, some of them fatal, to be due to reflex stimulation of inhibitory trophic nerves through the afferent nerves of the alimentary canal. In normal conditions the action of these hypothetical trophic nerves was postulated to be invisible. Only when the normal mechanism of the bodily activity is distorted is their action apparent.

On the basis of his work on the innervation of the heart Pavlov proposed the following hypothesis: There is a triple nervous control of each organ: (1) The functional nerves initiate or stop the specific activity of an organ (contraction of a muscle, secretion of a gland, etc.). (2) The vascular nerves regulate the supply of chemical material to an organ and the removal of waste products by changing the volume of blood flowing through the organ. (3) The trophic nerves determine the exact amount and rate of the utilization of the nutrient material. Pavlov concluded that "such a triple control we have proved exists in the heart."

Nobody will deny the results established by Pavlov concerning the effect of stimulation of the augmentor nerve to the heart, but his general hypothesis of the existence of special trophic nerves for each organ of the body can by no means be considered as proved. In any one of those diverse pathological disturbances which he observed in his experimental animals, Pavlov did not, and probably could not, take into account the possible role of the endocrine glands or the effects of vitamin deficiencies. Thus, when describing the cases of osteomalacia which he had seen in some of his dogs with different fistulas of the gastrointestinal tract, Pavlov (1905) postulated two possible causes for this illness: the loss of digestive juice and consequent disturbance in intestinal digestion, and the displacement and strain on the abdominal organs, formation of adhesions, etc., which resulted from the operations performed in this part of the body. It was characteristic of Pavlov that he chose the latter, a nervous factor, rather than the former, a chemical factor, as the chief cause of osteomalacia. In 1905 Pavlov certainly could not foretell that almost twenty years hence ergosterol and vitamin D would be discovered and their role in the metabolism of calcium established.

CHAPTER TWENTY

Centrifugal Nerves of the Heart (Concluded)

THE facts established by Pavlov that in the dog stimulation of the sympathetic nerve produced not only an acceleration but also an augmentation of the heart contractions and that stimulation of the vagus effected their inhibition and diminution were accepted by all physiologists. His theory of rhythmic and dynamic nerves to the heart, however, was not accepted. The phenomenon of weakening of the heartbeats, coupled with their slowing, on vagus stimulation was seen long before by the Weber brothers in 1845. The acceleration of heart contractions by faradization of the sympathetic nerve supply to the heart was also a well-established fact (Bezold, 1863; Cyon brothers, 1867; Schmiedeberg, 1871).

Augmentation of the heart contractions upon stimulation of the vagosympathetic nerves was established in cold-blooded animals by Gaskell (1882) and Heidenhain (1882) during the same time that Pavlov was experimenting on the augmentor nerve in warm-blooded animals. Thus, it was only natural that the results obtained by these investigators and confirmed by others were readily incorporated into the physiology of the heart.[1]

Pavlov's theory of four separate cardiac nerves—two rhythmic and two dynamic—did not appeal to the cardiologists and is seldom ever mentioned in any treatise or textbook dealing with the circulatory system. The influence of Gaskell, who summarized in the second volume of *Schaffer's Textbook of Physiology* in 1900 the data concerning the innervation of the heart, and particularly the results of his own researches, was presumably dominant and determined the attitude of other physiologists. According to Gaskell (1900, pp. 209 ff. and 216 ff.), stimulation of the vagus nerve depressed the rhythm, the conductivity, the force of contraction, the excitability, and the tonus of the heart muscle. The sympathetic nerve "is in every respect the opposite of that of the inhibitory." Its faradization increased the rhythm of the heart, the force of its contractions, and the conductivity in the cardiac muscle. Thus, all the functions of the vagus on the heart are ascribed to one and the same nerve, and all the effects of the sympathetic nerve are transmitted to the heart from the central nervous system through the fibers of one and the same nerve. (In his article Gaskell did not even mention Pavlov's name in connection with the problem of the innervation of the heart, although Pavlov's articles were published in the *Archiv für Physiologie* in 1887). Gaskell's viewpoint is that of the majority of modern cardiologists.

Only in lengthy manuals, e.g., those of Abderhalden (1925, pp. 190 ff.) or McDowall (1938, pp. 174 ff., 233 ff.), and in such articles as those of Asher (1926) is Pavlov's work discussed. This negative attitude taken by physiologists to his findings was probably the reason why, in 1925, Pavlov renewed the study of the functions of the augmentor nerve of the heart with one of his pupils (Kalmikov, 1925).

How to explain this fate of Pavlov's discovery? It was not his facts, new and important, which were criticized but the theoretical interpretation he gave them. Pavlov's theory of the quadruple innervation of the heart undoubtedly was the result of the general tendency of the epoch, when the investigators were inclined to explain the regulation of the bodily functions exclusively through the action of the nervous system. For each function there was assumed to be a separate nerve. Gaskell's conception, according to which all effects produced by the stimulation of heart nerves are due to the action of only two nerves—sympathetic or vagus—was founded on a broader basis. It is easier to apply the modern theory of chemical transmitters than to give an adequate interpretation of Pavlov's theory.

Let us try to explain the facts observed by Pavlov. He showed, as we know, that different branches of the cardiac nerves have a predominant or exclusive effect on different chambers of the heart. Thus, the lower external branch (Fig. 3, *5*), stimulation of which produces chiefly acceleration, has an almost exclusive relation to the auricles, whereas the strong inner branch (Fig. 3, *3*), which augments the contractions of the heart in some dogs, innervates only the ventricles. Besides these extreme cases there can be found in some dogs nerve branches which produced acceleration alone, or acceleration and augmentation of all chambers of the heart. The results obtained by Pavlov concerning the separate sympathetic innervation of various parts of the heart were confirmed by subsequent physiological and histological investigations (McDowall, 1938, p. 231).

Could not different sympathetic nerve branches each have special relation to different structures in the heart? The accelerator branch may be exclusively related to the pacemaker, and faradization of this branch would therefore accelerate the beats of both auricles and ventricles. The augmentor branch may affect only the ventricular muscles, and the sympathin which is liberated during its stimulation will increase the contractions of the ventricles.

It is true that in both cases—acceleration of the heart contraction and augmentation of the ventricular beat—the same sympathetic nerve and the same sympathin, which is the active ultimate chemical mediator of the nerve impulse, participate in these phenomena. But the heart is a complicated structure, each part fulfilling a special role in the contraction process. Each of the nerves related to these various parts may have a different function.

Physiological processes usually are more complicated than they seem at first glance. The question naturally arises whether the different divisions of the sympathetic nerve in normal conditions discharge their impulses separately or whether the different effects of various nerve branches are an artificial laboratory phenomenon. Besides a direct action of the sympathetic nerve on the ventricular muscle in a whole animal with an impaired blood circulation, Pavlov admitted the possibility of an augmentation of the ventricular contractions through an improved coronary circulation. As we have seen in the preceding chapter, Pavlov was inclined to think that the augmentor nerve is chiefly a "trophic" one, but he never discriminated experimentally between the "trophic" effect and its dilator effect on the coronary blood vessels. Since in his investigation of the cardiac nerves Pavlov employed very primitive experimental methods, it would be desirable to repeat this work, using modern physiological methods of investigation.

HEART-LUNG PREPARATION

Upon his return from abroad in 1886, Pavlov at once had to solve an extremely difficult problem: the isolation in a functioning state of the heart of a warm-blooded animal. (The well-known method of heart isolation was introduced by Langendorf only in 1895.)

In the first part of this book (chaps. 2 and 11) it was recalled how Dr. N. J. Chistovich awaited Pavlov's return to Russia. Chistovich was Professor Botkin's intern and had been assigned as his M.D. thesis problem the study of the effects of the root extract of *Hellebori viridis* on the heart and circulation.

Pavlov solved for Chistovich the problem of the isolation of the heart in the dog in an extraordinary way. This method was improved and modified much later by E. H. Starling and is now known as a heart-lung preparation. Pavlov made two modifications of the isolated heart: in one of them the pulmonary circulation was preserved, whereas in the other the lungs were excluded altogether and the heart was completely isolated *in situ*.

The three schemes (Fig. 4) of the isolated heart represent Pavlov's two modifications and Starling's heart-lung preparation. (These schemes and the description of Pavlov's preparations are quoted from an article by Chernigovsky [1939], since the original work of Chistovich published in *Botkin's Archive* of 1886–87 was not available to me.)

In Pavlov's first modification (Fig. 4, *A*) the blood was permitted to flow from the left ventricle to the aorta, the left subclavian artery, a glass tube, the right external jugular vein, the anonymous vein, the superior vena cava, the right heart, the pulmonary blood vessels, and back to the left heart. In his heart-lung preparation Starling ingeniously included a resistance, as an imitation of the capillary resistance, on the way of the blood from the left to the right heart (Fig. 4, *B*). To get such resistance, Pavlov narrowed or enlarged the diameter of the blood vessels by means of ligatures tied around the aorta and the superior vena cava.

In order to isolate completely the heart in the second modification, Pavlov connected the pulmonary artery with the left auricle and thus excluded the pulmonary circulation altogether. In this preparation (Fig. 4, *C*) the blood flowed from the left ventricle to the aorta and left subclavian artery, then to the connecting tube and a water bath containing a glass vessel which received the blood from the left ventricle and passed it to the right external jugular vein, then to the anonymous right vein, the superior vena cava, and finally the right auricle. The blood from the right ventricle was directed through a connecting tube from the right pulmonary artery to the left auricle and then to the left heart. The lungs were thus excluded.

INNERVATION OF THE PANCREATIC GLAND

Two papers on the innervation of the pancreatic gland, one by Afanassiew and Pavlov (1878), the other by Pavlov (1878*d*) are of historical interest only. In this epoch neither was the knowledge of the secretory process in general profound enough nor were the experimental methods of investigation sufficiently adequate for an attempt to solve this difficult problem. Even now, as a matter of fact, seventy years after Afanassiew and Pavlov completed their investigation, one cannot clearly state what role the nerves play in the process of pancreatic secretion. To this may be added that the youthful enthusiasm of the authors and their solid belief in the correctness of their own interpretations do not increase the value of these papers. However, these early works of Pavlov introduced him into the circle of problems concerning the nervous regulation of the secretory processes on which he later worked with such great success.

The theme of Afanassiew and Pavlov's investigation was the secretory innervation of the pancreatic gland. The object of the study was the pancreatic gland of a dog possessing a so-called "permanent" fistula of Bernstein. This fistula is a very crude and primitive method, one of the first introduced for the investigation of the secretory function of the pancreatic gland (see Cyon, 1876, p. 283). The proof of the existence of the pancreatic secretory nerves was the arrest of the pancreatic secretion evoked by a meal after subcutaneous administration of a substantial dose of atropine (5–10 mg.).

However, the dose of atropine necessary to arrest the pancreatic secretion did not correspond to the weight of the animal, and in one experiment (Afanassiew and Pavlov, 1878*a*, Exp. VIII, p. 179), 10 mg. of atropine did not produce any inhibition of the pancreatic secretion after a meal of meat.

On the basis of these experiments, Afanassiew and Pavlov arrived at the conclusion that the pancreas possessed secretory nerves

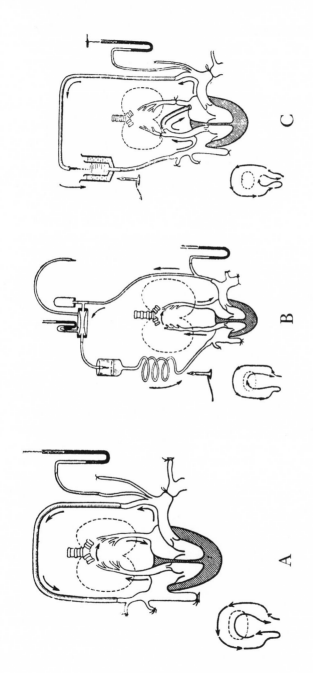

Fig. 4.—*A*, A scheme of Pavlov-Chistovich's heart-lung preparation. *B*, A scheme of Starling's heart-lung preparation. *C*, A scheme of Pavlov-Chistovich's isolated heart *in situ*. The drawings below the schemes show the course of the blood in each preparation. Explanations in the text (Chernigovsky, 1939).

which were paralyzed by atropine. This belief was expressed very forcibly: "The existence of the secretory nerves for the pancreatic gland may be considered to be proved without doubt." This conclusion was based presumably on an analogy with the paralysis of the salivary secretory (so-called "parasympathetic") nerves caused by atropine. However, whereas the existence of the salivary secretory nerves had been demonstrated, the secretory nerves of the pancreatic gland were not yet known. Another shortcoming is the fact that these authors did not take into consideration that the secretion of pancreatic juice depends upon the passage of the gastric contents into the duodenum.

At this point I must set aside Afanassiew and Pavlov's work for a while and continue with Pavlov's work (1878*d*).

In the summer of 1877, when Pavlov worked in Heidenhain's laboratory in Breslau, Heidenhain asked him to repeat the experiments he had performed in collaboration with Afanassiew on the inhibition of pancreatic secretion with atropine. The result was very unpleasant to Pavlov because in a dog with a Bernstein pancreatic fistula atropine arrested the secretion, whereas in a dog with a Heidenhain fistula (see Part III) it did not. This unsuccessful demonstration gave Professor Heidenhain reason to doubt the soundness of Afanassiew and Pavlov's conclusions about the effect of atropine. From his own previous experiments with atropine Heidenhain had already been convinced that this drug was unable to arrest the secretory activity of the pancreas.

On his return to Russia, Pavlov operated on four dogs with Heidenhain pancreatic fistulas and repeated the experiment with atropine. In all the animals he could substantially diminish the pancreatic secretion with small doses of atropine (5 mg.) and arrest it altogether with larger doses (20 mg.). Pavlov explained his failure in Breslau to demonstrate this fact to Professor Heidenhain as being due to the insufficient dosage of atropine used. He also checked another statement made by Heidenhain, namely, that the pancreatic secretion in the rabbit cannot be stopped with atropine. He confirmed this fact. In Pavlov's experiment the rabbit's pancreas continued to secrete in spite of 150 mg. atropine administered to the animal.

To be quite sure that the inhibition of the pancreatic secretion in the dog was due to the paralysis of the pancreatic secretory nerves by atropine and not to the inhibition of the motility of the stomach and hence to the arrest of the evacuation of the gastric contents into the duodenum, Pavlov (1878d) performed the following experiments which he omitted in his work with Afanassiew (1878). In a dog possessing both a pancreatic and a duodenal fistula, he was able to follow simultaneously the course of the pancreatic secretion and the discharge of the gastric chyme into the duodenum. After subcutaneous injection of 10 mg. of atropine into the animal, Pavlov could see that both the discharge of the gastric chyme into the duodenum and the pancreatic secretion were arrested. However, the first stopped before the second, and this fact induced Pavlov to make a rather doubtful statement concerning the independent action of atropine on gastric peristalsis and on pancreatic secretion. In other words, he insisted that pancreatic secretory nerves did exist and that they were paralyzed by atropine.

Before proceeding with the discussion of all these facts, one more series of experiments performed jointly by Afanassiew and Pavlov (1878) should be mentioned. The incentive for this work was Bernstein's statement that stimulation of the vagus inhibited pancreatic secretion. Afanassiew and Pavlov showed that stimulation of any sensory nerve acted in the same way. (However, much later Pavlov himself ascribed to the vagus not only a secretory function toward the pancreas but also an inhibitory one.) Pavlov (1878d) repeated these experiments on a dog with pancreatic and duodenal fistulas. Stimulation of sensory nerves (dorsalis pedis, vagus) inhibited the pancreatic secretion but at the same time increased the discharge of chyme, which became less watery, from the stomach.

Unfortunately, most of Pavlov's theoretical conclusions were not correct. At that time it was not known that the hydrochloric acid of the gastric juice is the strongest stimulus of the pancreatic secretion. We know now that acid in the small intestine stimulates the formation of a hormone, secretin, which excites pancreatic secretion. The stimulatory effect of hydrochloric acid on the secretory function of the pancreas is not arrested by atropine. However, atropine does inhibit gastric peristalsis and evacuation.

Therefore, when Afanassiew and Pavlov administered atropine to their dogs, they prevented the passage of acid gastric chyme into the duodenum, where secretin is formed, and in that way they arrested or diminished the pancreatic secretion. Pancreatic secretion continued for a while after the discharge of gastric chyme into the duodenum had ceased, presumably because some preformed secretin was still present in the circulation. What part paralysis of the vagal secretory fibers to the pancreas played in the diminution of pancreatic secretion is difficult to say.

The inhibition of the pancreatic secretion on stimulation of sensory nerves is believed to be due chiefly to the strong constriction of the pancreatic blood vessels.

The work of Afanassiew and Pavlov failed to prove the existence of secretory nerves of the pancreatic gland. However, by the use of other methods, Pavlov subsequently demonstrated that stimulation of the vagus and of the splanchnic nerves evoked a pancreatic secretion and that these nerves can be considered as true secretory nerves of the pancreatic gland.

During this period, i.e., in 1877 and 1878, Pavlov worked on some other problems related to the process of secretion in the digestive glands. One of these experimental investigations was performed by Pavlov in 1877 during the summer vacation he spent in Professor Heidenhain's laboratory at Breslau. The problem dealt with the effect of occluding the pancreatic duct in the rabbit. It was probably proposed by Heidenhain, since Pavlov never returned to this problem and never again made use of the histological technique which was employed in this work (Pavlov, 1878a).

The pancreatic duct was tied and the animals were kept alive up to 30 days. The microscopic examination of the gland showed atrophic changes. Microscopically there was a marked diminution of the acini, the appearance of fat-droplets in the secretory cells and between the secretory tubules, and a powerful development of connective tissue, which gradually replaced the acinous tissue. The remaining acini, with their secretory cells intact, had the appearance of functional activity. Incomplete degeneration of the acinous tissue of the pancreas was probably due to the relatively short period of observation of the gland after occlusion of the duct. Pavlov did not mention the islands of Langerhans in his description.

[205]

Although these were described by Langerhans in his thesis (Berlin University) in 1869, they were probably looked upon at first as an unimportant curiosity.

Another investigation performed by Pavlov during this period dealt with the reflex inhibition of salivary secretion (Pavlov, 1878c). Pavlov disagreed with the statement made by Claude Bernard that, whereas the secretory activity of the pancreatic gland is easily inhibited by reflex (usually painful) stimulation, the salivary secretion is not. Pavlov showed that faradization of the sciatic nerve, opening of the abdominal cavity, or drawing out an intestinal loop from the abdomen, all inhibited the secretion from the dog's submaxillary gland. Pavlov stated that the inhibition could not be due to reflex vasoconstriction in the gland because it was not prevented by section of the vagosympathetic nerve in the neck. Nothing was known at that time, of course, about the reflex discharge of adrenaline as a result of stimulation of the sensory nerves. Since in his experiments the secretory nerve to the sub-maxillary gland (n. chorda tympani) was not cut, Pavlov was inclined to explain the inhibition of salivary secretion as due to interference in the state of excitation in two centers: the center of salivary secretion and in the center of sensory stimulation. This explanation was purely theoretical.

A review of Pavlov's early work on the physiology of the secretory processes of the digestive glands reveals that it was not mature and added very little of importance. The interpretation of the few new facts he discovered was based on theoretical conceptions which were founded on the scanty contemporary knowledge in this field of physiology.

This period of Pavlov's experimental research must be looked upon as one in which he learned logical thinking and in which he trained himself in experimental technique. He acquired at this time a deep interest in gastroenterology and prepared himself for the great work in this field which he began ten years later.

THE EFFECT OF VAGOTOMY

The effect of sectioning both vagi nerves (the left one being cut in the neck and the right one in the chest below the inferior laryngeal nerve and the cardiac branches of vagus) attracted Pa-

vlov's attention for the first time while he was working in 1887
with Mme Shumov-Simanovsky on dogs with esophagotomy and
a gastric fistula. For the next fifteen years the cause of the death
of vagotomized animals interested him deeply. Three M.D. theses
of his pupils (Jurgens, 1892; Kachkovsky, 1899; and Cheshkov,
1902) dealt with the condition, survival, and death of dogs with
both vagi cut. There are also three papers by Pavlov himself on
this problem (1895, 1896, and 1901; cf. Pavlov, 1941, pp. 326, 344,
and 355). The last paper was Pavlov's address to the Thirteenth
International Congress of Medicine at Paris in 1900 under the title:
"Experimental Therapy as a New and Extremely Fruitful Method of Physiological Investigation." To prove his ideas, Pavlov
based his discussion on the example of the survival of vagotomized
dogs.

Section of both vagi nerves in the neck leads to the inevitable
death of animals. This fact was known long before, but its causes
were not properly understood and formed the subject of a great
controversy among scientists. At the time when Pavlov was interested in the survival of his dogs with double vagotomy, four causes
were considered to be responsible for their death: (1) the closure
of the glottis, usually in young animals, which may lead to asphyxi-
ation; (2) the lack of closure of the glottis in older animals during
swallowing, resulting in the penetration of saliva and food parti-
cles into the lungs, followed by pneumonia; (3) paralysis of the
lower third of the esophagus with the cardia only half opened,
as a result of which not all the swallowed food could pass into
the stomach but would stagnate in the lower part of the esophagus; the frequent vomiting of the animal would exhaust it; and
(4) intoxication by the abnormal products of decomposition and
putrefaction of the stagnant food masses.

Pavlov developed the following procedure to keep vagotomized
animals alive indefinitely. Each animal had an esophagotomy and a
gastric fistula. Food was never given by mouth but only through
the gastric fistula. The esophagotomy prevented the saliva from
entering the esophagus and accumulating in the lower third part.
Before each feeding the stomach was washed with tepid water.
Since in the vagotomized animals there was no powerful vagal
gastric secretion, the flow of gastric juice was stimulated by the

introduction of meat broth into the stomach. After a while, when the reaction of the broth became acid, food was introduced into the stomach, very often with the addition of gastric juice collected from normal dogs. At the termination of digestion in the stomach the gastric fistula was reopened and the stomach again washed with water. This whole procedure was repeated twice daily. As a result of these measures, the nutrition in vagotomized dogs remained quite normal. The animals slowly regained after vagotomy their preoperative weight and remained in perfect health.

The interest and, if one may say so, the beauty of this work were that Pavlov analyzed all the causes of death of such animals and eliminated them one by one. With his co-worker, Dr. Cheshkov, he also studied the results of vagotomy (in the neck) on different functions of the body.

Vagotomized animals are invalids. They can survive only under special laboratory care. If unattended, they are bound to perish in a very short time. Several functions of the body are rendered abnormal following the operation. These deviations from normality are partly due to the elimination of the influence of vagi nerves on some organs, such as the gastrointestinal tract, the respiratory apparatus, the heart. Partly, these defects are of a general character, e.g., a loss of the ability properly to regulate the temperature of the body, both in response to changes in environmental temperature and increased heat production during work. In this sense the vagotomized animals are similar to cold-blooded ones. The respiration is very slow, 4–8 times per minute. The activity of the heart changes markedly, becoming faster after vagotomy. There are marked changes in the excitability of the heart; if the heart is accelerated by some means, e.g., by high temperature, physical work, etc., it takes a very long time (up to 2 hours) for it to return to the normal postoperative rate, whereas in a normal dog, under the same conditions, it takes only a few minutes.

PART III

The Work of the Digestive Glands

Introduction

PAVLOV received world recognition as one of the leading physiologists of his time for his experimental physiological investigations of the digestive glands. This recognition was confirmed by the award to him in 1904 of the Nobel Prize.

The experimental material and its theoretical treatment was presented by Pavlov in the form of a book first published in Russian in 1897 under the title: *Lectures on the Work of the Principal Digestive Glands*. These lectures were reprinted in Russian without alteration in 1917 and in 1924. The German translation was made by Pavlov's pupil, Dr. A. A. Walther; it appeared one year after the first Russian edition as J. P. Pawlow, *Die Arbeit der Verdauungsdrüsen*, Übersetzung von A. Walther (Wiesbaden: J. F. Bergman, 1898). The French edition, translated by Pachon and Sabrazes, *Le travail des glandes digestives*, was printed by Masson & Cie in Paris in 1901. The first English edition appeared in 1902. It was translated by a professor of Dublin University, W. H. Thompson, under the name *The Work of the Digestive Glands: Lectures by Professor J. P. Pawlow* (London: Charles Griffin & Co., 1902). A paper given in 1899 by Pavlov at the memorial meeting of the Society of Russian Physicians in St. Petersburg in honor of the famous Russian clinician, the late S. P. Botkin, was added to this book and formed its eleventh chapter. In this paper, entitled "The Experimental Method—an Indispensable Requirement of Medical Research," Pavlov reported on the results of further researches in physiology, as well as on experimental pathology of the digestive glands. This paper was first published as a separate pamphlet in German, *Das Experiment als zeitgemässe und einheitliche Methode medizinischer Forschung* (Wiesbaden, 1900).

The second English edition of *The Work of the Digestive Glands* appeared in 1910. It was substantially enlarged by Professor Thompson, who included in it the physiological facts obtained in Pavlov's laboratory between 1902 and 1910 and also made his own additions, as, e.g., two chapters on the motility of the alimentary canal. Thompson was not familiar with the Russian language, and to learn the new facts discovered in Pavlov's laboratory, he used an article in *Nagel's Handbuch der Physiologie des Menschen* (Braunschweig: F. Vieweg & Sohn, 1907), 2:666–743, on "Die äussere Arbeit der Verdauungsdrüsen and ihr Mechanismus" which Pavlov had written not long before that. The chapters on motility of the gastrointestinal tract were well written, but they contained only a few data which could be ascribed to Pavlov (e.g., the so-called "acid control of the pylorus") because Pavlov never worked systematically on the movements of the alimentary canal. On the whole, it must be said that the second English edition of Pavlov's work was more useful for those who were making their first acquaintance with gastroenterology, but undoubtedly it lost the originality, the typical mode of exposition of the facts, the somewhat excited character of their discussion, and even the style of the first edition.

In the following chapters I shall, as a rule, quote from the first English edition of Pavlov's lectures to be sure that Pavlov's original expressions and thoughts are used. However, if the translation of certain passages is better in the second edition than in the first, I shall use the second.

The above-mentioned article of Pavlov in *Nagel's Handbuch* was satisfactory as a review of the contemporary investigations in the field of the external secretion of the digestive glands. However, it was one of his weakest literary works. It was written by him without interest and, one would think, even with disgust. He wrote it, as far as I remember, in the first half of the summer of 1903, which forced him to stay in St. Petersburg instead of going to his country house. He began to write it in the style of J. N. Langley's article on "The Salivary Glands" in *Schaffer's Textbook of Physiology* (Edinburgh and London: Y. J. Pentland, 1898), 1:475, but a systematic and detailed exposition of physiological facts was not what Pavlov could do with success. The form of writing which suited him best and which he exploited so admirably in his *Work of the Digestive Glands* was that of lectures. There he could present in a conversational manner the experimental material in the order which it seemed to him would communicate to his readers his thoughts in the most convincing way. Several times when he was writing the article for Professor Nagel, Pavlov himself told all of us in the laboratory that he was not qualified to write for a handbook and that he had the hardest time trying to do so. He called himself a fool for consenting to do this, but alas! he had to be true to his promise to Professor Nagel. Writing was becoming more and more difficult for him, and the summer days, which he loved so much to spend in the country looking after his flowers, were quickly running away, one after another, leaving less and less time for a well-deserved rest. I think it was about the end of June that he made a drastic decision—he left the article unfinished and went to the country. Only three chapters were written: i, "The Work of the Salivary Glands"; ii, "The Work of the Peptic Glands"; and iii, "The Work of the Pancreatic Gland." The secretion of bile and of succus entericus was completely omitted, although at that period Pavlov's laboratory had already accumulated many important facts concerning the discharge of bile into the duodenum and the secretion of the intestinal juice and its enzymes. Many facts not mentioned by Pavlov, yet discovered in his own laboratory, were discussed by O. Cohnheim in another article of the same volume of *Nagel's Handbuch* ("Die Physiologie der Verdauung und Aufsaugung," pp. 516–665). The operative technique of the digestive tract was discussed by Pavlov in two special articles, one in the *Ergebnisse der Physiologie* of 1902 and the other in Tigerstedt's *Handbuch der physiologischen Methodik* (1908).

Before the appearance of Pavlov's *Lectures on the Work of the Digestive Glands* his name outside Russia was known only to a few physiologists, although at this epoch he already had to be credited with such first-class discoveries as the dynamic nerves of the heart and the role of the vagus as a secretory nerve of the gastric glands and of the pancreas and other glands. The extraordinary success of Pavlov's *Lectures* was undoubtedly due to an unexpected revelation in them of a large number of new and striking facts and to the description of startlingly new physiological methods. Some of the facts had never been published before either in Russian or in foreign languages. However, these were not the only reasons why his work aroused such universal interest. Besides the factual material presented in the *Lectures*, there was given for the first time in the history of gastroenterology a comprehensive and coherent picture of the secretory activity of the alimentary canal as a whole, instead of separate unrelated though important facts. After 1898—the date when the German translation of Pavlov's book appeared—every physiologist and every clinician based his study of the normal or abnormal physiology of the alimentary canal on Pavlov's *Lectures*. It would not be an exaggeration to say that the facts discovered by Pavlov and his ideas became the foundation of modern gastroenterology. Almost half a century has passed since his *Lectures* were published; nevertheless, Pavlov's influence is felt to the present day.

The functions of the alimentary canal had interested Pavlov from his early days. When in 1929 Pavlov visited Montreal and was shown the physiological laboratory of McGill University, he took from a shelf in the library G. H. Lewis' *Physiology of Common Life*, Volume 1 (1859), opened it at page 230, and showed the late Professor J. Tait and me the diagram of the gastrointestinal tract which is reproduced here (Fig. 5). "When in my very young days I read this book, in a Russian translation," he said, "I was greatly intrigued by this picture. I asked myself: How does such a complicated system work? My interest in the digestive system originated at this epoch." (In his obituary notice of Pavlov in the *Scientific Monthly*, 42:374, 1936, J. F. Fulton also pointed out that Lewis' book greatly influenced Pavlov's scientific career, but he does not specifically mention the impression this chapter on the digestive system made on Pavlov.)

The first experimental work which Pavlov, then a third-year student in science in St. Petersburg University, performed in 1874 jointly with M. I. Afanassiew was on the innervation of the pancreatic gland. The secretory nerves of the pancreas were discovered by Pavlov much later, in 1888, but in this work there were, as Savich (1924) pointed out, some novelties for that time. Thus, for example, a new method for the preparation of a permanent pancreatic fistula was proposed. A T-tube was fixed in the pancreatic duct. For this purpose a slit was made in the duct, and a small tube was passed into it, then a longer vertical tube, through which

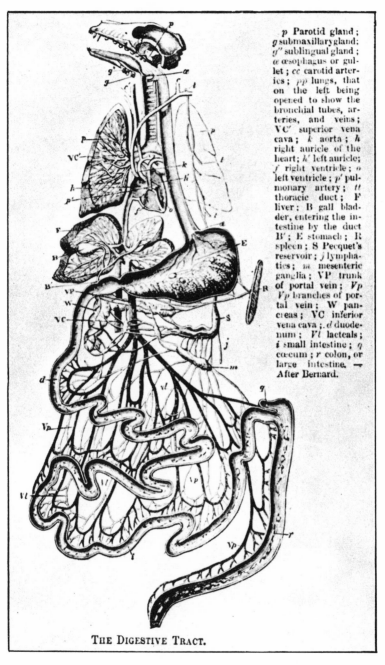

p Parotid gland; *g* submaxillary gland; *g″* sublingual gland; *œ* œsophagus or gullet; *cc* carotid arteries; *pp* lungs, that on the left being opened to show the bronchial tubes, arteries, and veins; VC′ superior vena cava; *k* aorta; *h* right auricle of the heart; *h′* left auricle; *f* right ventricle; *o* left ventricle; *p′* pulmonary artery; *tt* thoracic duct; F liver; B gall bladder, entering the intestine by the duct B′; E stomach; R spleen; S Pecquet's reservoir; *j* lymphatics; *m* mesenteric ganglia; VP trunk of portal vein; *Vp* branches of portal vein; W pancreas; VC inferior vena cava ; *d* duodenum ; *Vl* lacteals; *i* small intestine ; *q* cœcum ; *r* colon, or large intestine. — After Bernard.

THE DIGESTIVE TRACT.

FIG. 5.—Internal organs of a mammalian animal. (From F. H. Lewis, *The Physiology of the Common Life* [Edinburgh and London: W. Blackwood & Sons, 1859], 1:230.)

the pancreatic juice had to flow outside the body, was screwed into the opening in the middle of the horizontal tube already placed in the duct. Neither Pavlov himself nor anybody else afterward used this method for obtaining pancreatic secretion. This work was never published, although the university awarded Pavlov a gold medal for it.

The physiology of the digestive system continued to interest Pavlov after he graduated from St. Petersburg University. About 1876, when Pavlov occupied the position of an assistant in the Veterinary Institute in St. Petersburg, he evolved another method for the preparation of a permanent pancreatic fistula (1879). This new method, far more practical than the first one, was used extensively by Pavlov and his students.

In 1877 Pavlov worked for a couple of months in R. Heidenhain's laboratory in Breslau. The sojourn in Breslau's laboratory undoubtedly deepened Pavlov's interest in the physiology of the secretory processes because Heidenhain and his pupils performed first-class work in this field.

From 1876 until 1888 there was a gap in Pavlov's gastroenterological investigations. During this period Pavlov's interest centered on cardiovascular problems.

The year 1888, however, marks the return of Pavlov to the problems of the secretory activity of the digestive glands. In this year appeared Pavlov's paper in Russian in which he showed that the vagus is a secretory nerve of the pancreas. In the next year, 1889, Pavlov, jointly with Mme E. O. Shumov-Simanovsky, using dogs with esophagotomy and gastric fistula and the method of sham feeding, demonstrated that the vagus is also a secretory nerve for the gastric glands.

When in 1891 Pavlov became head of the Department of Physiology in the Institute of Experimental Medicine, he and his co-workers devoted all their time for at least ten years to the investigation of the functions of the gastrointestinal tract. The results of these investigations were collected in the above-mentioned books and articles. However, at the turn of the new century Pavlov's interest in the functions of the alimentary canal began to diminish gradually. He devoted more and more time to the study of the conditioned reflexes, and by about 1910 all his time and thoughts were given to this subject.

In the physiology of the gastrointestinal tract Pavlov was chiefly interested in the secretory function of the digestive glands and in the co-ordination of their activity. The phenomena of gastrointestinal motility attracted him far less, and only a few investigations in this field were performed in his laboratory. He was probably interested theoretically in the fate of food substances and the chemical changes which they undergo in the alimentary canal and also in the phenomena of absorption, but he never studied any of these problems experimentally.

In the following short review of Pavlov's work concerning the functions of the alimentary canal a few leading ideas which guided his investigation in this field will first be discussed and afterward his achievements will be described.

Some of the hypotheses used by Pavlov in his work had already been formulated by his predecessors. He accepted and elaborated them further. However, he enriched physiology with new ideas and supported them by a wealth of experimental material.

CHAPTER TWENTY-ONE

Physiological Surgery

PAVLOV was the first to apply systematically antiseptic and aseptic surgery to the study of the functions of the digestive glands. The idea of applying surgical methods to the experimental investigation of the physiology of the gastrointestinal tract was inspired by Beaumont's famous exploration of gastric functions in a wounded Canadian trapper, Alexis St. Martin. Two investigators —one Russian, Bassov (1842); another French, Blondlot (1843)— were the first to perform permanent artificial gastric fistula in dogs, but it was Thiry (1864) who introduced a new method of study of the secretory functions of the alimentary canal. His method consisted in the isolation of a short piece of small intestine in a manner which kept the mesentery, blood vessels, and nerves intact. The distal end of this cylindrical piece was closed with sutures and the proximal end sewed into the abdominal wall; the loose ends of the intestine, from which the short piece was cut out, were connected end to end. This so-called "Thiry's intestinal fistula" permitted the collection of intestinal juice uncontaminated with food masses or other digestive juices. In the case of the Bassov-Blondlot gastric fistula, the gastric secretion was practically never pure; usually if there was no food in the stomach, saliva or juices secreted into the duodenum and thrown back into the stomach were admixed with the gastric juice. Klemensiewicz (1875) used Thiry's method for isolation of the pyloric part of the stomach, and R. Heidenhain (1879) employed it for the isolation of a portion of the corpus.

Circumstances at the beginning of Pavlov's scientific career were favorable for the appreciation and further development of the surgical method in physiology. Pavlov graduated from the Medico-Chirurgical Academy in St. Petersburg at a time when Pasteur's bacteriological teaching and Lister's antiseptic method of operation were still new. These epoch-making achievements of the medical sciences had greatly impressed the mind of the young physician-physiologist and induced him to apply the antiseptic and later the aseptic methods of operating for his own purely physiological aims. However, Pavlov could realize his plans only after he became head of the Department of Physiology in the Institute of Experimental Medicine in St. Petersburg in 1891. Here was built according to his design a very modest physiological laboratory which was nevertheless the first in the world specially adapted to the performance of aseptic operations on animals and their postoperative care. A description of this operating department in the physiological laboratory may be found in Pavlov's *Lectures* (1902, p. 18; 1910, p. 20).

THE THEORETICAL BASIS OF PHYSIOLOGICAL SURGERY

There were more profound reasons, however, why Pavlov used so extensively the method of "physiological surgery," as he called it. He belonged to the school of physiological thought according to which a physiologist studying the functions of a certain organ has to take into consideration the whole body and never to forget the possibility of the reciprocal functional relationship of the organ in question with other organs. Such physiology may be called "synthetic" or "integral" in contradistinction to "analytical" physiology. It is not so much the methods of the analytical and integral physiologies which differ from each other (though they are not often alike) as the ultimate aims of the one and the other. By separating a complicated phenomenon into its integral parts, analytical physiology attempts to determine the cause or the causes which are responsible for it. The aim of analytical physiology is to find out what physical, chemical, or physicochemical processes are at the basis of the investigated phenomenon. These fundamental functions of organs may be studied in a whole animal by using the so-called method of "acute" experimentation when the anesthetized animal is sacrificed at the end of a short-term experiment. Isolated organs, pieces of tissue, or separate cells may also be employed for this purpose. Integral physiology, however, always takes the whole body into consideration. No organ in the body is independent of others, and the functions of every one of them may change with the changing conditions of the body.

[218]

It was the doctrine of "milieu interne" expounded by Claude Bernard (1878–79) which greatly emphasized the interrelations of all organs of the body. He wrote: "Tous les méchanismes vitaux, quelque variés qu'il soient, n'ont toujours qu'un but, celui de maintenir l'unité des conditions de la vie dans le milieu intérieur" (1878–79, p. 121). Further development of this doctrine and its experimental foundation was made by several outstanding physiologists, such as J. S. Haldane, C. S. Sherrington, W. B. Cannon, and especially Pavlov.

In his later years, i.e., in the conditioned-reflexes period, Pavlov formulated the following conception of an animal body. An animal body is a highly unstable, labile system. However, this instability is an essential condition of its existence. The outer world acts incessantly on the animal body. Some of the changes in the outer world may easily lead to the destruction of an animal; others are not so noxious, but if they are permitted to produce their effects unopposed, they will lead to some grave disturbances, structural or functional. To maintain the equilibrium with the surrounding medium and to prevent its destructive influence, an organism must counteract outside pressure by a change or by a number of successive changes in its activity. There is going on a constant neutralization of various effects produced on the organism by changes in the external world. The reaction of the body in response to a stimulus may involve a chain of organs or even the whole body (Pavlov, 1927, pp. 7–8). Cannon's theory of "homeostasis" is very close to Pavlov's point of view of an organism as an unstable labile system.

Undoubtedly, a conception similar to this was the reason why from his early days Pavlov as an experimenter always gave preference to investigations performed on normal animals. It would be wrong, however, to assume that Pavlov neglected the method of so-called "acute" experiments. He used this method extensively, was a great master of operative technique, and achieved with this form of animal experimentation outstanding results, such as the discoveries of the dynamic nerves of the heart, the secretory nerves of the pancreas, etc.; but whenever it was possible to substitute a "chronic" for an "acute" experiment, he always did so.

As early as 1897 Pavlov clearly realized what a hindrance the shortcomings of the "acute" experiment are for analytical physi-

[219]

olⅰogy. For synthetic physiology they are an unsurpassable obstacle. He wrote:

> The crude damage done [in an "acute" experiment] to the integrity of the organism sets up a number of inhibitory influences which react upon the functions of its different parts. The body as a whole, in which an enormous number of different organs are linked together in the most delicate fashion for the performance of a common and purposive work, cannot in the nature of things remain indifferent to forces calculated to destroy it. It must, in its own interest, restrain some functions while others are allowed free course, and thus, by appropriately economising its energies, rescue that which it is possible to save [Pavlov, 1902, p. 15].

Pavlov, therefore, warmly recommended the introduction of surgical methods into physiology and pointed out that the physiologists of his time (i.e., of the end of the nineteenth century) either did not realize the importance of these methods or had no means for their solution. He continued:

> The clearest testimony in proof of the fact that surgical methods have not assumed their legitimate position in physiology is evidenced by the fact that in the buildings for a physiological laboratory of the present day, while provision is made for chemical, physical, microscopic and vivisecting departments, none is made for an efficient, well-equipped set of surgical rooms [p. 16].

He pointed out that physiological surgery had already been employed by some investigators before him, thus, e.g., Minkowski extirpated the pancreatic gland in dogs; Goltz removed the hemispheres; and so on. However, these were rare and not systematic attempts to solve the physiological problems by surgical methods; most of the experimenters were satisfied by "acute" experiments. Modern physiology owes to Pavlov, therefore, the introduction into practice of the method of physiological surgery and a brilliant demonstration of its validity.

PHYSIOLOGICAL SURGERY OF THE DIGESTIVE TRACT

Pavlov (1902) himself formulated in his *Lectures* the experimental conditions which are essential for the proper investigation of the functions of the digestive glands. The secretions must be obtained by repeated samplings; they must be collected in an absolutely pure condition; their quantities must be estimated accurately; the digestive canal should function normally; and the experimental animal should be in perfect health (p. 4). To this must be added that the innervation of the gland or glands, whose functions are studied, should be preserved intact.

Several surgical methods were employed by Pavlov to obtain pure gastric juice without admixture of food masses or other juices. By adding esophagotomy to an ordinary gastric fistula, Pavlov could obtain pure gastric juice by sham feeding of the animal. Using this preparation, he discovered with Mme E. O. Shumov-Simanovsky that the vagus is the secretory nerve of the gastric glands. The same method permitted him to establish finally that there exists a real "psychic secretion" of gastric juice, a fact which had been denied by several investigators (Pavlov, 1902, p. 71; Babkin, 1928, p. 208).

Another surgical principle consisted in the isolation of a glandular duct (salivary, pancreatic, or common bile duct) with a small piece of mucous membrane surrounding the orifice of the duct. This so-called "papilla," with the opening of the duct exactly in the middle, was fixed by a few stitches to the edges of a wound or a stab wound in the skin. The small piece of the mucous membrane marvelously resisted the formation of a scar in the wound. If a duct of a gland was cut across and transplanted into the skin without a disk of mucous membrane surrounding it, a scar was rapidly formed and usually closed the duct in about two weeks. Fistulas with a "papilla" were really permanent and lasted as long as the animal lived.

For the study of the intestinal secretion, besides the Thiry and Thiry-Vella's fistulas, Pavlov used another method proposed by himself. He implanted three metal fistulas into the small intestine of a dog at a distance one from another (work of Glinski, 1891). When all three fistulas were open, the food masses were discharged from the two proximal ones. From the lowest fistula intestinal juice could be collected free of chyme on local stimulation of the intestine mechanically or chemically. This method, however, was not practical for the study of the intestinal secretion. Only Glinski in 1891 and nobody else in Pavlov's laboratory used it. However, this method could be very suitable for the investigation of the changes which the ingested food undergoes during its movement along the gastrointestinal tract, but this problem did not interest

Pavlov at all. Later, with substantial modifications, E. S. London used Pavlov's method for the study of the gastrointestinal chemism. He gave the name of "poly-fistulas method" to this method.

The crowning achievement of Pavlov in the physiological surgery of the alimentary canal was the operation of the so-called "Pavlov gastric pouch" (in Pavlov's laboratory it was always called the "Heidenhain-Pavlov pouch").

R. Heidenhain in 1879 had made a gastric pouch by cutting off part of the stomach in the region of the corpus near the greater curvature. The continuity of the gastrointestinal tract was restored by suturing the edges of the incision in the stomach. The excised part, which consisted of two flaps of the stomach, attached to the mesentery, was formed into a pouch of which one open end was sewed into the abdominal wound. The "Heidenhain pouch" for the first time permitted obtaining, during the course of digestion, pure gastric juice uncontaminated by food and saliva. However, the Heidenhain pouch had a great drawback because during the operation all vagus nerve fibers, which are secretory fibers, were sectioned in the walls of the stomach.

After discovering that the vagus is the secretory nerve of the gastric glands, Pavlov set himself to the task of making a gastric pouch which would retain the vagal as well as sympathetic innervation. Such a pouch had to reflect all phases of gastric secretion, i.e., the first or nervous phase and the second or chemical phase. It is impossible to go here into the detailed description of how Pavlov achieved his aim. The principle of the operation consisted in the preservation of vagal fibers which pass to the pouch in the muscular sheets of the stomach and in the separation of the main stomach from the pouch by a partition formed from only two layers of the gastric mucous membrane.

After the fundamental facts concerning the secretory activity, especially of gastric glands, were established, Pavlov began to analyze the secretory process in the gastrointestinal tract. For this purpose he isolated the different parts of the alimentary canal, which permitted him to study separately the secretory function of each of them and to determine the role which they were playing in the regulation of the secretory activity of other parts of the alimentary canal. Thus were isolated the whole stomach, the stomach

minus the pyloric part, the pyloric part, the Brunner's glands section of the duodenum, the caecum, etc.

The physiological surgery of the digestive tract was used, modified, and improved by many investigators. However, it must be
said that even now the original Pavlov methods are still of great
value for physiological, pharmacological, and pathological investigations of the secretory processes of the alimentary canal.

CHAPTER TWENTY-TWO

Nervous Regulation of the Secretory Activity of the Digestive Glands

A STUDY of the first Russian edition (1897) or of the first edition of the English translation (1902) of Pavlov's *Lectures on the Work of the Digestive Glands* leaves no doubt that he was convinced that the secretory activity of these glands is regulated exclusively by nervous reflex action. Moreover, he denied vehemently the possibility of humoral transmission of impulses from the alimentary canal to its glands. Such an attitude can be explained only by the epoch in which he studied physiology and medicine and began his scientific career.

Physiology and medicine stepped from infancy to maturity in the second half of the nineteenth century. Physiology became an exact science, and medicine rid itself of the doctrine of humoral pathology which had dominated it for more than two thousand years. No longer were diseases explained as being due to changes in the "body humors." This old conception had led only to further speculations since nothing was known about the "body fluids" or humors. Metabolic researches had hardly begun, biochemistry hardly existed, and endocrinology was still a science of the distant future.

In the second half, and especially the last third, of the nineteenth century the doctrine of humoral pathology received one severe blow after another (Bouchut, 1873). After 1854 the cellular pathology of Virchow occupied a dominant position. Pasteur's quickly developing bacteriological teaching brought an unheard-of clarity into the pathogenesis of many diseases, replacing old obscure theories of their origin. Antiseptic surgery, based on Pasteur's teaching, was a miracle in itself. Investigations in experimental physiology and biochemistry were now based on physics and chemistry. New and exact facts were discovered daily, forcing out obsolete theoretical and philosophical conceptions of bodily functions. The role which abnormal body humors played in pathogenesis of disease was rapidly discredited. There was no endocrinology which could counteract this new and extreme point of view (except for a few unsystematic investigations of Fagge, 1871, and Brown-Séquard, 1889). Even the nutrition of tissues and organs soon came to be believed to be under the control of the nervous system, due to Samuel, who in 1860 formulated his theory of so-called "trophic nerves."

As early as 1883 Pavlov expressed in his M.D. thesis a definite preference for the explanation of the regulations of bodily functions by a nervous mechanism. This was the so-called theory of "nervism" which Pavlov evolved under the influence of Botkin, with whom he worked at the time. He gave the following definition of "nervism" (in his M.D. thesis *The Centrifugal Nerves of the Heart*): "I understand by nervism a physiological theory which tries to prove that the nervous system controls the greatest possible number of bodily activities."

This tendency to explain the regulation of the functions in the body almost exclusively by the action of the nervous system was fully applied by Pavlov to the physiology of the gastrointestinal tract. Thus, when discussing the fine adaptation of the secretory activity of the digestive glands to the kind of stimulus that was acting on the surface of the alimentary canal, he wrote (1902, p. 45): "A probable answer is easily given, and naturally an explanation of the adaptability of the glands is first of all to be sought in their innervation. It is only when such a supposition proves untenable that we must seek another."

It is probable that it was the regulation of the secretory function of the salivary glands that impressed physiologists of this period most. The regulation is purely nervous, showing quantitatively a relationship between the stimulus applied to the mucous membrane and the response of the secretory organ. Pavlov was also impressed deeply, but he clearly understood that to draw an analogy between the innervation of the salivary glands and other deep-lying digestive glands was a mistake. "To me," he wrote (1902, p. 66), "it appears that the unjustified analogy drawn between the abdominal and salivary glands has to be credited with another important misapprehension." Nevertheless, though aware of its shortcomings, he applied, with slight modifications, the scheme of salivary gland regulation to the regulation of the gastric glands and the pancreatic gland.

GASTRIC GLANDS

Undoubtedly Pavlov was right when he insisted that the nervous mechanisms participated in the so-called "psychic" gastric secretion and in the first or nervous phase of gastric secretion. However, he also explained the second or chemical phase of gastric secretion as involving a nervous reflex mechanism.

According to Pavlov, when food was introduced directly into the stomach of a dog in a manner not arousing the dog's awareness of this and therefore with a complete exclusion of psychic gastric secretion, a reflex was originated and an impulse transmitted through the central nervous system which reached the peptic gland. The main proof of this thesis was that the same substances (e.g., Liebig's meat extract) were ineffective when introduced into and absorbed from the large intestine. Additional confirmation of the nervous character of the second or chemical phase of gastric secretion came from Pavlov's observation that the volume of secretion from an innervated pouch in response to each stimulus remained constant for many years, whereas that from a vagally denervated pouch gradually diminished and then became very scanty.

Although Liebig's meat extract does not provoke gastric secretion on intrarectal administration, it does do so when it is introduced intravenously and especially subcutaneously (Babkin, 1928, pp. 345 and 348). We know now that this effect is probably due in part to the presence of histamine in the meat extract. Of course, nothing was known about histamine and its stimulating effect on the gastric glands in the nineties of the last century. Therefore it is understandable that Pavlov, taken up so completely by the idea of "nervism," did not evaluate properly an important experiment of his own student, Lobassov (thesis, 1896, p. 95). Lobassov obtained a definite, though scanty, secretion of gastric juice from a Heidenhain pouch and the main stomach of a dog on intravenous injection of 100 cc. of 10 per cent Liebig's meat extract. This secretion was considered abnormal. Pavlov and Lobassov argued that a meat extract introduced directly into the blood acted as a substance foreign to the body. The organism used all possible means to free itself of it, including that of excreting it by way of the gastric glands. No experimental proof of this rather doubtful theory was given.

It must be mentioned that Pavlov explained nowhere how the chemical stimulants present in the stomach were able to evoke a gastric secretion from a Heidenhain pouch which was completely deprived of vagal innervation. Presumably Pavlov supposed that the transmission of the impulses from the surface of the main stomach to the glands of the Heidenhain pouch was of reflex nature, the efferent paths being conveyed through the splanchnic nerves. There is no experimental evidence in Pavlov's *Lectures* of such mode of transmission of secretory impulses, but twice (Pavlov, 1902, pp. 61 and 62) he mentioned that there was very little doubt that the secretory fibers of the gastric glands were present not only in the vagus but also in the sympathetic nerves. This undoubtedly was a conclusion by analogy with the innervation of the salivary and pancreatic glands. It was not justified by subsequent investigations.

Gradually at the very beginning of the twentieth century the problem of the regulation of the gastric secretion moved toward its solution, although even now, almost half a century later, it is not yet fully understood. The most important step in the elucidation of the mechanism of the chemical phase of gastric secretion was made by Edkins (1906). Like Bayliss and Starling for the pancreatic gland, Edkins similarly established for the gastric glands the existence of a special hormonal mechanism of transmission of secretory impulses from the pyloric part of the stomach to the peptic glands of the fundus and corpus of this organ. Unfortunately, mechanisms usually proved far more complicated than they seemed to the early investigators. It now appears probable that the gastric secretion is regulated during the chemical phase partly by a hormone and partly by the local nervous system. The limits to which each participates still remains unknown.

The Pancreatic Gland

Four fundamental facts were discovered by Pavlov and his pupils concerning the regulation of the secretory work of the pancreas. They found that (1) both vagus and splanchnic nerves contained secretory fibers for this gland; (2) the presence in the duodenum of weak solutions of hydrochloric or other acids stimulated the secretion of pancreatic juice; (3) the same effect was produced by fat or soap; and (4) the composition of the pancreatic juice, especially its enzyme power, varied with the nature of the stimulus.

It was only natural that Pavlov considered that the secretagogue effects of acid or fat were transmitted through long reflex paths, the efferent channels of which were vagi or splanchnic nerves. To be certain that this was so, a control experiment was performed with the introduction per rectum of 0.25 per cent hydrochloric acid into the large intestine of a dog with a permanent pancreatic fistula. This experiment, of course, gave a negative result because, as we know today, the mucous membrane of the large intestine does not contain the hormone secretin (or its precursor, prosecretin), which is liberated by the hydrochloric acid and then, with the blood stream, is brought to the pancreatic gland. Secretin is present only in the mucosa of the duodenum and of the upper part of the jejunum. On the basis of this experiment and of some theoretical considerations, Pavlov denied altogether any possibility that the acid would stimulate the pancreatic secretion after its absorption from the small intestine (see Pavlov, 1902, p. 136).

I remember well the time when the preliminary communication on secretin by Bayliss and Starling appeared in 1902 in the *Physiologisches Centralblatt*, Volume 15, No. 23. Before the discovery of secretin the problem of the action of acid from the duodenum on the pancreas was made extremely complicated by Popielski and Wertheimer, who supposed the existence of different short reflex arcs connecting the duodenal mucosa with the secretory (acinous) cells of the pancreas. (The full story of the discovery of secretin has been told by me in detail elsewhere [Babkin, 1944, pp. 491 ff.].) The theory of humoral transmission of impulses from the intestine to the pancreas not only was new and startling; it also simplified at once the involved problem of the regulation of the pancreatic secretory activity. Bayliss and Starling's article produced almost a sensation in our laboratory. It shook the very foundation of the teaching of the exclusive nervous regulation of the secretory activity of the digestive glands, a concept which seemed to be established so solidly and supported by so many experimentally proved facts.

Pavlov's reaction to the discovery of a humoral regulation was that which one would expect from him. He did not give up at once the idea of the exclusive nervous regulation of pancreatic secretion but rather the reverse. He tried to confirm facts obtained by himself earlier on the secretory functions of the vagus and splanchnic nerves and to disprove Bayliss and Starling's hormonal theory.

Two of Pavlov's co-workers, Borisov and Walther (1902), showed that (very crude) acid extracts of many organs (duodenum, small and large intestine, stomach, and even striated muscles) stimulated the secretion not only of the pancreatic juice but of saliva also. From this it was concluded that the acid extract of duodenal mucosa did not contain a specific pancreatic hormone but a substance or number of substances foreign to the body.

Very soon, however, Pavlov began to change his opinion. In the article in *Nagel's Handbuch* (2:742), published in 1907 but written by Pavlov in the summer of 1903, he again pointed out the presence of foreign substances in the extracts of the duodenal mucous membrane but added: "Thus there remain certain things, as a matter of fact a very few, which have to be cleared up to make us absolutely sure of the participation of secretin in the normal mechanism of the action of acid on the pancreas."

Pavlov radically changed his opinion about the new fact discovered by the English physiologists probably in the fall or in the winter of 1902–3 after reading Bayliss and Starling's complete and excellent paper on secretin in the *Journal of Physiology* (1902). In this article Bayliss and Starling reported experiments with highly purified extracts of the duodenal mucosa which stimulated a profuse secretion of the pancreatic juice and produced hardly any side effects (e.g., fall of the blood pressure, etc.). Pavlov always bowed to facts, so he did not hesitate any longer to recognize the existence of a humoral mechanism of pancreatic secretion. I think it was in the fall of 1902 that Pavlov asked V. V. Savich to repeat the secretin experiment of Bayliss and Starling. The effect of secretin was self-evident. Pavlov and the rest of us watched the experiment in silence. Then, without a word, Pavlov disappeared into his study. He returned half an hour later and said, "Of course, they are right. It is clear that we did not take out an exclusive patent for the discovery of truth."

The recognition of secretin as a part of the normal secretory mechanism of the pancreas did not mean at all that the well-established role of the nerves in it had to be denied. Pavlov's laboratory adopted now a theory of a dual mechanism—nervous and humoral—of the regulation of pancreatic secretion. A great deal of valuable information concerning the participation of the nervous system in the process of pancreatic secretion has been added recently by J. E. Thomas and his co-workers (see Babkin, 1944, p. 508). However, we must confess that it is not quite clear through what nervous paths the impulses are transmitted from the small intestine to the pancreatic gland. The matter is still more complicated by the discovery of Harper and Raper (1943) of a hormone "pancreozymin" which promotes the secretion of pancreatic enzymes, i.e., acts on the gland in the same way as do the secretory nerves.

In England the enthusiasm over the discovery by Bayliss and Starling of a new way of transmitting impulses from the gastro-intestinal canal to the pancreas was so great that the function of the pancreatic secretory nerves was neglected completely. In their article in the *Ergebnisse der Physiologie* (1906, 5:675) Bayliss and Starling went so far as to explain the secretory effect of vagus nerve faradization on pancreatic secretion by the increased gastric motility and by the passage of acid gastric juice into the duodenum with subsequent formation of secretin. In other words, according to these investigators, the vagus was not at all a secretory nerve for the pancreas. It required several years of work on the part of my colleagues and myself and actual demonstration of the secretory effect of vagus nerve stimulation to persuade them that the pancreatic gland possessed secretory nerves.

A New Field of Investigation

It has always seemed to me that the discovery of secretin, and soon afterward of other hormones which regulate the activity of the digestive glands, was one of the reasons why Pavlov gradually abandoned the study of the secretory processes and became involved in the investigation of the functions of the cerebral hemispheres. It was in the years 1901–2 that Pavlov began to think more and more about the physiological mechanism of the special type of salivary and gastric secretion which at one time he called "psychic." At that period Pavlov founded with his co-worker, Dr. I. Ph. Tolochinov, the method of investigation of the conditioned salivary reflexes.

In confirmation of the above I may quote Pavlov's own words. The conversation took place after the discovery of secretin. Pavlov said: "Of course, we may continue to study with success the physiology of digestion, but let other people do it. As for myself, I am getting more and more interested in the conditioned reflexes."

In his scientific work Pavlov was a pioneer, a discoverer of new lands. He did not like to meddle in debatable or fashionable problems, though he never shrank from any fight for the cause he believed was right. He was not a man of compromise. He liked to see before him a wide and virgin field which he could plow himself.

THE MAMMARY GLANDS

Although Pavlov was always fascinated by the nervous regulations of bodily activities and was inclined to explain by them the response of different organs to various stimuli acting on the body from outside or inside it, one cannot say that he was blind altogether to the humoral way of transportation of impulses. The best proof of this is the work on the mammary gland of the goat and of the dog which he performed with his student, Dr. M. M. Mironov (1894). The following facts were established:

1. Stimulation of a sensory nerve in dogs inhibits the production of milk up to 50 per cent; the composition of milk changes, it becomes thicker. Pavlov and Mironov looked on this phenomenon as an inhibitory reflex and an undoubted proof that the central nervous system influences the secretion of milk.

2. After section of all the nerves going to the milk gland in the goat, the volume of milk produced daily diminished from 30 to 40 per cent.

3. Another proof that the central nervous system has a definite relation to the process of elaboration of milk by the mammary gland was afforded to Pavlov and Mironov by an experiment in which a goat with a denervated mammary gland was subjected to stimulation of the sensory nerves. No diminution of milk secretion was noted in this animal. (No such experiment, as far as I can know, was performed on lactating dogs.)

4. In two goats during early stages of pregnancy all nerves supplying the mammary gland were sectioned. In spite of this, both animals began to lactate profusely after parturition, though somewhat less than under normal conditions, i.e., when the nerves were intact. From these experiments Pavlov drew the conclusion that lactation is not only regulated by the central nervous system but depends on the act of parturition and is influenced in some way by the sexual organs. According to him, parturition produced changes in the chemical composition of the body fluids which now stimulate the peripheral endings of the mammary secretory nerves. Although we know at the present time that at least three hormones—estrogen and progesterone (glandular development of mammae) and prolactin of the anterior pituitary gland (promotion of milk secretion)—participate in the process of lactation, the nervous factors cannot be excluded altogether.

CHAPTER TWENTY-THREE

Specific Excitability of the Endings of the Afferent Nerves in the Gastrointestinal Tract

THE theory of the specific excitability of the endings of the afferent nerves guided Pavlov throughout his investigations of the functions of the gastrointestinal tract. He opposed vehemently the conception of general excitability of the alimentary canal. According to this last theory the secretory activity of the digestive glands may be evoked by any stimulation—mechanical, chemical, or thermal—affecting the gastrointestinal mucous membrane.

The following are Pavlov's own words, an exposition of his *profession de foi*, so to speak:

The utmost importance must be attached to the fact that only the peripheral endings of centripetal (afferent) nerves, in contrast to the nerve fibres which possess a general excitability, are endowed with specificity, that is to say, are able to transform definite kinds of external stimuli into nervous impulses. The functions of the organs with which they are connected are therefore purposive. In other words, these organs are called into play by certain definite conditions, suggesting the startling idea that the organs possess a mind and are, so to speak, conscious of their duty. We have long known that the peripheral endings of the nerves in the organs of sense possess a high degree of specific excitability and we cannot therefore have any doubt regarding the specific nature of the end-organs of other centripetal nerves. The last question is the sick child of contemporary physiology. . . . To correct the conception of physicians on this point is my chief object in giving these lectures. I hope to furnish convincing evidence to show that the alimentary canal is endowed with no mere general excitability, that is to say, it does not respond in a similar way to every conceivable agency, but on the contrary responds only to special conditions which vary in its different parts [Pavlov, ed. Thompson (1st ed., 1902), pp. 63–64; (2d ed., 1910), pp. 66–67].[1]

[233]

Pavlov tried to obtain confirmation of his theory of specific excitability of the end organs of the sensory nerves of the alimentary canal from a great number of experiments. Since every chapter of his book brings evidence supporting this theory, repeating here these experimental proofs would mean quoting most of the pages of his *Lectures*. Therefore I shall enumerate briefly only the most important facts on which Pavlov based his theory.

1. A highly specialized response of the salivary glands to different stimuli was demonstrated.

2. Different quantitative and qualitative secretory responses of the gastric glands to the three typical food substances—meat, bread, or milk—was established.

3. It was shown that a gastric juice with a much lower digestive power was produced during the chemical phase, when the food substances come in direct contact with the gastric mucosa, as compared with the high peptic power of sham-feeding juice.

4. The inability of mechanical stimulation of gastric mucosa to evoke gastric secretion and the striking response of the gastric glands to certain chemical stimulations was demonstrated. Pavlov considered this point to be of paramount importance.

5. Acids, and especially hydrochloric acid, which is the normal component of gastric juice, served as a specific stimulant of pancreatic secretion. On the other hand, the same acid did not stimulate at all the work of the gastric glands. (At this time Pavlov believed, of course, that the secretion of pancreatic juice was stimulated reflexly through the nervous system.)

6. The end organs of the afferent nerves, which were specifically stimulated by acid and initiated a reflex pancreatic secretion, were present in the duodenum only but not in the stomach. Other substances, however, were specific stimulants for the gastric glands. Thus for each component gland of the alimentary canal there existed in the mucous membrane specific nervous receptors for special chemical substances.

7. In response to acid the pancreatic gland secreted a juice of a special composition; its alkalinity was high, and its enzymatic power was low.

[234]

8. Pavlov explained the adaptation of the enzymes of the pancreatic juice to the kind of food ingested by stimulation in each case of different specific end organs of the sensory nerves in the intestine. (This statement, made before the discovery of enterokinase and based chiefly on Walther's data of 1897, had to be modified considerably in view of subsequent investigations in this field.)

9. Different types of mechanical stimulation of the mucosa of the small intestine produced different kinds of intestinal secretion (Glinski, 1891).

10. In later years Pavlov was still guided in his investigations by the theory of specific excitability of the gastrointestinal tract, although this theory could not be formulated as strictly as before. For example, V. V. Savich (1904) discovered in Pavlov's laboratory that, of a number of substances tested, only pancreatic juice when introduced into a Thiry loop of the small intestine increased the production of enterokinase. This was considered a specific reaction of the intestinal mucosa to a special stimulus.

Pavlov recognized in his *Lectures* (1902, p. 111) his indebtedness to his predecessors Blondlot and Heidenhain. He wrote: "The talented author of the *Traité analytique de digestion*—Blondlot—spoke in plain words of the importance of the act of taking food and of the specific excitability of the gastric mucous membrane. . . . Of the other investigators we must mention Heidenhain who has enriched the physiology of secretion in general, but more especially in connection with secretory work of the stomach, has discovered important facts and given birth to many fruitful ideas" (see chap. 25 of this book).

ORIGIN OF THE THEORY OF SPECIFIC EXCITABILITY

The theory of the specific excitability of the gastrointestinal mucous membrane, as Pavlov pointed out himself (Pavlov, 1902, p. 111), originated with Blondlot (1843), who spoke very definitely about it in relation to the secretory activity of the stomach. Gastric secretion in the dog was intermittent. Only special chemical stimulants, namely, those which were present in food substances, were able to evoke gastric secretion on coming into contact with the gastric mucous membrane. Neither mechanical stimulation of the mucosa (with a rubber tube, pebbles, pieces of wood, etc.) nor chemical stimulation with such substances as pepper, common salt, potassium carbonate, etc., introduced directly into the stomach through the fistula, stimulated a secretion of acid gastric juice. All these irritants of the gastric mucosa increased chiefly the production of mucus (pp. 211–13).

The facts adduced in the working up of his [Blondlot's] theory [Pavlov wrote (1902, p. 111)] were naturally insufficient, but we must not forget that the first experiments on dogs with artificial gastric fistulae had only just been performed. It is truly incomprehensible that the researchers of Blondlot and his view on the secretion of gastric juice, have received during the last fifty years no completion and no addition, but, on the contrary, have passed out of sight thanks to the faulty experiments and erroneus presentations of later authors.

BEAUMONT'S INFLUENCE

It is possible that the stubborn adherence of physiologists and medical men to the theory of the general irritability of the gastric mucous membrane was due to the strong and lasting influence of the remarkable investigation of Beaumont (1833) on Alexis St. Martin. In accordance with the views of his epoch, and especially those professed by Spallanzani, Beaumont (p. 90) believed that the secretion of gastric juice was evoked by contact of any object—alimentary or indigestible—with the gastric mucosa. In his experiments Beaumont did not take into consideration the "psychic secretion" of gastric juice. This was discovered much later, in 1852, by Bidder and Schmidt. Beaumont, however, being a careful observer, remarked that the irritation of gastric mucosa by indigestible substances, such as an elastic tube or the stem of a thermometer, stimulated a smaller secretion than did food. He explained this fact by saying that ordinarily a meal would come in contact with a much greater area of the gastric mucous membrane than did the above-mentioned inert objects. He dealt presumably in both cases with conditioned alimentary gastric reflexes which were manifested more strongly in the case of food substances than in the case of the purely mechanical stimulation of the mucous membrane. Besides this, in the first case the chemical properties of food exerted their secretagogue effect. The mechanical stimulation was also undoubtedly associated with ingestion of food because in almost all experiments the subject, Alexis St. Martin, received his breakfast after the introduction of the tube through the fistula into the stomach for collection of fasting secretion.

THE MODERN CONCEPTION OF THE SPECIFIC EXCITABILITY OF THE DIGESTIVE GLANDS

The discovery of gastrin and pancreatic secretin makes Pavlov's theory of specific excitability of the end organs of the afferent nerves in the gastrointestinal mucosa untenable in the form in which it was proposed by him. There is strong evidence that, in the case of the stomach and the pancreas, the secretory cells of these glands may be stimulated in a purely humoral way without any participation of the nervous system. However, this phenomenon does not exclude the fundamental fact established by Pavlov that different food substances, like meat, bread, or milk, or different chemical agencies, like meat extract, peptone, hydrochloric acid, sodium oleate, etc., coming into contact with gastric or duodenal mucosa, stimulate the gastric and pancreatic glands, respectively, to produce secretions of different composition. Although the mechanism of transmission of impulses from the surface of the stomach to the gastric glands is still not clear, Pavlov's theory of the typical response of the gastric glands to different stimulants remains unquestioned. This is true also for the pancreatic gland. Thus, for example, a weak solution of hydrochloric acid or of olive oil or sodium oleate may evoke the same volume of pancreatic secretion, but the composition of the juice will be different in each case. Whether the secretory nerves somehow participate in the second case or whether different types of hormones—secretin or secretin plus pancreozymin—are produced, we do not know. Several modern investigators (Ivy, Thomas, and others) are inclined to think that in pancreatic secretion and in the second phase of gastric secretion both hormones responsible for the transmission of impulses from the mucous membrane to the corresponding glands and nervous reflexes are involved (see Babkin, 1944, pp. 417 ff. and 508 ff.).

The conclusion which has to be drawn from all that has been said in this chapter about Pavlov's theory of the specific excitability of the nerve endings in the gastrointestinal mucous membrane is that it must now be replaced by a more general conception of specific excitability of the gastric and pancreatic glands themselves. This conception, however, does not exclude the possibility of reflex transmission of impulses from the surface of the alimentary canal to its glands. By what means a typical response of these glands is achieved in each special case is not yet fully known; nevertheless, it is evident that the facts themselves observed by Pavlov were absolutely correct.

We now believe that in only one type of gland does the regulation of glandular activity proceed in a manner exactly as conceived by Pavlov. This is the salivary gland. The salivary glands respond to each stimulus, at least in dogs, with a typical quantitative and qualitative secretory reaction. The substances act in each case on specific nerve endings in the mouth cavity, and the nervous impulse thus originated is transmitted along the afferent nerves to the salivary centers.

CHAPTER TWENTY-FOUR

Secretory and Trophic Glandular Nerves

PAVLOV accepted R. Heidenhain's theory of secretory and trophic glandular nerves without reservations and believed that many of his own experiments confirmed it. Heidenhain's theory was based on the investigations he had made on salivary glands. Each salivary gland is supplied by two nerves—a cerebral or, as we now call it, parasympathetic nerve and a sympathetic nerve. According to Heidenhain, these nerves contain two different kinds of nerve fibers which are related to the secretory process. One group of these fibers regulates the production of the liquid parts and the inorganic constituents of a secretion. Heidenhain called these "secretory" fibers. The effect of stimulation of another group of nerve fibers was the conversion of the organic colloidal material, stored in the glandular cells, into a soluble form and the discharge of it, together with enzymes, into the secretion. Heidenhain called these fibers "trophic." The parasympathetic nerve, e.g., chorda tympani, contained a great number of "secretory" nerve fibers and a small number of "trophic" ones. The sympathetic nerve contained, on the other hand, a great number of "trophic" fibers and a very small number of the "secretory" type. Thus, a faradization of chorda tympani evoked from a submaxillary gland a copious flow of saliva which was poor in organic material. Faradization of the sympathetic nerve produced a very scanty flow of saliva which was, however, very rich in organic material.

Pavlov applied Heidenhain's theory of "secretory" and "trophic" nerves to the innervation of the gastric and pancreatic glands (Pavlov, 1902, pp. 46, 53, 62). He wrote:

We have seen that the vagus nerve, already laden with other duties, is employed to transmit impulses to the gastric glands and the pancreas. We must also assign to the sympathetic nerve a similar role. This cannot be questioned as regards the pancreas, and is highly probable as regards the stomach. Moreover, we saw good reasons for believing that these two nerves contain two different classes of fibres—secretory and trophic. This condition had already been proved by Heidenhain to exist for the nerves of the salivary glands. We might almost have proceeded a step further and divided Heidenhain's trophic nerves into fibres controlling the secretion of the individual ferments [quoted from Pavlov, 1910, p. 65, because here the translation of the same passage is better than p. 62 of Pavlov, 1902].

Heidenhain's influence on Pavlov may also be seen in the fact that he used exactly the same argument as the former when he wanted to prove the true secretory nature of gastric vagal innervation. Thus Heidenhain was convinced that the transformation of the precursor of mucin into soluble mucin in the cells of the submaxillary gland during the stimulation of chorda tympani was an active process and was not due simply to its solution by fluid coming from the glandular blood vessels.

Speaking of vagal gastric secretory fibers, Pavlov asked: "What kind of fibres are these? Are they special secretory fibres, or do they only influence the glands indirectly—through the medium of vessels, for example?" (Pavlov, 1902, p. 52). He then quoted his experiments in which it was demonstrated that the greater the secretion of the gastric juice, the more pepsin the juice contained and concluded that "this fact is . . . the best proof of the specific activity of the nerve fibres supplying the glands. If only vasomotor (dilating) fibres for the glands were contained in the vagi nerves, an augmented flow of juice from strong excitation would mean a *lessening* of the concentration. The more rapidly the flow passes through the glands, other things being equal, the less specific the constituents that it can carry away in solution from them."

The experimental evidence which rallied Pavlov to the support of the theory that the gastric and pancreatic glands have a secretory and trophic innervation was neither convincing nor notable. It is true that the impulses reaching the gastric glands through the vagus nerve evoke a secretion of a great volume of juice which is extremely rich in pepsin; and therefore, in agreement with Heidenhain's theory, it may be concluded that the vagus contains a great number of both secretory and trophic fibers. But data concerning the second nerve supplying the stomach, namely, the sympathetic nerve, are very confusing. By analogy from the salivary and pancreatic glands, Pavlov supposed that the sympathetic also was a secretory nerve for the gastric glands. Said he: "It is permissible to fill up gaps in our knowledge of one of the schemes of innervation by analogy from the other. We cannot doubt, for example, that secretory fibres for the stomach are present not only in the vagus, but also in the sympathetic" (Pavlov, 1902, p. 61).

It seems that the only experimental evidence to back up Pavlov's belief was gained from the fact that a Heidenhain gastric pouch, owing to the nature of the operation performed on the stomach, was deprived completely of vagal innervation and yet responded with a secretion when food was introduced into the organ. This was a logical conclusion since Pavlov knew nothing at this time about the humoral transmission of impulses from the stomach to its glands.

It is true that thirty years after Pavlov's *Lectures* were written, two of his pupils, Volborth and Kudryavzeff (1927), demonstrated in his laboratory that faradization of the splanchnic nerve, cut freshly or five days previously (to eliminate the effect of vaso-constrictors), evoked a secretion of gastric juice from the whole stomach or from the Heidenhain pouch. But this secretion was extremely scanty and did not always contain free hydrochloric acid. Even at the present time the problem of the relation of the sympathetic nerves to gastric glands still cannot be considered as solved (cf. Babkin, 1944, pp. 241 ff.).

To apply the Heidenhain theory of secretory and trophic nerves to the digestive work of the pancreatic gland, Pavlov had to evolve even more purely hypothetical suppositions than in the case of the gastric glands. The real secretory impulses, as we now know, are received by the pancreas from secretin. But Pavlov did not believe in the humoral transmission of impulses from the duodenum and upper jejunum to the pancreatic gland. According to him, a solution of the hydrochloric acid stimulated pancreatic secretion reflexly. He never explained, however, why the faradization of the vagus or splanchnic nerve produced such extremely scanty secretions of the pancreatic juice and why it was so rich in enzymes and protein material, in other words, why both pancreatic nerves were "trophic."

In a series of publications Thomas and his co-workers (see, e.g., Crider and Thomas, 1944) arrived at the conclusion that in all probability there exists a nervous, as well as a hormonal, regulation of the extrinsic secretion of the pancreas. Certain substances, such as the products of protein digestion, for example, stimulate the pancreatic secretion reflexly through a peripheral reflex mechanism. These peripheral reflex arcs are under the control of the vagi. Through the vagi nerves the central nervous system sends impulses which may either augment or inhibit the local reflexes. Although this explanation differs greatly from Pavlov's original conception of the regulation of the external pancreatic function, it rehabilitates to a certain degree his conviction of the important role which the nervous system plays in transmitting the secretory impulses to the digestive glands.

Adaptation of Pancreatic Enzymes

Pavlov's hint (see above) that Heidenhain's trophic nerves could perhaps be divided into fibers controlling the secretion of individual enzymes was based on an unavoidable mistake which Walther and other of Pavlov's co-workers were bound to make when they studied the secretion in dogs with a permanent pancreatic fistula.

As mentioned before, Pavlov's method of operation of a pancreatic fistula consisted in the transplantation onto the abdominal skin of the natural opening of the main pancreatic duct with a small piece of the surrounding intestinal membrane. The work of Walther (1897) and others was performed before the discovery in Pavlov's laboratory of the enzyme enterokinase. Certainly no one could have suspected that the little piece of intestinal mucosa, which surrounded the orifice of the pancreatic duct in the papilla, might produce an enzyme which was able to activate the protrypsin of the pancreatic juice. Besides activating the protrypsin, the intestinal juice secreted by the papilla facilitated, to a certain degree, the lipolytic and the amylolytic actions of the pancreatic juice. This latter action of the intestinal secretion was not of enzymatic nature.

Walther established the adaptation of pancreatic enzymes to the types of food ingested by the animal. He found, for instance, that the greatest amount of trypsin was found in the pancreatic juice secreted on a meal of milk; less was secreted on meals of bread and meat. The juice richest in amylase was one secreted on bread; it was less rich on milk and much less so on meat. On the other hand, lipase was found in the greatest amount in the juice secreted on milk meals and in the smallest amount on bread meals. Pancreatic juice secreted on a meal of meat occupied an intermediate position (Pavlov, 1902, p. 39).

The experiments of Vasiliev (1893), Jablonski (1894), and Lintvarev (1901)—all students of Pavlov—also spoke, according to him, in favor of adaptation of pancreatic enzymes to a particular type of food. These co-workers of Pavlov found that when a dog was maintained on some one diet, such as meat, or bread-and-milk, for any length of time, there was an adaptation of pancreatic enzyme secretion similar to that observed by Walther (Pavlov, 1902, p. 41). In its final form, after enterokinase had been already discovered, the teaching of the adaptation of the pancreatic enzymes to a prolonged diet of one or another type took the following form (Lintvarev): on a meat diet, trypsin and lipase were in an active state and did not require enterokinase and bile, respectively, for their activation. On a prolonged bread-and-milk diet these two pancreatic enzymes gradually acquired a zymogenic form: that is, they were in an inactive state, and without the help of their activators—enterokinase and bile—they produced only a weak effect on their corresponding substrates. Amylase under all circumstances was secreted in an active form.

Pavlov was extremely pleased with Lintvarev's work; it confirmed his fundamental idea of the adjustment of the bodily functions to the needs of the organism. As early as 1897 in his *Lectures* (1st English ed., 1902, p. 3) Pavlov wrote: "The differences and complexity of the reagents indicate that the work of the digestive canal in every single case is elaborately contrived, beautifully performed, and most carefully adapted to the task in hand."

The more severe, then, was the blow to Pavlov when two French physiologists, Delezenne and Frouin (1902), declared only one year after publication of Lintvarev's thesis that the trypsin of the pancreatic juice was secreted by the gland in an absolutely inactive form under all circumstances. They claimed that the data on the adaptation of the pancreatic enzymes to the type of food were the result of a faulty experimental technique adopted by Pavlov. The variations in the concentration of enzymes were explained thus: in dogs with Pavlov's pancreatic fistula, the juice became activated in a greater or lesser degree, depending on the rate with which the pancreatic gland was secreting, because the juice flowed over the papilla which produced the enterokinase. However, when Delezenne and Frouin introduced a catheter directly into the pancreatic duct through its orifice on the papilla, they obtained a juice which contained an inactive trypsin—one which was unable to digest the coagulated protein without the help of the succus entericus. This finding was confirmed by many investigators (cf. Babkin, 1928, p. 467).

However, it developed finally that Pavlov was right: the theory of the adaptation of pancreatic enzymes to different alimentary regimes was, to a certain extent, rehabilitated. The new evidence, however, did not come from Pavlov's laboratory but from that of the talented French physiologist, Frouin, in 1907.

The French scientist demonstrated that there was a very great variability in the property of the pancreatic protrypsin which was secreted by a dog on a meat or bread regime to be activated by the intestinal juice containing the enterokinase. To a certain amount of pancreatic juice obtained from a dog on a meat regime, the addition of one five-hundredth to one one-thousandth of its volume of intestinal juice was enough fully to activate the protrypsin. For the same purpose, the protrypsin secreted when the animal was on a bread diet required one-tenth to one-twentieth by volume of the intestinal juice. Much later, Chechulin (1923), working in Pavlov's laboratory, repeated Frouin's experiments and confirmed them (Babkin, 1928, p. 498). Pavlov, although at that time fully absorbed in the study of conditioned reflexes, was still interested in rehabilitation of his old theory of the adaptation of the pancreatic enzymes.

But the fact discovered by Frouin and confirmed by Chechulin only partially rehabilitated Pavlov's theory of the adaptation of the pancreatic enzymes to different sorts of food. It explained satisfactorily why in dogs with Pavlov's pancreatic fistula the pancreatic juice secreted on a meat diet seemingly possessed more trypsin and why it was discharged by the gland in an active form as compared to the juice secreted in response to a bread-milk diet. However, Pavlov's theory in its original form cannot be accepted at the present time. We know now that all three enzymes of the pancreatic juice are secreted by the pancreas of the dog and cat under all normal circumstances in a parallel fashion. The more trypsin there is in the pancreatic secretion, the richer it is in lipase and amylase and vice versa.

KATABOLIC AND ANABOLIC NERVES

Each epoch, with its dominant scientific ideas, is always reflected to some degree in the general conceptions of a particular scientist. And Pavlov did not escape the influence of the scientific ideas which were current in his time.

Presumably influenced by Gaskell's work, he labeled the secretory nerves "katabolic" and the trophic nerves "anabolic." But he did not elaborate on these definitions and did not discuss the controversy which existed in the physiological literature of the eighties and nineties of the last century. Speaking of the innervation of the salivary glands, Pavlov mentioned only briefly that one type of the glandular nerve received the name "secretory" or "katabolic" nerve and that the "trophic" nerve had also been termed an "anabolic" nerve (Pavlov, 1902, p. 46).

It is also possible that Pavlov ascribed to the glandular nerves an anabolic function because he (Pavlov, 1888, 1890) and his student Verkhovski (1890) thought that in the submaxillary gland there was a synthesis of the protein material going on during the secretion evoked by stimulation of chorda tympani (see Babkin, 1944, p. 15). Although the chorda tympani contained, according to Heidenhain, chiefly secretory fibers, it still carried a certain number of trophic fibers which Pavlov considered anabolic.

Gaskell (1887) tried to draw an analogy between the heart nerves and the nerves of the salivary glands, and, according to him, the effect of the two heart nerves was exactly the opposite. Stimulation of the sympathetic nerve increased the activity of the heart, which increase was followed by its exhaustion. This was a definite sign of katabolic action of the nerve. On the other hand, stimulation of the vagus nerve diminished the activity of the organ, and this was followed by repair of function. This was a symptom of anabolic action.

Gaskell's (1887, p. 51) explanation of the effect of Heidenhain's trophic nerves in the salivary glands was as follows: These nerves did not necessarily produce constructive changes in the gland but did make some alterations which were responsible for the formation of some constituents of the secretion from the protoplasm of the glandular cells. Thus, these nerves produced katabolism rather than anabolism of the protoplasm. "It would be better, therefore," Gaskell concluded, "to call such nerves 'katabolic' rather than 'trophic.'"

But this statement seems to have been based on a misunderstanding. Heidenhain spoke of the conversion of unsoluble organic material which was deposited in the form of granules into soluble material under the influence of the trophic nerves. He did not speak, as did Gaskell, about "the formation of the essential constituents of the gland secretion from the protoplasm of the gland," under the influence of the glandular nerves. Heidenhain (1878) was convinced that the mass of the zymogene granules was formed during the rest period of the gland and not during its activity. The granular material was formed from the protoplasm of the gland, hence the "katabolism" in the gland in Gaskell's sense went on without much participation of the nervous system, which was contrary to Gaskell's theory.

Gaskell ascribed the anabolic effect to the secretory nerves. He based this conclusion on Langley's (1886) work on paralytic salivary secretion. According to Langley, the growth of the protoplasm in the gland cells did not take place when a trophic nerve was stimulated, e.g., the sympathetic nerve to the parotid gland, but when the gland received its impulses from the cerebral (parasympathetic) nerve. In the cerebral nerve, which was predominantly secretory, two sets of nerve fibers must be discriminated, according to Langley: one was "secretory" (through it the impulses for discharge of water and granules reached the gland); the other was "anabolic" (this set was in charge of the building of protoplasm).

Gaskell thought that anabolism excluded katabolism and vice versa, an idea which was similar to Hering's (1889) theory of assimilation and dissimilation—processes which were antagonistic to each other. Langley (1900, p. 674) was opposed to Gaskell's theory. He did not think it probable that anabolism interfered with, or, indeed, arrested, katabolism, because during secretion in most of the glands both processes were going on actively at the same time.

Probably the restoration of the granular material lost during secretion goes on independently of the nervous system. Anrep and Khan (1924) demonstrated that the return to normal of the mucin content in the saliva of the submaxillary gland, exhausted by prolonged stimulation, was not at all affected by the antropinization of the animal or by extirpation of the superior cervical sympathetic ganglion.

All these facts and considerations make one very reluctant indeed to accept the theory of katabolic and anabolic nerves in its original form. In that sense, Barcroft (1934, p. 268) is most outspoken. He said:

The theory of anabolic and katabolic nerves seems to have died a natural death. . . . The modern view does not present metabolism as a process which divides itself into anabolism and katabolism. It is natural, therefore, that the theory of antagonistic nerves should cease to be of interest from the old standpoint, namely, that of its being the key to the essential process of living matter. Yet, if the antagonism of nervous action has been dethroned from its former high estate, the fact of its existence remains.

CHAPTER TWENTY-FIVE

Secretory Inhibitory Nerves

TO PAVLOV must go the credit for the discovery of the secretory (vagus) nerves of the stomach and the pancreas (vagus and splanchnic), the existence of which has now been firmly established. This discovery will always provoke admiration for the deep understanding which this great physiologist had of the whole problem of innervation and for his experimental skill.

But Pavlov also introduced another conception of the innervation of glands: he claimed that besides the secretory nerve fibers the gastric and the pancreatic glands were supplied with nerve fibers which were able to inhibit the secretion of these glands. He called these "secretory-inhibitory" nerves in contradistinction to "secretory-excitatory" nerves. However, this theory regarding them is open to criticism. Whereas the existence of secretory-excitatory nerves to the stomach and pancreas is easily demonstrated, the proofs Pavlov gave in support of the theory that the vagus nerve contained secretory-inhibitory fibers and that their stimulation might arrest—under certain circumstances—the gastric and the pancreatic secretions independently of any vascular effect are doubtful.

Let us begin with the gastric glands.

According to Pavlov, the chief evidence that the vagus carried secretory-inhibitory as well as the secretory fibers to the gastric glands (Pavlov, 1902, p. 555) was the fact that in acute experiments there existed an extremely long latent period of gastric secretion in response to faradization of vagi nerves. Pavlov's pupil Oushakov, who performed these experiments on dogs which had had their spinal cords cut below the medulla and were under conditions of artificial respiration, noted that the latent period for gastric secretion lasted, in most of his experiments, from 45 to 60 minutes. Very rarely was the period as short as 15 or 20 minutes, and only in some experiments did it last for $1\frac{1}{2}$ hours.

Since the vagus nerve did not supply the stomach with vaso-constrictor fibers and since special stimulation not affecting the vasomotors, such as Heidenhain's tetanomotor (Pavlov, 1902, p. 60), did not shorten the latent period, Pavlov came to the conclusion that the exceedingly long latent period must be due to the presence in the vagus nerve of special secretory-inhibitory fibers for the gastric glands. When the vagi were stimulated rhythmically with an induction current, both the secretory and secretory-inhibitory fibers were excited. The latter, being more excitable than the former, dominated the picture and suppressed, for a while, the gastric secretion. However, they gradually lost their excitability, and the secretory fibers were able to act on the gastric glands without hindrance.

Pavlov wrote in 1902 (p. 55): "We are forced to conclude that in artificially stimulating the vagus, both exciting as well as restraining impulses are transmitted to the glands. This view would find its simplest expression in a hypothesis which assumes the presence of inhibitory nerves acting in antagonism to the secretory, in a manner similar to what we know exists in the innervation of the heart, the vessels, and other organs."

It is well known that the gastric secretion in normal dogs with a permanent gastric fistula or a pouch and in man may be easily inhibited by painful stimulation or certain emotional states. However, this kind of inhibition is little concerned with the action of the secretory-inhibitory nerves and is best explained by the constriction of gastric blood vessels due to excitation of the sympatho-adrenal system.

The extremely long latent period of gastric secretion in the Pavlov-Oushakov experiments thus may be explained without recourse to the secretory-inhibitory vagal fibers. The experimenters believed that immobilization by cord section excluded all the inhibitory influences on the gastric glands. As a matter of fact, division of the spinal cord below the medulla was, as we now see, a very unfavorable condition for the secretory action of the vagus nerve on the gastric glands.

Browne and Vineberg (1932) demonstrated in dogs that stimulation of the vagus nerves with a faradic current produced a secretory effect only if the CO_2 content of plasma did not fall below the critical level (30 vol. per cent), the gastric secretion induced by vagal stimulation greatly diminished or stopped altogether. Admixture to the respiratory air of CO_2 restored the gastric secretion. All of Oushakov's animals were under artificial respiration for hours and undoubtedly were in a state of acapnia, the magnitude of which, of course, was never determined.

The pancreatic gland, according to Pavlov, was, like the gastric glands, also supplied with two types of nerve fibers—secretory and secretory-inhibitory (Pavlov, 1902, pp. 57 ff.). But he and his pupils brought forward more evidence in favor of the presence in the vagi of special secretory-inhibitory nerve fibers for the pancreas than for the gastric glands. Here are the most important facts: a long latent period of pancreatic secretion in response to stimulation of vagi with induction current; the gradual increase of the volume of pancreatic secretion through repeated stimulation of the vagi; at the beginning of the experiment the flow of pancreatic juice occurs during the first few stimulations of vagus nerve only as an aftereffect, i.e., after the cessation of stimulation, while during the actual period of faradization there is inhibition of the secretion; arrest of the pancreatic secretion resulting from faradization of one vagus occurs when the induction current is applied to the other vagus, which has not yet been stimulated; the existence of a special, purely inhibitory branch of the vagus.

After the work of Anrep in 1915 and 1916, and later of Korovitzky in 1923, as well as of Crittenden and Ivy (1937), who demonstrated that the vagus is also a motor nerve for the pancreatic ducts, it became doubtful whether all the phenomena enumerated above were due to the action of secretory-inhibitory nerves. Anyhow, some of them could be more easily explained by contraction and relaxation of the pancreatic ducts under the influence of special and, it seems, more excitable motor fibers in the vagus than as a result of stimulation of the secretory-inhibitory nerves.

The theory of secretory-inhibitory nerves, however, need not be forgotten forever. There still appear from time to time observations which indicate that the external secretory function of the pancreas may be inhibited through the vagi or splanchnic nerves without concomitant changes in the blood supply of the gland. Thus, La Barre and Destree (1928), using the method of cross-circulation in two dogs, found that the pancreatic secretion was inhibited in the recipient, the blood in whose body had a normal concentration of sugar but in whose head a hypoglycemia was established by administration of insulin or decamethylene-diguanidine to the donor. Section of both vagi abolished this effect. Dr. Baxter (1932) demonstrated that insulin hypoglycemia caused a diminution of the output of enzymes by the spontaneously secreting pancreatic gland of a rabbit, very often independently of the changes in the rate of the pancreatic secretion. This "negative trophic," or, better, "negative ecbolic," effect was transmitted through the vagi nerves.

Harper and Vass (1941) thought that the splanchnic nerves contained fibers inhibitory to the acinous cells of cat pancreas. On stimulation of the splanchnic nerve, they noted the diminution of the secretion and of the concentration and minute output of pancreatic amylase. The fall in enzyme concentration was observed when the rate of the secretion was kept constant by injection of secretin. Tanturi and Ivy (1938) believed that true inhibitory-secretory fibers were also contained in vagi nerves for the liver. Thus the problem of the secretory-inhibitory nerves for the digestive glands is not yet solved and deserves further study.

The theory of the secretory-inhibitory nerves was another expression of Pavlov's belief in a certain general plan of organization of the animal body according to which every organ possessed a double antagonistic innervation. Speaking of the nature of the secretory-inhibitory nerves as genuinely inhibitory and antagonistic to the secretory nerves, Pavlov (1902, p. 59) said: "But when it has been proved beyond doubt for several organs that the nerves which regulate them belong to two opposite groups, the same may be rightly assumed for the glands. It is quite possible that an antagonism of this nature belongs to the general principles of innervation."

Such ideas were current in the epoch when Pavlov worked on the problem of the innervation of the digestive glands, i.e., in the eightiest and nineties of the last century. Thus, for example, Gaskell (1887), who had done so much for the understanding of the organization of the autonomic nervous system and particularly on the innervation of the heart, wrote, "The evidence is becoming daily stronger than ever that every tissue is innervated by two sets of nerve fibres of opposite characters, so that I look forward hopefully to the time when the whole nervous system shall be mapped out into two great districts of which the function of the one is katabolic, of the other anabolic, to the peripheral tissues" (p. 50).

However, as we now know, things are not so simple as Gaskell believed.

To the very end of his life, Pavlov firmly believed in the existence of secretory-inhibitory nerves for the gastric and pancreatic glands. When, in 1930, I wrote to him about the experiments of Baxter, whose paper was published in 1932 and who worked in my laboratory on the effect of hypo- and hyperglycemia on the pancreatic secretion in rabbits and demonstrated the existence of "trophic inhibitory" vagal influence on the pancreas, he answered me: "Your experiments with the pancreatic secretion in the rabbit interest me very much. On my part I never doubted the existence of genuine inhibitory nerves for the gastric as well as for the pancreatic secretion, in spite of Anrep's experiments" (he wrote this letter on December 24, 1930).

PURPOSIVENESS OF THE PHYSIOLOGICAL FUNCTIONS

The idea of purposiveness (in Russian, *tselesoobraznost;* in German, *Zweckmässigkeit*) of functions of the bodily organs is very old, and at the beginning was based on a teleological conception of life. Pavlov, who often spoke about it, held to something quite different. He never believed in a special plan of creation or in the theory which said that the structure and function of any organ was developed for the purpose which an organ might serve. Under "purposiveness" Pavlov understood an adaptation of bodily functions to the needs of the organism. In the special cases of the secretory work of the disgestive glands, "purposiveness" was for Pavlov another expression of his belief in the specific excitability of the alimentary canal, which determined the special response of each digestive gland to various types of stimuli. Pavlov's argument could be presented as follows: The definite and exact reaction of the secretory apparatus of the gastrointestinal tract to the type of stimulus acting on its mucous membrane was not created at once, as comparative physiology showed us. Endless generations of animals struggled, perished, or survived, until the more resistant forms were able to withstand the merciless impact of the surrounding medium in which they lived. As a result, there was an "adaptation," in the Darwinian sense of the word, of an animal or, in our particular case, of its digestive functions to the conditions of life.

It is not a mere coincidence that in the eleventh edition of the *Encyclopaedia Britannica* (**26**:542, 1911) the word "teleology" is explained in the following way: "The term is applied to the doctrine that the universe as a whole has been planned on a definite design, or, at least, it tends towards some end." And, further, "the modern theory of evolution . . . has reintroduced a scientific teleology of another type. Teleology, in this narrow sense, as the study of the adaptation of organic structure to the service of the organisms in which they occur, was completely revolutionized by Darwinism and the research founded on it." Undoubtedly, in the epoch in which Pavlov worked, the term "purposiveness" was understood quite differently from Aristotle's "final causes" or the medieval theistic conception "which postulates God as the Creator, omniscient and all-good."

The specific excitability of the alimentary canal, first clearly demonstrated by Pavlov and understood by him as a fine adaptation of one of the fundamental functions of the body to its needs, naturally roused in him great admiration. It was, therefore, while studying the digestive glands, that he spoke so often about "purposiveness." We find "purposiveness" spoken of in many pages of his *Lectures*. Here are a few quotations:

It appears to me that the facts here given lend strong support to our previous conclusions, that the variations in secretion which occur during the progress of a digestion period must have some essential meaning. When, for example, a characteristic curve of secretion is peculiar to every single kind of food, surely this must have a definite aim [in the 2d ed., p. 38–"purpose"] and possess a special significance [Pavlov, 1902, p. 35].

. . . the work of the digestive glands is, if I may say so, elastic to a high degree, while it is at the same time, characteristic, precise, and purposive. It is to be regretted that till now the *rationale* of the latter feature had remained a field of investigation but little touched upon [*ibid.*, p. 36].

At the beginning of the third of the *Lectures* (1902, p. 45), Pavlov declared that "the gastric and pancreatic glands have what we may call a form of instinct." In the original Russian text (p. 56)

Pavlov expressed this idea even more forcibly, saying that the glands "seem to possess a mind." The use of such expressions could easily give the reader the impression that Pavlov had a teleological conception of life. However, such a hasty conclusion would be utterly unjustified. Here is, in his own words, Pavlov's definition of "purposiveness" (see chap. 23):

> The utmost importance is to be attached to the fact that only the peripheral endings of centripetal (afferent) nerves, in contrast to nerve fibres themselves, respond to specific stimuli; that is to say, are able to transform definite kinds of external stimuli into nervous impulses. The function of the end organs with which they are connected is therefore of a purposive nature; in other words, these organs are only called into play by certain definite conditions, and impart the idea of being aware of their purpose, of being conscious of their duty [Pavlov, 1902, p. 63].

It was typical of Pavlov's style to begin his *Lectures* on the "Work of the Digestive Glands" by comparing the digestive canal to a chemical factory. (Perhaps that is why he entitled it the "*Work of the Digestive Glands.*") Again, in his address entitled, "Experiment: The Only Adequate Method for Present-Day Medical Research" (included in the Thompson edition of Pavlov), he recommended research in experimental therapeutics and boldly compared the animal body to a man-made machine (Pavlov, 1902, p. 174).

Much later, in 1903, speaking in Madrid for the first time about conditioned reflexes, Pavlov (1928, p. 49) again touched on the problem of adaptation. He defined it as the "exact co-ordination of the elements of a complicated system, and of their complexes, with the outer world." He could not see in this respect any difference between the inanimate, e.g., chemical, system and a living organism; for their existence both must be maintained on an equilibrium between their parts and between the whole body and the outer world. He said that the words "adaptation" and "fitness," in spite of Darwin's work, still continued to denote a certain subjectiveness. Those who looked on living organisms from a "physico-mechanical" point of view "see in these words an anti-scientific tendency— a retreat from pure objectiveness to speculation and teleology." Of course it was not so, because the study in the dog of the higher nervous activity, usually called "psychic," which he, as a physiologist, planned to investigate would be conducted strictly objectively, as any other physiological investigation.

It is interesting to note that almost forty years after Pavlov wrote his *Lectures*, a very distinguished physiologist, J. Barcroft, devoted the last chapter of his book, *Features in the Architecture of Physiological Function* (1934), to the question: Could a significance be ascribed to every phenomenon? (Chap. xv has as title: "The Chance that a Phenomenon Has a Significance," pp. 334 ff.) Barcroft asked himself:

> Were it conceded that every phenomenon has a significance, would it be a proof of teleology—in other words, were it clear that everything had a function, would it mean that everything had a purpose? The answer, surely, is "no." I have heard L. J. Henderson use some such phrase as that "the mill of evolution very soon grinds out anything which does not justify its existence." That is not teleology in the ordinary sense, it is something quite different from the conception that every part of the body had been made "just so" as part of an intelligent design [p. 356].

Undoubtedly Barcroft spoke the same language as Pavlov but wisely avoided the dangerous word "purposive," which, as was shown above, has two different meanings which exclude each other.

On the other hand, W. B. Cannon, in his last book, *The Way of an Investigator* (1945), spoke freely about the teleological conception of bodily functions: "The view that there are organic adjustments which promote bodily welfare and consequently are useful," said Cannon, "involves the conception that these activities are *directed*, i.e., that the parts operate *teleologically* for the good of the entire group of parts that constitute the organism . . . the various stages in the response that lead to the consequences may then be looked upon as *purposive*" (p. 108). But, of course, Cannon looked on all these reactions in an organism as adaptive arrangements favorable to survival in the struggle for existence, and certainly he never considered the fact that the bodily reactions involved an "intelligent foresight working towards a predetermined end" (p. 112). Whereas the approach of Pavlov, Barcroft, and Cannon to the interpretation of complex physiological phenomena is perfectly justifiable, it is very doubtful whether the use of words which for centuries have had a different meaning from the one they acquired

[255]

comparatively recently was desirable. It would be better to coin new words for new ideas.

Blondlot's Influence on Pavlov

Although Pavlov undoubtedly was familiar with Beaumont's (1833) classical work on gastric digestion on Alexis St. Martin, it influenced him less than Blondlot's experimental investigation. This was partly due to the fact that some of Beaumont's startling observations and conclusions had become firmly established in science and did not rouse any doubt in the mind of physiologists and medical men (thus, e.g., that in the gastric juice there was present hydrochloric acid or that the digestive power of the gastric juice was due not to the acid alone but to something else present in the secretion and known since Schwann's [1836] time, namely, pepsin, etc.). One must not forget also that between the publication of Beaumont's *Experiments and Observations on the Gastric Juice and the Physiology of Digestion* in 1833 and the time Pavlov began to work on the function of the digestive glands, more than half a century had elapsed. New and fundamental facts were established in the physiology of digestion during this period, and quite different theoretical conceptions now directed the thoughts of scientists as compared to those in use in Beaumont's time. (The influence of Beaumont's work on the medical thought of his contemporaries is discussed by Rosen, 1942.)

We have seen in chapter 23 that Pavlov highly valued Blondlot's work on gastric secretion and recognized that Blondlot spoke definitely of the importance of the act of taking food and of the specific excitability of the gastric mucosa.

Here are, in brief, Blondlot's observations on dogs with gastric fistula, confirmed experimentally by Pavlov, further elaborated by him, and often explained on the basis of new theoretical conceptions:

The secretion of the gastric juice in dogs was intermittent. No gastric juice was produced between meals, but only a small amount of mucus, slightly acid, or neutral, or alkaline (Blondlot, 1843, pp. 206–7 and 454–55). Blondlot could leave the gastric fistula open for hours and only a small amount of more or less thick mucus flowed out (p. 207).

If a solid food (meat or bones) was given a dog, the flow of gastric juice began in 10–15 minutes. A certain time also passed before the secretion started when food was introduced directly into the stomach through the fistula. The volume of secretion was less in this case than after ingestion of food through the mouth (p. 210).

The mechanical stimulation of the gastric mucous membrane by introduction through the fistula of pebbles, pieces of wood, or an elastic tube did not stimulate the secretion of acid gastric juice. When Blondlot energetically moved the elastic tube inside the stomach, only a certain amount of thick and viscous mucus appeared (pp. 211–14).

Irritation—undoubtedly local—of the gastric mucosa with small amounts of chemical substances, such as sodium chloride, potassium carbonate, pepper, presumably *in substantia,* etc., evoked a production of slightly acid mucoid fluid (p. 213).

The food substances were true stimulants of acid gastric secretion. After ingestion of food, the gastric mucosa, pale and covered with a thin film of mucus before that, became turgid and red and produced gastric juice. In this state, the mechanical and especially the chemical stimulation of the mucosa increased the volume of gastric secretion (pp. 216–20). For the mechanical stimulation of the mucous membrane, Blondlot used an elastic rubber tube which he introduced through the fistula. Under these circumstances, was there not a better drainage of gastric juice rather than a stimulation of its production? The chemical substances, e.g., sodium chloride, sodium and potassium bicarbonate, sugar, or pepper, were rolled into pieces of meat and given by Blondlot to his dogs to eat. Undoubtedly some of these substances, as for instance sodium chloride or sodium bicarbonate in hypertonic concentrations, stimulated the gastric secretion. This was demonstrated by Lönnquist (1906) in Pavlov's laboratory.

It is significant of the fine capacity of observation possessed by Blondlot that he noted the inhibitory effect of acid on gastric secretion. He wrote cautiously that "it seems" that acids slow the gastric secretion (p. 219). The inhibitory effect on gastric secretion of 0.5 per cent hydrochloric acid, acting on the gastric mucosa, was first established in Pavlov's laboratory by Sokolov (see Pavlov, 1910, p. 115, and Babkin, 1928, p. 270).

According to Blondlot, two modes of stimulation of gastric secretion were supposed to exist: one through the action of palatable food substances on the organ of test, i.e., it was connected with the act of eating; and the other when food was introduced directly into the stomach (pp. 221–24). This corresponded to Pavlov's first, or nervous, and second, or chemical, phases of gastric secretion. Blondlot compared the reaction of the gastric glands in the first case with the secretory reaction of the salivary glands. Stimulation of the gustatory nerves of the mouth cavity by food evoked in sympathy (*sympathiquement*) the activity of the gastric mucous membrane.

The volume of gastric secretion depended on the nature and quantity of food ingested. The more food Blondlot gave to his dogs, the more gastric juice they secreted (pp. 224–26). The importance of investigation of different foodstuffs as stimulants of gastric secretion was emphasized by Heidenhain (1879) and was recognized by Pavlov (1902, p. 111). However, only in Pavlov's laboratory was this subject studied systematically in qualitative as well as in quantitative aspects on dogs with innervated, i.e., Pavlov, pouch (cf. Pavlov, 1902, pp. 20 ff.).

Blondlot had several other sound ideas, one of them being that the gastric juice which contains a "special substance" (pepsin) digested only the protein material but did not affect carbohydrates and fats (pp. 254–93, 456–58). Another was that acid chyme stimulates the secretion of the pancreatic juice (p. 461) and that the alkaline pancreatic juice neutralized the acid gastric juice, but only at a certain distance from the stomach, where the intestinal chyme became slightly alkaline (p. 464).

In his explanation of the processes which took place in the digestive tract, Blondlot held a strictly mechanistic point of view. "The physical and chemical forces are the only ones which participate in digestion . . . ," he said (p. 466). The "vital forces" do not take any direct part in it. Blondlot compared the processes going on in the alimentary canal with the processes employed in a chemical laboratory, an analogy reminding one of Pavlov's comparison of the alimentary canal with a chemical factory (Pavlov, 1902, p. 2).

There was much in common between the sincere enthusiasm Blondlot and Pavlov had for their subject and in the admiration they had for the perfection and fine adjustment of the bodily functions. They both were especially struck by the ability of the alimentary canal to respond with different secretory reactions to various stimuli, which they ascribed to the specific excitability of the gastrointestinal mucosa. Blondlot expressed in the following poignant sentence his leading idea: "Il faut donc admettre que l'estomac est doué d'une sensibilité particulière, d'une véritable intuition chimique, qui, ainsi que nous l'avont dit, lui permet d'apprécier la nature nutritive des substances mises en contact avec ses parois" (p. 221). How these words remind one of Pavlov's definition of the work of the gastric and pancreatic glands! He wrote, fifty-four years after Blondlot: "It is evident that the gastric and pancreatic glands have what we may call a form of instinct" (Pavlov, 1902, p. 45).

This short review of Blondlot's achievements shows what a sharp observer he was and what sound opinions he had. His points of view in many instances coincided with those of Pavlov. Does that mean that Pavlov simply borrowed Blondlot's ideas and repeated his experiments, using more adequate and more modern methods of investigation? Certainly not! Undoubtedly, Blondlot's work influenced Pavlov, and the Russian scientist himself admitted it. But Pavlov's experiments and his thoughts developed independently of the conceptions of his predecessor. Moreover, and this is a point of paramount importance, Pavlov always based his conclusions on facts. Blondlot, on the other hand, quite often speculated and theorized, having at his disposal but few data and these not well controlled.

To this must be added that some of Blondlot's statements were absolutely erroneous. For example, he thought that the gastric juice owed its acidity to acid calcium phosphate (p. 456), although already in 1824 Prout had shown the presence of hydrochloric acid. Blondlot's immediate predecessor in the study of gastric functions, Beaumont, fully agreed with the analyses of Professors Dunglinson of the University of Virginia and Sullivan of Yale, to whom he had sent samples of really pure human gastric juice, that the acidity was due to hydrochloric acid (Beaumont, 1833, p. 79). Blondlot turned a deaf ear to this valuable piece of information.

Blondlot also did not believe that pepsin, discovered by Schwann in 1836 in the gastric mucous membrane, was present in the gastric juice (pp. 369–75). Nevertheless, he ascribed peptic properties to the gastric juice and thought that they were due to "un principe organique particulier" which was very alterable and which seemed to be "a kind of mucous substance in a certain state of modification" (p. 456).

Again, Blondlot had no evidence whatever to back up his claim that acid stimulated the pancreatic secretion. His was mere speculation and a conclusion by analogy. He noted that acid inhibited and alkali increased the gastric secretion; and of course he knew that any acid fluid, e.g., vinegar, stimulated the flow of saliva. From this he deduced a general rule, that the alkaline substances stimulated the secretion of acid digestive juices and that acid substances evoked the secretion of the alkaline juices: "contraria contrariis excitantur" (p. 220). They inhibited the production of the corresponding secretions in reverse order (p. 202). Now we know that the alkalies stimulate the salivary secretion and, under certain circumstances, inhibit the gastric secretion.

Several other examples might be given of such vague speculations of Blondlot. The conclusion is that very many of his statements were not justified by his experimental data, though sometimes he guessed correctly.

The Blondlot-Pavlov case is a good example of how the work of one serious and honest investigator may influence the work of his successors. Every scientist is a product of his epoch. He may foresee the further development of his science, and some geniuses indeed do divine it, but hardly anyone can predict with accuracy the actual achievements of those who will follow him half a century later.

There is no need to say that Heidenhain, under whom Pavlov worked in 1877 and in 1884, greatly influenced him. This Pavlov recognized himself. Thus, Pavlov's idea of obtaining an innervated gastric pouch grew from Heidenhain's method of pouch preparation; the theory of secretory and trophic nerves of Heidenhain became the basis of Pavlov's theoretical conceptions concerning the mode of action of the nerves on the glands; the idea of studying the secretory response of the gastric glands by giving different kinds of food to the animals also belonged to Heidenhain, and so on.

CHAPTER TWENTY-SIX

Pavlov's Contribution to the Physiology and Pathology of the Gastrointestinal Tract

IN ORDER to appreciate the originality, novelty, and importance of the work which Pavlov and his pupil-associates did in the field of gastroenterology, it would be interesting to compare physiology textbooks on the subject of the digestive glands which were published a few years earlier (i.e., before 1897–98) with Pavlov's *Lectures*. Space does not permit us to make this instructive comparison; only a brief summary of Pavlov's achievements can be presented in this chapter.

SALIVARY GLANDS

Pavlov replaced the theory of the general excitability of the mucous membrane of the tongue and of the mouth cavity by its specific excitability. He demonstrated that in the dog the secretion of the salivary glands varied both quantitatively and qualitatively in accordance with the nature and strength of the stimulus acting on the mucosa of the mouth.

Although the reaction of the tongue and buccal mucosa test organs to different chemical and mechanical stimulants was known long before Pavlov, it was not connected in any way with the secretory work of the digestive glands and, in this specific case, with the work of the salivary glands. It was a part of the physiology of organs of sense and seemingly had no relation to the digestive glands. As far as the physiologist was concerned, the salivary glands responded with secretion to any stimulus, as if the mouth mucosa possessed a general excitability only! Pavlov replaced this crude conception with a picture based on indisputable facts, that

[261]

of different quantitative and qualitative work of the salivary glands in response to various stimuli.

GASTRIC GLANDS

Especially noteworthy were Pavlov's studies in the physiology of the gastric glands. The chief facts discovered and firmly established by Pavlov and his pupils may be summarized here (see the 1st English ed. of Pavlov's *Lectures* of 1902).

1. It was demonstrated beyond doubt that vagus was the secretory nerve of the gastric glands.

2. It was shown that "psychic" gastric secretion was a fact of extreme importance.

3. A typical course of gastric secretion in response to different food substances—meat, bread, milk—was established.

4. For the first time it was demonstrated that the peptic power of the gastric juice varied with the nature of the food ingested and the phase of gastric secretion.

5. The constancy of the acidity of the gastric juice was demonstrated.

6. The stimulation of gastric secretion by food introduced directly into the stomach was shown to be due not to the mechanical but to the chemical stimulation of the gastric glands.

7. New secretagogue substances, e.g., water and meat extract, were discovered.

8. The ability of starch to stimulate a greater output of pepsin was shown.

9. The inhibitory effect of fat on gastric secretion was established.

10. The three phases of gastric secretion—the nervous, the pyloric, and the intestinal—were disclosed.

To this imposing list of new facts related to the functions of the stomach and discovered by Pavlov must be added a new, or, rather, revised, conception of specific excitability; introduction of aseptic surgery into physiology and new experimental procedures for the study of gastric secretion, namely, esophagotomy combined with gastric fistula as well as with the Pavlov gastric pouch; application of a new method of faradization of the partly degenerated nerve to discover one of its functions; and many others. Little wonder that

Pavlov's ideas regarding the secretory function of the stomach produced an extraordinary impression on his contemporaries.

It must be emphasized that the completeness of the picture of the physiology of gastric secretion presented by Pavlov was in a great measure due to the systematic study of all the properties of the gastric juice—its volume, acidity, content of mucus, and peptic power. Unfortunately, this is not always done even by modern investigators.

PANCREATIC GLAND

The following is a summary of the facts obtained by Pavlov and his pupils in respect to the external secretion of the pancreas:

1. Action of the vagus and splanchnic nerves as secretory and secretory-inhibitory nerves of the pancreatic gland was demonstrated.

2. A typical course of pancreatic secretion after ingestion of different food substances—meat, bread, and milk—was described.

3. The variations in the composition of the pancreatic juice secreted in response to different foods were analyzed. Although the original Pavlov-Walther conception of the adaptation of the enzymatic power of the pancreatic juice to the kind of food was erroneous, owing to lack of knowledge of the existence of enterokinase, it still was valid in a modified form. The same was true of the adaptation of the pancreatic secretion to different alimentary regimes (see chap. 24 of this book, as well as Babkin, 1928, p. 497).

4. Stimulants of pancreatic secretion were discovered—acid, fat, and water.

5. Localization of the surface of the alimentary canal was found from which acid and fat acted as pancreatic stimulants, i.e., the duodenum and upper part of the jejunum.

6. The inhibition of pancreatic secretion by alkali was established.

7. Weak "psychic" secretion of the pancreatic juice was described.

For the reader of Pavlov's *Lectures* the following were new: the methods of operation of permanent pancreatic fistula; methods of stimulation of partly degenerated vagus and splanchnic nerves to demonstrate that they were secretory nerves of the pancreas; a special technique of "acute" experiments, which consisted in the section of the spinal cord below the medulla, by means of which the "inhibitory" influences on pancreas were eliminated. (In all probability, these "inhibitory" influences were nothing other than vasoconstriction of abdominal blood vessels [see the work of Edmunds and of Babkin in Babkin, 1928, pp. 624 ff.].)

DISCHARGE OF BILE INTO THE DUODENUM

The following facts were obtained by Pavlov and his pupils regarding dogs with permanent fistula of the common bile duct:

In fasting animals there was no discharge of bile from the common bile duct, except during the periods of hunger contractions. After a meal of meat, bread, or milk, the discharge of bile began following a rather long latent period which was different for each sort of food and had a course similar to the course of the pancreatic secretion. The investigation of the effect of the constituents of the three food substances on the discharge of bile showed that it was not evoked by water, acid, or egg white. The real stimulants of the discharge of bile were the products of protein digestion, possibly extractive substances of meat, and especially fat in all its forms. Pavlov considered that the chief role of bile was to activate the lipase of the pancreatic juice and to inhibit peptic digestion by neutralizing the hydrochloric acid of the gastric juice and precipitating the pepsin.

INTESTINAL JUICE

The importance of succus entericus as a digestive reagent became evident after Shepovalnikov discovered in Pavlov's laboratory an enzyme of a new type—enterokinase.

Enterokinase does not act on any substrate in the food, but it activates the inactive protrypsin of the pancreatic juice into active trypsin. Therefore, Pavlov called enterokinase a "ferment of a ferment." The search for enterokinase was initiated by a successful investigation of bile as an activator of pancreatic lipase. Pavlov asked himself: Would not intestinal juice, like bile, also help some of the enzymatic functions of the pancreatic juice? The discovery of enterokinase was the brilliant answer to this question.

Another of his pupils, Savich, demonstrated that the specific stimulant of enterokinase production was the trypsin of the pancreatic juice (Pavlov, 1902, p. 160). The mechanism by which the pancreatic juice, which comes into contact with the intestinal mucous membrane, increases the concentration of enterokinase in the intestinal juice is still not at all clear.

MOTILITY OF THE GASTROINTESTINAL TRACT

Another group of facts which was discussed by Pavlov in the last lecture of his book—the ninth lecture, which was actually an address delivered in 1899 before the Society of Russian Physicians in St. Petersburg—was the motility of the gastrointestinal tract (Pavlov, 1902, pp. 163 ff.). Here, as everywhere else, Pavlov approached the problem from a different angle than most investigators. He was not interested in the type of movements which the stomach or the intestine performed or in the nerves which regulated the motility of the alimentary canal. His chief interest was directed toward the following problem:

Why was the progress of various foods along the gastrointestinal tract different, and what role was played by the food substances and their products of digestion, and what role did different secretions play in the regulation of the gastrointestinal motility? "The synthesis of the actual progress [of food masses] and the mechanism of the movements have been, until recently, as little brought under investigation as had the synthesis of the secretory work of the digestive apparatus," Pavlov said (1902, p. 164).

Pavlov with his student Serdukov proved the existence of the so-called "acid reflex control of the pylorus." His experiments showed that the presence of diluted hydrochloric acid in the duodenum greatly delayed the evacuation of a neutral fluid from the stomach. He believed that this was due to the closure of the pyloric sphincter. Besides acid, it was found in Pavlov's laboratory (Lintvarev, 1901) that fat, coming into contact with the duodenal mucosa, also delayed the evacuation of the stomach. By analogy from the effect of acid, it was supposed that fat also evoked a reflex closure of the pyloric sphincter.

Facts observed by Pavlov and his pupils were absolutely correct, but time has brought substantial changes in their interpretation. It was chiefly J. E. Thomas and his co-workers who demonstrated that acid in the duodenum delayed the evacuation of gastric con-

[265]

tents not because there was a spasm of the pyloric sphincter—as a matter of fact the sphincter was now more relaxed than before—but because the whole motility of the stomach itself was substantially slowed down. Thomas (1931) spoke of an "enterogastric reflex." Besides initiating a nervous reflex on the motor apparatus of the stomach, acid, fat, and carbohydrates present in the duodenum probably also stimulate the formation of an inhibitory hormone, "enterogastrone," which depresses the motility of the stomach. The effect of this hormone ocurs even in a transplanted gastric pouch which is deprived of extrinsic innervation.

Also in chapter 9 of his *Lectures* (p. 165), Pavlov described for the first time the periodic movements of the empty stomach (experiments of P. O. Shirokikh), which could be arrested by giving food to the animal or by introducing acid into the stomach. Pavlov thought that the periodic movements appeared "probably as the result of psychic impulse." Somewhat later, this phenomenon was studied very thoroughly and systematically in Pavlov's laboratory by Boldyreff (1904), who established the existence not only of the periodic movements of the stomach but also of the small intestine and the periodic secretion of pancreatic and intestinal juices, as well as the periodic discharge of bile. The American physiologists W. B. Cannon and, especially, A. J. Carlson continued the study of these periodic contractions as they occur in animals as well as in man and named them "hunger contractions."

Experimental Pathology and Experimental Therapeutics

In the same address of 1899 Pavlov emphasized the importance of experimental pathology and experimental therapeutics as methods of physiological investigation.

The observation that an occasional disease in the laboratory animal might lead to gastrointestinal disorders suggested to Pavlov the idea of intentionally inducing pathological disturbances and studying the changed activity of the alimentary canal.

"What," asked Pavlov, "is a pathological condition? Is it not the effect produced upon the organism by the encountering of an unusual condition, or more correctly said, an unusually intensified ordinary condition?" (p. 166).

To re-establish the normal state, the various physiological

mechanisms were called into play. These special activities of the organism might be observed only during an illness; their experimental investigation would permit better understanding of the physiological process which under normal conditions regulated the activity of a diseased organ. "Have we not therefore in this a method which is quite commonly used in physiology for the investigation of the functions of a given organ, a method put into operation by nature with a delicacy which is quite unattainable by our crude technical measures?" (Pavlov, 1902, p. 167).

Only a few experiments in the field of the pathological physiology of the alimentary canal were reported this time by Pavlov. The most interesting were the effects of irritating chemical substances (solutions of sublimate or of silver nitrate, strong emulsion of mustard oil) on the mucosa of the Pavlov pouch. As a result of these measures, a profuse secretion of gastric mucus appeared and developed a state of astenia of the peptic glands. Introduction of ice-cold water or of a solution of silver nitrate into the main stomach depressed the gastric secretion in both the main stomach and the Pavlov pouch, although the noxious agent never came into contact with the mucosa of the latter. Of special interest were the experiments which demonstrated the vicarious properties of the gastric mucous membrane. When the mucosa of the main stomach was damaged by hot water and stopped secreting, the Pavlov pouch began to secrete gastric juice in amounts equal to the whole secretory production of the main stomach when the latter was in a normal state. With the subsiding of the pathological process in the main stomach and gradual restoration of gastric secretion in it, the secretory work of the pouch correspondingly diminished and finally again became only a fraction (usually about one-tenth) of the former .

However, experimental pathology as a method of physiological investigation did not fully satisfy Pavlov. "Are we, as experimenters, however, to rest satisfied with this? I think not," he said, "for no one can say that he fully comprehends the physiology of an organ until he is able to restore its disordered function to a normal state. Hence, experimental therapeutics is essentially a test of physiology" (Pavlov, 1902, pp. 173 ff.).

As an example of experimental therapeutics, Pavlov gave the

facts regarding treatment and care of dogs in which the vagi nerves were divided in the neck (see chap. 22).

Another problem which Pavlov discussed in his *Lectures* was the inhibitory effect of alkali on gastric secretion in normal and pathological conditions (Pavlov, 1902, pp. 95, 145 ff., 175). His feelings on the matter were contrary to the opinion current among medical men at the end of the nineteenth century and contrary to Blondlot's experimental evidence that meat sprinkled with sodium bicarbonate evoked in dogs with gastric fistulas a greater gastric secretion than meat taken alone (Blondlot, 1843, p. 220). The controversy concerning the inhibitory, or stimulatory, effect of alkali on the gastric secretion continued into the present century. Different explanations of the effects of alkali were probably due, as it was demonstrated later in Pavlov's laboratory, to the fact that they act as stimulants from the stomach and as inhibitors from the duodenum (see Babkin, 1928, p. 290). Besides this, after discontinuation of alkali treatment, which diminishes the gastric secretion, there is a "rebound" when the gastric secretion is markedly increased.

Although Pavlov considered the two new lines of investigation—experimental pathology and experimental therapeutics—very important and promising, he never developed them further. His failure to delve into them was rather unexpected. And the reason for it is this: In the first years of the twentieth century his interest began to shift from the physiology of the alimentary canal to investigations of the functions of the cerebral cortex by means of conditioned reflexes. The transition from one field of investigation to the other took some time, although Pavlov's decision to devote the time of his students and his own to the study of the physiology of the cerebral hemispheres was irrevocable. He reached the decision after a long and painful mental struggle. At first the laboratory investigation was conducted in both—physiology of the central nervous system and physiology of digestion; but in a few years, as mentioned previously, Pavlov's interest was centered exclusively on conditioned reflexes.

When all the results achieved by Pavlov in the normal and pathological physiology of the gastrointestinal tract are considered, it becomes evident why he occupied one of the first places in the ranks of physiologists and was the first such scientist ever to receive the Nobel Prize, which he was awarded in 1904.

Even now, Pavlov's *Lectures* in their original form, e.g., the first English edition, makes most absorbing reading. It is not difficult to see how the small book, less than two hundred pages long but full of facts, then new, which were obtained through the medium of a new and brilliant experimental technique and which were bound together with a novel theoretical treatment of the whole subject, fascinated Pavlov's contemporaries. It may be said without exaggeration that Pavlov's work is the foundation on which modern normal and pathological gastroenterology is based. His theoretical conceptions may be replaced, and some have already been replaced by new ones, but most of the facts established by him will remain as a permanent acquisition of science and as a testimony to his genius.[1]

PART IV

Conditioned Reflexes

Introduction

THE last thirty-four years of his life (from 1902 until 1936) Pavlov devoted almost exclusively to the study of the functions of the cerebral cortex by the method of conditioned reflexes.

The fundamental point of Pavlov's teaching was that all nervous activity of such a highly organized animal as a dog, including what is usually called its "psychic activity," is based on reflex action. Thus even the most complicated behavior of a dog is nothing else than a response of the animal to certain stimuli which act on it from outside or from inside its body. This response is effected through the nervous system.

Pavlov discriminated between two kinds of reflexes: unconditioned and conditioned. By an unconditioned reflex he understood a definite nervous, inborn reaction of the organism to a certain external or internal stimulus. Conditioned reflexes were acquired by an animal during life. When the action of an indifferent external or internal phenomenon, which was able to stimulate one of the receptive surfaces of the body, coincided several times with an unconditioned reflex action, it was converted into a conditioned stimulus. A conditioned stimulus reproduced the same response as an unconditioned stimulus; this connection between the conditioned stimulus and a certain activity of the body was temporary.

It is commonly considered that the cerebral cortex is the seat of the psychic activity of an animal and that at the same time it is a part of the central nervous system whose pattern of action, according to Pavlov, as in the rest of the central nervous system, is reflex. Therefore Pavlov excluded all considerations of the subjective states of the animal, to penetrate into which is impossible, and concentrated his efforts on the study of conditioned reactions. Thus he studied with a purely physiological method of conditioned reflexes the physiology of the cerebral cortex. Pavlov regarded his work on conditioned reflexes as his greatest scientific achievement, and it was truly his beloved child.

As we shall see later, Pavlov never denied the right of psychology to study the inner world of man. His aim was to build a physiological basis for psychic phenomena, and he hoped that the time would come when physiology and psychology would coalesce and make one science. Pavlov was convinced that a conditioned reflex is an elementary cortical reaction. On this physiological foundation are built the highest and most refined forms of nervous activity, which permit an animal or a man to establish their most complicated relations with the outer world.

It is only natural that such an approach to the study of the "psychic" phenomena in so highly organized an animal as a dog met with strong objections on the part of many psychologists (see Hilgard and Marquis, 1940), physiologists (Sherrington, 1940; Denny-Brown, 1932–33), psychoanalysts (Masserman, 1943), and others.[1] One may suspect that some of Pavlov's opponents thought that his primary aim was the investigation of the psychic life of the dog, whereas he repeatedly emphasized that his objective was the physiology of the cerebral cortex. However, owing to the fact that the physiological processes in the cortex may be related, and often are, to the "psychic" phenomena, Pavlov believed that he was justified in saying that the study of conditioned reflexes would cover the whole activity of the cortex, including the "psychic" one.

Sight is often lost of the fact that the investigator of natural phenomena, no matter how brilliant his procedures or arduous his efforts, does not invent a particular process but merely exposes it to our view. Pavlov with remarkable clearness and ingenuity brought out certain information on the physiological mechanisms of higher nervous activity. An attempt is made in the following pages to show the relationship of Pavlov's work to that of his predecessors, especially Sechenov and Hughlings Jackson, as well as that of present-day neurophysiological investigators, such as Wilder Penfield.

I intend to discuss briefly the teaching of the conditioned reflexes and to show why Pavlov decided to apply a purely physiological method for the study of "psychic" phenomena in animals; how inevitable this step was on his part, owing to the historical development of the physiology of the central nervous system as well as of the psychology; and what right he had to reject altogether the accepted psychological interpretation of the behavior of such a highly organized animal as a dog and replace it by what he called an objective study of the "higher nervous activity."

CHAPTER TWENTY-SEVEN

Origin of the Conditioned Reflexes

IN THE Preface to the first Russian edition on conditioned reflexes, *Twenty Years of Objective Study of the Higher Nervous
Activity (Behavior) of Animals* (Leningrad, 1922), Pavlov[1] related
how he began his studies of "psychic" phenomena by objective
physiological methods:

> More than twenty years ago I independently began these experiments,
> passing to them from my former physiological work. I entered this
> field under the influence of a powerful laboratory impression. For many
> years previous, I had been working on the digestive glands. I had studied
> carefully and in detail all the conditions of their activity. Naturally I
> could not leave them without considering the so-called psychical stimu-
> lation of the salivary glands, i.e. the flow of saliva in the hungry animal
> or person at the sight of food or during talk about it or even at the
> thought of it. Furthermore, I had demonstrated myself a psychical exci-
> tation of the gastric glands. I began to investigate a psychic secretion
> with my collaborators, Drs. Wolfson and Snarsky. Wolfson collected
> new and important facts for this subject; Snarsky, on the other hand,
> undertook to analyze the internal mechanism of the stimulation from a
> subjective point of view, i.e., he assumed that the internal world of
> the dog—the thoughts, feelings and desires—is analogous to ours. We
> were now brought face to face with a situation which had no prece-
> dent in our laboratory. In our explanation of this internal world we
> diverged along two opposite paths. New experiments did not bring us
> into agreement nor produce conclusive results, in spite of the usual lab-
> oratory custom according to which new experiments undertaken by
> mutual consent are generally decisive. Snarsky clung to his subjective
> explanation of the phenomena, but I, putting aside fantasy and seeing
> the scientific barrenness of such a solution, began to seek for another exit
> from this difficult position. After persistent deliberation after a con-
> siderable mental conflict, I decided finally in regard of the so-called
> psychical stimulation and to maintain the role of a pure physiologist,
> i.e. an objective external observer and experimenter, having to do exclu-
> sively with external phenomena and their relations [Pavlov-Gantt I,
> 1928, p. 37].

The urge to investigate the problem of the psychic secretion of
the salivary and the gastric glands arose in Pavlov long before the

incident with Dr. Snarsky. In the nineties of the nineteenth century, when he studied the secretory activity of the digestive glands, he was struck by the regularity with which a certain type of psychic influence produced a secretory effect upon the gastric glands. By 1897 he could write in his lectures on the *Work of the Digestive Glands* (Thompson's translation of 1902, p. 74):

Consequently, in the sham feeding experiment, by the act of eating the excitation of the nerves of the gastric glands depends upon a psychical factor which has here grown into a physiological one, that is to say, is just as much a matter of course and appears quite as regularly under given conditions as any other physiological result. Considered from the purely physiological view, the process may be said to be a complicated reflex act.

Very gradually a new idea concerning an objective study of the "psychic" phenomena in higher mammalian animals began to crystallize in Pavlov's mind. If a physiologist was able to study with such astounding success all the functions of the animal body, including the physiology of the central nervous system with its subcortical ganglia, why must the functions of the cerebral cortex, which was only a part of the brain, be discussed from a subjective point of view and be investigated by a psychologist instead of a physiologist? That the processes in the cortex were usually coupled with a state of consciousness (a belief which, by the way, has yet to be proved) was not a handicap for the application to their study of the methods of exact science. Pavlov never denied that psychology was a legitimate approach to the understanding of the inner world of man, but he vehemently defended the right of physiology, with its objective methods, to investigate in animals the manifestations of what is ordinarily called the "psychic" life, or, to use a modern term, their "behavior."

In one of his most brilliant orations, in 1909, entitled "Natural Science and the Brain" (Pavlov-Gantt I, 1928, p. 120), Pavlov said:

I should like to elucidate that which might be misunderstood in these statements concerning my views. I do not deny psychology to be a body of knowledge concerning the internal world of man. Even less am I inclined to negate anything which relates to the innermost and deepest strivings of the human spirit. Here and now I only defend and affirm the absolute and unquestionable rights of natural scientific thought everywhere and until the time when and where it is able

[276]

to manifest its own strength, and who knows where its possibilities will end!

Even more definitely in another oration, in 1923 ("The Latest Success of the Objective Study of the Highest Nervous Activity" [Pavlov-Gantt I, 1928, p. 329]), Pavlov fully recognized the rights of psychology to investigate the inner world of man but denied any legitimacy of psychological, i.e., subjective interpretation of the state of mind of animals. He said:

Certainly psychology, insofar as it concerns the subjective state of man, has a natural right to existence, for our subjective world is the first reality with which we are concerned, but though the right of existence of human psychology be granted, there is no reason why we should not question the necessity of animal psychology. Indeed, what means have we to enter into the inner world of the animal! What facts give us the basis for speaking of what and how an animal feels? The word "zoopsychology," it seems to me, is a misnomer, the results of misunderstanding . . . but though zoopsychology as a science is to be condemned, the data which zoopsychologists have collected are worthwhile. These data are derived from a study of the influence of the external world on animals and of their responding reactions.

All this valuable material, concluded Pavlov, must be handed to the physiologist who is studying the functions of the higher sections of the brain. It would be ridiculous to say that Pavlov did not recognize the extraordinary value of the application of subjective methods to the investigation of the physiology and pathology of the organs of sense in man. It is well known that many fundamental facts in the physiology of the organs of sense were obtained by such great physiologists as Helmholtz, Hering, and others with the help of the analysis of their own subjective impressions, which they received by stimulating in one way or another their organs of sense or by collecting corresponding data from the persons on whom they experimented. However, all this, of course, referred to man and not to animals.

Pavlov's protest against the pretenses of psychology to explain the phenomena taking place in the inner world of animals and his defense of the rights of physiology to investigate with the help of physiological methods all the manifestations of the activity of the central nervous system without exception are quite comprehensible. He pointed out that there was no such physiology before 1870 when Fritsch and Hitzig found that stimulation of the front part of the hemispheres in dogs with a weak induction current evoked co-ordinated movements of the limbs. They also found that extirpation of these same parts led to disturbances in the regulation of the normal functioning of the corresponding groups of muscles (Pavlov-Anrep, 1927, p. 1). Although later Ferrier (1876), Munk (1890), and others found that, besides the motor zone discovered by Fritsch and Hitzig, there were other areas of the cortex which had definite relations to some of the organs of sense—eye, ear, skin receptors, and so on—the functions of the cortex were always discussed from the psychological viewpoint. Munk spoke about "psychic blindness" and "psychic deafness"; Goltz (1892), and all those who repeated his experiment with the extirpation of the cerebral cortex in animals, explained the behavior of such animals as a result of "weakness of mind," "destruction of intellect," and so on. No attempt was made to understand the physiological mechanisms, normal or abnormal, which regulated the complex behavior of an animal such as a dog. "The problem of the mechanism of this complex structure [cerebral cortex]," wrote Pavlov, "which is so rich in function, has been hidden away in a corner and this unlimited field, so fertile in possibilities for research, has never been adequately explored" (Pavlov-Anrep, 1927, p. 2).

The transition from the usual psychological mode of thinking about the behavior of such an intelligent animal as a dog to a purely objective physiological mode was not an easy matter with Pavlov. He testified several times how painful were his doubts concerning the legitimacy of the purely physiological study and interpretation of animal behavior. The difficulties were manifold. Quite naturally they arose from the novelty of the physiological approach to the study of "psychic" phenomena, an approach of almost revolutionary character. The main difficulty, however, was chiefly seated in Pavlov himself. For a long time he doubted whether the path of objective study of animal behavior was correct. He questioned whether he did not deceive himself when he tried to explain physiologically the psychological phenomena and whether the study of conditioned reflexes would not lead him into a blind alley from which there would be no exit. The old habit of explaining psychologically the behavior of animals still possessed him strongly. I re-

[278]

member well that during the first years of my work in Pavlov's laboratory (1902–5), when the work on conditioned reflexes was already under way, he would often say that if ever he should have some free time, he would write a psychological study of the dog's characteristics and temperament. So many animals passed through his laboratory and he so closely observed many of them that he was convinced that in their psychological aspect they differed from each other as human beings differ. Pavlov attained his desire, though not until much later, in 1927, and he discussed the types of nervous system, i.e., the temperaments of dogs. However, he then discussed this subject not from a psychological but from a purely physiological point of view, which was based on the study of conditioned reflexes in different types of dogs.

As was pointed out above, the transition from the study of the functions of the digestive tract to the investigation of the "higher nervous activity" was a gradual one. Pavlov's first work on conditioned reflexes in 1901–2 with I. F. Tolochinov was only a "test balloon," so to speak. He wanted to know whether the "psychic" phenomena in the dog could be studied purely physiologically without recourse to psychological interpretations. This first attempt proved to be a success. Already Tolochinov observed facts which were impossible to explain psychologically. Thus, for example, when food was shown to a dog and the conditioned stimulus was not reinforced by giving the animal this food to eat, the salivary reaction gradually diminished and then disappeared altogether. Now the sight or smell of food did not evoke any salivation or positive motor reaction toward the food. However, the conditioned reflex extinguished in that way could be easily restored by giving the dog some of this food to eat. This fact, of course, was very easy to explain from the psychological viewpoint, but how could the restoration of an extinct alimentary conditioned reflex be explained by pouring acid into the mouth of a dog or by giving him mustard oil to smell, both undoubtedly highly unpleasant procedures to the animal? In spite of this "offense" the dog again reacted with positive salivary and motor reaction to the presentation of food.

Tolochinov's pioneer work encouraged Pavlov very much and strengthened his determination to study the "psychic" phenomena in the dog. This change in attitude is reflected in his Madrid oration on "Experimental Psychology and Psychopathology in Animals" in 1903 (Pavlov-Gantt I, 1928, p. 47). Here Pavlov for the first time attempted to give the theoretical foundations of his teaching of conditioned reflexes and the justification of the objective physiological study of the "psychic" phenomena.

It is interesting to note that as late as 1899 Pavlov had not as yet any intention of abandoning the field of gastroenterology. From his address "The Experimental Method—an Indispensable Requirement of Medical Research" (Pavlov, 1902, p. 148) one may gather that he intended to begin a thorough study of the pathology of the gastrointestinal tract. Pavlov wrote: "We shall in the end arrive at a knowledge as accurate and complete of the process of diseases in the alimentary canal as we now possess of its admirably beautiful work under normal conditions" (Pavlov, 1902, p. 173). This was never done, either by him or by anybody else because Pavlov radically changed the course of his scientific work. It is highly interesting to speculate what might have been the outcome if he had pursued his original intention.

Pavlov's abandonment of the physiology of the gastrointestinal tract for the study of conditioned reflexes must not be looked upon as "Serendipity." By this word Cannon (1945, p. 68), who borrowed it from Horace Walpole's fairy tale (1754, "The Three Princes of Serendip"—an ancient name of Ceylon), understood "the happy faculty or luck, of finding unforeseen evidence of one's ideas or, with surprise, coming upon new objects or relations which were not being sought." As we shall see later, the whole history of psychology and of physiology led inevitably to the application of objective scientific methods to the investigation of the functions of all the parts of the brain, including the cerebral hemispheres. Furthermore, the personal spiritual history of Pavlov made him the one who was destined to break this new path in science. Conditioned reflexes were not the result of Pavlov's "faculty of making happy and unexpected discoveries by accident" (definition of "Serendipity" in *Shorter Oxford Dictionary*, 2:1847 [Oxford, 1933]). The incident with Dr. Snarsky only threw a strong light on some conceptions and thoughts which were lying dormant in Pavlov's mind.

The Evolution of Psychology

In spite of their novelty and originality, Pavlov's ideas on conditioned reflexes were only the logical conclusions which could be drawn: they were only the inevitable ideas which could occur in the course of psychological and physiological thinking. The development of psychology and of physiology, especially during the second half of the nineteenth century, was such as to force a mentalistic, introspective interpretation of "psychic" phenomena in man and animals to give way to an interpretation based on objective physiological study. Application of the concept of a reflex in the form of a conditioned reflex to the investigation of these phenomena by Pavlov and his consideration of the "psychic" reactions of an animal as one of the forms of the activity of the central nervous system designated as "higher nervous activity" crowned the thought and work of many generations of investigators.

The history of psychology fully justified Pavlov's attempt to study the "psychic" phenomena in animals from a purely physiological point of view. As a matter of fact, the whole history of psychology shows a slow but continuous retreat under the pressure of natural sciences from pure dualism to monism. Dualism supposes that the soul or mind (which is the seat of consciousness, thought, volition, and feeling) and the body are two separate entities. The conception of dualism, through all kinds of intermediate stages tinged with a spirit of compromise, has been largely replaced by a teaching of monism, by which most psychologists and philosophers understand the doctrine of the identity of mind and body relations. Monism in one of its most modern forms of behaviorism claims that the subject matter of psychology is not the consciousness but the behavior of a human being (Watson, 1930, p. 2).

The Evolution of the Physiology of the Central Nervous System

The history of physiology shows us that to interpret the reaction of the whole central nervous system, including the cerebral cortex, to stimulation as reflex action was a logical result of the development of this science.

[281]

Up to the middle of the nineteenth century and even later the great majority of physiologists definitely discriminated between the physiological and psychological functions of the brain. Thus one of the leading physiologists of the nineteenth century—Pflüger —who studied in 1853 the reflexes in spinal animals, found them to be exact, co-ordinated, and directed to a certain aim (e.g., a "wash reflex" in a spinal frog [see Fig. 6]). He concluded that not only the brain but even the spinal cord possessed a "soul." He wrote: "It is undoubtedly proved that we are dealing with the animal's fragments which feel and will" (p. 129). A modern physiologist now sees in the reactions of spinal animals only complicated co-ordinated reflexes, like the "wash reflex" in the frog, the "scratch" or "stepping" reflex in a dog, and so on.

The same physiological interpretation was applied to the far more complicated reactions of animals in which the higher sections of the central nervous system took part. Thus the "postural" reflexes are considered as inborn involuntary reflexes which are displayed without any participation of consciousness. It is a matter of common knowledge that a cat thrown from a height with its back turned down lands on its feet. This behavior of the animal, which has all the appearance of a conscious purposive reaction, could be reproduced in "thalamic" animals, in which the cerebral hemispheres are separated from the rest of the central nervous system by section above the thalamus. Though the "thalamic" animals (cats, dogs, rabbits) are able to perform very complicated movements, they behave like automatons (Magnus, 1924, p. 210).

ORIENTATION REFLEXES

The optic thalami are not the uppermost point in the central nervous system which is responsible for involuntary reflexes quite independent of any acts of volition or consciousness. The existence of some of the reflexes in man and mammalian animals depends on the integrity of the cerebral cortex. These are the so-called "orientation reflexes" (Beritov, 1937, p. 440). The following examples of such reflexes in man and animals may be mentioned: the turning of the head toward the source of a sudden noise or sound; the turning of the eyes in the direction of an object at the periphery of the visual field; the enlarging of the nostrils and deeper breathing at the onset of an unusual smell, and so on. These reactions are

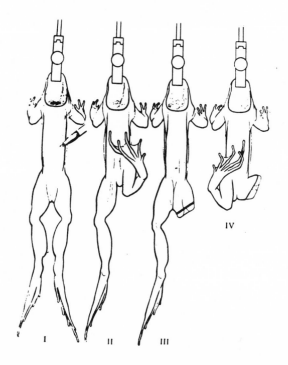

IV

I   II   III

FIG. 6.—"Wash reflex" in a spinal frog. *I*, The back of a frog on the right side is painted with a solution of acetic acid. *II*, "Wash reflex" is performed with the right hind leg. *III*, The amputation of the right femur. *IV*, Stimulation with acid of the same spot on the right side of the back has induced the "wash-reflex" movements of the left leg (Verworn, 1932).

all involuntary and not learned. It requires a certain training in man to inhibit them (which can be done if they are not too strong), as is often required by standards in human society.

The facts presented above have shown us that all parts of the central nervous system, from the spinal cord to the cerebral cortex, are able to respond with very complicated inborn involuntary reactions to definite stimuli. These reactions have all the characteristic features of a reflex in spite of the fact that from the psychological point of view they all are purposive as, for example, the "wash reflex" in the spinal frog, the postural reflex of a cat landing on its feet, or the orientation reflexes in man and mammalian animals.

CEREBRAL CORTEX

Why could not the conception of a reflex, which was so useful in the study of the functions of the lower parts of the central nervous system, be applied to the cerebral hemispheres? It is true that the hemispheres are the higher and phylogenetically more lately developed parts of the brain, which undoubtedly have in man a close relation to his mental capacities; and exactly this latter circumstance, i.e., the belief that the hemispheres are the seat of conscious processes in the brain, was the chief obstacle on the part of physiologists to the use of the conception of a reflex in the discussion of the functions of the cerebral cortex. The habit of psychological interpretation of the more complicated reactions of an animal to his surroundings and of its behavior in general was too strongly implanted (and still is!) in the mind of physiologists. Human motives and feelings were transferred to animals, and their behavior was explained by analogy with human behavior. This situation reminds one of the attitude of a child toward its doll which, in the child's mind, is endowed with exactly the same mental capacities as is the child itself.

The turn from this attitude toward the investigation of the functions of the cerebral hemispheres and the application to its study of the conception of a reflex came independently from two quarters, from the Russian physiologist, I. M. Sechenov, in 1863, and the British neurologist, Hughlings Jackson, in 1874 (Jackson, 1931, 1:37). They claimed that the higher functions of the brain, usually called "psychic," are based on the reflex activity of the cerebral cortex. In their minds this conception did not exclude entirely psychological interpretation of phenomena induced by the action of some stimuli on the brain through some organs of sense. Descartes's conception of a reflex action, which both he and others after him applied to the explanation of the simpler forms of nervous reactions only, was thus for the first time extended to the activity of the higher parts of the nervous system.

Both Sechenov's and Jackson's contributions to the physiology of the cerebral hemispheres were theoretical. However, their deductions were based on contemporary physiological data and on clinical observations.

Sechenov had no known predecessors who appear to have influenced his thoughts. At the conclusion of his famous book *Reflexes of the Brain* he wrote: "I must confess that I have built up all these hypotheses without being well acquainted with psychological literature. . . . Professional psychologists will probably point out the resulting defects of my work. But my task was to show the psychologists that it is possible to apply physiological knowledge to the phenomena of psychic life, and I believe that my aim has been partly attained" (Sechenov, 1935, p. 335).

Jackson's convictions of the reflex nature of the function of the cerebral hemispheres were influenced by early impressions formed during an association with Dr. Laycock, who later became professor of medicine at the University of Edinburgh. In a paper written in 1845 (*British and Foreign Medical Review*, 19:298) Laycock stated that as early as 1841 he had expressed the opinion that "the brain, although the organ of consciousness, is subject to the laws of reflex action, and that in this respect it does not differ from the ganglia of the nervous system." Jackson begins his article of 1874 "On the Anatomical and Physiological Localization of Movements in the Brain" (Jackson, 1941, 1:37) by quoting these words of Laycock's.

Since Sechenov's and Jackson's theories of the functional mechanisms regulating cerebral activity are important for the proper understanding of Pavlov's attitude toward the investigation of the "psychic" phenomena in animals, they will be discussed in some detail in the next two chapters. It is surprising how much of what these two remarkable men thought in the sixties and seventies of the last century has become the foundation of today's knowledge.

CHAPTER TWENTY-EIGHT

I. M. Sechenov

ONE of the strongest impulses which moved Pavlov to investigate the "psychic," "higher nervous" activity in animals by a purely physiological method was the deep impression made on him by Sechenov's remarkable treatise *Reflexes of the Brain*. This Pavlov acknowledged in the Preface to the first Russian edition of his *Twenty Years of Objective Study of the Higher Nervous Activity (Behavior) of Animals* (Pavlov-Gantt I, 1928, p. 39). He stated that a physiologist, for a successful study of the psychic phenomena in the higher forms of animals, such as a dog, must abandon the subjective point of view and use in his work objective physiological methods and appropriate terminology. Pavlov decided to apply this point of view to the study of the psychic activity of the dog, "the intimate and faithful companion of man since prehistoric time." He continues:

The most important motive for my decision, even though an unconscious one, arose out of the impression made upon me during my youth by the monograph of I. M. Sechenov, the father of Russian physiology, entitled Cerebral Reflexes [or *Reflexes of the Brain*] and published in 1863. The influence of thoughts which are strong by virtue of their novelty and truth, especially when they act during youth, remains deep and permanent even though concealed. In this book a brilliant attempt was made, altogether extraordinary for that time, to represent (of course only theoretically as a physiological outline) our subjective world from the standpoint of pure physiology.

In every respect Sechenov was an outstanding man. He was born in 1829, youngest son of a landowner who belonged to the provincial gentry of Simbirsk district. He graduated from the medical faculty of Moscow University in 1856 and died in 1905. He was the first Russian physiologist to use the experimental method. Before him physiology in Russian medical schools was taught by medical men or by physiologists who knew their subject only theoretically. Among Sechenov's principal contributions to physiology were the discovery of the "inhibitory centers" in the brain, studies of the reflex activity of the spinal cord, investigation of the effect of acute intoxication by alcohol, and physicochemical studies of the absorption of CO_2 in salt solutions and in blood.

Sechenov's daring attempt to consider psychic phenomena as reflexes is the more remarkable when it is realized that it was made before Fritsch and Hitzig in 1870 discovered the cortical motor centers and before Wundt founded experimental psychology (about 1879). Sechenov still adhered to Flourens' teaching in considering the cerebral hemispheres the only part of the central nervous system which does not give rise to muscular contractions when stimulated directly. "In other words," he wrote, "the hemispheres do not contain fibres with the properties of motor nerves" (Sechenov, 1935, p. 275). The psychology of the fifties and sixties of the nineteenth century also could not help Sechenov to build his reflex theory of brain activity because with rare exceptions psychology in this period was philosophical. Even for Wundt, who followed to a marked extent the teaching of psychophysiological parallelism, the psychic phenomena were something quite different from physiological phenomena.

Sechenov's pupil, Professor M. N. Shaternikov, pointed out in the biography of his teacher (Sechenov, 1935, p. xxi) that the idea of a reflex nature of psychic phenomena had been maturing in Sechenov's mind for several years before the publication of his treatise *Reflexes of the Brain*. Thus in his M.D. thesis, presented in 1860, one of the general statements was: "All movements known in physiology as voluntary are reflex movements in the strictest sense of the word."

Sechenov's monograph *Reflexes of the Brain* appeared in 1863 as a journal article and in 1866 was released in book form. The basic idea discussed in his book was that the origin of all acts of unconscious and conscious life was reflex. He considered voluntary activity to be

composed of reflexes which begin with sensory excitation, continue by means of a definite psychical act, and end in muscular movements; [and again] a given sensory stimulus inevitably leads to the other two components of the whole phenomenon and always in the same sense, granted, of course, that the external and internal conditions are the same and the physiological state of the person who is performing the action is unchanged. The final member of every voluntary act, i.e. the muscular movement, is identical with the action of muscles in pure reflexes, i.e. in elementary involuntary movements [Sechenov, 1935, p. 291].

Sechenov's argumentation was as follows:

1. "All the endless diversity of the external manifestations of the activity of the brain can be finally regarded as one phenomenon—that of muscular movement. Be it a child laughing at the sight of a toy, or Garibaldi smiling when he is prosecuted for his excessive love for his fatherland, a girl trembling at the first thought of love, or Newton enunciating universal laws and writing them on paper—everywhere the final manifestation is muscular movement" (p. 264). He proceeded to discuss separately the involuntary and voluntary movements.

2. The origin of every involuntary movement, simple or complicated, inborn or learned, is the excitation of the sensory nerve. A sensory stimulation, external or internal, may or may not call forth a conscious sensation.

3. The possibility of frequent repetition of involuntary muscular movements presupposes the existence of definite mechanisms in the body, inborn or acquired by learning. This mechanism consists of sensory and motor nerves with their center in the central nervous system. Along these paths a reflex is transmitted from the endings of a sensory nerve to the muscle (p. 290).

4. What is true of involuntary movement is true of voluntary: here, too, in spite of seeming independence of a voluntary movement from a sensory stimulation, the latter also may be looked upon as machine-like. To prove his thesis, Sechenov discussed the formation in a child of various associations of gradually increasing complexity (optico-tactile, acoustico-tactile, optico-acoustico-tactile, and so on), which become the basis for corresponding images. The mechanism of the formation of these associations is purely reflex. If a child touches a bell, for instance, the muscular and tactile sensations produced by this act, together with visual impressions, are accompanied by stimulation of the acoustic nerve and the sensation of sound. If the process of ringing a bell is repeated often, the child begins to recognize the bell not only by its sound but by

its appearance. "Now see what this leads to," wrote Sechenov; "the consecutive series of reflexes gives a very complete idea of the object, it imparts knowledge in its elementary form" (p. 297).

Sechenov purposely discussed the origin of voluntary movements in infants rather than in adults because it was difficult to demonstrate in the latter that sensory excitation was always the cause of a voluntary movement. He emphasized that character in man develops very gradually from his cradle; a very important part in this process is played by "contact with life," i.e., the influence on an infant and afterward on a child of the medium in which he is brought up (p. 292). This approach to the study of the formation of the habits in man anticipated by more than half a century the attitude of behaviorists toward this problem. They have gone even farther than Sechenov because they believe that habit formation probably starts in embryonic life and continues after birth with great rapidity (cf. Watson, 1930, pp. 100 ff.).

5. When a child has received a concrete impression of some object, say, a person standing in front of him, he is able to produce an analysis of it. This is a process of disintegrating a concrete impression into its elements. Owing to the properties of the retina and eye muscles, the child is able to discriminate among the different parts of the body of the person standing in front of him—head, body, arms, legs—and later, when the vision becomes more acute, among different parts of the face. The capacity to analyze various impressions depends on the physiological properties of the corresponding organ of sense (pp. 299 ff.).

6. A child's differentiation between various sensations which he has received from his own body and those derived from external objects forms the basis of self-consciousness. This process is based also on some complex reflexes (p. 304).

7. The capacity to reproduce sensations is based on memory, and memory has very much in common with the aftereffects of stimulation of sensory nerves. These sensations are preserved in a latent state.

8. The most complex association is nothing more than "an interrupted series of contacts of the end of every preceding reflex with the beginning of the following one" (p. 312). The merest hint of any part of an association results in the reproduction of the

entire association. The reproduction of a long chain of associated thoughts appears to be spontaneous but, as a matter of fact, is induced by a sensation, often hardly noticeable. In other words it is of reflex nature. Sechenov gives the following example:

I devote my daytime to physiology, but in the evening, while going to bed, it is my habit to think of politics. It happens, of course, that among other political matters I sometimes think of the Emperor of China. This acoustic trace [Sechenov means the sound of the four words] becomes associated with the various sensations (muscular, tactile, thermic, etc.) which I experience when lying in bed. It may happen one day, that owing to the fatigue or to the absence of work, I lie down on my bed in the daytime and lo! all of a sudden I notice that I am thinking of the Emperor of China [p. 316].

9. In most cases a reflex ends in a contraction of a group of muscles or in a movement of the whole body. However, there are reflexes in which inhibition is the end of the arc and movement is absent. The capacity to inhibit movement is the property of the central nervous system, but man must learn to inhibit his movements in the same way as he learns to perform them. The arrest of a movement is not due to the contraction of the antagonistic muscles but to a mechanism acting in the central nervous system (p. 326).

Sechenov's ideas of central inhibition of reflexes were based on his own work. He was the first to demonstrate that the stimulation of certain parts of the brain in a frog (a crystal of sodium chloride was placed on the optic thalami, which were cut across) inhibited the reflex withdrawal of the legs when they were dipped into a weak acid solution. Prior to this it was believed that only organs with autonomic functions, such as the heart or the intestine, could be inhibited by the stimulation of their nerves. Sechenov's discovery of central inhibition of the movements of voluntary skeletal muscles made a great impression on the leading physiologists of his time—Ludwig, Brücke, Du Bois-Reymond, and others. Sechenov's enthusiasm over his discovery is quite understandable, and it is no wonder that he tried to generalize it and to apply it to the explanation of certain psychic phenomena.

10. To the phenomenon of the inhibition of motor reflexes Sechenov ascribed a great importance. He believed that to such reflexes, in which the last member of the reflex action, i.e., move-

ment, was inhibited, man owed his capacities to think, deliberate, and judge. "A thought," he wrote, "is the first two thirds of a psychical reflex" (p. 231).

11. On the other hand, emotions and passions are psychic reflexes, the end of which is augmented. Emotions are coupled with desires; their external manifestations are often exaggerated. Not only pleasure but a suppressed desire may be a source of emotion. Such negative emotions are subjected to the same laws as positive ones. The origin of an emotion lies in the instinctive craving to satisfy the senses, and an emotion arises owing to frequent repetition of the psychic reflex. In other words, an emotion is induced by an external stimulation. However, the emotional state, which grows at first with repetition of the stimulation, diminishes after many repetitions or even vanishes. A child grows tired of old toys (pp. 322–26).

12. Thus the stimulation of all forms of the human psychic activity depends on the impressions which our organs of sense receive from outside or from the inner parts of the body. If the impulses from the organs of sense do not reach the central nervous system, the psychic life is annihilated. In his *Reflexes of the Brain* Sechenov expressed the purely theoretical thought that "a man in dead sleep and without sensory nerves would sleep to his death" (p. 336).

Many years after Sechenov's book was published, his supposition was confirmed to a certain degree by observations on some patients who were deprived of almost all organs of sense (Strümpell, 1877; Heyne, 1871; Ziemssen, 1891). Here is a description of one of these interesting cases (Strümpell, 1877). It was a boy sixteen years of age whose skin was deprived of any sensibility (touch, heat, pain). The same was observed in mucous membranes. Muscular sensation was lost; there was no feeling of tiredness in the muscles. There was a complete absence of taste and smell sensations. He was blind in his left eye and deaf in his right ear. Only two channels for communication with the external world were left to him, i.e., his right eye and his left ear. If these two channels were closed, his brain was completely isolated from the outside world and in two or three minutes the patient always fell into a deep sleep. Waking up could be effected only by a sound acting on his normal ear or by a light acting on his normal eye. Shaking the body did not wake him. When sleeping by himself, he was awakened by some internal stimulations or through the action of sound or light on his normal ear or eye. One of Pavlov's students, Dr. A. D. Speransky, reproduced partially in dogs the famous clinical case of Strümpell. The fili olfactorii and the optic nerves were cut, and both cochleae were destroyed. Such dogs, completely deprived of the senses of smell, sight, and hearing, slept almost $23\frac{1}{2}$ hours a day and woke up only when they were hungry or needed to empty their pelvic reservoirs. It was very difficult to awaken such dogs in an ordinary way, e.g., by petting them. One had to shake them rather strongly; only then did they recover from their slumber and only very gradually (see Pavlov, 1940).

Sechenov looked upon his conception of psychic life as a hypothesis. "My teaching," he wrote, "is a pure hypothesis as far as the presence in man of three separate mechanisms directing the phenomena of conscious and unconscious life is concerned (viz. the mechanism of the pure reflex and those of reflex inhibition and augmentation)" (p. 334). He formulated his hypothesis as follows: "Under similar external and internal conditions man must act in the same way. The choice of one of many possible ends of the same psychical reflex is definitely impossible, and its apparent possibility is only an illusion of our consciousness. . . . The real cause of every human activity lies outside man" (pp. 333–34).

From this short exposition of Sechenov's teaching it is evident how new and daring were his ideas, expressed in such definite form in the sixties of the last century. He realized this himself when he wrote: "I have decided to communicate to the world some ideas concerning the psychical activity of the brain—ideas which have never been expounded in the literature of physiology" (p. 264). His book was written brilliantly; the argumentation was logical and convincing. No wonder that Sechenov's treatise, according to his pupil, N. E. Wedensky (a distinguished physiologist who at the end of the eighties succeeded Sechenov as professor of physiology in St. Petersburg University), produced an enormous impression on the contemporary Russian society and was read by every educated Russian in the sixties and seventies of the past century. As was mentioned in the first part of this book, this was a period of Russian political spring. After the gloomy barrack-like regime of Emperor Nicholas I, which ended in 1855, the new Czar Alexander II began his liberal reforms. The old clashed with the new, and enthusiasm, especially among the young generation, ran extremely high. Turgenev in masterly fashion depicted this period in his famous novel *Fathers and Sons*, written in 1861.

I am under the impression that there was a contemporary French translation of the *Reflexes of the Brain*. In spite of this, Sechenov's teaching passed unnoticed in western Europe, perhaps because it was too radical for its time. Thus, e.g., in the German textbooks of physiology of this period outstanding scientists, such as Funke, Vierordt, and others, spoke about "der Sitz der Seele" ("seat of the soul") in the central nervous system.

Sechenov was a follower of Locke, according to whom the psychic development of man was acquired entirely through the activity of his organs of sense, and, as we have seen, he was definitely opposed to philosophical psychology (see, e.g., Sechenov, 1935, pp. 377–78). Therefore, the mental development of man or of the higher forms of mammals, according to Sechenov, depended on the impulses which arrived in the brain from the organs of sense. These latter in their turn were set into activity only when they received certain external or internal stimulation which they transformed into a nervous process and transmitted to the brain. The mental activity, with the exclusion of some special cases discussed above, was usually expressed in a form of movement. In other words, at the foundation of mental processes must lie a well-known phenomenon of reflex action. Thus Sechenov emphasized the possibiilty of approaching the study of psychic phenomena by the objective methods of the natural sciences. He never attempted to do this himself, but his theoretical considerations had an extraordinary methodological value: if the psychic life is based on reflex action, then there is a possibility of studying it with physiological methods. This is exactly what Pavlov attempted to do.

CHAPTER TWENTY-NINE

J. Hughlings Jackson

ONE of the outstanding neurologists of England, J. Hughlings Jackson (1834–1911), and Sechenov were contemporaries but were not acquainted with each other's work. Their interpretation of the mechanism of the brain activity had very much in common. Both firmly believed that the activity of the nervous system was based on reflex action, but neither held materialistic conceptions concerning the psychic phenomena.

Jackson was a clinician who was especially interested in the phenomena and causes of the epileptic states. One must bear in mind that Jackson was under the exceptionally great influence of the philosopher Herbert Spencer, who was then at the crest of his fame. This extraordinary influence of Spencer on Jackson finds its explanation in the fact that Jackson himself had a natural inclination toward philosophy and at one time even considered devoting his life to philosophy rather than to medicine. Jackson's admiration for Spencer was so great that most of Jackson's articles, published in special medical journals, were filled with quotations from Spencer's works. Jackson continuously used Spencer's terminology (e.g., "evolution" and "dissolution," "statical" and "dynamical" qualities of objects) and applied it to the physiology and pathology of the nervous system.

A great part of Spencer's philosophy is now very much disputed, and a great deal of it is forgotten altogether while, on the other hand, most of Jackson's contributions to normal and abnormal neurology still remain valid. The reliability of Jackson's clinical conclusions was due not only to his fine capacity for observation but also to the fact that he always tried to correlate his observations on patients with the experimental data obtained on animals by his contemporaries, Fritsch and Hitzig, Ferrier, Horsley, and others.

The Three Levels of Evolution

Jackson divided the central nervous system into three parts or, following Spencer's terminology, "three levels of evolution." In his Croonian Lectures of 1884 Jackson (2:45 ff.)[1] gave the following definitions of "evolution" and "dissolution."

"Evolution," in the nervous system, was the passage from the most organized, most simple, and most automatic to the least organized, most complex, and most voluntary, i.e., from the lowest to the highest centers. "Dissolution" was the reverse process; it was a degradation from the least organized and more complex, to the most organized, most simple, and most automatic. In diseases the "dissolution" might be only partial, since complete dissolution was equivalent to death.

Jackson's division of the nervous system is not a morphological one but a functional one. At the basis of this scheme is the conception of "the degree of indirectness" with which the different centers in the nervous system represent the different parts of the body (Jackson, 1:348, 366, 412; 2:45, 76, 422; and in many other articles). The hierarchy of the nervous centers, according to Jackson, is as follows:

1. The lowest level extends from the tuber cinereum to the conus medullaris. It is made up of sensory and motor centers and interconnecting fibers of the spinal cord, medulla oblongata, pons, and aqueduct. The motor centers extend from the lowest anterior horns up to the nuclei of the ocular muscles. Besides these sensory-motor centers which represent the whole body from "nose to feet" there are present in the same parts of the central nervous system "superior centers of the lowest level," such as respiratory, vasomotor, etc. The lowest centers are the simplest and most organized centers; each of them represents some limited region of the body. They are "representatives."

2. The Rolandic region of the cerebral cortex (Jackson calls it "Ferrier's motor region"), with its motor centers and also possibly the ganglia of corpus striatum, is the province of the middle level.

[294]

These centers are more complex and less organized than the lowest centers; they represent indirectly wider regions of the body, from ocular muscles to the perineum, which were already represented in a simpler form by the lowest level. They are "re-representatives."

3. The highest level of the nervous system comprises the centers of the prefrontal and occipital lobes. This level consists of highest motor centers in the first and highest sensory centers in the second. (Jackson always believed that the middle and highest centers were chiefly motor and that the corresponding centers were chiefly sensory [Jackson, 2:79].) The highest motor centers are the most complex and least organized and represent the widest regions of the body triply indirectly; thus they are "re-re-representatives." "The highest centres (sensory and motor division of the highest level)," wrote Jackson, "the 'organ of mind,' or anatomical substrata of consciousness—are the acme of evolution; they have the same kind of construction as lower centres; they are sensory-motor as certainly as the lumbar enlargement is" (Jackson, 1:349 ff. and 414).

Already during Jackson's lifetime there arose a controversy between him and Ferrier (see Jackson, 2:63 ff.). Ferrier did not agree with Jackson's division of the motor cortical centers into two groups, middle and highest. From his experiments on monkeys, Ferrier concluded that the stimulation of the frontal lobes evokes only lateral movements of the eyes and head. According to Jackson, on the other hand, the frontal lobes, in which he believed were located the highest motor centers, represented the movements of all parts of the body. The modern conception of the functions of the frontal lobes disagrees with Jackson's teaching. However, the following remarkable fact must not be passed by. Presumably independently of Jackson's teaching, Pavlov arrived at conclusions concerning the organization of the central nervous system reminding the Jacksonian three levels of organization. In the last years of his life Pavlov held the opinion that there exist three "signaling" systems in the brain: one subcortical and two cortical (Pavlov-Gantt II, 1941, pp. 126, 179). The first cortical system subserves the conditioned reflexes; the second cortical system is situated in the frontal lobes and is a purely human evolutionary achievement.

The Reflex Mechanism of the Centers

What is the mechanism which sets into activity the centers of the different levels, and what is the difference between the functions of the lowest and of the highest centers?

The mechanism which is responsible for the activity of the centers in all three levels is reflex. A peripheral impression evokes a movement. (By "impression" Jackson understood stimulation—the word which is used at the present time—of the endings of the sensory nerves. He was not satisfied himself with the word "impression" but did not know any better one. In several articles he explained that he used it in a purely physiological sense [see 1:238 and 367].)

"So far for resemblances; there is reflex action in each case," wrote Jackson. "Now for certain differences. The difference is not that reflex action is the characteristic of the lower centres, but that exact and perfect reflex action is characteristic of them" (1:60). The lower centers respond with a few simple movements to certain peripheral "impressions." The reflex action in the highest centers is, according to a special expression of Jackson's, "imperfect." By "imperfection" Jackson understood a certain delay in the action of the highest centers, owing to the fact that they are widely separated "geographically" in the cerebral hemispheres. But, what is more important, there are no "absolute connections" in the highest cortical centers between their afferent and efferent parts, whereas in the lower reflex action some definite movement inevitably follows a certain afferent impulse.

This was written by Jackson in 1875. The same idea was expressed by him twenty-three years later, in 1898, even more forcibly. "If the 'vital' centres of the lowest level were not strongly organized at birth, life would not be possible; if the centres of the highest level ('mental centres') were not little organized and therefore very modifiable we could only with difficulty and imperfectly adjust ourselves to new circumstances and should make few new acquirements" (Jackson, 2:437).

This last statement is nothing else than a recognition of the existence in the cerebral cortex of a mechanism subserving conditioned reflexes. Time was not yet ripe at the end of the nineteenth cen-

tury, even for the most advanced thinkers of the generation like
Jackson, who were then approaching the concluding period of life,
to speak in purely physiological terms about the processes taking
place in the cerebral cortex. As the new wine requires new bottles,
so the new ideas require new men to put them into practice.

NERVOUS STATE AND MENTAL STATE

From the exposition of Jackson's doctrines, presented above, it
is evident that for him the difference between the three levels of
centers in their constitution and function was not so much one of
kind as of degree. All nervous centers are of sensory-motor constitution, and the mechanism of their functions is reflex. Man has
body and mind. Regarded physically he is a sensory-motor mechanism, but the highest nervous centers, aside from their representation of most complex movements, are the physical basis of consciousness and mind (Jackson, 2:64).

What is the relation of the mental state to the nervous state?

Jackson rejected the materialistic hypothesis. As in many other
instances, when philosophy was involved, he closely followed
Spencer, who considered materialism an "utterly futile" hypothesis. Spencer insisted on an "absolute difference between states of
consciousness and nervous states," but he believed in the existence
of "parallelism between a certain psychic evolution and the correlative physical evolution" (quotations from Spencer's *Psychology*,
made by Jackson, 2:63). On his part Jackson tended to be thoroughly materialistic in the study of the nervous system. "But,"
wrote he, "we must not be materialistic at all as to mind" (Jackson,
1:367). What did Jackson actually mean when speaking thus?

He formulated the relations between the consciousness and the
nervous state in the following ways:

1. States of consciousness (or states of mind) are utterly different from nervous states.

2. The two things occur together, i.e., for every mental state
there is a correlative nervous state.

3. Although the two things occur in parallelism, there is no
interference of one with the other.

Jackson called this hypothesis of his the "doctrine of concomitance." The cardinal point in Jackson's teaching is that he recognized that the conscious process arises whenever the "highest nervous centers" are stimulated reflexly. He expressed this thought very definitely in several of his articles (1:242, 367; 2:65 ff., 85 ff.).

Jackson insists on the motor compound of the reflex action, which gives origin to the mental process. Our "ideas," according to Jackson (1:240 ff.), are acquired by experience; in other words they are "acquired during the correspondences betwixt the organism and its environment. . . . The sensory-motor arrangements we have been speaking of constitute the inherited mechanism by which these correspondences can be effected." Thus, e.g., in a "visual idea," obtained by looking at a red brick, stimulation of purely sensory highest centers may give only an incomplete knowledge of the object, i.e., of its color. To obtain ideas of the size and shape of the brick, movement, in this particular case of the eye muscles, is absolutely necessary (cf. Jackson, 1:53 ff.). In such case the reflex action is complete and strong, since the highest centers are engaged along with the lower centers.

Jackson's conception of obligatory participation of the centers of muscular movements in each psychic act, when the stimulus acts on one of the receptive surfaces of the body, resembles closely Sechenov's conception of mental brain function. "All the endless diversity of the external manifestations of the activity of the brain can be finally regarded as one phenomenon, that of muscular movement," wrote Sechenov (p. 264). Translating this sentence into Jacksonian language, one would say that each mental activity of the brain requires the participation of both the highest sensory and the highest motor centers in the cerebral cortex.

If we have seen the red brick one day and the next day we think about it in its absence, the reflex action is incomplete and weak because only the highest centers are involved in this process but not the sensory and motor lower centers. "The highest sensory and motor centres are alone engaged; there is still reflex action, but only the central links of the great sensory motor chain are engaged" (Jackson, 2:70). What is the mechanism of the origination of a thought when there is no object which may act on our organs of sense, when we think about the red brick but do not see it? Jackson does not explain this fact.

In his discussion of the brain functions Sechenov was more logical than was Jackson. He explained the seemingly spontaneous appearance of an unexpected thought by a hidden reflex stimulation, direct or indirect, through a chain of associations. (Remember his example of his thoughts about the Chinese emperor, which sometimes appeared when he was lying on his bed.)

In other respects Sechenov's and Jackson's conceptions of thought had very much in common. "A thought," wrote Sechenov, "is the first two thirds of a psychical reflex." In the process of thinking, the reflex action is curtailed by inhibition of the last member of the reflex act—the movement. According to Jackson, movement is also excluded in the case of thought. This, he believed, was due not to the central inhibitions of the movement but to the weakness of the stimulation of the highest sensory and motor centers and the resulting inability of the motor impulse to overcome the resistance in the middle and lower motor centers.

How closely the conceptions of Sechenov and Jackson about the function of the brain coincided is shown in the following example. Speaking about the acoustic sensations, Sechenov pointed out that in early childhood they are closely associated with the muscular sensations which arise in the chest, throat, and especially in the tongue and in the lips. Thus arises speech, and speech is closely related to thinking. Small children cannot think without speaking. Most grown-up people also think in words. The words are usually not spoken, but when emphasis is put on some words or a sentence, these are whispered, or even pronounced loudly. "It seems even to me," wrote Sechenov (p. 312), "that I never think in words, but always in those muscular sensations which accompany my thought when it is spoken." "I have urged for years that the anatomical substrata of words are motor processes," wrote Jackson (1:50). He quoted Ferrier (1:51), whose conclusions he considered to be very close to his.

In his fundamental article "Investigation of Epilepsies," published in 1874–76, Jackson (1:178 ff.) actually arrived at the same conclusions as Sechenov about the reflex nature of speech and the relation of speech to thinking. "The nervous arrangements forming the substrata of mind are only in great degree different from the nervous arrangements of the pons or spinal cord." There is an external speech and an internal speech; "there are discharges of the highest sensory-motor processes when we think, just as there are of the lower processes when we walk." The difference between the internal speech, i.e., thinking, and the external speech is only quantitative. The nervous process engaged in both cases is one and the same, but in the case of internal speech the discharge in the corresponding center is weak and limited to the center, whereas in the case of external speech the impulse from the higher center spreads to the lower centers and to the muscles (see also Jackson, 2:222 ff.).

It is interesting to note that Sechenov's and Jackson's ideas about speech and thinking have been expressed again, more than half a century later, by some modern psychologists. Thus, e.g., Watson (1925) wrote in our time that the behaviorist advances the view that a "thought is in short nothing but talking to ourselves" (p. 238). "My theory," he stated further (p. 239), "does hold that the muscular habits learned in overt speech are responsible for implicit or internal speech (thought)." As one of many evidences in favor of this view he quoted (p. 241), Dr. Samuel Gridley Howe, superintendent of the Perkins Institute and Massachusetts Asylum for the Blind, who was teaching the hand-and-finger language to the deaf, dumb, and blind Laura Bridgman, stated that even in her dreams Laura Bridgman expressed her thoughts by using the finger language with great rapidity.

CHAPTER THIRTY

From Sechenov and Jackson to Pavlov

FROM the discussion of Sechenov's and Jackson's work it is evident that the scientific thought of more profound thinkers at the end of the nineteenth century was moving toward the purely physiological interpretation of the functions of all parts of the brain without exception and to unification of physiology and psychology. Although these investigators were definitely stating that the psychic phenomena were of a different order than the physiological ones, they nevertheless believed that the former were based on and controlled by the latter. However, it required another great mind, that of Pavlov, to approach the study of all the functions of the brain, including the hemispheres, from a strictly physiological point of view. The work of Pavlov was the continuation of the work of Sechenov and Jackson, and the conditioned reflexes were a logical sequel to their teaching.

CONDITIONED REFLEXES

The following is a brief history of the development of the method of study of conditioned reflexes and a résumé of the theoretical foundations on which the method is based.

During his studies of the gastrointestinal functions Pavlov, like many other investigators, could not fail to notice that the mere sight, smell, or sound of food evoked the salivary and the gastric secretions. The food substances obviously acted on the digestive glands indirectly, not by coming in contact with the appropriate receptive surface of the mouth but on other receptive surfaces, as, e.g., those of the eye, nose, and ear and, moreover, from a distance. Secretion of this type had always been called "psychic." Pavlov was very much interested in "psychic" salivary and gastric secretions and made a special study of them. As late as 1899 (see Pavlov, 1902, p. 152) Pavlov still interpreted these phenomena from a psychological point of view. He wrote: "In the psychology of the salivary glands, as it has displayed itself to us, we find all the elements of what we usually attribute to 'mental activity'—namely, sensation, choice, dispassionate consideration, and judgment with respect to the substance introduced into the buccal cavity."

But three years later, after the laboratory incident with Dr. Snarsky, described above, Pavlov radically changed his attitude in this respect. He approached the study of the "psychic" secretion in the dog from a purely physiological point of view. Any purely psychological interpretation of the observed facts was now absolutely rejected, and the phenomenon, insignificant in itself, of "psychic" salivary secretion became a powerful method of investigation of the functions of the cerebral cortex.

A very important fact may be brought out in the case of "psychic" salivary secretion. The object does not act by its essential properties on the appropriate receptive surface of the body (e.g., in the case of food, on the mucous membrane of the mouth cavity) but acts on the other receptive surfaces (eye, nose, ear) by its unessential properties, such as sight, color, smell, or sound. The participation of the central nervous system is essential for the display of the "psychic" secretion. An especially important role is played by the cerebral cortex, which may be considered the chief organ transmitting the impulses from the unessential properties of the stimulating object to the gland. The removal of the cerebral cortex in animals almost completely abolishes these reactions. Since the salivary secretion at a distance is only a part of a more general reaction of a dog to the sight or smell of food, the enormous significance of the response acquired by experience becomes evident. Any animal would starve to death if the effect of food were limited to its action on the surface of his mouth only. To find food, to select between the edible and inedible foodstuffs, an animal must react to certain properties of food other than its taste or consistency. Often these properties are apparently insignificant. Pavlov called such stimuli "signaling stimuli" (Pavlov-Anrep, 1927, pp. 14 and 17). A decorticated dog is practically deprived of the ability to react to the signaling stimuli and cannot find food which is placed in front of him; eating movements are begun only when the food touches the lips.

The next problem concerning the "psychic" secretion was its

origin: is it inborn or acquired? The reaction of the salivary glands to food substances from the mouth cavity is undoubtedly inborn. It was observed in the earliest stages of the animal's life and is not abolished by decortication or moderate anesthesia. On the other hand, the "psychic" salivary or gastric secretion to food or to a rejectable substance such as a weak solution of acid or alkali is always acquired. This has been proved repeatedly by scores of Pavlov's pupils.

Thus, for instance, one of Pavlov's former pupils, Dr. Zitovich (1911; see Pavlov-Anrep, 1927, p. 22), kept puppies for more than half a year on a diet of milk alone. In these animals only the sight and smell of milk or milk products, like cheese, or the sound of splashing fluid behind a screen evoked a salivary secretion from a distance. No other food substances—meat or rusk—were effective stimulants of the salivary or gastric secretion under similar circumstances. Sight or smell of these substances or sounds produced by them (e.g., breaking of a rusk) left the animals indifferent. However, when any one of these food substances was placed in the mouth of a puppy and he ate it, the salivary glands began to secrete copiously. Moreover, after a puppy ate several times of the new food, its sight, smell, or sound began to stimulate the work of his salivary glands, just as before the sight and smell of milk alone stimulated them and formed a "natural" conditioned reflex.

These experiments (extremely difficult, by the way) revealed the astounding fact that the seemingly most natural reaction of a dog to the ordinary food substances is only partly inborn but in a very great part acquired.

A most convincing proof that the ability of an animal to react to signaling stimuli is not inborn but is acquired during life was given by experiments in which any unrelated event in the outside world or inside the animal could become a signaling stimulus. To achieve this, it was sufficient to let an indifferent stimulus inadequate to affect the salivary secretion, such as light, sound, or smell, or stimulation of the skin by a brush, coincide with the act of eating or introduction into the mouth of a rejectable substance, for example, a weak solution of acid, alkali, or bitter stuff. After several repetitions of such combination of stimuli, the signaling stimulus

[303]

alone provoked a positive or negative motor reaction and salivation. This was called an "artificial" conditioned reflex.

Different phenomena taking place in the body of an animal could
also be made signaling stimuli for the salivary secretion, for example, stimulation of the sensory nerve endings (proprioceptors) in
the muscles, distention of the stomach, and so on.

How should a physiologist look on this peculiar nervous reaction
of the animal formed during its life? Is it legitimate to consider a
"psychic" salivary secretion or a motor response or any other form
of animal behavior elicited by a command or a special signal as a
reflex? Can a cortical reaction occur without any impulse? May it
originate spontaneously, or is a stimulus always necessary to set
the cortical machinery into activity? In other words: is a conditioned reflex a reflex? If it is not, then the very foundation of
Pavlov's teaching is shattered.

As far as we know, everything speaks in favor of the interpretation of the reaction of an animal to the signaling stimuli of the
objects, i.e., of the "psychic" secretory or motor response, as a
reflex. Undoubtedly the type of reaction is of a reflex nature. Since
special conditions were always necessary for the formation of a
response—secretory or motor—to some objects at a distance and
since this reaction had the fundamental features of a reflex, Pavlov
called it "conditioned reflex" to distinguish it from the inborn or
"unconditioned reflex." For the formation of a conditioned reflex,
it is only necessary that the essential properties of a substance, like
its taste, consistency, and so on, act on the receptors in the mouth
coincidently with the stimulation of one of the other organs of
sense. In other words, the specific receptor (the mouth) and some
other sense organs must be stimulated at the same time. After several such combinations the conditioned stimulus evokes secretory
and motor reactions.

Motor conditioned reflexes may easily be formed if an unrelated
stimulus be combined, for example, with weak electric stimulation
of a dog's leg. As in response to sound, smell, or light, and so on,
the dog will now raise its leg to avoid the electric shock. Several
investigators (e.g., Bechterev and his students, Beritoff, and others)
preferred to work with the motor rather than with the secretory
conditioned reflexes. However, the use of salivary conditioned re-

flexes offers certain advantages, such as the more quantitative reaction of the salivary glands and their much more restricted physiological function as compared to skeletal muscles. But one may surmise that one of the chief reasons why Pavlov preferred the salivary secretory reaction to the motor reaction of the skeletal muscles was the absolute absence of a "voluntary" salivary secretion. A dog with permanent salivary fistulas may not secrete a drop of saliva for hours. For the initiation of secretion there is always necessary the action of an unconditioned or conditioned stimulus.

Here are evidences in favor of the view that a conditioned reflex is a reflex indeed.

1. Does a conditioned reflex reproduce the unconditioned one with the help of which it was formed? Some psychologists (see Hilgard and Marquis, 1940, p. 37) believed that a conditioned reflex is seldom an exact replica of the unconditioned. This statement, however, is true only to a certain degree.

Since Pavlov's work was carried out chiefly with salivary conditioned reflexes, and not motor, we are interested here in the former. Very detailed investigations performed in Pavlov's laboratory (see Babkin, 1928, pp. 42 ff.) showed that a conditioned reflex was quantitatively and qualitatively a diminutive replica of the corresponding unconditioned reflex. Both the volume and composition of the saliva secreted in response to the signaling stimulus approximated those of the saliva evoked by introducing into the mouth the substance which served for the formation of the conditioned reflex.

Although a conditioned salivary reflex retains the general features of the unconditioned reflex on which it was based, it would be incorrect to speak of "substitution" of one by the other. A conditioned stimulus is a signaling stimulus. It is only a part of a very complex pattern of stimulation in which the conditioned stimulus and unconditioned stimulus act on the animal together and in an overlapping spatial and temporal manner. The latter, e.g., food, acts on a great number of the receptive substances—eye, ear, nose, mouth, etc.—and sends a powerful stream of nervous impulses to the brain, whereas the signaling stimulus acts usually on one receptor only. This is especially true when we deal with "artificial" rather than with "natural" conditioned reflexes.

Far more complicated relations were observed in the case of motor conditioned reflexes, particularly when the animal was not restrained. Here the investigators speak of a "preparatory response" during the action of the conditioned stimulus (Hilgard and Marquis, 1940, p. 39). This preparatory response, according to them, is different from the conditioned response. For example, during the action of the conditioned stimulus, such as food, a dog which is permitted to walk in the chamber approaches the food pan; but in the case of acid, in this example serving as an unconditioned stimulus, the animal may walk away from the stimulating device. Is not the approach of the animal to the food pan or the retreat from a damaging stimulus (acid) each a part of a corresponding conditioned reflex? The usual mistake of such investigations is that they are too complicated, and the experimenter has to use the psychological approach which he is accustomed to use in everyday life to explain the behavior of the animal.

2. A reflex arc consists of one or more afferent neurones, a center or number of centers, and an efferent secretory or motor neurone. Section of the latter will abolish permanently both unconditioned and conditioned reflexes. However, it was demonstrated in Pavlov's laboratory that section of the afferent nerves will only partly modify both types of salivary reflexes (see Babkin, 1928, pp. 74 ff.). The glossopharyngeal nerve, the lingual nerve of the fifth division, and the pharyngeal branch of vagus nerve were sectioned in dogs with permanent fistulas of the mixed and parotid glands. There was almost no change in the unconditioned reflexes to different food substances eaten by the dogs. The secretory impulses in these animals were presumably transmitted to the central nervous system through the trigeminal nerves distributed in the mouth cavity, which endings were stimulated by mechanical properties of food substances, and through the olfactory nerves. On the other hand, the secretory reaction to chemical stimuli, such as solutions of bitter, sweet, acid, or alkali substances, underwent marked quantitative and qualitative changes. The conditioned reflexes to food substances and to the enumerated chemical substances followed on a diminished scale the pattern of the unconditioned reflexes.

3. The part played by the cerebral cortex in transmission of the

conditioned reflex action from a receptive surface to a salivary gland (or muscle) is not clear. It is well known that an unconditioned salivary reflex may be evoked by stimulation of the mouth cavity after the removal of the whole anterior part of the brain (section at the level of the pons). Under these circumstances, however, no conditioned reflex can be obtained. The removal of the "cortical salivary center" does not abolish the conditioned reflexes, as claimed by Bechterev and his pupils (see chap. 9, above). However, the removal of the whole cerebral cortex leads to the loss of all conditioned reflexes which existed in the dog before the operation, and the formation of new conditioned reflexes becomes impossible. As early as 1907–8 Pavlov stated that "the cerebral cortex is the organ of conditioned reflexes" (Pavlov-Gantt I, 1928, p. 98) and regarded it as being built almost exclusively of the central ends of various receptors, or, as he called them, "analyzers."

In discussing in 1927 the results of the experiments on decorticated dogs, Pavlov concluded more cautiously: "To present the final conclusion of these experiments with the utmost reserve, the cerebral cortex should be regarded as the essential organ for the maintenance and establishment of conditioned reflexes, possessing in this respect a function of nervous synthesis of a scope and exactness which is not found in any other part of the central nervous system" (Pavlov-Anrep, 1927, p. 330).

Pavlov's conception of the function of the cerebral cortex in the dog was disputed by several authors who were able to form positive and negative conditioned reflexes in the decorticated animal (Poltyrev and Zeliony, 1930; Culler and Mettler, 1934; Lebedinskaia and Rosenthal, 1935, 1938; Girden, Mettler, Finch, and Culler, 1936). On the basis of these experiments some of these investigators claimed that conditioned reflexes could be formed in the absence of the cortex and utilized only some subcortical regions of the brain. In other words, Pavlov's statement that "the cerebral hemispheres constitute the organ of the conditioned reflexes" was challenged.

The possibility of formation of conditioned reflexes in decorticated dogs is indisputable, but two points must be emphasized in connection with these experiments: (1) Some parts of the cerebral cortex always remained intact after decortication (see Poltyrev and Zeliony, 1930). (2) Though some conditioned reflexes could be formed in the decorticated animal by using strong stimuli and some degree of discrimination could be achieved, the formation process was a very slow one and the sense of fine discrimination between two or more conditioned stimuli, so characteristic of the normal animal, was lost forever. Furthermore, the experiments were obscured by the choice of stimuli. The conditioned stimuli selected for the experiments on the decorticated dogs were unfortunately unusually strong and in most cases were such as to give rise to a generalized motor reaction rather than to a local reaction. Thus, an electric shock was used, and the usual result was an extensive defense reaction involving the whole trunk and all four limbs.

The conclusion which may be drawn from experiments on decorticated dogs is that the subcortical regions cannot replace functionally the cerebral cortex. A decorticated dog (one such dog lived in Pavlov's laboratory for four and a half years) was a helpless invalid (probably a lay observer would use the word "idiot") who could not learn anything and would have perished in a few days if left to its own devices. Nevertheless, the fact that crude conditioned reflexes could be formed in animals deprived of their cerebral cortex demonstrates that the capacity to establish temporary connections with the objects of the outer world is not limited to this part of the brain. The subcortical regions, the functional mechanism of which is based on reflex action, are able to react to signaling stimuli. Thus, although fish have hardly any hemispheres and no cerebral cortex, it has been possible to form conditioned reflexes in ten species of bony fishes (Frolov, 1925, 1928).

4. It has been said (Howell-Fulton, 1946, p. 530) that the conditioned reflex cannot be called a reflex because the minimal latent period is in the order of 100 m.sec. (This refers, of course, to motor conditioned reflexes, because the latent period of secretory reflexes is much longer.) A latent period of 100 m.sec. for a conditioned motor reflex, compared with the total reflex time of 10.4 m.sec. for the flexor reflex of the spinal cord, seems to be very long. However, in perfectly normal dogs the latent period for the lifting of a leg in response to electric stimulation (unconditioned reflex) was equal to 150–200 m.sec., according to Beritoff (1927). The conditioned motor response in this case appeared after 1.0 sec. Especially accu-

rate measurements of the latent period of conditioned reflexes in the dog were performed by Bykov and Petrova (1927) in Pavlov's laboratory. They took care to eliminate the inhibitory state which exists even in shortly delayed (say, 30 sec.) conditioned reflexes. They found that the latent period of a motor conditioned reflex based on an alimentary unconditioned reflex was 80 m.sec., whereas the latent period of a motor conditioned reflex based on a defense unconditioned reflex (electric stimulation of the leg) was only 60 m.sec. Undoubtedly, the passage of an impulse through the lower parts of the central nervous system requires less time than one which has to run along an additional path through the cerebral cortex. However, the difference is not great, and the longer latent period of a conditioned reflex as compared with an unconditioned reflex is not evidence against the reflex nature of the former. The latent period of a salivary conditioned reflex is much longer than of a motor one. Thus, when Pavlov suddenly introduced food into the mouth of a dog with a salivary fistula, the secretion began in 1–2 sec. This was an unconditioned response. When food was only shown to the animal—conditioned reflex—the secretion started after 5 sec. (Pavlov-Anrep, 1927, p. 22). However, such a latent period cannot be considered very long, because faradic stimulation of any parasympathetic secretory nerve evokes a secretion of saliva after only 2–5 sec. (see Babkin, 1928, p. 95).

The only logical conclusion to which Pavlov could come in studying the reaction of the salivary glands to food substances from a distance was that it was in the nature of a reflex action. But, to adopt such a physiological point of view, it was necessary to abandon altogether the psychological approach, which was not compatible with the fundamental conceptions of physiology. All considerations about the wishes, feelings, and thoughts of an animal had to be excluded from such studies altogether. Only physiological interpretation of observed facts could be permitted.

What other conceptions could Pavlov use in his studies of this special form of salivary secretion if he wanted to stay on the ground of physiology? There was none, and for almost half a century after the beginning of Pavlov's investigations in this field none was advanced. True, it has been proposed to call the salivary secretion evoked by sight, smell, etc., of food not a reflex but a "reaction" or "response" or some such term. However, another terminology did not explain anything and only made the analysis of the phenomenon in question even more difficult. Pavlov had the choice of either following the old and hopeless path of psychological interpretation of the so-called "psychic" phenomena in animals or of abandoning uncompromisingly such attempts and applying the well-established physiological conception of a reflex action.

The brief history of the elaboration of the method of conditioned reflexes presented above shows that Pavlov gave to neurophysiologists an entirely new method for the study of animal behavior, one which depended chiefly on the integrity of the cerebral cortex. This, of course, did not deny psychology the right to look from its own point of view on the processes taking place in the brain. The method of conditioned reflexes permitted more than any other method advanced hitherto the investigation of the course of a nervous process in the cerebral cortex, the mutual influence of two or more nervous processes going on at the same time in this part of the brain, and the mechanism of the formation of new and extremely fine relations between the outer world and the animal. Pavlov insisted that the study of the conditioned reflex mechanism permits one to reduce the problem of the activity of the central nervous system to a study of space relations, something psychology is unable to do. He wrote: "You must be able, so to say, to point with the finger where the excitation process was at a given moment, and where it has gone" (Pavlov-Gantt I, 1928, p. 192).

CHAPTER THIRTY-ONE

Conditioned Reflexes as a Physiological Discipline

S PACE does not permit presentation of a systematic exposition of the results obtained by Pavlov and his co-workers in their study of conditioned reflexes. There is no possibility of discussing even such very interesting problems, which Pavlov studied with this method, as sleep, hypnosis, experimental neuroses, different types of nervous systems in dogs, genetics, and others. (Incomplete reviews of Pavlov's achievements in this field may be found in most of the modern textbooks of physiology.) Only a few fundamental points of Pavlov's teaching will be discussed in this chapter.

MECHANISM OF THE FORMATION OF A CONDITIONED REFLEX

Pavlov formulated the following theory of the mechanism of the formation of a conditioned reflex. An unconditioned stimulus evokes a state of strong activity in the lower centers of the brain—for instance, in hypothalamus and medulla oblongata—and in some points in the cerebral cortex. When, for instance, a center of salivary secretion, which is in the medulla oblongata, is reflexly stimulated by substances present in the mouth, simultaneously a number of cortical "centers," such as gustatory, olfactory, visual, and others, are involved in this excitatory process. According to Pavlov, the center of the unconditioned reflex—salivary, in our example, or motor or vomiting—attracts to it the stimuli from the cortical cells, which were excited in a lesser degree than was the center of the unconditioned reflex. A "temporary" connection is formed between these points. It is now sufficient to send a stimulus into the corresponding cortical cells through the appropriate afferent paths to excite the secretory or motor centers in the lower parts of the brain. Any stimulus which is indifferent, when combined several times with the activity of these centers, will become a conditioned stimulus and originate a conditioned reflex (Pavlov-Anrep, 1927, p. 36; Pavlov-Gantt I, 1928, p. 101).

Since a conditioned—secretory or motor—reaction of an animal is a reflex and the integrity of the cerebral cortex is essential for the display of this reflex, it is legitimate to ask what part of the reflex arc the cerebral cortex represents. Pavlov believed that almost the whole cortex is composed of the central ends of the analyzers.

Under "analyzer" Pavlov understood a complicated nervous mechanism which begins at the periphery of the body as an organ of sense or even just a simple sensory nerve ending and which is connected by means of a chain of neurones with centers in the lower and then in the higher parts of the central nervous system. The central ends of various analyzers—optic, acoustic, dermal, muscular, and so on—are situated in the cerebral cortex. The peripheral end of each analyzer is a receptor for one definite kind of stimulus, e.g., visual, auditory, tactile, etc., and at the same time a transformer of these stimuli into a nervous process. Both the receptor at the periphery and the specially organized groups of the nerve cells in the central nervous system, which are called "centers" for the sake of brevity, are involved in the analysis.

According to Pavlov, the cerebral cortex is endowed with two fundamental properties: analysis and synthesis. These are essential for the establishment of a temporal and fine relationship of an animal organism with the outer world. For this purpose "the nervous system possesses" wrote Pavlov, "on the one hand a definite analyzing mechanism, by means of which it selects out of the whole complexity of the environment those units which are of significance, and, on the other hand, a synthesizing mechanism by means of which individual units can be integrated into an excitatory complex" (Pavlov-Anrep, 1927, p. 110).

The experiments with conditioned reflexes showed that analysis is not achieved at once. A conditioned reflex always passes through an initial period of generalization. If, for example, a conditioned salivary reflex is established on a tone of 1,000 double variations, the neighboring tones also acquire excitatory properties. The nearer these neighboring tones are to the one which is always reinforced by an unconditioned stimulus, the greater the secretory response. The same phenomenon was noted in the activity of all other analyzers. The initial generalization of a conditioned reflex is based on irradiation—a phenomenon which Pflüger had observed earlier in a spinal frog (see chap. 27 and Fig. 6).

At the initial stage of the formation of a conditioned reflex such generalized reactions of an animal to similar stimuli may be useful. The natural stimuli, acting on an animal, are not, as a rule, constant but vary somewhat. At first a crude conditioned reflex is formed which permits the animal to orient itself in the surrounding medium, but this reaction is unsuitable for exact learning.

Two methods of specialization of conditioned reflexes were tried in Pavlov's laboratory. The first method consisted in persistent repetition of the original conditioned stimulus only, always reinforced by the unconditioned one. No satisfactory results were obtained with this method. The conditioned stimulus could be repeated over a thousand times and no absolute discrimination from similar neighboring stimuli could be achieved. The second method gave quick and better results. A single definite stimulus, which was always reinforced by the unconditioned one, was contrasted with all other stimuli, which were never reinforced. This process was called "differentiation." The finest type of discrimination between two stimuli was achieved with this method. To mention only two examples: a dog could differentiate with his visual analyzer between an object rotating clockwise and anticlockwise; he showed discrimination between a certain tone of an organ pipe and an interval one-fourth or even one-eighth lower (for details see Pavlov-Anrep, 1927, pp. 117 ff.).

What is the nature of the nervous process which converts a generalized conditioned reflex into a strictly specialized one?

The fundamental theoretical conception of Pavlov concerning the functional properties of the nervous system, and of the cerebral cortex in particular, was that they were based on two equally important processes: the process of excitation and the process of inhibition. Very often he compared the nervous system with the ancient Greek god Janus, who had two faces looking in opposite directions. The excitation and the inhibition are only sides of one and the same process; they always exist simultaneously, but their proportion varies in each moment, at times the one prevailing, at times the other. Functionally the cerebral cortex is, according to Pavlov, a mosaic, consisting of continuously changing points of excitation and inhibition. The process of cortical inhibition by eliminating inessential stimuli prevents a chaotic state of the cerebral cortex.

Differentiation is based on inhibition which develops in those points of an analyzer which, when excited by accessory stimuli, are not reinforced by the unconditioned stimulus. Pavlov called this inhibition "differential inhibition" and included it in the group of "internal inhibition." The "internal inhibition" depends on processes which develop in those very parts of the brain where the reflex response was initiated. Pavlov distinguished between "internal inhibition" and "external inhibition." The latter is induced by extraneous stimuli of any kind which are strong enough to diminish or abolish a conditioned reflex. When repeated several times, an external inhibitory stimulus usually loses its inhibitory effect.

Whereas the phenomenon of "external inhibition" may be explained by interference of the activity of a more strongly excited point in the nervous system with the activity of a less excited one (i.e., that of the conditioned reflex), no adequate explanation can be given to the "internal inhibition." The latter arises in the very point which previously was in a state of excitation. Thus, for example, if a conditioned reflex is repeated without reinforcement by its unconditioned stimulus, the former undergoes "extinction" and the corresponding conditioned stimulus becomes ineffective. Moreover, if the extinction be "deep" enough, other conditioned reflexes are weakened for a while. In other words, they are inhibited. Another remarkable feature of inhibition is that like excitation it irradiates over the cerebral cortex and then concentrates in the initial point.

Let us take an example: Five tactile apparatuses are attached to the hind leg of a dog with a salivary fistula, one on the paw and the others higher up at a distance of 3, 9, 15, and 22 cm. along the leg. The lower tactile apparatus (N) is made negative and has never been reinforced with food. The four upper ones (I, II, III, and IV) are positive stimulants and are always reinforced with food.

N	I	II	III	IV
−	+	+	+	+

If, one minute after the negative tactile apparatus has produced its invisible effect (invisible since, of course, it does not stimulate the flow of saliva), each of the positive apparatuses is tested, it may be seen that the secretory effect of Apparatus I is completely abolished, that of II is diminished to a half, Apparatus III gives an almost normal, and Apparatus IV a normal, volume of secretion. These facts were interpreted by Pavlov as follows: The position of tactile receptor cells in the cortex is probably in the same relative order as on the skin. The inhibitory process initiated by the tactile Apparatus N spreads in the cutaneous analyzer, that is, the inhibition irradiates, but its influence diminishes in proportion to the distance of the point of positive conditioned stimulation from the point of negative stimulation. After a while the inhibition gradually disappears from the points of the positive conditioned reflexes; the farther the positive point lies from the negative point, the sooner the disappearance. Thus, for example, in another experiment arranged as above, the farthest Point IV was found 15 sec. after the application of the negative stimulus (N) to be inhibited by a half, while in 30 sec. it was completely freed of inhibition. (This explains the normal amount of salivary secretion found in the experiment cited above 1 min. after the application of the negative stimulus.) Point II was free of inhibition in 5 min. and Point I in 10 min. Pavlov gave the name of "concentration" to this process.

When the arrangement of the experiment was reversed, i.e., when the stimulated point on the skin was positive and the tested points were negative, the results fully agreed with the first series of experiments. After the application of the positive stimulus, a temporary disinhibition of the negative points could be seen; this denoted the irradiation and concentration of the excitatory process in the cerebral cortex. The process of concentration of an irradiating wave of excitation or of inhibition may be best explained by the phenomenon of induction (Orbeli, 1945, p. 64): an excitatory process originates an inhibitory process and vice versa. The phenomenon of induction was first discovered by E. Hering when studying the physiology of organs of sense and later was observed in spinal reflexes by Sherrington. Pavlov adopted the conception of induction and applied it to physiology of the cerebral cortex.

Whereas the impulses irradiated very rapidly over the cortical analyzer, a certain amount of time was required for them to reach a maximum concentration. This time often amounted to several minutes. The time of irradiation and concentration of the negative or positive process varied in different animals (Pavlov-Anrep, 1927, pp. 152–87).

THEORETICAL CONCEPTIONS OF PAVLOV

Almost all theories formulated by Pavlov on the basis of his experimental observations in conditioned reflexes were criticized at one time or another. Included were his theory of the formation of the conditioned reflexes, theory of irradiation and concentration of excitation and inhibition in the cerebral cortex, and the theory of inhibition (Denny-Brown, 1932–33; Beritoff, 1937, pp. 562 ff.).

At first Pavlov was forced to explain the activity of the cerebral cortex, as it was revealed by the study of the conditioned reflexes, with the help of theories formulated by previous generations of physiologists, i.e., prior to 1901. He spoke of excitation and inhibition, *Bahnung*, or fatigue. He then added new theoretical conceptions gradually, such as irradiation and concentration of a nervous process in the cerebral cortex, or borrowed from Hering and Sherrington the idea of positive and negative induction, or recognized three systems in the brain, etc. Pavlov needed his theories to organize his facts in a comprehensible whole and to have a stepping-stone for further experimental research.

Pavlov had no illusions about the permanency of his theoretical considerations. He wrote in 1925, after almost a quarter-century of work with conditioned reflexes: "It is obvious that the time has not yet come for a theory to explain all the enumerated phenomena [of excitation and of inhibition] and to assign them a common basis, although many hypotheses have been proposed, each one of which has a certain justification. In the present situation, one may use various conceptions in the work if only they permit a systematization of the material, and suggest new and detailed problems" (Pavlov-Gantt I, 1928, p. 349).

Although the criticism of Pavlov's theoretical conceptions is in some cases justified, the weakness of most such attempts is that the critic is unable to deal with the enormous volume of factual material accumulated by Pavlov. The criticism consequently usually covers only part and not all of the facts established by Pavlov. (A more detailed discussion of Pavlov's theoretical conceptions may be found in Orbeli's [1945] *Lectures*.)

Pavlov formulated the functions of the central nervous system, and of the cerebral cortex in particular, in the following way:

All the nervous activity and all the behavior of the higher animals may be included in a scheme containing six principal nervous phenomena: (1) excitation; (2) inhibition; (3) spreading of both excitation and inhibition; (4) reciprocal induction—inhibition by excitation process (negative phase), and the excitation by the inhibition process (positive phase); (5) the opening and closing of paths between different points of the system, and finally, (6) analysis—the decomposition by organism of the external *milieu* and its own internal world (everything which proceeds within it), into their units [Pavlov-Gantt I, 1928, p. 296].

THREE SYSTEMS IN THE BRAIN

Another of Pavlov's theoretical conceptions of general nature has to be mentioned. On several occasions in the last years of his life Pavlov expressed the opinion that in the human brain there exist three signaling systems: one subcortical and two cortical (Pavlov-Gantt II, 1941, pp. 126, 170).

The subcortical system is the region where centers dealing with complex chain reflexes, instincts, are located (see Pavlov-Anrep, 1927, pp. 9 ff.). These centers regulate the most essential functions of the body, such as those of self-defense, sexual impulse, alimentation, and others. The state of excitability of these centers depends on the internal conditions of the organism (hunger and satiety, influence of various hormones, and other factors), but the actual discharge of energy by these centers depends on stimuli acting on them from outside through afferent reflex channels. In spite of the very great importance of these centers for the maintenance of life, they do not acquire a high degree of adaptation in relation to the surrounding medium. This system of centers predominates in the lower vertebrates. While it gives them a certain chance to survive, the absence or scarcity of other signaling systems in their nervous system keeps them on the lower level of evolution.

The first cortical system is the system subserving the conditioned reflexes. It comprises the afferent paths from different receptors with their cortical ends, i.e., the analyzers, a number of connector paths to the subcortical centers, and further paths to the efferent brain or spinal centers of the corresponding organs. From the functional point of view, this system permits the animal to establish, with the help of the temporary connections, fine relationships with the outer world. A fine degree of adaptation is thus achieved. In some animal forms this first cortical system remains probably the highest level of evolutionary achievement. "To an animal," wrote Pavlov, "the reality is signalled almost exclusively by the stimulations—and the traces that they leave in the cerebral hemispheres—conveyed directly to the special cells of the visual, auditory and other receptors of the organism" (Pavlov-Gantt II, 1941, p. 179).

The second cortical system, which, according to Pavlov, is situated in the frontal lobes, is a purely human evolutionary achievement. It is the function of speech. The signals of reality in us are the sensations and concepts which we receive with the help of conditioned reflexes from the surrounding world. Speech is based predominantly on kinesthetic stimulations originating in the organs of speech. These stimulations arrive in the second cortical system; they are signals of signals. In 1935 Pavlov wrote in one of his last articles:

> Words have built up a second system of signalling reality, which is only peculiar to us, being a signal of the primary signals. The numerous stimulations by word have, on the one hand, removed us from reality, a fact we should constantly remember so as not to misinterpret our attitude towards reality. On the other hand, it is nothing other than words which have made us human, but this, of course, cannot be discussed here in great detail. However, it is beyond doubt that the essential laws governing the work of the first system of signalling necessarily regulate the second system as well, because it is work done by the same nervous tissue [Pavlov-Gantt II, 1941, p. 179].

In his division of the brain into three functional systems, Pavlov approached closely Hughlings Jackson's conception of the three levels of evolution in the central nervous system (see chap. 29).

Conditioned Reflexes and Psychology

Nothing is further from the truth than the often cited misstatement that Pavlov "denied psychology." As we have seen, he considered it utterly wrong to interpret the behavior of *animals* from a psychological point of view. Since we are unable to penetrate their thoughts, feelings, and wishes, this was, of course, a sensible stand. But he certainly recognized that psychology, as a science devoted to the study of the *subjective states of man*, has a right to a separate existence. This view he expressed on numerous occasions. Thus he wrote: "Our subjective world is the first reality with

which we are concerned" (Pavlov-Gantt I, 1928, p. 329). He believed, however, that the time would come when it would be possible to fuse the subjective with the objective. "Marching forward
and pressing onward, the natural and unavoidable approach and
final fusion of psychology with physiology, of the subjective with
the objective will be achieved—the actual question so long dis-
quieting the human thought" (this was written by Pavlov about
1932 [Pavlov-Gantt II, 1941, p. 71]).

In another article, also written about 1932, Pavlov expressed the
opinion that the most important problem of the present day is
"uniting or identifying the physiological with the psychological,
the subjective with the objective" (Pavlov-Gantt II, 1941, p. 117).

These quotations in Pavlov's own words show clearly his attitude. His chief aim was to assert the right of the physiologist to
investigate by objective physiological methods, as he called it, the
"higher nervous" activity of the dog. He was concerned with a
purely physiological investigation of certain aspects of animal behavior, those which are usually called "psychic," and thus showed
that the teaching of conditioned reflexes is part of the physiology
of the central nervous system and nothing else.

Conditioned Reflexes from a Psychological Point of View

The fact that a conditioned response is in all probability coupled
with some kind of psychic state of the animal in no way can diminish the value of conditioned reflexes as a purely physiological method of investigation of the cerebral functions. However, we do not
know what relation a physiological cortical process bears to the
subjective state of the mind. Since modern psychology, especially
the American, is so closely linked with physiology, it is very interesting to know how Pavlov's teaching of conditioned reflexes has
influenced psychology. The very title of a book by E. R. Hilgard
and D. G. Marquis, *Conditioning and Learning* (1940), indicates
that certain psychologists consider the conditioned reflex as a conception applicable to psychological study. This book should be
consulted by all those who are interested in this problem.

Professor Lashley's Point of View

It gives me very great pleasure to quote, in part, Professor K. S.
Lashley's letter (of February 8, 1946) which he wrote to me in

answer to my question: How does Pavlov's work on conditioned
reflexes influence the development of psychology? Besides giving
firsthand information about the influence of the conditioned reflexes on the course of American psychology from the beginning
of this century, Professor Lashley also expressed his thoughts on
the position in science of the teaching of the conditioned reflexes.
Professor Lashley's opinion is that the greatest value of the work
of Pavlov for psychology was his insistence that explanation of behavior is to be sought in nervous activity and his formulation of
definite theories of cerebral physiology which pointed the way to
possible neurological explanations of more complex behavior. His
rigorous exclusion of mentalistic concepts and terminology from
physiological theory avoided the confusion that arises again whenever people intermingle two approaches to the study of behavior.
The weakness of Pavlov's position, according to Professor Lashley,
was his acceptance of a simple associationist doctrine and his failure
to grasp the complexities of the problems of stimulus analysis and
of adaptive motor co-ordinations.

The following excerpts from Professor Lashley's letter, which
I am quoting with his kind permission, give an account of the influence of conditioned reflexes on American psychology.

I have been fairly close to the development of objective psychology
in this country since its beginning and shall give you my impression
of the role that Pavlov's work has played in that development. His work
came to the serious attention of American psychologists between 1909,
when attention was called to it by the review of Yerkes and Morgulis,
and 1915, when Watson proposed the conditioned-reflex method as a
substitute for introspection. At that time subjective psychology, represented by a structuralism of Titchener and the functionalism of Angell,
was dominant, but a trend toward objectivism was developing in the
work of students of animal behavior, of learning, and of the testing
methods of Cattell and Binet. This trend was without coherent expression and did not yet constitute a systematic position opposed to sub-
jectivism. Watson's *Psychology As the Behaviorist Views It* was the first
attempt here to formulate an objective program. It was written in 1912
before Watson had been significantly influenced by Pavlov's work.
Only in the following year did we begin a study of the writings of
Pavlov and Bechterev.[1] The ground was then already prepared for acceptance of an objective and physiological point of view. The conception of reflex basis of behavior, sketched by John Dewey about 1896,
was exemplified in the work of Russian investigators. They provided

not only theory but an experimental method and concrete results in support of their views. Bechterev was actually more influential than Pavlov in the early days. He appeared to have a more comprehensive grasp of psychological problems than did Pavlov, and the French edition of his *Objective Psychology* provided a more complete account of his position than was available for that of Pavlov. The early experimental work, presented in Watson's presidential address, was based on Bechterev's accounts and designed to test his interpretations.[2]

However, Bechterev held to psycho-physical parallelism which did not fit with the anti-introspection movement which characterized behaviorism, and his terminology was rejected in favour of Pavlov's more rigorously physiological one. Without the earlier growth of the movement toward objectivism, Pavlov's work would probably have aroused little interest in America, as was the case in Germany and France. Without his work, behaviorism would have developed, though perhaps in a different way. Few details of Pavlov's experiments were available to English readers until the translation of his book in 1927. (In 1914 I compiled a bibliography of more than three hundred Russian titles on the conditioned reflex, of which only seven were available in the major libraries of America.) In consequence, there was little understanding of his physiological theories.

According to Professor Lashley, the early influence which Pavlov's teaching exerted on psychology was derived chiefly from three main sources:

(1) He formulated learning in terms of association between stimulus and response, thus avoiding the association of images or of ideas, which had offered difficulties to objective psychology; he insisted that all learning could be reduced to that formula; and he provided evidence which could be cited in support of such an interpretation. (2) The conditioned reflex offered a potential method for study of psychological processes which had been considered accessible only to introspection and so provided an argument against one of the chief criticisms of the objective movement. (3) He emphasized the possibility of a psychology without mentalistic elements and gave some evidence of progress toward such goal. In actual practice his work provided a set of slogans for the objective movement rather than an influence on the direction of development of that movement. Pavlov believed, I am sure, that an understanding of behavior could be gained only by study of the physiology of the brain and that such studies should be as direct as possible. He was primarily an experimenter and had little use for the construction of conceptual systems, except as they could be supported step by step by direct experimental evidence.

[321]

Although Pavlov "pointed the way to fundamental investigation of the physiology of the brain," continued Professor Lashley,

this way, unfortunately, was not followed systematically in America and very little was added to further analysis of the cerebral functions with the help of his method.[3] Paradoxically, many psychologists, in whose current work the influence of Pavlov's theories can be most clearly traced, have turned to the development of conceptual systems from which all neurological interpretations are rigorously excluded. Thus the chief influence on psychology in America of conditioned-reflex theory seems to have been diametrically opposed to Pavlov's expectation of using his studies as a basis for the physiological explanation of behavior.

All this is no fault of Pavlov. He was one of the great pioneers in experimenting and inductive reasoning. But it seems to me that these characteristics of his work which gave him greatest claim to genius have been least influential in American psychology. It has been his misfortune to fall into the hands of philosophers. His influence has been rather that of a Descartes than of a Pasteur.

CHAPTER THIRTY-TWO

Conclusion

WE HAVE seen that Pavlov's primary aim was to study the physiology of the cerebral cortex. Since the physiological processes taking place in the cortex are tied up in some way with the phenomena of consciousness and since the surgical removal of the cerebral hemispheres invalidates tremendously the psychic life of a dog, Pavlov concluded that with the help of the conditioned reflex method he would be able to express the whole behavior of an animal in purely physiological terms. It is too early to say whether or not this aim could be attained, because the application of an objective method to the study of the cerebral cortex in a fully conscious and, in the majority of cases, quite normal animal is hardly forty-odd years old. One fact, however, is evident: the conditioned reflex study, being a physiological investigation of the functions of the cerebral cortex, is of paramount importance for neurophysiology. This statement is contrary to the opinions of some psychologically minded investigators, for whom the coupling of a conditioned reflex with a conscious state puts this type of reaction of the nervous system into a special category. The study of the conditioned reflexes, according to these critics, has very little of importance to offer neurophysiology.

This is undoubtedly a misunderstanding. Pavlov's teaching of conditioned reflexes is certainly neurophysiology and not psychology in any form or under any name. Actually, it is a more physiological method than those used by the neurophysiologist, which require anesthetics, the breaking of the skull, the implanting of the electrodes into the tender mass of the brain, the application of drugs like strychnine, and so on. Yet the aim of all these crude methods is to explain the normal functions of the cerebral hemispheres, which is precisely the purpose for which the method of conditioned reflexes is employed!

Not better than the method of acute experiments is the method of the total or partial extirpation of the cerebral cortex. Ludwig once compared this method with the attempt to understand the mechanism operating a watch by striking it with a sledge hammer. Speaking about the investigation of cortical localization by the extirpation method, Pavlov said: "The only method so far available for such a study consists in observing the effects of partial destruction or complete extirpation of different parts of the cortex. This method naturally suffers from fundamental disadvantages, since it involves the roughest form of mechanical interference and the crude dismembering of an organ of a most exquisite structure and function" (Pavlov-Anrep, 1927, p. 320).

One may marvel indeed that, with such primitive methods as electric stimulation or the removal of different parts of the brain, physiologists achieved so much. Because of the necessity for a special laboratory, equipment, and trained personnel, the method of conditioned reflexes is employed by exceedingly few neurophysiologists outside Russia. Most of the investigators in this field employ the motor conditioned reflexes, although the salivary conditioned reflexes are more reliable because they give quantitative results. This choice is determined chiefly by the relative simplicity of the technique of the motor conditioned reflexes, as well as by the impossibility of using the salivary conditioned reflexes in some animals. I know of only one investigator outside Russia—Dr. W. Horsley Gantt of Johns Hopkins University—who has taken full advantage of the salivary conditioned reflex method for the study of cortical processes in the dog, combining it in his studies with the registration of the motor reactions of the animal.

It would, of course, be erroneous to think that Pavlov's conditioned reflex method is the only one with the help of which the cortical functions may be studied. Thus, for example, the electroencephalogram promises to become an important method for the study of the normal and abnormal functions of the cerebral cortex. It was shown, for instance, that the so-called "alpha" waves are present when the eyes are closed and disappear as a result of visual activity or during a mental effort.[1] The electroencephalogram proved valuable, for example, in the study of epilepsy. Undoubtedly, still other methods, finer than those we now possess, will be found for the objective study of the functions of the cere-

bral cortex, but, up to the present, the conditioned reflex method
has contributed more to the understanding of the physiology of
this part of the brain than has any other method.

Localization of "Consciousness" in the Brain

How farsighted Pavlov was in excluding any reference to "consciousness" from his studies of the physiological functions of the
cerebral cortex is seen from the remarkable work of Penfield
(1938), confirmed by Le Beau (1942).

Observations resulting from electrical stimulation of the human
cerebral cortex during operations under local anesthesia led Penfield to the conclusion that the cerebral cortex is not essential for
the conscious process. Consciousness depends on the integrity of
the region below the cortex and above the midbrain, probably in
the anterior and inferior parts of the lateral walls of the third ventricle. Le Beau, on the basis of his studies of the clinical neurosurgi-
cal material, arrived at similar conclusions. Both Penfield and
Le Beau used a purely practical approach in their determination of
"consciousness," leaving aside any psychological or philosophical
considerations. The patient is "conscious" when, during the operation under local anesthesia, he answers properly the questions
which the surgeon asks him and afterward remembers well all that
happened during the operation.

Penfield came to the conclusion that "consciousness" or the
"center of consciousness" (if I may be permitted to use the term)
is not localized in the cortex but below it. Stimulation by thyrotron
of the cortical motor area produced movements in the corresponding parts of the body—arm, leg, mouth, etc. However, the patient
was convinced that he did not evoke these movements himself, that
he had no intention at all of making them, and that these parts of his
body moved of their own accord. Stimulation of a certain point of
the cortex (Brodman's point 5) evoked vocalization, and the patient
asserted that he produced the cry involuntarily, even against his
own will. This experiment was repeated many times. Stimulation
of the sensory-motor area near the fissure of Rolando provoked a
sensation of "electricity" in the corresponding part of the body, for
instance, in one of the hands, but the patient never realized that it
was, so to say, imaginary.

Penfield's observations of the effect of the stimulation of the remaining two-thirds of the cerebral cortex are especially interesting. Stimulation of these areas produced hallucinations only in those patients who previous to the brain operation had suffered from repeated epileptic attacks. It seemed that the artificial stimulation of these parts of the cortex always resulted in bringing back to life what became, owing to the illness, a typical response of these cortical regions. Penfield concluded that the visual and the auditory cortical areas were involved in the epileptic patients in the paths of the conditioned reflexes. Electrical stimulation of the corresponding cortical areas revived the dormant reactions.[2]

Either one or both frontal lobes, with the inclusion of the whole extra-motor cortex, could be removed in patients while they retained full consciousness during the entire operation. After the operation they remembered quite well and even in detail their sensations during the operation. This fact is of great significance because the frontal lobes have been considered by some investigators to be in charge of the higher mental functions. The "association" centers of the brain in man have been supposed to be located in this area. The ablation of both the frontal lobes appears to have affected finer and not easily definable mental capacities, but the simpler associative processes remained unaffected. No brain surgeon ever spoke of the loss of consciousness of his patients after lobectomy.

Epileptic attacks also gave indications that some cortical phenomena, such as progressive involvement into a convulsive state of the leg, arm, and face, are separate from the loss of consciousness, which occurs some time after the beginning of the convulsions. On the other hand, in cases of petit mal the loss of consciousness is the primary phenomenon, without other manifestation, with the exception perhaps of *l'expression vide* and loss of speech. In other cases of epileptic seizures there is a paleness of the face and loss of the ability to maintain the vertical position of the body, as a result of which the patient suddenly falls to the floor.

Penfield believes that all these facts indicate that somewhere below the cerebral hemispheres there must be a region which is in charge of the conscious state in man. The size and position of this region is not yet known exactly, but it appears to be situated near the third ventricle, close to the thalamic vasoconstrictor center, the center of visceral sensations, and the center of the equilibrium. Le Beau thinks that the "center" of the consciousness is in the anterior portion of the brain stem, in the third ventricle, near the centers which provoke an epileptic attack and a sudden cerebral edema. Moreover, he believes that the centers of the psychomotor activity may be located in the same region.

Further evidence that the "center" of consciousness is not in the cerebral cortex but below it has been supplied by cases of brain tumors with the loss of consciousness. Such tumors usually compress the region of the brain lateral to the third ventricle (Le Beau), or they develop above but not very far from the midbrain and its neighborhood (Penfield). Penfield described the case of an unconscious patient who began to wake up and to return to a conscious state six weeks following the surgical removal of one of these tumors.

Summarizing the results, which were obtained by himself and by other investigators, Penfield arrived at the conclusion that there are many proofs of the existence in the brain of a level of integration functionally higher than that which exists in the cerebral cortex. There is no doubt that consciousness cannot be denied to many vertebrate animals which have a very weakly developed cerebral cortex. It cannot be denied also to a decorticated dog. Penfield believes that this special region is located not in the cerebral cortex, which must be looked upon from the phylogenetic point of view as a rather recent acquisition of the vertebrate brain, but in its older parts, below the cortex and above the midbrain. Unlike the analytical properties of the brain, it was not transferred during evolution from its original position to the cerebral cortex (cf. Babkin, 1948).

CONDITIONED REFLEXES AND CONSCIOUSNESS

One may ask what place consciousness has in the scheme of a conditioned reflex. Is it the actual cause of the new conditioned reaction of the nervous system—as some physiologists and the majority of psychologists think—or is it a phenomenon which may be coupled with the formation and reproduction of a conditioned reflex? Although the "center" of consciousness is presumably a central point around which the system of analyzers developed, a conscious state does not appear to be indispensable for the higher nervous activity in the form of conditioned reflexes. Everyday experience shows that conditioned reflexes can be formed in a conscious state, but without any special participation of consciousness or its direction toward the stimulus acting in a given moment. The acquiring of new words by infants and even by grown-up persons when they learn a new language, the learning to walk in man and by many animals, and the unconscious formation of many associations in adult life are representative examples. We have all experienced the so-called *je l'ai déjà vu* ("I have seen it already") when a place or a phenomenon seems to be familiar but which one does not recall having seen. Actually, the phenomenon or place was seen, but a corresponding association, or a conditioned reflex, which is the same thing, was formed unconsciously. Probably consciousness does participate, especially in the formation of finer or complicated conditioned reactions, but such participation is not obligatory at all.

Penfield's work supports Pavlov's conception that the chief function of the cerebral cortex is the analysis of the stimuli arriving there from the surface or from the inside of the body and their synthesis of their integral parts with one or other function of the body.

Conditioned Reflexes and Psychic Phenomena in Man

The experimental results obtained with the help of the conditioned reflex method can be applied to man. However, from the very beginning Pavlov warned that this may be done in general terms only. Detailed application of the experimental results obtained on dogs to the complicated problems of human psychology is, as yet, not possible (Pavlov-Anrep, 1927, p. 395). A great deal of care must be exercised when one tries to explain in man the function of organs even simpler than the brain, like the heart, those of the digestive tract, etc., by facts established through animal experimentation. While the structure and the function of many internal organs in the higher mammalian animals are very much like those in man, there is a tremendous advance in the structural and functional development of the brain, especially of the hemispheres, in man.

Nevertheless, some facts established by the study of conditioned reflexes in the dog may find their parallel in man, since fundamentally the activity of the lower and of the higher parts of the central nervous system is the same in all higher mammalian forms.

In an article written in 1935 Pavlov enumerated the following phenomena of our subjective world which may perhaps find their counterpart in the facts which were established in the dog with the help of conditioned reflexes (Pavlov-Gantt II, 1941, p. 178).

A conditioned reflex is apparently an association by simultaneity. The generalization of a conditioned reflex corresponds to the association of similarity. The analysis and the synthesis of conditioned stimuli is the same fundamental process which we perform during our mental work. Complete absorption in work or conversation to the exclusion of conscious perception of sound or sight may be explained by negative induction. In such instances a strong point of excitation in the central nervous system inhibits all other points. In the complex reflexes (instincts) like hunger, sex attraction, anger, and others it is almost impossible to separate the psychic from the physiological phenomena. Contrast emotions, according to Pavlov, are the manifestation of reciprocal induction. When a strong process of excitation is irradiating over the cerebral cortex, we do things which we would never do when composed; presumably the wave of excitation transforms the inhibitory state of certain cortical points into an excitatory one. Loss of memory in old age for things of the present is explained by Pavlov by the inertness of the excitatory process.[3]

VOLUNTARY MOVEMENTS

One of the most controversial points which hinder unification of the physiological and psychological points of view is the problem of the voluntary control of behavior. Although the psychologists in their laboratory experiments could not establish a sharp line demarcating voluntary activity from reflex response, they still prefer to retain these two conceptions (Hilgard and Marquis, 1940, pp. 257 ff.). Pavlov, on the other hand, believed that all behavior of the animal is based on unconditioned and conditioned reflexes. Every act performed by the animal is determined by external or internal stimuli which are able to evoke an unconditioned or conditioned response. The voluntary acts are not excluded from this scheme.

We are fortunate to have Pavlov's own formulation of the mechanism of voluntary action, as expressed in voluntary movements. It is given by Pavlov in his Introduction to the work of G. Konorsky and S. Miller, *Conditioned Reflexes of the Motor Analyser* (1936).

At the beginning of this Introduction, Pavlov reminded the reader that it was established in his laboratory by N. I. Krasnogorsky that any passive movement of a skeletal muscle, i.e., a kinesthetic stimulation, could be made a signal for a conditioned reflex and that the afferent nature of the cortical motor area in the dog was thus established. The fundamental facts which supplied the basis for the interpretation of the physiological mechanism of voluntary movements were the following:

Stimulation of the kinesthetic cells of the cerebral cortex (e.g., by a faradic current) provokes a definite muscular movement. But a passive movement of the corresponding muscles sends impulses to those very cortical cells, the artificial stimulation of which was responsible for the movement. The latter was illustrated by Pavlov by means of the ordinary method of training a dog to give his paw. The dog is told, "Give me your paw," and his paw is taken and lifted by his master. The animal is rewarded with a piece of food which he likes. After several repetitions of this procedure the words of the command produce the desired effect. The stimulation of the auditory (and probably of the visual) cortical cells coincides under such conditions with the stimulation of the corresponding kinesthetic cortical cells and the gustatory cells. A temporary connection is formed between them. If the animal is hungry and his food center, between which and the gustatory center there exists a close relationship, is in a state of excitation, the dog lifts his paw himself without the words of command. These facts signify that (1) the kinesthetic cells which are stimulated by a passive movement of the muscles evoke the same movement when they are stimulated centrally and (2) the corresponding kinesthetic cells become connected with the auditory and gustatory cells. From this it is evident that the nervous process may move in two opposite directions: either from the kinesthetic cells to the auditory and gustatory cells in case of the formation of the conditioned reflex or from the gustatory cells and food center to the kinesthetic cells when the dog is in a hungry state. An analogous phenomenon takes place during the teaching of piano- or violin-playing; the impulse passes from the visual cells to the kinesthetic cells. Similarly, the kinesthetic cells may be connected with any other cortical cells which represent in the cerebral cortex all the external stimuli acting on the body and all the processes taking place inside it. Thus, the voluntary character of the movements is due to the activity of almost the whole cortex. This physiological interpretation of the voluntary movements, as Pavlov admitted himself, left unsolved the problem of the connection in the cortex of the kinesthetic with the motor cells which give origin to the pyramidal tract. Of the two possible solutions of this problem, that these connections are inborn or that they are acquired in postnatal life, Pavlov was inclined to accept the latter.

It is not possible to say whether Pavlov's theory of voluntary movement explains adequately and in detail one of the most complicated phenomena taking place in the living body. There is very little doubt that Pavlov's fundamental postulate concerning the reflex nature of the cortical processes is correct, but the actual value of his theories, including the theory of voluntary movements, has to be subjected to further experimental study. Whatever the ultimate fate of these theories may be, one will always be amazed by the extraordinary ingenuity of Pavlov, who always found a logical and, at the same time, as simple as possible explanation of the mass of facts discovered by him. This is exactly what made the theoretical conceptions of Pavlov the foundation of so many physiological and psychological investigations of the higher forms of nervous activity.

Here are a few examples. The method of conditioned salivary and motor reflexes was applied directly to man, chiefly to the study of acquired reactions of the nervous system in children (see Krasnogorsky, 1931; Ivanov Smolensky, 1930, 1933). A very interesting conception of the development of binocular vision was proposed by Chavasse (1939). According to him, the binocular reactions to unity, direction, distance, and size are conditioned reflexes which develop on the basis of older (unconditioned) pro-

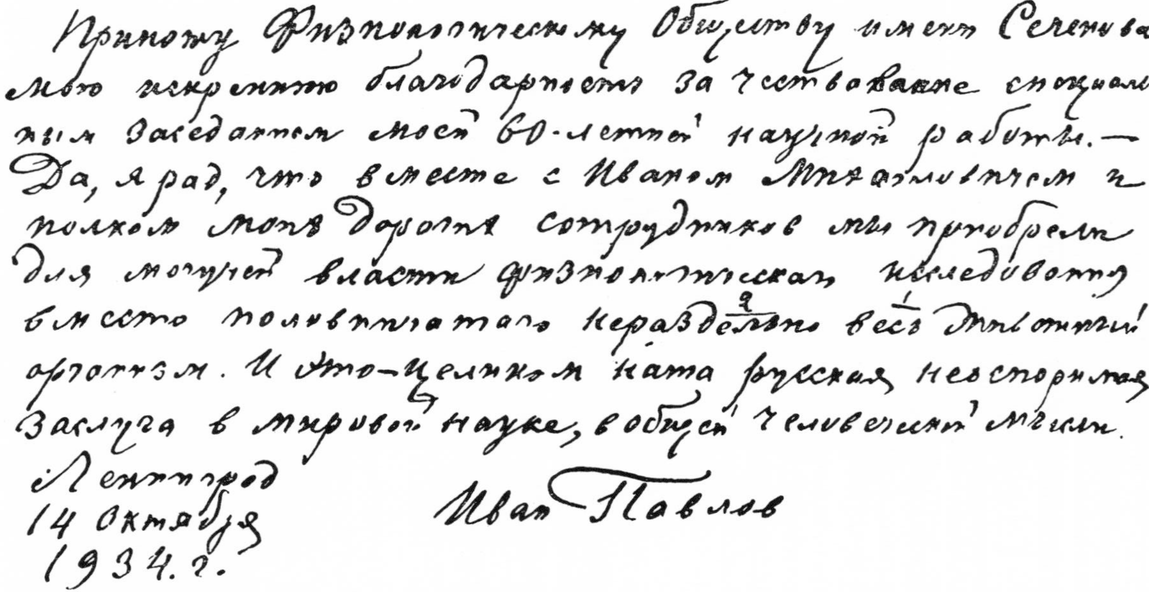

Приношу Физиологическому Обществу имени Сеченова мою искреннюю благодарность за чествование специальным заседанием моей 60-летней научной работы. — Да, я рад, что вместе с Иваном Михайловичем и полком моих дорогих сотрудников мы приобрели для могучей власти физиологического исследования вместо половинчатого нераздельно весь животный организм. И это — целиком наша русская неоспоримая заслуга в мировой науке, в общей человеческой мысли.

Ленинград
14 Октября
1934 г.

Иван Павлов

Fig. 7.—The facsimile of a letter written by I. P. Pavlov in response to a letter of congratulation on his eighty-fifth birthday, sent to him by the members of the Sechenov Physiological Society in Leningrad (*Physiological Journal of U.S.S.R.*, 1934).

CONCLUSION

prioceptive and tactile reflexes. In infancy the binocular reflexes are in a state of flux, but at the age of five years the conditioned reflexes assume unconditioned fixity. We have also seen how extensively the psychologists used the method of conditioned reflexes in its various modifications in man and animals. There is no doubt that the method of conditioned reflexes is making deep inroads into different branches of science dealing with the higher nervous functions. This is a great achievement, the credit for which must go to Pavlov. In his scientific activity Pavlov was always a pathfinder and opened new roads along which other investigators could follow.

The most appropriate way to conclude the review of Pavlov's work on conditioned reflexes is to use his own words, in which he concisely defined the importance of the new, strictly physiological method of studying the cortical functions. It is his reply to the congratulations sent to him on the occasion of his eighty-fifth anniversary by the Sechenov's Physiological Society in Leningrad. The facsimile of this reply (Fig. 7) is on page 1152 of Volume 17 of the *Physiological Journal of U.S.S.R.* (1934), and here is its translation:

I convey my sincere thanks to Sechenov's Physiological Society for the celebration by a special meeting of my sixty years of scientific work. Yes, I am happy that together with Ivan Michailovich [Sechenov] and an army of my dear co-workers, we subordinated to the mighty power of physiological investigation the whole animal organism. This is entirely our Russian achievement and a contribution to world science and human thought.

IVAN PAVLOV

LENINGRAD
October 14, 1934

NOTES

Notes

FOREWORD

1. The original, unabridged typed manuscript of this biography, together with letters written to me by I. P. Pavlov and Mrs. Pavlov, will be deposited in the Osler Library, McGill University, Montreal.

CHAPTER 1

EARLY YEARS

1. September 14 according to the Julian calendar, which was used in Russia up to 1917; September 27 according to the Gregorian calendar of western Europe.

2. Cyon was a worthy successor to the father of Russian physiology, I. M. Sechenov, who shortly before (1870) had relinquished the chair of physiology at the Medico-Chirurgical Academy in St. Petersburg and had accepted the chair of physiology in the University of Odessa. However, Cyon held his professorship at the Academy for only three years, being obliged to resign in 1875. His resignation was due to political factors, according to Kogan (1938). After Sechenov's departure, the Conference of the Academy elected Shkliarevsky to the chair of physiology by a majority of votes. Cyon received the fewer votes. In spite of this, the Minister of War appointed Cyon to the chair on account of the extremely favorable recommendations made by European scientists (Cl. Bernard, Ludwig, Helmholtz, and Pflüger) on his behalf. This was a step which obviously violated the autonomy of the Academy, and those belonging to the Russian liberal group among the professors were naturally opposed to their new colleague. Supporting Cyon there was a minority made up of conservative professors, who were largely German or of German extraction. Thus Cyon found himself aligned with the conservative group and this definitely influenced him for the rest of his life. Cyon, it should be added, had rather an unpleasant personality; he was aggressive, conceited, and extremely ambitious. What most damaged his reputation at the Academy was the fact that he mercilessly failed the students in their examinations. For instance, in 1874 there were in the second year of the medical course one hundred and thirty students who had to repeat the year because they had failed in physiology. All this eventually led to students' riots at the Academy, for which many students were punished, and a campaign began to be

waged against Cyon in the newspapers. At last the students, supported by some of the professors, declared a strike and demanded Cyon's dismissal. Finally the Minister of War was obliged to acquiesce. In 1875 Cyon left the Academy and, departing from Russia for good, settled permanently in Paris. (Cyon's latter history is given in great detail by Kogan.)

CHAPTER 2
Medico-Chirurgical Academy

1. Quoted from the article of Professor Savich, who made this extract from the minutes of the Academy Conference for the year 1890.

CHAPTER 4
Married Life

1. The life of Richard Wagner, by Ernest Newman, in four volumes (New York: Alfred A. Knopf, 1933–46), is a masterpiece. Each statement in the biography is supported by documents, and each piece of evidence is analyzed and scrutinized. Newman had no intention of "painting a portrait" of Wagner, but a living Wagner steps out from the pages of his book with all his greatness and all his faults. This seems to be the only right way to write a biography, which differs so much from the fashionable "art of portrayal" of great men, in our times.

CHAPTER 5
The Military-Medical Academy

1. For the benefit of those who are unfamiliar with this system, I should explain that the period of governmental service in Imperial Russia was twenty-five years, after which the employee was retired on full pension. At the Military-Medical Academy and at all universities a teacher who had served twenty-five years could, on recommendation being made to the minister concerned by the principal of the academy or the rector of the university, be retained for a further five-year term of service, as usually happened. Very few remained for a second five-year term. Since young people of twenty-three or twenty-five on completing their college education immediately entered the government service, their enforced retirement at the end of twenty-five years meant that the work of the professors was often terminated when they were most active.

2. In 1922 I was put in prison by the Bolsheviks in Odessa and after ten days was exiled from Russia. After spending two years in England, doing research work at University College, London, and being unable to find a permanent position in England, I finally, through Professor H. S. Gasser, received an appointment as instructor in pharmacology at Washington University, St. Louis, Mo. Before I could take up this position, however, I was appointed to the chair of physiology at Dalhousie University, thanks to the recommendations of Professor A. V. Hill (see my article, How I came to Dalhousie, Mt. Sinai Hosp., 9:168, 1942). During my stay in England I received two invitations to return to Russia and occupy a chair of physiology. One came from the University of Moscow, the other from Pavlov himself, who offered me his chair in the Military-Medical Academy. I refused both these offers.

CHAPTER 7

I Enter Pavlov's Laboratory

1. V. V. Savich, E. A. Hanike, A. A. Walther and P. G. Borisov, A. P. Sokolov, I. F. Tolochinov, and myself. Abstracts of all these papers may be found in the proceedings of the congress, Förhandlingar vid Nordiska Naturförskare och Läkaremötet (Helsingfors, 1902).

2. Pavlov's last remark had reference to the tragic death in a railway accident of Dr. Walther, who was a *Privatdocent* of physiology at the Military-Medical Academy and Pavlov's favorite pupil. (Soon after the Helsingfors congress in which he had taken part, Walther was journeying from St. Petersburg to be married, and during the night by some accident he fell off the train, which was traveling at full speed. Next morning he was found dead beside the track. He must have been thrown from the platform by a sudden lurch of the train, since his body bore no marks of violence.)

CHAPTER 10

Pavlov's Sense of Reality

1. "Volia"—diminutive for Vladimir.

2. As far as I remember, the sum of money stolen from Pavlov was about $800, although W. B. Cannon (1945) in relating this incident in his book, The way of an investigator (p. 185), stated that it amounted to "over fifteen hundred dollars."

3. The late Professor W. B. Cannon (1945) in his interesting book, The way of an investigator, which actually is his autobiography as a scientist, enumerated the conditions which are essential for successful and productive scientific work. It is interesting to compare Cannon's

recommendations for the production of proper physiological research with the above-described attitude of Pavlov toward experimental work and the requirements which he demanded of himself and of his co-workers. It is amazing how seldom Pavlov was guilty of any of the mistakes enumerated by Cannon, such as "error of incomplete test," "error of omitted control," "error of faulty technique," "neglect of multiple causes," "neglected details," and so on (see pp. 120 ff.).

CHAPTER 13

PAVLOV'S DAY—THE NOBEL PRIZE

1. It seems to me that this statement of Mrs. Pavlov's is not quite exact. Pavlov's Work of the digestive glands, published in Russia in 1897, aroused unusually widespread interest, for translations of it appeared in several languages some years before Pavlov received the Nobel Prize. A German edition was published in 1898, a French edition in 1901, and an English edition in 1902. Few scientific books have had such success.

CHAPTER 14

PAVLOV, THE WRITER

1. Mrs. Pavlov noted in her "Reminiscences" that Pavlov's paper passed unnoticed at the Madrid Physiological Congress. Only a few of the older physiologists became interested in his new approach to the study of the so-called "psychic phenomena" in animals, and they visited the Pavlovs several times.

CHAPTER 15

CLASSICISTS AND ROMANTICISTS

1. Osler's valedictory address, The fixed period, produced an unexpected effect in the United States and caused its author a great deal of trouble. In speaking about the uselessness of men above sixty years of age, Osler in jest quoted Anthony Trollope's novel, The fixed period (*inde nomen* of the valedictory address), in which "the plot hinges upon the admirable scheme of a college into which at 60 men retired for a year of contemplation before a peaceful departure by chloroform" (see Cushing, 1926, p. 667). This joke of Osler's was misunderstood and created a furore in the newspapers and among the public.

CHAPTER 16

PAVLOV'S POLITICAL VIEWS

1. According to Nature (1946) the number of the academicians in the Academy of Science of the U.S.S.R. is 142 and of the corresponding members 208.

CHAPTER 17

Pavlov and the Bolsheviks

1. Although this whole incident gives evidence of the nobility of character, the intelligence, and the farsightedness of Professor X, I cannot bring myself to name him. It is completely uncertain how life in conquered Germany will work out and whether those persons will be persecuted who did not at the proper time bow themselves to the hypnotism of Hitlerian folly and who were able to distinguish true patriotism from an obsession of grandeur.

2. Besides Professor H. J. Muller, five British scientists—S. C. Harland, C. D. Darlington, R. A. Fisher and J. B. S. Haldane (see The Lysenko controversy, The Listener, 40:873, December 9, 1948), and E. Ashby (see Genetics in Soviet Union, Nature, 162:912, December 11, 1948)—expressed their views on Lysenko's teaching. They all, with the exception of J. B. S. Haldane, were highly critical about Lysenko's claims and his attitude toward other geneticists. Haldane obviously had some sympathy with the Soviets' views, but his article was written very guardedly.

CHAPTER 20

Centrifugal Nerves of the Heart

1. The question of priority in the discovery of the augmentor nerves was discussed by Pavlov in his article in the Archiv für Physiologie, 1887, p. 564. Pavlov began to work on the innervation of the heart indedependently of Gaskell in 1882. The preliminary communication of Gaskell on the augmentation of the heart contractions on stimulation of the vagus in the frog, which was printed in the August number of the Journal of physiology for 1882, came to Pavlov's knowledge only at the beginning of the next year, 1883. Before that, several articles on the action of the cardiac nerves were published by Pavlov in the Weekly clinical gazette of Botkin in 1882 and 1883; his M.D. thesis was published in 1883, and in the same year there appeared a preliminary communication of his result in the Centralblatt für die medicinische Wissenschaften, Nos. 4 and 5, 1883.

CHAPTER 23

Specific Excitability of the Afferent Nerves

1. This quotation is taken from the first and second editions of Thompson's translation of Pavlov's book. The translations in the first and in the second editions varied somewhat and did not quite coincide with the Russian text, some sentences being changed or even omitted.

I have restored the original rendition. Why these changes were made in the English translation and by whom it is difficult to say because Professor Thompson was not familiar with the Russian language and probably used the German (A. A. Walther's) or French editions of Pavlov's Lectures as his text for translation.

CHAPTER 26

The Gastrointestinal Tract

1. In C. C. Mettler's History of medicine (Philadelphia and Toronto: Blakiston Co., 1947) in chap. 3, dealing with the physiology of the nineteenth century (Digestive function, p. 159), and in the Selected readings for chap. 3, neither Blondlot's nor Pavlov's name was mentioned although many far less important investigators were quoted. Pavlov's name appears in this book only once, and incorrectly, in connection with the Eck fistula. The author claims that Pavlov was the first who performed the Eck operation in the dog, but this is not correct. The credit must go to Dr. Eck. About the conditioned reflexes the reader is not informed at all.

INTRODUCTION TO PART IV

1. To the chorus of Pavlov's critics must be added the noisy voice of George Bernard Shaw. This vociferous playwright unfortunately was unable to grasp a new scientific idea. In his book Everybody's political what's what (1944) Shaw dedicated to Pavlov a whole chapter (chap. xxiii, The man of science, pp. 200–213). Shaw considers the whole teaching of conditioned reflexes "a crackle of blazing nonsense from beginning to end" (p. 208) and Pavlov himself a "scoundrel" (p. 209), which means a person who repudiates common morality in the pursuit of his personal or professional interest, or, according to Shorter Oxford English dictionary (1933), "an audacious rascal, one destitute of all moral scruple." However, Shaw did make a slight concession and said that Pavlov reached imbecility not in a single jump but gradually (p. 207). Shaw fabricated and ascribed to Pavlov opinions which Pavlov never expressed and never could express, e.g., that Pavlov pretended that "the laboratory-made science is the whole science" (p. 212). One may only feel sorry for Shaw, who gave clear evidence of his inability to understand rather simple things. Thus, for example, he wrote in this chapter on Pavlov: "The natural mouth watering at the sight and smell of food he [Pavlov] called an unconditioned reflex. The watering provoked by some sensation which became connected in the dog's experiment with food, . . . he called conditioned reflex" (p. 206). Undoubtedly Shaw wasted his time in reading and discussing Pavlov's book on Conditioned reflexes (trans. Anrep).

CHAPTER 27
ORIGIN OF THE CONDITIONED REFLEXES

1. The results of Pavlov's work on conditioned reflexes were collected by him in two Russian books, the one mentioned above, Twenty years, etc., which up to 1932 had five editions, and another, Lectures on the work of the hemispheres of the brain (Moscow and Leningrad, 1927). The first book was translated by W. Horsley Gantt under the title of Lectures on conditioned reflexes (New York: International Publishers, 1928). Some of Pavlov's articles which appeared in subsequent Russian editions of this book and separate articles and pamphlets in which he discussed the neuroses formed another volume which was also translated by Dr. Gantt under the title Conditioned reflexes and psychiatry (New York: International Publishers, 1941). For brevity's sake I shall quote the Lectures on conditioned reflexes as "Pavlov-Gantt I, 1928" and Conditioned Reflexes and psychiatry as "Pavlov-Gantt II, 1941"]. Pavlov's own systematic exposition of the teaching of conditioned reflexes, Lectures on the work of the hemispheres of the brain, was translated by G. V. Anrep under the title Conditioned reflexes: an investigation of the physiological activity of the cerebral cortex (London: Oxford University Press, 1927). This book I shall quote as "Pavlov-Anrep, 1927." We must be especially thankful to Dr. Gantt, who spent several years in Leningrad working in Pavlov's laboratory, mastered the Russian language, translated and supplied with introductions and footnotes all of Pavlov's articles, addresses, speeches, etc., and brought to the United States Pavlov's original method of conditioned reflexes, with the help of which he continues to work most successfully himself.

The useful book by E. R. Hilgard and D. G. Marquis, Conditioning and learning (New York: D. Appleton–Century Co., 1940), may be recommended to those who are interested in the psychological approach to the teaching of conditioned reflexes.

CHAPTER 29
J. HUGHLINGS JACKSON

1. Jackson was a very prolific writer. He wrote more than two hundred articles. The most important of these were collected in two volumes: Selected writings of John Hughlings Jackson (London: Hodder & Stoughton, Ltd., 1931 and 1932). Jackson's articles will be quoted by me by the volume and page of his Selected writings.

CHAPTER 31
PHYSIOLOGICAL DISCIPLINE

1. At that period Professor Lashley worked with J. B. Watson in his psychological laboratory at Johns Hopkins University.

2. J. B. Watson, The place of the conditioned reflex in psychology, Psychol. Rev., 23:89, 1916 (a presidential address delivered in 1915 before the American Psychological Association).

3. [We must not forget the work of W. H. Gantt, S. Dworkin, and H. S. Liddell.–B. P. B.]

CHAPTER 32
CONCLUSION

1. It is interesting to note that according to Beritoff and Vorobjev (1943) the appearance of alpha waves is due not only to the darkening of the retina but to the exteroceptive and proprioceptive excitation of the eye muscles, of the eyelids, and of the surface of the eyeball when it comes in contact with the eyelid. The appearance of alpha waves in these cases is not an inborn reflex but a conditioned one. Beritoff and Vorobjev were able to form a corresponding conditioned reflex and to obtain the alpha waves by producing a sound which was combined several times with a darkening of the retina.

2. In a personal communication Dr. Penfield added the following: The visual responses from the occiput are on the basis of inborn structure and do not require epileptic conditioning. The same is true of sound-responses arising in the first temporal convolution. The hallucinations and illusions obtained by the stimulation of the temporal lobes are, on the other hand, dependent on acquired patterns. They must be properly facilitated by repeated epileptic discharges before they are capable of being evoked by the stimulating electrode.

3. A psychological subdivision of the conditioned reaction into its different forms led to the introduction into the theories of learning of a concept of different "principles," such as "principle of substitution," "principle of effect," "principle of expectancy," and many others. Those who are interested in these problems may find them discussed by Hilgard and Marquis (1940, pp. 76 ff.). An elaborated theory of learning, based on principles established by Pavlov in his conditioned reflex studies, was proposed by Hull (Hilgard and Marquis, pp. 207 ff.).

REFERENCES

References

ABDERHALDEN, E. Lehrbuch der Physiologie, Vol. 2. Berlin and Vienna: Urban & Schwarzenberg, 1925.
AFANASSIEW, M., and PAVLOV, I. Pflüger's Arch. f. d. ges. Physiol., 16: 173, 1878.
ANREP, G. V. J. Physiol., 50: 421, 1915–16.
ANREP, G. V., and KHAN, H. N. J. Physiol., 58: 302, 1924.
ASHER, L. Handb. d. norm. u. path. Physiol., 7, Part 1, 402. Berlin: J. Springer, 1926.
BABKIN, B. P. Die aüssere Sekretion der Verdauungsdrüsen. Berlin: J. Springer, 1928.
———. Rev. Canad. de biol., 2: 416, 1943.
———. Secretory mechanism of the digestive glands. New York: Paul B. Hoeber, Inc., 1944.
———. Arch. Neurol. & Psychiat., 60: 520, 1948.
BARCROFT, J. Features in the architecture of physiological function. London: Cambridge University Press, 1934.
BASSOW. Bull. de Soc. d. natur. de Moscou, 16: 315, 1842. (Quoted from PAVLOV, I. P. 1902.)
BAXTER, S. G. Quart. J. Exper. Physiol., 21: 355, 1932.
———. Am. J. Digest. Dis. & Nutrition, 1: 36, 1934.
BAYLISS, W. M. Principles of general physiology. 4th ed. London: Longmans, Green & Co., 1924.
BAYLISS, W. M., and STARLING, E. H. J. Physiol., 28: 325, 1902.
———. Ergebn. d. Physiol., 5: 664, 1906.
BEAUMONT, W. Experiments and observations on the gastric juice and the physiology of digestion. Plattsburgh: F. P. Allen, 1833.
BECHTEREV, W. Objective psychology. 1907. (Quoted from IVANOV-SMOLENSKY, A., p. 103. 1929. [Russian.])
———. Problems in study and education of character, Nos. 4 and 5. 1922. (Russian.)
———. Allgemeine Grundlagen der Reflexologie des Menschen: Leitfaden für das objektive Studien der Persönlichkeit. Leipzig and Vienna: F. Deutike, 1926.
BELITSKI, I. S. Rev. Psychiat., Neurol. & Exper. Psychol., p. 34, 1906. (Russian.)
BERITOFF, I. S. J. f. Psychol. u. Neurol., 33: 113, 1927.
———. The general physiology of the muscular and nervous systems. Moscow and Leningrad: Biomedgiz, 1937.

REFERENCES

BERITOFF, I. S., and VOROBJEV, A. Tr. Beritashvili's Physiol. Inst., Tiflis, 5:369, 1943.
BERNARD, CL. Leçons sur les phénomènes de la vie communs aux animaux et aux végétaux, Vol. 2. Paris: Baillière, 1878–79.
BIDDER, F., and SCHMIDT, C. Die Verdauungssäfte und der Stoffwechsel. Mittau and Leipzig, 1852.
BLONDLOT, N. Traité analytique de la digestion considérée particulièrement dans l'homme et dans les animaux vertébrés. Paris: Fortin, Masson & Cie; Nancy: Grimblot, Raybois & Cie, 1843.
BOLDYREFF, V. N. Arch. d. Sc. biol., St. Petersburg, 10: 361, 1904.
BORISOV, P., and WALTHER, A. Förh. Nord. Naturförsk. Läk., p. 42. Helsingfors, 1902.
BOUCHUT, E. Histoire de médecine et des doctrines médicales, Vol. 2. Paris: Baillière, 1873.
BROWNE, J. S. L., and VINEBERG, A. M. J. Physiol., 75: 345, 1932.
BROWN-SÉQUARD, C. E. Lancet, 2: 105, 1889.
BYKOV, K. M., and PETROVA, M. K. Tr. I. P. Pavlov's Physiol. Lab., 2, No. 1, 91, 1927. (Russian.)
CANNON, W. B. The way of an investigator. New York: W. W. Norton & Co., 1945.
CHAVASSE, F. B. Worth's squint. 7th ed. London: Baillière, Tindall & Co., 1939.
CHERNIGOVSKY, W. N. Arch. Biol. Sc., 54, No. 2, 80, 1939. (Russian.)
CHESHKOV, A. M. One year and seven months of life of a dog after a simultaneous section of both vagi nerves in the neck. St. Petersburg, 1902. (Russian.)
CHISTOVICH, N. J. Reminiscences on work under I. P. Pavlov in 1886–87, in Jubilee volume dedicated to I. P. Pavlov on his 75th birthday, p. 27. Leningrad: State Publishers, 1924. (Russian.)
CREED, R. S.; DENNY-BROWN, D.; ECCLES, J. C.; LIDDELL, E. G. T.; and SHERRINGTON, C. S. Reflex activity of the spinal cord. London: Oxford University Press, 1932.
CRIDER, J. O., and THOMAS, J. E. Am. J. Physiol., 141: 730, 1944.
CRITTENDEN, P. J., and IVY, A. C. Am. J. Physiol., 119: 724, 1937.
CULLER, E., and METTLER, F. A. J. Comp. Psychol., 18: 291, 1934.
CUSHING, HARVEY. The life of Sir William Osler, 1: 666. London: Oxford University Press, 1926.
CYON, E. Methodik der physiologischen Experimente und Vivisection, mit Atlas. Giessen: G. Rickersche Buchhandlung; St. Petersburg: Carl Ricker, 1876.
CZERMAK, J. Sitzungsb. d. Akad. Wien, Math.-naturw. Kl., 25: 3, 1857.
DELEZENNE, C., and FROUIN, A. Compt. rend. Soc. de biol., 54: 691, 1902.
DENIKE, J. The new ideological politics, New Rev., 19: 165, 1948. (Russian.)

REFERENCES

DENNY-BROWN, D. J. Neurol. & Psychopath., 13:52, 1932–33.

EDKINS, J. S. J. Physiol., 34:133, 1906.

ELIASON, M. M. Proc. Soc. Russ. Physicians, St. Petersburg, Vol. 75, 1907–8. (Russian.)

FAGGE, C. H. Tr. Med.-Chir. Soc. London, 54:155, 1871.

FERRIER, D. Functions of the brain. London: Smith, Elder & Co., 1876.

FROLOFF, J. Pflüger's Arch. f. d. ges. Physiol., 201:261, 1926; 220:339, 1928.

FROUIN, A. Compt. rend. Soc. de biol., 63:473, 1907.

GASKELL, W. H. J. Physiol., 7:1, 1887.

———. The contraction of the cardiac muscle, in Schäfer's textbook of physiology, 2:169. Edinburgh and London: Y. J. Pentland, 1900.

GERVER, A. V. Rev. Psychiat., Neurol. & Exper. Psychol., p. 191, 1900. (Russian.)

GIRDEN, E.; METTLER, F. A.; FINCH, G.; and CULLER, E. J. Comp. Psychol., 21:367, 1936.

GLINSKY, D. L. On the physiology of the intestines. Thesis. St. Petersburg, 1891. (Russian.)

GOLTZ, F. Pflüger's Arch. f. d. ges. Physiol., 51:570, 1892.

GORSHKOV. Thesis. St. Petersburg, 1901. (Quoted from PAVLOV, I. P. Lectures on conditioned reflexes. Translated by W. HORSLEY GANTT. New York: International Publishers, 1928.)

GRAHAM, E. A. Harvey Lect., 29:176, 1933–34.

HARPER, A. A., and RAPER, H. S. J. Physiol., 102:115, 1943.

HARPER, A. A., and VASS, C. C. N. J. Physiol., 99:415, 1941.

HEIDENHAIN, R. Pflüger's Arch. f. d. ges. Physiol., 17:62, 1878.

———. Ibid., 19:148, 1879.

———. Physiologie der Absonderungsvorgänge, in Hermann's Handb. d. Physiol., Vol. 5, Part 1, 1880.

HERING, E. Zur Theorie der Vorgänge in der lebendigen Substanz, Lotos, 9:35–70, 1889.

HEYNE, M. Deutsches Arch. f. klin. Med., 47:75, 1891.

HILGARD, E. R., and MARQUIS, D. G. Conditioning and learning. New York: D. Appleton–Century Co., 1940.

HOWELL-FULTON. Text-book of physiology. 15th ed. Philadelphia: W. B. Saunders Co., 1946.

IPATIEFF, V. N. Life of one chemist, Vols. 1 and 2. New York, 1945. (Russian.)

IVANOV-SMOLENSKY, A. Natural science and the science of human behavior. Moscow, 1929. (Russian.)

JACKSON, J. H. Selected writings. Edited by J. TAYLOR. London: Hodder & Stoughton, Vol. 1, 1931; Vol. 2, 1932.

JURGENS, N. P. The condition of the alimentary canal as a result of the chronic paralysis of the vagi nerves. Thesis. St. Petersburg, 1892. (Russian.)

REFERENCES

KACHKOVSKY, P. Survival of dogs after a simultaneous section of both vagi nerves in the neck. Thesis. St. Petersburg, 1899. (Russian.)

KALMIKOV, M. Russian Physiol. J., Vol. 8, 1925. (Quoted from CHERNIGOVSKY.)

KAMENSKI, D. A. Jubilee volume, Arch. d. sc. biol., suppl., 11:xii, 1904.

KHIZIN, P. P. The secretory work of the stomach in the dog. Thesis. St. Petersburg, 1894. (Russian.)

KLEMENSIEWICZ, R. Sitzungsb. d. Akad. Wien, Math.-naturw. Kl., 71, Abt. III, 249, 1875.

KOGAN, S. R. M. Rec., 148:331, 1938.

KONORSKY, G., and MILLER, C. Tr. I. P. Pavlov's Physiol. Lab., 6:115, 1936. (Russian.)

KOROWITZKY, L. K. J. Physiol., 57:215, 1923.

KOSHTOYANZ, C. S. A page from the life of I. P. Pavlov: work on the physiology of digestion. Moscow and Leningrad: Academy of Science of U.S.S.R., 1937. (Russian.)

KRASNOGORSKY, N. I. Ergebn. d. inn. Med. u. Kinderh., 39:613, 1931.

LA BARRE, J., and DESTRÉE, P. Compt. rend. Soc. de biol., 98:1237, 1928.

LANGLEY, J. N. J. Physiol., 6:71, 1886.

———. Schäfer's textbook of physiology, 2:674. Edinburgh and London: Y. J. Pentland, 1900.

LANGSTROTH, G. P.; MCRAE, D. R.; and KOMAROV, S. A. Canad. J. Research, Part D, 17:137, 1939.

LE BEAU, J. Rev. Canad. de biol., 1:134, 1942.

LEBEDINSKAIA, S. I., and ROSENTHAL, J. S. Brain, 58:412, 1935.

———. Tr. I. P. Pavlov's Physiol. Lab., 8:463. 1938. (Russian.)

LINTVAREV, I. I. The influence of different physiological conditions on the diverse state and quantity of the enzymes in the pancreatic juice. Thesis. St. Petersburg, 1901. (Russian.)

LOBASSOV, I. O. The secretory work of the stomach in the dog. Thesis. St. Petersburg, 1896. (Russian.)

LÖNNQUIST, B. Skandinav. Arch. f. Physiol., 18:194, 1906.

LOGANSKY. (Quoted from FLOROV, Y. P. Pavlov and his school. London: Kegan Paul, Trench, Trubner & Co., 1938.)

McDOWALL, R. J. S. The control of the circulation of the blood. London: Longmans, Green & Co., 1938.

MAGNUS, R. Körperstellung. Berlin: J. Springer, 1924.

MASSERMAN, J. H. Behavior and neurosis. Chicago: University of Chicago Press, 1943.

MIRONOV, M. M. See Pavlov's remarks about the work of Dr. MIRONOV. Proc. Soc. Russ. Physicians, St. Petersburg, Vol. 60, May, 1894. (Quoted from PAVLOV, I. P. Collected works, 1:319. Moscow and Leningrad, 1940. [Russian.])

MULLER, H. J. Letter to the president, the secretary and the membership of the Academy of Science of the U.S.S.R., Science, 108:436, 1948.

REFERENCES

MUNK, H. Die Funktionen der Grosshirnrinde. Berlin: A. Hirschwald, 1890.

ORBELI, L. A. Proc. Soc. Russ. Physicians, St. Petersburg, Vol. 75, 1908. (Russian.)

———. Introduction, in Collected works of I. P. Pavlov. Moscow and Leningrad: Academy of Science of U.S.S.R., 1940. (Russian.)

———. Lectures on problems of higher nervous activity. Moscow and Leningrad: Academy of Science of U.S.S.R., 1945. (Russian.)

OSTWALD, WILHELM. Grösse Männer, Vol. 1. Leipzig: Akademische Verlagsgesellschaft, 1909; 2d, 3d, and 4th eds., 1910.

PAVLOV, I. P. a. Pflüger's Arch. f. d. ges. Physiol., 16:123, 1878.

———. b. Ibid., p. 266.

———. c. Ibid., p. 272.

———. d. Ibid., 17:555, 1878.

———. a. Ibid., 20:210, 1879.

———. b. Ibid., p. 215.

———. Tr. Soc. Biologists Univ. St. Petersburg, 11:51, 1879. (Russian.)

———. Week. Clin. Gaz., Nos. 26 and 38, 1882. (Russian.)

———. The centrifugal nerves of the heart. Thesis. St. Petersburg, 1883. (Russian.)

———. Pflüger's Arch. f. d. ges. Physiol., 37:6, 1885.

———. a. Arch. f. (Anat. u.) Physiol., p. 452, 1887.

———. b. Ibid., p. 498.

———. a. Week. Clin. Gaz., p. 469, 1888. (Russian.)

———. b. Innervation of the pancreatic gland, Week. Clin. Gaz., p. 667, 1888. (Russian.)

———. Fifth Pirogov's Convention of Physicians, 1:216, 1894.

———. Tr. Soc. Russ. Physicians, Vol. 61, April, 1895. (Russian.)

———. Ibid., Vol. 63, March–June, 1896. (Russian.)

———. Lectures on the work of the principal digestive glands. St. Petersburg, 1897. (Russian.)

———. Compt. rend. 13ᵉ Cong. internat. de méd., Paris, p. 55, 1901.

———. Lectures on the work of the digestive glands. Translated by W. H. THOMPSON. London: Charles Griffin & Co., 1902; 2d ed., 1910.

———. Die physiologische Chirurgie des Verdauungskanals, Ergebn. d. Physiol., 1, Abt. 1, 46, 1902.

———. Tr. Soc. Russ. Physicians, Vol. 72, March–May, 1905. (Quoted from PAVLOV, I. P. Collected works, 1:365. Moscow and Leningrad, 1940. [Russian.])

———. Die äussere Arbeit der Verdauungsdrüsen und ihr Mechanismus, in Nagel's Handb. d. Physiol. d. Menschen, 2:666 ff. Braunschweig: Vieweg & Sohn, 1907.

———. Die operative Methodik des Studiums der Verdauungsdrüsen, in Tigerstedt's Handb. d. physiol. Methodik, 2, Part 2, 150, 1908.

[351]

REFERENCES

PAVLOV, I. P. A. A. Nechaiev's jubilee volume. Petrograd, 1922. (Russian.)
———. Twenty years of objective study of the higher nervous activity (behavior) of animals. Moscow and Petrograd: State Edition, 1923. (Russian.)
———. Skandinav. Arch. f. Physiol., 47:7, 1925.
———. Conditioned reflexes. Translated by G. V. ANREP. London: Oxford University Press, 1927.
———. Lectures on conditioned reflexes. Translated by W. HORSLEY GANTT. New York: International Publishers, 1928.
———. Collected works, Vol. 1. Moscow and Leningrad: Academy of Science of U.S.S.R., 1940. (Russian.)
———. Conditioned reflexes and psychiatry. Translated by W. HORSLEY GANTT. New York: International Publishers, 1941.
PAVLOV, I. P. and SHUMOV-SIMANOVSKY, E. O. Innervation of the gastric glands in the dog, Vratch, No. 41, 1890. (Russian.)
PAVLOV, I. P., and STOLNIKOV, J. J. Arch. Botkin's Clin. Intern. Dis., Vol. 6, 1879. (Russian.)
PENFIELD, W. L'Année psychologique, Vol. 39. Paris: Presses universitaires de France; Paris: Alcan, 1938. Also in Arch. Neurol. & Psychiat., 40:417, 1938.
PFLÜGER, E. Die sensorischen Funktionen des Rückenmarkes der Wirbelthiere, 14:1–145. Berlin: A. Hirschwald, 1853.
POLTYREV, S. S., and ZELIONY, G. P. Ztschr. f. Biol., 90:157, 1930.
PROTOPOPOV, V. P. Associative motor reaction to acoustic stimuli. St. Petersburg, 1909. (Russian.)
PROUT. J. de physiol. expér., 4:294, 1824. (Quoted from LOEPER, M. Histoire de la sécrétion gastrique, p. 99. Paris: Masson & Cie, 1924.)
ROSEN, G. The reception of William Beaumont's discovery in Europe. New York: H. Schuman, 1942.
SAMUEL, S. Die trophischen Nerven. Leipzig: O. Wigand, 1860.
SAVICH, V. V. The secretion of the intestinal juice. Thesis. St. Petersburg, 1904. (Russian.)
———. Ivan Petrovich Pavlov, in Jubilee volume dedicated to I. P. Pavlov on his 75th birthday. Leningrad: State Publishers, 1924. (Russian.)
SCHWANN, TH. Arch. f. Anat. u. Physiol., p. 90, 1836.
SECHENOV, I. Selected works. Moscow and Leningrad: State Publishing House, 1935.
SHERRINGTON, SIR CHARLES. Man on his nature. London: Cambridge University Press, 1940.
SHWARTZ, S. Debacle of science in U.S.S.R., Socialist Courier, September 27, 1948, p. 147. (Russian.)
SIPPY, B. J.A.M.A., Vol. 64, May 15, 1915.
SPIRTOV, N. I. Rev. Psychiat., Neurol. & Exper. Psychol., p. 120, 1909. (Russian.)

REFERENCES

STRÜMPELL, A. Pflüger's Arch. f. d. ges. Physiol., 15:573, 1877.

TANTURI, C. A., and IVY, A. C. Am. J. Physiol., 121:270, 1938.

THIRY, L. Sitzungsb. d. Akad. Wien, Math.-naturw. Kl., 1:50, 77, 1864.

THOMAS, J. E. Proc. Soc. Exper. Biol. & Med., 28:968, 1931.

TICHOMIROV, N. P. Thesis. St. Petersburg, 1906. (Russian.)

TIGERSTEDT, R. Arch. d. sc. biol., suppl., 2:iii ff., 1904.

VAN DEN BERGH, A. A. H. Brit. M.J., 2:498, 1924.

VELIKI, V. N., and PAVLOV, I. P. Tr. Soc. Biologists Univ. St. Petersburg, 5:lxvi, 1874. (Quoted from PAVLOV, I. P. Collected works, Vol. 1. Moscow and Leningrad, 1940.)

VERWORN, M. Physiologisches Practicum für Mediziner, p. 202. Jena: G. Fischer, 1932.

VOLBORTH, G. W., and KUDZYAVZEFF, N. N. Am. J. Physiol., 81:154, 1927.

WALTHER, A. A. The secretory work of the pancreatic gland. Thesis. St. Petersburg, 1897. (Russian.)

WATSON, J. B. Behaviorism. New York: W. W. Norton & Co., 1925.

YOUGOV, ALEXIS. Ivan Petrovich Pavlov. Edited by L. N. FEDOROV. Moscow and Leningrad: People's Commissariat of Education, 1942. (Russian.)

ZIEMSSEN, H. VON. Deutsches Arch. f. klin. Med., 47:89, 1891.

INDEX

Index

Abderhalden, E., 199
Academy of Science, St. Petersburg, 113, 156
Adaptation, 254
Adonis vernalis, 20
Afanassiew, M. I., 14, 202, 203, 204, 205, 214
Albitsky, P. M., 57, 63, 64
Alexander II, 11, 105, 158, 159, 292
Alexander III, 158, 159
Alkali: effect of, on gastric secretion, 268
Alley, Armine, 77
Anabolic nerves, 245 ff.
Analyzer, 307, 312
Andreyev, L. A., 179
Angell, 320
Anrep, G. V., 247, 250, 252, 343
Artificial sutures, 74, 75, 77
Ashby, E., 341
Asher, L., 199
Atropine: effect of, on pancreatic secretion of dog and rabbit, 203
Augmentor nerve of the heart, 22, 23, 189 ff.; as trophic nerve of the heart, 194, 195

Barcroft, J., 247, 255
Bauman, 153
Baxter, S., 251, 252
Bayliss, W. M., 101, 102, 227, 228, 229
Beaumont, W., 217, 236, 256, 259
Bechterev, V. M.: laboratory of, 75; and his attendant Peter, 76; and reflexology, 87; and objective psychology, 88; controversy of, with Pavlov, 89 ff.; asked by Pavlov to repeat Belitski's experiment, 93; and failure of Spirtov's demonstration, 94; preferred to work with motor conditioned reflexes, 304; and view that cortical salivary center is nec-

essary for conditioned reflexes, 307; American psychologists and, 320–21
Beethoven, L. van, 150
Belitski, J., 90, 93, 94
Beritoff, I. S., 282, 304, 308, 316, 344
Bernard, Claude, 206, 219, 337
Bernstein, N. O., 204
Bezold, 198
Bicha, 149
Bichurina, A., actress, 29, 30
Bidder, F., 236
Bile: discharge of, into duodenum, 264
Binet, 320
Blondlot, N., 235, 236; influence of, on Pavlov, 256 ff.; on the effect of alkali, 268, 342
Blood circulation, 187 ff.
Bochefontaine, 90
Bock, M. M., 181
Boldyreff, V. N., 73, 266
Borisov, P., 229, 339
Botkin, S. P., 18, 19, 163
Bouchut, E., 224
Brest Litovsk peace treaty, 104
Bridgman, Laura, 300
Browne, J. S. L., 249
Brown-Séquard, C. E., 225
Brüke, 289
Buchstab, J. A., 100
Burdon-Sanderson, 151
Bykov, K. M., 309

Cannon, W. B., 106, 179, 219, 255, 266, 280, 339, 340
Carlson, A. J., 106, 266
Cattell, 320
Cerebral cortex: as a seat of psychic activity, 273; Pavlov's desire to study functions of, physiologically, 276; reflexes of, 283; as chief organ

[357]

INDEX

of conditioned reflexes, 302, 306, 307; in decorticated dog, 308; analysis and synthesis in, 312; processes of excitation and inhibition in, 313; and mosaic of function, 313
Chavasse, F. B., 331
Chechulin, S. I., 244
Chekhov, A. P., 119
Chemical phase of gastric secretion, 226, 227
Chernigovsky, W. N., 201
Cheshkov, A. M., 207, 208
Chistovich, N. J., 22, 120, 201
Churchill, Winston, 150
Classicists in science, 144 ff.
Conditioned reflexes, 140, 273 ff.; formation of, 273; origin of, 275 ff.; Jackson's three levels of evolution and, 296; history of the method of study of, 301; natural, 303; artificial, 304; are they reflexes? 304; motor, 304; proofs of the reflex nature of, 305 ff.; as a physiological discipline, 311 ff.; mechanism of formation of, 311; generalization of, 312; differentiation of, 313; irradiation and concentration of, 313, 314, 315, 316; and different kinds of inhibition, 314; and induction, 315; and three signaling systems in the brain, 317; psychology and, 318 ff.; importance of, for neurophysiology, 323; consciousness and, 327; psychic phenomena and, 328, 329; voluntary movements and, 329 ff.
Congress of Northern Naturalists and Physicians, in Helsingfors, 82
Congress of Physiologists, All-Russian, 154
Consciousness, 325 ff.
Convallaria majalis, 20, 190
Crider, J. O., 241
Crittenden, P. J., 250
Culler, E., 307
Cushing, Harvey, 149, 151, 340
Cyon, Ilya, 13, 58, 198, 337, 338

Danilevski, A. J., 59, 68
Danilevski, V. J., 68

Darlington, C. D., 341
Davy, Sir Humphry, 144
Delezenne, C., 243, 244
Denny-Brown, D. E., 274, 316
Destree, P., 250
Dolinski, I. L., 189
Dostoevski, F. M., 29, 30, 150
Dualism, 281
Du Bois-Reymond, 289
Duma, Imperial, 153
Dworkin, S., 344
Dynamic nerves, 190, 198

Eck, Dr., 342
Edkins, J. S., 227
Eliason, M. M., 91
Enterogastric reflex, 266
Enterogastrone, 266
Enterokinase, 242, 264
Enukidze, secretary of ZIK, 156
Ergosterol, 197
Experimental pathology, 266, 267
Experimental therapeutics, 266, 267

Fagge, C. H., 225
Faraday, Michael, 144
Fedorov, 175, 176
Ferrier, D., 278, 293, 295, 299
Finch, G., 307
Fisher, R. A., 341
Florinski, Dean, 55
Fritsch, G., 278, 286, 293
Frolov, Y. P., 111, 133
Frouin, A., 243, 244
Fulton, J. F., 214, 308

Gantt, W. Horsley, 3, 4, 13, 111, 324, 343, 344
Gaskell, W. H., 23, 190, 194, 195, 198, 199, 245, 246, 251, 252
Gasser, H. S., 339
Gastric glands, 226 ff.; Pavlov's contribution to the physiology of, 262
Gastric-juice factory, 69, 72, 131
Gastrin, 237
Gauss, 145
Gelman, H. I., 67
Gerhardt, C., 144
Gerver, A. V., 90
Giblin, Norris, 77

[358]

INDEX

Girden, E., 307
Glinski, D. L., 221, 235
Goltz, F., 220, 278
Gorodki: Pavlov's love of the game, 12, 13, 134
Gorshkov, 90, 91
Graham test, 174
Grekov, 175, 176
Gustav, King of Sweden: his reception of Pavlov, 136

Haldane, J. B. S., 341
Haldane, J. S., 219
Hanike, E. A., 69, 71, 339
Harland, S. C., 341
Harper, A. A., 230, 251
Heart-lung preparation, 200 ff.
Heidenhain, R., 17, 190, 198, 203, 205, 215, 217, 222, 235, 239, 240, 241, 245, 258, 260
Heidenhain pouch, 222
Hellebori viridis, 20, 22, 301
Helmholtz, H. von, 144, 148, 277, 337
Henderson, L. J., 255
Heparin, 194
Hering, E., 246, 277, 315, 316
Heyne, M., 290
Hilgard, E. R., 274, 305, 306, 319, 329, 343, 344
Hill, A. V., 339
Histamine, 226
History of medicine, 77 ff., 83
Hitler, Adolf, 167, 168, 169
Hitzig, E., 278, 286, 293
Homeostasis, 219
Horsley, V., 293
Howe, S. G., 300
Howell, W. H., 194, 308
Hull, 344
Humoral pathology, 224
Huxley, Julian, 172

Ibsen, Henrik, 104
Institute of Experimental Medicine, 67 ff.; as chief place of Pavlov's work, 67, 70, 73; physiological laboratory of, 68; budget of, 69; and preparation of gastric juice, 69, 70, 72; graduate students in, 70

Institute of Postgraduate Studies, St. Petersburg, 18
Intestinal juice, 264
Ipatieff, V. N., 155, 157
Islands of Langerhans, 205
Ivanov Smolensky, A., 331
Ivy, A. C., 237, 250, 251

Jablonski, J. M., 243
Jackson, J. Hughlings: as Pavlov's predecessor, 274, 283, 284; influenced by Spencer, 293; and three levels of evolution, 294, 318; ideas of, on the nervous and mental state, 297; and doctrine of concomitance, 297; and theory of the motor compound of a reflex, 298; and theory of origin of speech, 299
Jurgens, N. P., 207

Kachkovsky, P., 207
Kaiser-Wilhelm-Gesellschaft zur Förderung der Wissenschaften, 67
Kamenski, D. A., 56, 57
Karlsbad, 174, 175, 176
Kasso, 167
Katabolic nerves, 245 ff.
Khan, H. N., 247
Khijin, P. P., 99
King of Sweden: and reception of Pavlov, 136
Klemensiewicz, P., 217
Kogan, S. R., 337
Koltushi: Pavlov's laboratory in, 133, 165
Komarov, S. A., 60
Komsomol, 110
Konorsky, G., 330
Kopilov, Comrade, 158
Korovitzky, L. K., 250
Koshtoyanz, C. S., 4
Kosturin, 57, 63, 64
Krasnogorsky, N. I., 124, 125, 330, 331
Kraushkin, V. A., 67
Kravkov, N. P., 58
Krylov, fables of, 9
Kudryavzeff, N. N., 241

La Barre, J., 250
La Bohème, Puccini's opera, 101

Langendorf, 201
Langerhans, islands of, 205
Langley, J. N., 212, 246
Lannelong: artificial sutures of, 75
Lashley, K. S., 319 ff., 343
Laycock, 284
Le Beau, J., 325, 327
Lebedinskaia, S. I., 307
Lectures on Conditioned Reflexes, by Pavlov (1926), 139, 140
Lectures on the Work of the Principal Digestive Glands, by Pavlov (1897), 139, 140
Ledentzov's Society, 73
Lepine, 90
Levene, P. A., 106, 107
Liddell, H. S., 344
Liebig, J., 144
Liebig's meat extract, 226
Lintvarev, I. I., 243
Lobasov, I. O., 140
Locke, John, 292
Lönnquist, B., 257
Logansky, 133
London, E. S.: "poly-fistulas method" of, 222
Ludwig, Carl, 19, 289, 324, 337
Ludwig, King of Bavaria, 53
Lukianov, 67
Lysenko controversy, 158, 170 ff.

McDowall, R. J. S., 199, 200
Magistrate's wife: story of, 126
Magnus, R., 282
Mammary glands, 231
Manasein, V. A., 21, 25
Marquis, D. G., 274, 305, 306, 319, 329, 343, 344
Martinov, 175, 176
Masserman, J. H., 274
Mayer, J. R., 144
Medico-Chirurgical Academy: Pavlov's entrance into, 10, 14; graduation from, 18
Melnikov, 29, 30
Mendeleev, D. I., 44
Mendelism, 164
Mett, S. G., 51
Mettler, C. C., 342

Mettler, F. A., 307
Minkowski, 220
Military-Medical Academy: Pavlov as professor of, 55, 57; Pashoutin as principal of, 57, 63 ff.; new laboratory of, 59, 73, 113, 132; Clinical Military Hospital of, 130; retiring system in, 338
Miller, H. J., 170, 341
Miller, S., 330
Mislavski, N. A., 90
Mitchurin, 170–71
Mörner, Professor (Count), 135, 136
Monism, 281
Morgulis, 320
Morozov: attendant in the Physiological Laboratory, as an experimentalist, 16; gambled Pavlov's military uniform, 62
Motility of the gastrointestinal tract, 265
Mozart, W. A., 149
Munk, H., 278

Napalkov, 175
Nencki, M. V., 67, 68
Nerves of the heart, 189 ff.
Nervism, 20, 21, 225
New Economic Policy (NEP), 104
Newman, E., 338
Nicholas I, 292
Nicholas II, 159
Nikitin, M. P., 181
Nobel, Alfred, 135
Nobel, Emmanuel, 135, 136
Nobel Prize: and laureates of 1901, 1902, and 1903, 82; awarded to Pavlov, 134, 211, 269; value of, 136; money from, lost by Pavlov, 136; attitude of Pavlov's colleagues toward his winning of, 137, 138

Objective psychology, 88
Oldenburg, Prince Alexander Petrovich, 55, 67
Orbeli, L. A., 90, 91, 153, 161, 163, 171, 172, 179, 315, 316
Osler, Sir William: and theory of the "Fixed Period," 149, 151, 340

Ostankov, A. P., 92
Osteomalacia, 197
Ostwald, Wilhelm, 144, 145, 146, 147, 148, 149, 151
Oushakov, V. G., 248, 249, 250
Ouskov, P. V., 67

Pancreatic duct: occlusion of, in the rabbit, 205
Pancreatic fistula: Bernstein's, 202, 203; 'Heidenhain's, 203; Pavlov's, 214
Pancreatic gland, 202 ff.; reflex inhibition of secretion of, 206; Pavlov's contribution to the physiology of, 227 ff., 263; and adaptation of enzymes, 242; and secretory nerves, 248
Pancreozymin, 237
Paraschuk, S. V., 82
Pashoutin, V. V., 57, 66
Pasteur, Louis, 149
Pasteur Institute in Paris, 67
Pavlov, Dmitri Petrovich, 9, 12, 27, 28, 35, 36, 40, 44
Pavlov, Ivan Petrovich: biography of, by V. V. Savich, 3; parentage of, 5; his father, 6; and love for learning and reading, 6; importance of experimental work of, 7; and gardening, 7, 8; letter of, to Donetz Coal Miners, 8; godfather of, 8; influence of Pisarev on, 11; and his bashfulness, 12; as student in St. Petersburg University, 12; influence of I. Cyon on, 13; surgical methods of, 13; as student in Medico-Chirurgical Academy, 14; and Tarkhanov incident, 15; assistantship of, in the Veterinary Institute, 16; and summer in Heidenhain's laboratory, 17; as director of research in Botkin's ,laboratory, 19, 20; and theory of nervism, 21; on co-operation between laboratory and clinic, 21; work of, on *Hellebori viridis* with Chistovich, 22; M.D. thesis of, 22, 23; promoted to lectureship, 23; devotion of, to science, 24; married S. V. Karchevskaya, 27; Shakespeare in life of, 32; and beloved philosopher Spencer, 32, 35; fell in love with Sara, 34; and Sara's shoe, 37; wedding of, 37; married life of, 40; and inability to manage his financial affairs, 41; jealousy of, 47; as a traveler, 48; intimate life of, 49; irritability of, 51, 52; appointed professor of physiology in Tomsk, 55; as professor of pharmacology in the Military-Medical Academy, 55; as professor of physiology, 57; and method of teaching of physiology, 58 ff.; and special course in physiology, 59; resignation of, from Military-Medical Academy, 62; and incident with General Kuropatkin, 62; and conflict with Pashoutin, 63 ff.; and cowardice of Academy professors, 65; as director of the department of physiology in the Institute for Experimental Medicine, 67; graduate students of, 70; and relations with senior workers, 72; began to work on conditioned reflexes, 72; as scientist, 84; indifference of, toward honors, 84; and belief in science, 85; and controversy with Bechterev, 87 ff.; asks Bechterev to repeat Belitski's experiment, 93; integrity of, 95 ff.; sense of duty of, 96; and incident with Dr. V., 97; tenacity of, 98; ability of, to concentrate, 100; and discovery of secretin, 101; and "riders" in science, 102; and sense of reality, 103 ff.; and importance of observation, 103; and public lecture of 1918, 103; and Americans, 105 ff.; creative imagination of, 108 ff.; theories of, 109; legacy of, to students, 110; and method of directing scientific work, 111 ff.; and help to students, 112; and school of experimental physiology, 115 ff.; influence of, on students, 117 ff.; temperament of, 119 ff.; swearing by, 123 ff.; and reading of thesis, 127; and assistance at operations, 128; Pavlov's day, 130 ff.;

received Nobel Prize, 134; festivities for, in Helsingfors and Stockholm, 135, 136; attitude of colleagues toward, 137, 138; as a writer, 139 ff.; children of, 139; as neither classicist nor romanticist, 147 ff.; chronological list of works of, 150; political views of, 152 ff.; and Bulyginsky Duma, 153; letter of, to All-Russian Congress of Physiologists, 154; and incident with Zabolotny, 156, 157; criticized the Soviet regime, 157; attitude of, toward the Royal House, 158, 159, 160; and Bolsheviks, 161 ff.; addressed the Fifteenth International Congress, 162, 169; on vivisection, 162; depressed by Bolsheviks' favors, 166; changed attitude of, toward Germans, 167; illnesses of: gallstones, 173 ff., severe grippe, 177–78; death of, 179 ff.; funeral of, 182; work of, on blood circulation, 187 ff.; and centrifugal nerves of the heart, 190 ff.; on trophic innervation, 194 ff.; and criticism of his theory of the quadruple innervation of the heart, 199; early work of, on pancreatic functions, 202 ff.; and occlusion of pancreatic duct in rabbit, 205; and *Lectures on the Work of the Principal Digestive Glands*, 211 ff.; introduced physiological surgery, 216 ff.; chronic experiments of, 219; and nervous regulation of the digestive glands' activity, 224 ff.; and unsatisfactory explanation of the chemical phase, 226, 227; reaction of, to the discovery of secretin, 229; on specific excitability of the alimentary canal, 233 ff.; Blondlot's influence on, 235 ff., 256 ff.; adopted Heidenhain's theory of secretory and trophic nerves, 239 ff.; and adaptation of pancreatic enzymes, 242 ff.; and anabolism and katabolism, 245; and secretory-inhibitory nerves, 248 ff.; on purposiveness, 252 ff.; contribution of,

to gastroenterology, 261 ff.; introduced the conception of the conditioned reflex, 273; and origin of this theory, 275, 276; attitude of, toward psychology, 276, 277; doubted his theory of conditioned reflex, 278; studied temperament of the dog, 279; Madrid oration of, 280; abandoned gastroenterology, 280; acknowledged the influence of Sechenov, 284, 285; and three signaling systems analogous to Jackson's three levels of evolution, 295; arrived at the conception of conditioned reflexes, 301 ff.; was convinced that a conditioned reflex is a reflex, 304; stated that the cerebral cortex is the organ of conditioned reflexes, 307; and conception of analyzers, 307, 312; and decision to study the "psychic reaction" physiologically, 309; and theory of conditioned reflexes, 311 ff.; American psychologists and, 320; and importance of conditioned reflexes for neurophysiology, 323; on voluntary movements, 329 ff.

Pavlov, Peter Dmitrievich, 6; opposition of, to the marriage of Pavlov to Sara, 35, 37, 42

Pavlov, Vladimir, 51, 52, 106, 107, 108

Pavlov gastric pouch, 98, 222

Pavlova, Seraphima Vasilievna: "Reminiscences" of, 4; and her biography, 27 ff.; religion of, 28, 29; love of literature of, 29; and her memoirs, 31; at Pedagogical Institute, 31; Shakespearean plays attended by, 32; and Pavlov's courtship, 34; love of, 35; wedding of, 37; and meetings with Turgenev, 39; married life of, 40; miscarriage of, 42; and death of Mirchik, 43; and visit to Professor Botkin, 43, 44; as a wife, 44; effect on, of Pavlov's jealousy, 47; intimate life of, 49; corresponded with us, 126; on Pavlov's illness, 173 ff.; on his severe grippe,

INDEX

177; on his death, 179 ff.; cared for by Soviet government, 183
Pavlova, Vera, 139, 177
Penfield, Dr. Wilder, 274, 325, 326, 327, 328, 344
Petrova, M. K., 309
Pflüger, E., 282, 313, 337
Physicians' Athletic Society, 134
Physiological Congress, International: Eleventh, 106, 107; Fifteenth, 178 ff.
Physiological surgery, 217 ff.
Physiology: analytical and integral, 218, 219
Pisarev, 11
Plescheev, 29
Pletnev, D. D., 177, 181
Podvisotski, 67
Poltyrev, S. S., 307
Ponomarev, Z. I., 83
Popielski, L., 96, 140
Poussep, L. M., 92
Protopopov, V. P., 88, 89
Prout, 259
Psychic secretion: gastric, 221, 236; salivary, 275, 302; as acquired, 303
Psychology: Pavlov's attitude toward, 276, 277, 310; evolution of, 281; and "seat of the soul," discussed by Funke, Vierordt, etc., 292; and three signaling systems, 295
Purposiveness, 252 ff.; Pavlov's definition of, 254; Barcroft on, 255; Cannon on, 255
Pushkin, A. S., 149

Raper, H. S., 230
Raphael, 149
Reflex: of purpose, 98; spinal, postural, etc., 282, 283; orientation, 282; Descartes's conception of, 284
Reflexes of the Brain, 11, 284, 285, 286, 290, 292
Reflexology, of Bechterev, 87
Revolution: of 1904–5, 152; of 1917, 154, 155
Rhythmic nerves, 190, 198
Riazantsev, N., 121
Romanticists in science, 144 ff.
Roosevelt, F. D., 150

Rosanov, 175
Rosen, G., 256
Rosenthal, J. S., 307
Russo-Japanese War, 152, 153
Ryazan: Pavlov's birthplace, 5; life in, 9; Ecclesiastical High School Seminary in, 10; Sara's visit to, 42

St. Martin, Alexis, 217, 236, 237, 256
Salazkin, S. S., 155
Salivary glands, 225, 238, 247; Pavlov's contribution to the physiology of, 261; "psychology" of, 301
Savich, V. V., 3, 10, 11, 15, 72, 73, 82, 97, 98, 100, 125, 128, 137, 138, 147, 155, 169, 178, 179, 182, 183, 214, 229, 235, 264, 339
Schmidt, C., 236
Schmiedeberg, 198
Schwann, 256, 259
Sechenov, I. M.: *Reflexes of the Brain*, 11; and S. P. Botkin, 19; and Pavlov, 91; as Pavlov's predecessor, 150, 274, 283, 284; as son of a landowner, 163; theory of, in *Reflexes of the Brain*, 285 ff.; and motor compound of a reflex, 298; and origin of speech, 299; relinquished the chair of physiology, 337
Secretin, 96, 101, 228, 237
Secretory-inhibitory nerves, 248 ff.; of gastric glands, 248 ff.; of the pancreatic gland, 250 ff.
Secretory nerves, 239 ff.
Semenuta, P. P., Admiral, Mrs. Pavlov's godfather, 31, 32, 36
Serdukov, A. S., 265
Serendipity, 280
Sham feeding, 69, 131, 215
Shaternikov, M. N., 286
Shaw, George Bernard, 342
Shepovalnikov, N. P., 264
Sherrington, Sir Charles, 219, 274, 315, 316
Shirokikh, P. O., 266
Shkliarevsky, 337
Shumov-Simanovsky, Mme E. O., 43, 215, 221
Shuvalov, Vania, 129

Signaling stimuli, 302, 304
Sikorskaya, E. V., 28, 40
Sillomiagy, Pavlov's summer house, 7, 48
Simanovsky, N. P., 25, 43, 47, 65
Sirotinin, 65
Skorichenko, professor of history of medicine, 74, 78
Snarsky, A. T., 275, 276, 280, 302
Society of Russian Physicians, 137, 138
Sokolov, A. P., 69, 129, 257
Soviet government: and education, 164; attitude of, toward Pavlov, 164 ff.; and care of Pavlov during his illness, 177; reaction of, to Pavlov's death, 181 ff.; and care of Mrs. Pavlov, 183
Spallanzani, 236
Specific excitability, 233 ff.
Speransky, A. D., 291
Sperk, E. F., 67
Spirtov, N. I.: failure of his demonstration, 93, 94
Splanchnic nerve: secretory nerve of the pancreatic gland, 248
Starling, E. H., 101, 102, 201, 227, 228, 229
Stolnikov, J. J., 17, 18, 19, 32, 193, 194
Strajesko, N. V., 100
Strümpell, A., 290, 291
Suvorin, A. S., 152

Tait, J., 214
Tarenetski, A. I., 66
Tarkhanov, I. R., professor of physiology, 14; and defense of Professor Ovsyannikov, 15; and his attendant Morosov as an experimenter, 16; and dismissal from Military-Medical Academy, 57
Tchaikovsky, P. I., 150
Tchernoruchkin, M. V., 181
Teleology, 252, 253, 254, 255
Tetanomotor, 249
Thiry, L., 217
Thomas, J. E., 230, 237, 241, 265, 266
Thompson, W. H., 129, 211, 341
Tichomirov, N. P., 73, 90, 91
Tigerstedt, Robert: on Pavlov's surgical methods, 14; on Stolnikov, 19; on Nobel Prize, 45; as best friend of Pavlov, 82, 84; informed him about the award of Nobel Prize and entertained him in Helsingfors, 135
Tolochinov, I. F., 72, 140, 141, 231, 279
Tolstoy, Countess, 183
Tomsk University, 55
Trophic nerves, 194, 239 ff.
Turgenev, I. S., 29, 30, 39, 292
Twenty Years of Objective Study, etc. (1923), 141, 143

Unconditioned reflex, 304
Ushakov, V. G., 67, 189
Ustimovich, 16

Vagotomy, 206
Vagus nerve: secretory nerve of gastric glands, 221, 248; of the pancreatic gland, 248
Van den Bergh's test, 174
Vannovsky, war minister, 64
Vartanov, V. I., 58
Vasiliev, W. N., 243
Vass, C. C. N., 251
Veliki, V. N., 55, 187
Verigo, B. F., 96
Verkhovski, B., 245
Vineberg, A. M., 249
Vinogradski, O. N., 67, 68
Virchow, R., 224
Vitamin D, 197
Vivisection: Pavlov on, 162
Vladimirov, A. A., 67
Volborth, G. W., 73, 241
Volkov, M. M., 78, 80, 82
Voluntary movements, 329 ff.
Vorobjev, A., 344

Wagner, Cosima, 53, 54
Wagner, G., 32
Wagner, Richard, 53, 338
Walpole, Horace, 280
Walther, A. A., 140, 211, 229, 235, 242, 243, 339, 342
"Wash reflex," 282
Watson, J. B., 281, 288, 300, 320, 321, 343, 344

INDEX

Weber brothers, 198
Wedensky, N. E., 25, 291
Wednesdays, Pavlov's, 133
Wolfson, S. G., 275
Wundt, 286

Yerkes, 320
Yougov, A., 4, 122, 162
Yousha: and his *botiki absolutiki*, 33

Zabolotny, 156, 157
Zakharin, professor of medicine in Moscow, 19
Zavadsky, I. D., 124
Zeliony, G. P., 307
Zhebrak, 171
Ziemssen, H. von, 290
Zitovich, I. S., 303
Zoopsychology, 277